BY THE SPEAR

Ancient Warfare and Civilization

SERIES EDITORS:

RICHARD ALSTON   ROBIN WATERFIELD

In this series, leading historians offer compelling new narratives of the armed conflicts that shaped and reshaped the classical world, from the wars of Archaic Greece to the fall of the Roman Empire and the Arab conquests.

Dividing the Spoils: The War for Alexander the Great's Empire
Robin Waterfield

By the Spear: Philip II, Alexander the Great, and the Rise and Fall of the Macedonian Empire
Ian Worthington

Taken at the Flood: The Roman Conquest of Greece
Robin Waterfield

BY THE SPEAR

Philip II, Alexander the Great, and the Rise
and Fall of the Macedonian Empire

✒

Ian Worthington

OXFORD
UNIVERSITY PRESS

OXFORD
UNIVERSITY PRESS

Oxford University Press is a department of the
University of Oxford. It furthers the University's objective
of excellence in research, scholarship, and education
by publishing worldwide.

Oxford New York
Auckland   Cape Town   Dar es Salaam   Hong Kong   Karachi
Kuala Lumpur   Madrid   Melbourne   Mexico City   Nairobi
New Delhi   Shanghai   Taipei   Toronto

With offices in

Argentina   Austria   Brazil   Chile   Czech Republic   France   Greece
Guatemala   Hungary   Italy   Japan   Poland   Portugal   Singapore
South Korea   Switzerland   Thailand   Turkey   Ukraine   Vietnam

Oxford is a registered trademark of Oxford University Press
in the UK and certain other countries.

Published in the United States of America by
Oxford University Press
198 Madison Avenue, New York, NY 10016

Library of Congress Cataloging-in-Publication Data is available

ISBN: 978-0-19-992986-3

CONTENTS

Contents

WEST MET EAST IN the Macedonian Empire of the later fourth century B.C., which stretched from Greece to the Punjab and as far south as Egypt. It was the largest empire in antiquity before the Roman yet was created by only two men: Philip II and his son Alexander the Great. How they did so is an epic tale of warfare across thousands of miles and numerous cultures. Before Alexander physically landed in Asia in 334 B.C. he was said to have thrown a spear into the foreign soil, claiming it as his "spear-won land." Over the next decade he lived by the spear, waging bloody battles and sieges against numerically superior foes and demonstrating generalship skills and a strategic and tactical genius that arguably no other individual has ever fully matched. Yet his father, Philip II, had already established Macedonia as an imperial power, also by the spear. He conquered first the areas that bordered his kingdom and then Thrace and Greece and was all set to invade Asia when he was cut down by an assassin's dagger. Alexander inherited his father's plan and brought it to stunning fruition, but more than just defeating his enemies in fierce battles, his conquests spread Greek language and culture in the East and facilitated economic and cultural contacts between West and East. Thanks to him the Greeks were catapulted from the Mediterranean world they had been accustomed to for centuries into one far larger.

This book is the first to consider the achievements of Philip and Alexander within one set of covers to show how they together formed one of the most important epochs in Greek history. It is not a biography but, rather, a study of the rise and fall of their Macedonian Empire, which necessarily explores their reigns, challenges, achievements, and shortcomings.

I present Philip as the architect of the Macedonian Empire and Alexander as its master builder—and destroyer. In keeping with this series' intersection of war and civilization, the narrative is also used as a backdrop to discuss social and cultural matters in the West and East, the impact of an invading army on the societies and cultures of the conquered, and, as far as possible, what the Macedonians themselves thought of their empire and the experience of battle—what fighting in battles and sieges was like for combatants and how it affected them. Analogies to the modern era are also made, such as how the problems Alexander faced in dealing with a multi-cultural subject population and his successes and especially failures can inform makers of strategy in culturally different regions of the world today.

All dates are B.C. except where indicated.

ACKNOWLEDGMENTS

I THANK ROBIN WATERFIELD for inviting me to write this book and for all his help and advice throughout the writing process. His comments on the content of various chapters and then on a draft of the whole book were invaluable. Equally so were those of my editor, Stefan Vranka, at Oxford University Press, with whom it was a pleasure to work again. Likewise, I owe much to Sarah Pirovitz at the same press for arranging the permissions for the illustrations and a myriad of always cheerful e-mails. I am also grateful to the referees of the book proposal and submitted draft for their astute suggestions and questions.

I am indebted to the Research Council of my own institution for awarding me a Research Leave grant for the 2011–2012 academic year, which allowed me to finish my *Demosthenes of Athens and the Fall of Classical Greece* (Oxford: 2013) and to complete most of a draft of the present book. Then in 2013 the Research Council continued its generosity by awarding me a Summer Research Fellowship, thanks to which I was able to complete the final version of this book.

Last, but by no means least, I thank once again my family for putting up with me—and who might read this book one day.

IAN WORTHINGTON
University of Missouri
November 2013

LIST OF MAPS AND FIGURES

MAPS

FIGURES

ANCIENT WORKS AND ABBREVIATIONS

Q UOTATIONS FROM Diodorus, Justin, and Plutarch's lives are taken
from these translations (those of other ancient writers are translated
by me or referenced in the notes):

DIODORUS

C. L. Sherman, *Diodorus Siculus 15.20–16.65*, Loeb Classical Library, vol. 7
(Cambridge: 1952)
C. Bradford Welles, *Diodorus Siculus 16.66–17*, Loeb Classical Library,
vol. 8 (Cambridge: 1963)

JUSTIN

R. Develin and W. Heckel, *Justin. Epitome of the "Philippic History" of
Pompeius Trogus* (Atlanta: 1994)
J. C. Yardley and W. Heckel, *Justin. Epitome of the "Philippic History" of
Pompeius Trogus, 1: Books 11–12: Alexander the Great* (Oxford: 1997)

PLUTARCH

Alexander, Demosthenes, and *Phocion*
Ian Scott-Kilvert, *Plutarch, "The Age of Alexander,"* Penguin Classics
(Harmondsworth: 1973)

The following modern works are abbreviated in the notes to reduce repetition of bibliographical information:

Adams and Borza (eds.), *Macedonian Heritage*
W. L. Adams and E. N. Borza (eds.), *Philip II, Alexander the Great, and the Macedonian Heritage* (Lanham: 1982)

Anc. Macedonia
Ancient Macedonia (Institute for Balkan Studies, Thessaloníki)

BNJ
Ian Worthington (editor-in-chief), *Brill's New Jacoby* (Leiden: 2007–)

Carney and Ogden (eds.), *Philip and Alexander*
E. D. Carney and D. Ogden (eds.), *Philip II and Alexander the Great: Father and Son, Lives and Afterlives* (Oxford: 2010)

FGrH
F. Jacoby, *Die Fragmente der griechischen Historiker (The Fragments of the Greek Historians)* (Berlin/Leiden: 1926–)

Heckel and Tritle (eds.), *Crossroads*
W. Heckel and L. A. Tritle (eds.), *Crossroads of History. The Age of Alexander* (Claremont: 2003)

Heckel and Tritle (eds.), *New History*
W. Heckel and L. A. Tritle (eds.), *Alexander the Great: A New History* (Malden: 2009)

Roisman (ed.), *Companion to Alexander*
J. Roisman (ed.), *Brill's Companion to Alexander the Great* (Leiden: 2003)

Roisman and Worthington (eds.), *Companion to Macedonia*
J. Roisman and Ian Worthington (eds.), *A Companion to Ancient Macedonia* (Malden: 2010)

Worthington (ed.), *Ventures*
Ian Worthington (ed.), *Ventures into Greek History. Essays in Honour of N. G. L. Hammond* (Oxford: 1994)

FIGURE 1
Facial reconstruction of Philip II. Courtesy of the Whitworth Art Gallery, the University of Manchester.

FIGURE 2

Head of Alexander the Great (Pella). Photo: Ian Worthington, Pella Museum, Greece.

Epidamnus

THRACE

Byzantium

MACEDONIA

Strymon R.

Amphipolis

Eion

PROPONTIS

Stagira

Acanthus

Thasos

Aegospotami

Cyzicus

CHALCIDICE

Lampsacus

Dascylium

Potidaea

Cynossema

Scione

Troy

AEOLIS

MYSIA

Corcyra

THESSALY

AEGEAN
SEA

Lesbos

Ambracia

Mytilene

Anactorium

AETOLIA

Arginusae Islands

LYDIA

Sollium

ACAR-

Euboea

Sardes

NANIA

Delphi

PHOCIS

Chios

Erythrae

Naupactus

Gulf

Thebes

Delium

Chios

Notium

of Corinth

Oropus

ACHAEA

Plataea

Decelea

IONIA

Ephesus

Megara

Athens

Samos

Corinth

Piraeus

ATTICA

Icaria

Miletus

Zacynthus

ELIS

Argos

Laureum

Delos

ARCADIA

Olympia

Epidaurus

Aegina

Halicarnassus

Messene

LACONIA

MESSENIA

Pylos

Sparta

Melos

Rhodes

Cythera

100 miles

160 km

Crete

MAP 1
Greece.

xvii

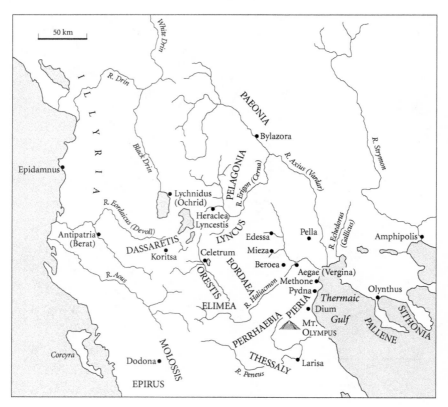

MAP 2

Macedonia.

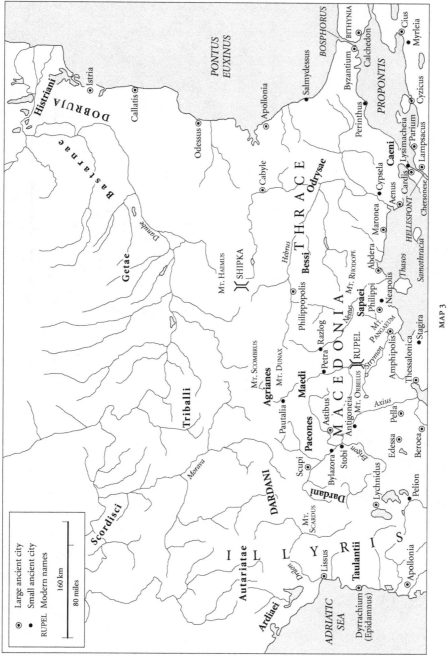

MAP 3

The Balkan area.

xix

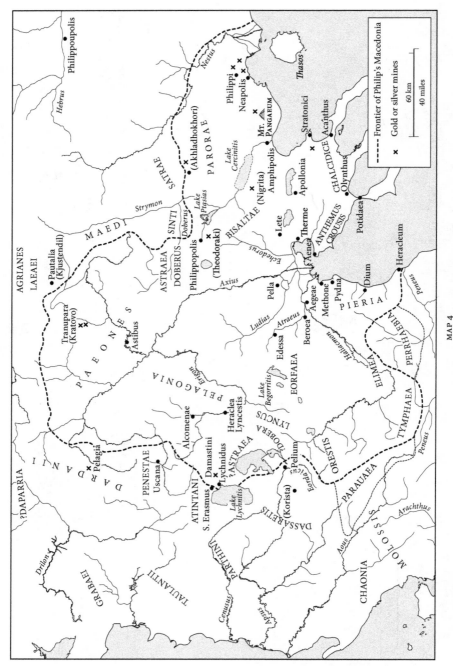

MAP 4

Macedonia's frontiers and Philip's mines.

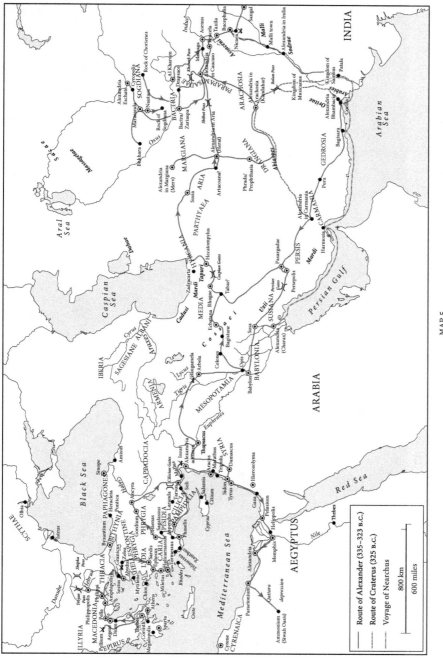

MAP 5

Alexander's empire.

INTRODUCTION

The Architect and the Master Builder

A T ITS HEIGHT THE Macedonian Empire of the later fourth century B.C. stretched from Greece in the west to India (present-day Pakistan and Kashmir) in the east, including Syria, the Levantine coast, and Egypt (Map 5). By contrast the Athenians' fifth-century empire at its height included over 160 allies from as far afield as Italy and Sicily to Asia Minor, but it could not measure up to the size of the Macedonian. Yet, while Macedonia and Athens were imperial powers, there were significant differences in how they achieved their empires and even what we mean by *empire* in this period, which we need to bear in mind as we examine the reigns of Philip and Alexander.[1]

Macedonia's empire consisted of a number of different states and geographical regions, all containing disparate ethnic and multicultural subject populations, which were ruled over by a single king. It was no voluntary federation though. The king had had to seize power by force and maintain it by military and diplomatic means, as we shall see. The pressure was thus always on him to retain control, since no one likes to be conquered, and to provide a stable succession. In that respect the Macedonian Empire was akin to the Persian Empire (discussed on pp. 142–143) but different in conception from that of its southern neighbor, Athens. The Athenians' fifth-century empire began as a voluntary league of allies (the Delian League), who united to resist any renewed threat from Persia after the Persian Wars. As the danger from Persia receded the Athenians maintained their league, imposing their rule over their allies and disregarding their autonomy and grievances. On the other hand, the Macedonian king included his conquered subjects in his administration and even allowed them some semblance of autonomy while ensuring that he was always in control. This aspect helps to explain why Athens never regained mastery of its allies when its empire came to a crashing end in 404, whereas for centuries after the downfall of its empire Macedonian rule of the various conquered areas continued under individual rulers of those regions.

The vast Macedonian Empire had not taken decades or even centuries to build, nor had a succession of conquerors fought to shape it. Only one man, in his twenties and early thirties, had brought it about, astonishingly in a mere decade—Alexander III of Macedonia, "the Great" (r. 336–323), who dubbed himself King of Asia. Alexander always intended to conquer Asia: even before he disembarked from his boat after crossing the Hellespont, separating Europe from Asia, he threw a spear into the foreign soil. In doing so he claimed all of Asia as his own spear-won land. Like his father, Alexander sought to extend his own personal power and that of Macedonia by the sword. Yet not even Europe and Asia were enough for him, for he also intended to invade Arabia and after that possibly attack Carthage and the western Mediterranean. These final campaigns never came to pass because on June 11, 323, on the eve of the Arabian expedition, Alexander died in Babylon, a few weeks before his thirty-third birthday.[2]

From his use of psychological warfare in Persia and India to his mastering of guerilla tactics in Afghanistan and the way he constantly rallied his men, Alexander was a great general. He fought battles against numerically superior Persian and Indian foes, prosecuted sieges against cities and strongholds that because of their strengths and locations ought to have beaten him, and demonstrated leadership skills and an innate strategic and tactical genius that arguably no other individual has ever fully matched. He strove to emulate the heroes of Homer in the fierce way he fought and lived, and he was also well educated, taught by Aristotle no less, and loved Greek philosophy and tragedy. His conquests also had the byproduct—as he intended—of spreading Greek language and culture in the areas through which he marched and of promoting economic and cultural contacts between West and East. In doing so, he introduced to the Greeks a world that was far larger than that of the Mediterranean to which they had been accustomed for centuries. He was worshiped by some of his subjects while he was still alive, and he died young, remaining a godlike example to all would-be conquerors.

Without doubt Alexander is one of history's most exciting people. Because of his spectacular military exploits he became a legend, and later fourth-century Greek history is commonly called "the age of Alexander." His legendary status began in his own time and grew especially in the medieval period, with its emphasis on chivalry, and in early modern Europe, when rulers were likewise gripped by "Alexander fever"—for example, the portraits of Louis XIV as the Macedonian king. Today the popular fascination with Alexander continues in the shape of TV documentaries, Hollywood movies, and of course books.

Yet Alexander's empire, on which so much of his posthumous reputation rests, had a rocky start. Mere weeks after he landed in Asia in 334 he was fighting for his life in his first battle against the Persians at the Granicus River (in modern Turkey). The Macedonians were gaining the upper hand over the enemy when all of a sudden a Persian javelin penetrated Alexander's breastplate. As he struggled to pull the javelin out of his armor another Persian sheared his helmet off his head, and even as the king ran him through with his sword yet another Persian lined up his weapon to split Alexander's bare head in two. He was saved at the last possible moment by his cavalry commander, Cleitus the Black, who slashed off the attacker's arm.

Alexander's desperate fight for survival probably lasted less than a minute, but it showed how he lived up to the expectations of a Macedonian warrior king: to lead from the front in battle and to involve himself in the thick of fighting. His near-death experience at the Granicus River never deterred him from engaging the enemy, often with no thought for his personal safety. Thus, eight years later, in 326, the Macedonian army was hard-pressed during its siege of the citadel at Malli in India. To goad his men into redoubling their efforts Alexander climbed the walls of the citadel at Malli, but then the scaling ladders broke behind him, stranding him and three others on the battlements. They were sitting ducks for the Mallian archers, so Alexander immediately jumped into the enemy's midst, the others following suit. Hopelessly outnumbered they nevertheless fought ferociously until one of the king's comrades was killed. Then Alexander fell to an enemy arrow, which punctured his lung. The remaining Macedonians prepared for the inevitable but were rescued in the nick of time when the besiegers stormed the citadel and slew everyone—men, women, and children. Alexander's doctor saved his life, but he had lost a great deal of blood and was so weak that his army feared for the worst. In a stirring show of true grit he mounted his horse shortly after and rode it in front of his troops to show that he was very much alive.

Had Alexander died at the Granicus or at Malli there would have been no Macedonian Empire and no age of Alexander. Yet this empire did not survive Alexander anyway. For one thing, the failure on his part to administer it effectively and recognize native religious beliefs and customs led to dissatisfaction with his rule and open revolt in part of it during the latter years of his reign. Moreover, he left no heir to succeed him—his wife Roxane was still pregnant when he died. When his generals crowded around his deathbed and asked him to whom he wished to leave his realm, there is a story that he merely replied, "To the best." The big question for these generals, who disliked each other intensely and had been bound together only by the force of Alexander's personality, was: whom did Alexander have in mind? Each man thought that he was the best. They held a meeting and carved up the self-standing empire among themselves. This settlement at Babylon was the preamble to an inevitable civil war, which turned Alexander's former conquests into a battleground for the next three decades and saw the creation of the three great kingdoms of the Hellenistic period: Ptolemaic Egypt, Seleucid Syria, and Antigonid Greece.

Alexander's legacy stands in stark contrast to his spectacular military exploits. Furthermore, his remarkable empire was the product of not only himself but also his father, Philip II. Without Philip's achievements for Macedonia there would have been no Alexander the Great. All historical figures are a product in some form or another of their predecessors of course, but the case of Philip and Alexander goes beyond that because history has arguably done Philip a disservice in relegating him to the periphery. When Philip came to power in 359 Macedonia was a backward, economically weak, and perilously unstable kingdom, prone to invasions from neighboring tribes and interference in its domestic politics by Greek cities, and with only a conscript army of poorly trained and equipped farmers. By the time he was assassinated in 336, Philip had turned Macedonia into an imperial power, to include modern Greece, much of Albania and Bulgaria, and all of what is present-day European Turkey (Map 3). He had created the most feared and powerful army in the Greek world, had brought about economic prosperity as never before, and had planned and even launched the invasion of Asia, which Alexander inherited.

However, Philip campaigned only in Greece and up to the Hellespont (Dardanelles), hardly as exciting as Alexander's exploits in far-flung places. Yet in battle he fought as hard and as valiantly as Alexander, in the process losing an eye, shattering a collarbone, and suffering a near-fatal leg wound that made him limp for the rest of his life. He was also a great general and strategist, a skilled diplomat, and a traditional Macedonian king—more than Alexander, in fact, whose penchant for Eastern luxuries and practices was resented by many of his men. Like his son, he lived large, drank copiously, and had no qualms in marrying for political ends, taking seven wives without ever divorcing any of them. His last marriage so infuriated Alexander's mother, Olympias (Philip's fourth wife), that she may have plotted to kill her husband. Nevertheless, ancient writers lavished more attention on Alexander, thereby casting Philip to live in the shadow of his famous son.

This book discusses the reigns and achievements of Philip and Alexander as the backdrop to understanding the rise and fall of the Macedonian Empire and compares and contrasts them as kings of Macedonia to decide if one of them ultimately better served his kingdom. It examines how different Macedonia was before it acquired its empire, the impact of Macedonian rule on the Greek world and Asia, and social and cultural changes on both conquered and conqueror. Because Alexander brought down the Achaemenid dynasty of Persia and defeated its Great King, Darius III, in a mere four years, there is a tendency to think of the army under Alexander as a steamroller, crushing everything in its path effortlessly and indefatigably. In fact Darius was a skilled general who commanded a vast army and posed a challenge to Alexander on more than one occasion. The extent of resistance on the part of the Persians to Alexander will also be discussed, as will the effect of the near-constant fighting on the Macedonian combatants, which proved that their army was anything but inexhaustible.

There is no doubt that Alexander was the empire's master builder, but Philip was certainly its architect. The reader is left to decide whether one has the edge over the other and if so, which one. To begin, we turn to Greece and Macedonia before Philip, to a period when events were dominated by a small handful of powerful cities, Athens in particular, and the Greeks viewed Macedonia as a political, military, economic, and cultural backwater that no one could have predicted would become a superpower of the ancient world.

1.

GREECE AND MACEDONIA

T HE PERSIAN WARS (480–479) had been a defining moment in Greek history.[1] When Xerxes invaded Greece in 481 with a land army supposedly in the hundreds of thousands and over 1,200 ships, it seemed that Greece would quickly fall victim to Persian aggression. Nevertheless, undaunted by the size of Xerxes's large army, 31 Greek cities hastily banded together to resist him. The Persians scored a victory at Thermopylae in northern Greece in 480 (against the famous "300 Spartans"), which allowed them to penetrate as far south as Athens and actually loot and burn the city. However, this success turned out to be the highlight of Xerxes's offensive. At the same time as Thermopylae the Athenian general Themistocles contributed to a defeat of the Persian navy at Artemisium, off the northern tip of Euboea, and shortly afterward he masterminded the near annihilation of the enemy fleet at Salamis. Xerxes turned tail and fled back to Persia, leaving behind his general Mardonius to rally the demoralized Persian troops and retreat north to Thessaly for the winter. In the following year, 479, Mardonius was soundly defeated thanks principally to Spartan resistance in battle at Plataea in Boeotia. The remnants of the Persian army then fled Greece, never to return. Thus the scene was set for the rise of Athens as an imperial power and the inevitable military clashes with the two other mainland powers of the Classical period, Sparta and Thebes (Map 1).

A TALE OF THREE CITIES

Athens's navy had contributed decisively to defeating the Persians, and it is no surprise that the Persian Wars feature prominently in Athenian literature and propaganda. Because of their naval strength, in 478 the Athenians put together an anti-Persian naval league (called the Delian League after the island on which its council of allies met and the allied treasury was stored) under their leadership. Athenian allies were located throughout the Mediterranean area and as far afield as the northern Aegean, the western Mediterranean, and the coastline of Asia Minor. Each one paid an annual tribute to the city in money or ships. The Delian League quickly grew into an Athenian empire and allowed Athens to become the most powerful and prosperous city in Greece.

Athens quickly established itself as a superpower but soon came into conflict with Sparta, which viewed the Delian League apprehensively. From the middle of the sixth century Sparta (located in Laconia in the Peloponnese) had been gaining influence in Greek affairs by means of its Peloponnesian League. The Spartans could boast the most daunting land army in Greece, but their military reputation had suffered a blow during the Persian Wars because of the Athenian naval victories that tipped the scales in the Greeks' favor. The Spartans' fear of the growth in the Athenians' power led to a series of clashes between the two cities and eventually the Peloponnesian War (431–404).[2] Despite the Athenian advantages of naval strength and financial resources, they suffered defeat, losing at least half and perhaps as much as 75 percent of their population. The Delian League was brought to a crushing end, and Sparta absorbed the Athenian allies into the Peloponnesian League, installing in Athens an oligarchy and a garrison.

Sparta dominated Greek affairs from the end of the war until 371, a period commonly called the Spartan hegemony.[3] However, they cared little for their allies and soon became unpopular leaders. In an effort to restore their waning influence in Greek politics they turned to the Great King of Persia. Under the terms of the resulting "King's Peace" or Peace of Antalcidas (after the Spartan diplomat who brokered it) of 386, they agreed to abandon the Greek cities of Asia Minor to Persian rule, an act that the other Greeks despised. In fact, in 337 Philip II of Macedonia made liberating these betrayed cities one of his main goals in invading Asia.

During the Spartan hegemony another city was flexing its muscles: Thebes in Boeotia. The Thebans had a formidable army, including the famed "Sacred Band," an elite infantry corps of 300 soldiers (150 pairs of lovers, who thus fought all the more ferociously to protect their partners). Viewing Thebes's military forces as a threat, the Spartans seized the Theban Cadmea (Acropolis) in 382, installed a garrison on it, and exiled 300 Theban citizens. Their action was completely unprovoked and led to the Thebans, in 379/8, expelling the garrison. They received support from the Athenians, even though the latter had a traditional hostility toward the Thebans, because of their hatred of the Spartans. Then in 371 the brilliant Theban generals Epaminondas and Pelopidas defeated the Spartans in battle at Leuctra (in Boeotia). The following year the Thebans invaded the Peloponnese to deliver the death blow: they liberated the helots (slaves) of Messenia, on whom the Spartans had depended for their economic livelihood since the mid–eighth century. Over the next decades the Spartans harbored hopes of returning to their former position in Greek affairs, but their hopes were never realized.

The Thebans' victory at Leuctra granted them a period of ascendancy in Greece, which lasted only until 362.[4] It was short-lived not so much because of Thebes's relatively small size but because of Athens's return to influence and the rebuilding of its economy over the years.[5] In 403, one year after the Peloponnesian War formally ended, a group of exiled Athenian democrats had overthrown the pro-Spartan oligarchy and restored democracy. Then in 378, partly for protection after helping to liberate Thebes from Spartan influence, the Athenians invited other Greek states to join them in an anti-Spartan league. Thus was born the Second Athenian Confederacy (or League), which comprised as many as 75 allies at its height and lasted until 338, when Philip abolished it.[6]

Just as the Spartans had viewed the Delian League with alarm, the Thebans now perceived the Athenian Confederacy as a threat to them. When Pelopidas was killed during a campaign in Thessaly against Alexander of Pherae in 364, Epaminondas took steps to strengthen Thebes, among other things planning to build 100 triremes and in 362 even threatening to move the Propylaea (the monumental gateway to the Acropolis) to the Theban Cadmea. To forestall his attack on their city the Athenians, helped by a handful of other states, brought him to battle in the same year at Mantinea. In the fighting, Epaminondas was killed, and the Thebans' ascendancy in Greece ended. Athens was again the dominant city in Greece.

The Athenians initially honored the terms of the charter of their new confederacy by not resorting to practices that had generated ill will toward them in their fifth-century empire. For example, they did not levy a tribute from their allies, install garrisons and governors in allied towns, or found cleruchies (settlements of their citizens that took over towns and territories and ousted the native population). Their attitude soon changed—among other things, they did impose a tribute (which they euphemistically called *syntaxeis*, "contributions") and established cleruchies. Eventually in 356 Chios, Rhodes, and Cos, with the support of Mausolus, the satrap of Caria, revolted from the Athenian League, and others followed suit. The Social War, as the revolt was called, ended the following year when the rebels defeated an Athenian fleet at Embata (perhaps off Erythrae). The Athenians had no choice but to recognize the independence of a number of allies, and their confederacy became a shadow of its former self, although thanks to their powerful navy they remained the major military force of the mainland.[7]

The Athenians also suffered financial hardship for many years after the Social War. Fortunately for them a politician named Eubulus instituted a series of austere financial and economic reforms to revitalize the Athenian economy and generate revenue.[8] Among other things he was well aware that peace brought prosperity, and so he persuaded the people not to involve themselves in costly wars or overseas ventures. Thanks to him, Athens's annual income increased from the 137 talents at the end of the Social War in 355 to 400 talents a few years later. He also created the Theoric Fund, into which surpluses from the city's annual income were paid. Originally constituted to provide the people with money to attend festivals and dramatic performances (in Greek *theoria* means "looking at"), this fund was soon used for other civic affairs, and the people referred to it as "the glue of democracy."[9] Its assets became so great that its treasurer played a role in political affairs, which explains Eubulus's influence in public life in the second half of the 350s.

Throughout the Classical period the constant feuding among the various Greek cities and the bickering and antics of large cities such as Athens, Sparta, and Thebes contributed to a lack of stability and unity on the Greek mainland. These woeful conditions permitted the kingdom of Macedonia under Philip II to rise to dominance as that king played off one city against another, eventually conquering the Greeks in 338 and suppressing the two ideals that they had cherished the most: autonomy and freedom.

GREEK AUTONOMY AND THE POLIS

Greeks mostly lived in independent poleis or "city states." The reasons why this polis system developed are not properly known, but at some point in the "Dark Age" period of Greece (from roughly 1100 to 750) geographical, racial, economic, and even ethnic reasons came together and caused one city to dominate the towns and settlements of the area in which it was located. These cities had common features such as a citadel (Acropolis) and a market area (Agora), which accounted for their particular rise to power. The people living in the area shared in the city's citizenship; thus Athens was the polis of Attica, a peninsula of some 900 square miles, and all those living in Attica were Athenian citizens.

A polis was autonomous: it had its own constitution, laws, coinage, weights and measures, and social customs and was responsible for all aspects of its domestic and foreign policy. It was completely individual. Travel from one polis to another within Hellas (as the Greeks called Greece) was not far removed from visiting a different country today, aside from the common language. A man, according to Aristotle, was part and parcel of polis life. Women, although citizens, did not have the right to vote and could not even represent themselves in the law courts. Women did maintain the *oikos* (household), on which the polis was grounded, but nevertheless a polis was a male preserve. The Greeks believed that their polis system was the best political and social structure because it focused on self-sufficiency. It provided them with autonomy (*autonomia*) in all their policy decisions and freedom (*eleutheria*) in how they lived and interacted with their fellow citizens and other Greeks, and they went to war to maintain these two ideals.

The focus on self-sufficiency, on the other hand, fostered in the Greek poleis a feeling of xenophobia toward each other that prevented them from actively uniting (even against a common foe) and even going to war with each other. Feelings of hostility were felt long after any conflicts were settled. Nor did the rise to power of cities such as Athens, Sparta, or Thebes in the Classical period bring any stability to affairs in Greece or reconcile the poleis to each other. Athenian unpopularity, for example, was one reason why the Social War broke out and why smaller states welcomed the later intervention of Philip II in Greek politics because they were tired of the self-serving activities of major cities. Philip exploited this bitterness as he slowly but surely built up Macedonian influence in Greece—as Justin soberly remarked of the Greek cities' interactions with one another, "For all their attempts to impose their rule on each other, they only succeeded in losing their ability to rule themselves. With no restraint they rushed into mutual destruction, and realised only in subjection that what they forfeited individually constituted a loss for them all."[10]

Greeks recognized the weaknesses of their polis system yet did nothing about it.[11] Aristotle, for example, criticized the frequent outbreaks of violent and bloody civil strife (*stasis*) within poleis and with each other and spent much of the eighth book of his *Politics* proposing ways to prevent it. He argued that if the Greeks could have formed a single political entity, they would have ruled the world. Aristotle had every reason to say this— he was writing in the 330s and 320s, when Greece had fallen under Macedonian hegemony. But even before Aristotle there were critics of the poleis and of the pitfalls of popular rule in them. Plato in the *Republic*, for example, believed that only philosopher kings could govern states and restore stability and that ideally cities should have no more than 5,040 families and an agricultural economy. In 380 Isocrates had written a treatise, the *Panegyricus*, calling upon the Greeks to invade Persia. His reason had nothing to do with military conquest; rather, he thought that the campaign would enable the Greeks to put aside their differences and reduce *stasis*. His appeal was unsuccessful, but he repeated it for much the same reasons in 346 in his *To Philip*.

Nevertheless, the Greeks continued to believe that their personal autonomy made them better than anyone else, which is one reason why they regarded the Macedonians as ignorant because they lived under a king and could not make their own decisions. They learned their mistake too late, as Justin remarked in the quotation above. In 338 at the Battle of Chaeronea Philip defeated a coalition of Greek states and imposed Macedonian rule on Greece by means of the League of Corinth, which comprised all Greek mainland cities (and probably those of Asia Minor and nearby islands after Alexander's campaign there). The league allowed them some semblance of autonomy in their daily affairs, although in reality the Macedonian kings could enforce major foreign and domestic decisions when they wanted—as when Alexander unilaterally decided to send exiles back to their native cities in 324. Yet the Greeks never abandoned their desire for *autonomia* and *eleutheria*—on Philip's death in 336 and Alexander's in 323 many cities revolted from Macedonian rule in pursuit of their liberty. These revolts came to nothing. After the second one ended the following year, in 322, Greeks living on the mainland and as far afield as Central Asia remained under the tight control of Macedonian rulers for all of the Hellenistic period and then fell under Roman masters.

Of course Macedonian rule did not destroy the polis; it merely curtailed personal freedom. Nor did the League of Corinth impose a common citizenship on its Greek members—an Athenian was still an Athenian, for example. The polis continued to exist during the Macedonian hegemony of Greece in the late Classical and especially Hellenistic periods, when its civic life and urban culture were no different from their Classical predecessors.[12] It still elected its public officials and held meetings of its political bodies as inscriptional evidence attests; social and cultural life also changed little, and economic and trading contacts were maintained and increased. The new cities of the Hellenistic East, often named after their rulers (Antioch from Antiochus, for example), were modeled on the Greek polis, and their culture was Greek—the legacy of Alexander's conquests.

MACEDONIA AND MACEDONIANS

Mount Olympus, Greece's tallest mountain at 9,461 feet, was the natural border between Macedonia and Greece (Map 2). In its early history Macedonia consisted of the valleys of the rivers Haliacmon (to the west) and Axius (the Vardar, extending up to Skpoje) and their various tributaries, which flow into the Gulf of Therme or Thermaic Gulf (Map 2). By the time he died in 336 Philip II had doubled the size of Macedonia to include the Greek mainland, the south of Yugoslavia, much of Albania, and all points east as far as Byzantium and had likewise doubled the population to as many as 500,000.[13]

The Pindus mountain range split the kingdom into two parts: Upper Macedonia (to the west) and Lower Macedonia (to the east).[14] Lower Macedonia and the southern area of Upper Macedonia are now in Greece; the rest of Upper Macedonia is in the independent Republic of Macedonia (previously Serbia, then Yugoslavia). Lower Macedonia consisted of a rich plain extending all the way eastward to the Thermaic Gulf and the Strymon River. Here were a number of towns scattered in the original center of Olympus, Pieria, the coastal plain of Emathia and Bottiaea, and the areas called Amphaxitis, Crestonia, Mygdonia, Bisaltia, Crousis, and Anthemus (Map 2). Thanks to its warm climate and fertile soil (*Pieria* means "rich land"), the people grew and lived off cereal crops, vegetables, grapes, and fruits and grazed their flocks and horses. In the early seventh century Perdiccas I, the first king of the Argead dynasty (which included Philip and Alexander),[15] founded Macedonia's capital Aegae, the "Place of goats" (modern Vergina), in the northern foothills of Pieria. He called it this because an Oracle had told him that goats would lead him to its site (*aix* being Greek for "goat").[16] Then in 399 King Archelaus established a new capital at Pella (Figure 3), after which Aegae was used only for royal weddings and burials.

Upper Macedonia, on the other hand, had a far harsher climate and was the highlands of the country. Here, Elimiotis (in the south), Orestis (to the west), and Lyncestis (to the northwest, by Lake Lychnitis) had been originally autonomous kingdoms, together with cantons such as Tymphaea, Elimea, Eordaea, Lyncus, Pelagonia, and Derriopus (Map 2).

FIGURE 3
Pella. Photo: Ian Worthington.

Their inhabitants were mostly nomadic tribes, ruled by individual chief-tains, who may have lived in basic settlements in the tribal areas instead of actual towns. Macedonia's rugged terrain made travel and communica-tions difficult because there were few passes through the mountains—the most famous and easiest to traverse was the Vale of Tempe by Mount Olympus and the later Via Egnatia. The Upper and Lower Macedonians might well have believed that they were descended from Macedon (they claimed that he was a son of Zeus, the most important god in their pan-theon), but the Upper Macedonian chieftains had more in common with their Illyrian and Paeonian neighbors than their supposed countrymen. They felt little loyalty to the Macedonian kings, although that too changed once Philip assumed the throne.

Macedonian kings had generally kept their distance from the Greeks, who viewed them with hypocritical disdain for their self-serving natures. For example, when Xerxes invaded Greece in 481 the Macedonian king,

Alexander I, had openly sided with Persia. It was only when the Persians had been defeated at the Battle of Plataea in 479 and were beating a retreat from Greece that he supported the winning side. Later, during the Peloponnesian War, Perdiccas II had flip-flopped so often between Athens and Sparta that he was never trusted by either of the two cities.

Politically, the Greeks considered that their polis system was superior to all other forms of government. This was especially so in the case of monarchy, which Greeks associated with autocracy. The Macedonian monarch was one half of the constitution—the other was the Assembly of male citizens—but in practice he ruled absolutely when it came to domestic and foreign policy and waging wars, during which time he was sole commander of the army.[17] He was also the chief priest in the state and final judge in cases of treason appeals. Powerful aristocrat Macedonians did lead factions that existed at court, but while the king was careful in his cultivation of relations with them, their power ultimately depended on him, and everyone knew that.[18] For advice he could turn to his closest friends and advisers, who were called Companions (Hetairoi), but he did not need to heed their guidance. Nor did he have to follow the directive of the Assembly, whose principal duty was deciding the next king, a process called acclamation, which involved the men dressing in full armor and clashing their spears on their shields.

These royal duties and expectations were incumbent upon kings, and they were never neglectful of them, even though the people always swore an oath of allegiance to the new king. However, once Philip began to expand Macedonia's territory, especially after he conquered Thrace and Greece, the duties and responsibilities of kings necessarily expanded because of the different subject populations and the need to administer and maintain control over new regions. Likewise Alexander was forced to adapt and extend his duties in Asia, coming to see himself not as a traditional Macedonian warrior king but as King of Asia.

More than just episodes from history and the nature of monarchic rule, the whole fabric of Macedonian society was alien to Greeks and so abhorred by them. A Macedonian male was an entirely different animal from his Athenian counterpart, for example, who came of age at 18, was then eligible to attend the Assembly (the main political body, which debated and voted on domestic and foreign policy), served in the army as and when required, was eligible for jury service when he turned 30, and—if he came from a well-to-do family—attended symposia (drinking parties) to engage in intellectual discussion before letting his hair down and swapping talk for sex with the ever-present courtesans.

Macedonia was utterly different. No one was allowed to wash in warm water except women who had just given birth. No man could recline at a banquet until he had speared and killed one of the ferocious wild boars without using a net to trap it (perhaps reminiscent of Heracles's slaying of the Erymanthian boar). A soldier had to wear a rope or sash around his waist until he had killed his first man in battle. To achieve these expectations boys from an early age were taught to fight, ride a horse, and hunt wild boar, foxes, birds, and even lions. Hunting in fact was more than just a sport: it allowed time for the king and his nobles to interact socially, which affected their relations politically.[19] These hunts were clearly dangerous, as a mosaic depicting a lion hunt from Pella attests. Although the figures on the mosaic have been disputed, most likely we have Alexander to the animal's left, trapped by its paw, and Craterus (who became one of Alexander's generals) to its right, coming to his rescue (Figure 4). Both are wearing next to no protective clothing and are armed only with short swords—they thus had to get up close and personal with their deadly prey and rely on split-second instincts.

Macedonian society, then, was rugged and had more in common with the tough love of Homeric heroes or even Viking society than with Classical Greece. Not even members of the ruling dynasty enjoyed any privileged treatment as they grew up: boys in line to the throne would be expected to be as hardy and well trained as anyone else and so grow into their role as warrior kings. Kings even dressed in the same manner as the people, steering clear of any regalia such as a crown and preferring a purple cloak and the distinctive, wide-brimmed felt hat known as the *kausia*.[20] No one called the king "his highness" or "your majesty" but, rather, addressed him by name, and the king's personal name was used on official documents. These expectations explain the dissatisfaction of the army with Alexander in Asia as he began to favor Asian dress, Asian customs, and even Persian personnel over his own men.

FIGURE 4

Mosaic of a lion hunt (Pella). Photo: Ian Worthington, Pella Museum, Greece.

Even the Macedonians' symposia were utterly different from Greek ones and reflected the people's coarser lifestyle.[21] In Athens symposiasts discussed literature, philosophy, or public affairs while they ate and drank wine mixed with water—they considered that drinking wine neat was a barbarian practice. Not so the Macedonians. At their symposia, which the king routinely attended, they drank their wine "unmixed" (*akratos*) and had no time for highbrow deliberation. They quickly became drunk and rowdy and often fought among themselves as they strove to outdo each other with stories of their valor.

According to ancient writers, the Macedonians "were drunk while they were still being served the first course and could not enjoy their food":[22] Philip was interested only in "a life of drunkenness, debauchery and indecent dancing,"[23] while Alexander the Great "would sleep without waking up for two days and two nights" after some of his drinking contests.[24] These kings were not alcoholics in the modern sense of the word but more like binge drinkers, who restricted their drinking to parties. Still, these parties could turn deadly. An angry exchange between Philip and Alexander at the former's wedding feast in 337 led to the king drawing his sword on his son and rushing to attack him before drunkenly falling over a table. Far worse was the alcohol-fueled argument between Alexander and his general Cleitus the Black at Maracanda in 328, which ended with the king murdering him.[25]

Equally distasteful to Greeks, who placed high value on the nuclear family, was the Macedonian practice of polygamy, at least among the kings. It is strange that the Macedonians never abandoned this custom, given the dynastic problems that multiple heirs from several mothers legally married to the same king caused for the throne.[26] Most often marriages were for diplomatic and military reasons—Philip married seven times without ever divorcing a wife, but his first six marriages were political—he "made war by marriage," as an ancient biographer stated.[27] The king's wives or, rather, queens had equal status and lived together in the same palace. Olympias, Philip's fourth wife, was an exception, perhaps because she was the mother of Alexander, the heir to the throne. She felt that she could interfere in political affairs, which led to a rapid deterioration in relations with her husband: by the time he died in 336 they hated each other.

The Greeks routinely referred to the Macedonians as "barbarians" even in the late fourth century after they had fallen under their control.[28] In a speech of 341, Demosthenes of Athens, Philip's most vocal adversary, claimed bluntly that the king was "not only not Greek and unrelated to the Greeks...but a miserable Macedonian, from a land from which previously you could not even buy a decent slave."[29] This slur had nothing to do with Macedonian culture, or lack thereof, for Pella had been a cultural center since the time of Archelaus, who ruled from 413 to 399.[30] Archelaus had invited Socrates and the Athenian tragic playwrights Agathon and Euripides to his court. Socrates declined, but Euripides moved to Pella, where he wrote the *Bacchae* and the *Archelaus* (of which only fragments survive), and may have died in Macedonia in 406. Archelaus also attracted Zeuxis, the foremost fresco painter, to move from Italy and set up a school in Pella that pioneered mosaic painting. Macedonian gold, silver, and bronze artwork, mosaics, tomb paintings, and jewelry were of the very highest quality, as can be seen in the lion hunt mosaic (Figure 4) and the painting from the north wall of Tomb I at Vergina of Hades abducting Persephone (Figure 5).[31]

Some themes and images, such as hunts, are almost uniquely Macedonian and spread first to Greece and then, thanks to Alexander's conquests, to the east and even influenced Roman artists and styles. Further, some kings, including Philip II, had contacts with intellectuals and philosophers, including Plato, Aristotle, and Speusippus.

Culture, therefore, had nothing to do with being a "barbarian." What Greeks meant by the term was someone who did not speak Greek. Twice during his reign Alexander was said to speak in Macedonian, the first time at the trial of his general Philotas in 330 and the second time in a verbal fight with Cleitus in 328.[32] Thus, the Macedonians may have been a Slavic people who came into contact with Greeks and embraced their culture. However, the ethnicity of the ancient Macedonians is controversial because of the nature of the evidence, which is all Greek and so biased. Also complicating the issue is the intervention of modern politics, especially after 1991 when the "new state" of the Republic of Macedonia was formed.[33]

Nonetheless, ancient writers, from Hesiod in the eighth century to Herodotus and Thucydides in the fifth, and even to Strabo in the early

FIGURE 5
Hades abducting Persephone (Tomb I, Vergina). Macedonian School/Vergina, Macedonia, Greece/
The Bridgeman Art Library.

first century A.D., accept that the Macedonians were Greek and so Greek speaking.[34] When Athenian ambassadors visited the court at Pella or Macedonian envoys visited Athens, neither side needed interpreters, whereas Greeks needed interpreters to understand the Illyrians, for example.[35] Moreover, the written archaeological evidence discovered in Macedonia is all in Greek, Macedonian proper names are Greek, and the correct term for the people—*Makedones*—is Greek in root and ethnic terminations and may have meant "Highlanders."[36] Even Macedonian religion is more Greek than anything else—the Macedonians particularly revered Zeus, Dionysus, and Heracles.[37] It is therefore more likely that the Macedonians spoke a dialect, not a different language (as the Persians and Illyrians did), probably peppered with Illyrian and other border vocabulary, and it was this that was foreign to the Greeks.[38]

Macedonia, then, was looked upon as having more in common with northern tribes than with the Greeks—politically, socially, and culturally. It was different, it was on the periphery of Greece, and its people knew that—perhaps why they relished their hard-living, hard-drinking, "different" image, because it was how they wanted to be seen.[39] Certainly Philip (and Alexander) must have been influenced by Greek attitudes to his people and the geographical location of Macedonia. It was so far north that Greeks thought civilization ended there, just as those living in southern England used to think that "civilization ended north of Watford Gap" (about 15 miles north of London).[40] Philip must have enjoyed getting his own back as he increased Macedonian influence in Greece; so too must Alexander, who treated Greeks as what they were by his time: his subjects.

PHILIP BECOMES KING

The Greeks south of Mount Olympus could never have imagined their country ruled by another, let alone one like Macedonia, which on top of all its troubles had a stagnant economy. The kingdom possessed abundant natural resources, such as silver, gold, copper, iron, lead, and in particular forests of oak, pine, fir, and cedar, which the Greeks to the south coveted.[41] The kings ex officio owned all of these resources, but the poor to nonexistent exploitation before Philip meant that their truth wealth was never realized. That is why Macedonian coinage was almost always bronze, unlike the silver and even gold of their neighbors and Greek states. Philip, however, thoroughly reformed the economy and expanded mining interests (Map 4). Among other things he minted silver and gold Macedonian coinage that became the strongest currency in Europe.[42]

Most of the kings' income before Philip derived from their timber supplies, which often accounted for the disruptive and meddling contacts between the Macedonians and the Greeks.[43] Interested only in the kingdom's timber for their fleet, the Athenians in 437 had founded a colony named Amphipolis on the border of Macedonia and Thrace (between the Aegean and the Danube) to guarantee them access to the region's timber (Map 2). Along with the Thebans and the Chalcidian League, headed by Olynthus, the Athenians had a long history of interfering in Macedonian domestic politics. To make matters worse for Macedonia, marauding tribes (*ethnoi*) on its borders seized livestock, crops, and possibly timber.[44] Principal among these were the tribes to the northwest (in the western Balkan Peninsula), collectively called the Illyrians,[45] and the Paeonians in the Axius Valley to the north, whose lands bordered on northern Lyncestis.

During his reign Archelaus (413–399) had striven to unite Upper and Lower Macedonia as well as relocated the capital to Pella as part of a series of wide-sweeping military and economic reforms. After his death five kings assumed the throne in just six years and just as quickly lost it, contributing to dynastic upheavals and anarchy over the next three decades that undid all of Archelaus's achievements. Another blow came during the reign of Amyntas III, Philip II's father (393/2–369), when an Illyrian invasion forced him out of Macedonia for some time.[46] His son Alexander II became king in 369 but was assassinated the following year, sparking off four more years of dynastic chaos until in 365 Perdiccas III (Philip's brother) came to the throne and enforced some stability. His reign was cut brutally short in 359 when he marched against a band of invading Illyrians led by the octogenarian chieftain Bardylis. In a bitter battle Perdiccas and 4,000 Macedonian soldiers were killed; to make matters worse, his son and heir, Amyntas, was only a boy.

Ordinarily, when the heir was a minor the Macedonian Assembly appointed a regent over him until he came of age.[47] The Assembly, however, set Amyntas aside and acclaimed his uncle Philip, who was then in his mid-twenties, as king.[48] The reason for this extraordinary action was a series of sudden threats to Macedonia. The first threat was that posed by the triumphant Illyrians, who were pressing deeper into Macedonia, perhaps even intent on seizing lands in Lower Macedonia. The second came from the Paeonians, who were preparing to invade the kingdom.

The third and fourth threats were pretenders to the throne: Pausanias, supported by Berisades, king of Western Thrace, and Argaeus, whom the Athenians had landed at Methone on the Thermaic Gulf with 3,000 troops. It is small wonder that the Greeks expected Macedonia to spiral further downward into the abyss of a second- or even a third-rate power.

As history proves, the Assembly's decision in 359 was the best it made for Macedonia's history. Philip neutralized these four external threats within a matter of months and went on to unite Macedonia, centralize the capital of Pella, increase the size and prosperity of his kingdom, create the best army in the ancient world before the Roman, and subdue lands from Greece to Thrace, in the process laying the foundations for Alexander's empire. A typical warrior king, Philip always led his army into battle, suffering the loss of an eye, a shattered collarbone, and a life-threatening leg wound—his reconstructed face from the skull fragments discovered in his tomb testifies to the life he led (Figure 1). How he accomplished all of these things, given the adversities he faced throughout his reign, is a remarkable story of military and diplomatic prowess, personal sacrifice and injury, shameless deceit, and sheer endurance.

2.

PHILIP II AND THE RISE OF MACEDONIA

A NCIENT WRITERS SPENT LESS time on Philip because they were more concerned with his son Alexander's dazzling exploits.[1] Most information about Philip's reign is provided by two later narrative writers: the Greek historian Diodorus Siculus (of Sicily), who in the first century B.C. composed a universal history from mythological times to the early Roman Empire, and Justin's epitome (written between the second and fourth century A.D.) of a first-century B.C. work by Pompeius Trogus.[2] The contemporary speeches of the Athenian politicians Aeschines and Demosthenes provide substantial information about Philip and his aims, although they are biased and have to be read with a large pinch of salt.

PHILIP'S BIRTH AND YOUTH

Philip was born in either 383 or 382 and was the son of King Amyntas III and his wife Eurydice, a princess most likely from Lyncestis in Upper Macedonia (Map 2). He had two older brothers—who reigned as Alexander II (369–368) and Perdiccas III (368–359)—and a sister. His father later married a lady named Gygaea, possibly an Argead,[3] and with her he had three more sons—Archelaus, Arrhidaeus, and Menelaus—and a daughter. These stepbrothers may also have made a bid for the throne in 359, prompting Philip to order their executions.

We do not know for sure what Philip looked like. Statues of him have not survived, and his portrait is found on only a few coins, such as a silver tetradrachm where he appears as a bearded horseman wearing the distinct

Macedonian felt cap or *kausia* (Figure 6), and on a gold medallion from Tarsus (Figure 7). His features are also probably represented on a small, carved ivory head (Figure 8), found in what is believed to be his tomb at Vergina. It depicts a bearded man with trauma around the right eye, which is consistent with a blinding wound he received at the siege of Methone in 355–354. Also in the tomb were skeletal remains including skull fragments that indicate an eye wound—when reconstructed the face bears a remarkable similarity to the ivory head. The assembled skeleton, along with the occupant's arms and armor that were also placed in the tomb, suggests that Philip was between 1.67 and 1.71 meters tall (see pp. 124–126 on the tomb).

FIGURE 6
Portrait of Philip on a silver tetradrachm. © The Trustees of the British Museum/
Art Resource, New York.

FIGURE 7
Portrait of Philip on a gold medallion. Alfredo Dagli Orti/The Art Archive at Art Resource, New York.

FIGURE 8

Ivory head of Philip from Tomb II, Vergina. Gianni Dagli Orti/The Art Archive at Art Resource, New York.

Philip would have had a typical Macedonian upbringing, with its emphasis on physical activities, fighting, riding, and hunting. He would have attended symposia and heard the stories that were raucously told there— including those about Macedonia's enemies. His intellectual education would have included the poems of Homer, other genres of Greek literature such as tragedy and lyric poetry, and philosophy.[4] He did not receive the same uninterrupted formal education as his son, who was tutored from the ages of 14 to 16 by Aristotle, but he was still seen as an intellectual, whose patronage was cultivated by Speusippus, Plato's successor as head of the Academy in Athens.

When Philip was 13 or 14, in 368, his education in Macedonia was interrupted when he was sent to live for two years in Thebes (Map 1). In that year his brother Alexander II had been forced to enlist Theban assistance against a challenger to the throne, Ptolemy. Pelopidas, the Theban general, supported Alexander, but in return Pelopidas imposed terms on Alexander, which included sending hostages (one being Philip) to Thebes. The young Philip's academic education continued in that city, for the Pythagorean follower Lysis of Tarentum taught him for at least some of his time there. But what impressed Philip the most was the military life to which he was exposed. He lived in the house of the Theban politician and general Pammenes and enjoyed close contacts with Pelopidas and another general, Epaminondas. From the latter, the tradition goes, Philip learned about shock tactics and the various ways to combine infantry and cavalry deployments in battle.[5] He also watched the famed 300-strong Sacred Band train and much admired them—so much so that when he came across all their corpses after his victory at Chaeronea in 338 he burst into tears. Despite his young age the military experiences Philip gained in Thebes influenced him the most after he became king—it was these that Justin claimed "most served to develop his exceptional genius."[6]

Also of benefit to Philip was the fact that for two years he lived in a Greek polis and so experienced life in Greece from the inside. He saw the weaknesses inherent in the polis system, such as the factionalism, the divide between the rich and poor strata in society that Demosthenes's speeches in Athens often pointed to, and the inefficiency and slowness of democracies—not to mention the feelings of outright hostility on the part of one Greek city to one another. These experiences were at the core of his most dangerous traits when he became involved in Greek affairs: acting fast and decisively while a city was still debating how to deal with him and playing off one city against another.

Philip returned to Pella in probably 365, shortly after the accession of his brother Perdiccas III. The new king appointed him governor of part of the kingdom, perhaps Amphaxitis, which stretched from the Axius to the Thermaic Gulf (Map 2), and put him in command of cavalry and infantry troops. Perdiccas may have been drawing on the military skills his brother had gained in Thebes since he tasked him with preventing the Thracians and the Paeonians from penetrating Macedonia's borders. For three, possibly even four, years Philip performed his duties admirably, which may well have influenced the Assembly to proclaim him king, not Amyntas, in 359. During Philip's governorship Perdiccas—as was his right as king—most likely arranged for his brother to marry Phila, the daughter of Derdas II of Elimeia.[7]

The threats posed by the two invading tribes and the two pretenders to the throne at the time of Philip's accession were very grave. However, he "was not panic-stricken by the magnitude of the expected perils, but, bringing together the Macedonians in a series of assemblies and exhorting them with eloquent speeches to be men, he built up their morale."[8] In systematically reducing each threat, he set what would become a lethal pattern in his reign of speed, diplomacy, deceit, and hard fighting when necessary that always outmaneuvered his opponents. As king he always preferred diplomacy, for which he had an uncanny ability, over military action, but when diplomacy failed he struck fast and ruthlessly.[9] A king like that was certainly needed to save Macedonia. Philip's appetite, however, was not merely for rescue—after securing his borders he grew hungry for empire.

BUYING TIME

Philip's most urgent need in 359 was to neutralize the threats to his vulnerable kingdom, and he did so with speed and determination.[10] He negotiated with the Illyrians, who represented the greatest danger, agreeing to marry Bardylis's granddaughter Audata (his second wife).[11] Bardylis retained control of Upper Macedonia, but at least he now returned home, presumably expecting to dominate Philip and Macedonia because of the marriage settlement. Next, Philip bribed the Paeonians to abandon their invasion of Macedonia. A bribe likewise convinced Berisades of Thrace to abandon support for the pretender Pausanias and put him to death.

Then Philip turned to deal with the crisis perpetuated by the Athenian support of Argaeus, who was intent on marching to the old capital of Aegae.[12] The pretender had a formidable military force of 3,000 soldiers at his disposal; if he had successfully rallied any barons at Aegae who had opposed Philip's elevation to the throne, then the new king might well have been toppled. This concern perhaps explains why Philip took steps to eliminate his three stepbrothers, who may have been laying claim to the throne. One of them, Archelaus, was executed, but the others fled, and it was not until 348 that the king finally caught up with them and had them killed. Interestingly, Philip took no measures against his nephew and the actual heir to the throne, Amyntas. He allowed him to live at Pella in some luxury and arranged for him to marry his daughter Cynnana (from his marriage to Audata), thus binding uncle and nephew closer together.

The Athenians had long desired to regain their former colony Amphipolis, on the border of Macedonia and Thrace, which had defected from them in 424 during the Peloponnesian War. They had made several attempts on it over the years, and to assist its independence Perdiccas III had installed a Macedonian garrison there. Philip now withdrew that garrison, which the Athenians interpreted as a precursor to his returning the city to them. They immediately ordered their troops to stand fast at Methone. Argaeus was thus forced to march the 20 miles to Aegae with only a few supporters. His attempt to gather support there failed utterly, and he turned back to Methone, only to be ambushed by Philip at the Livahdi ridge—and to disappear from history. Philip followed up his action by sending a letter to the Athenians, who at the time were debating a union with the Chalcidian League, in which he called for an alliance. He further insisted that he laid no claim on Amphipolis for himself. They accordingly rejected the Chalcidian initiative in favor of Philip.

Philip had therefore saved Macedonia at one of the gravest times in its history. However, the enforced agreements with his opponents were simply to buy him time—he had no intention of honoring any of them. Instead, he planned to take the fight to Macedonia's enemies for a change and for the first time in his kingdom's history properly secure its borders. Therefore he embarked on an ambitious series of military reforms that revolutionized the Macedonian army—for himself and Alexander.

COMBAT IN GREECE

During the Archaic and Classical periods poleis were almost constantly at war with each other for all sorts of reasons—personal, economic, religious, and strategic.[13] It might even be said that treaties and truces interrupted warfare rather than the other way around. Take as an example the Peace of Nicias in 421, which was meant to end hostilities in the Peloponnesian War and last for 50 years, but had been abandoned within two years, and fighting resumed until 404. While the Greeks appear to have waged war at the drop of a hat, they were well aware of the personal and financial costs involved in warfare and did not go to war lightly. Yet pitched battles between rival armies in Greece were quite rare in the Archaic and the first half of the Classical periods.[14] The pace of combat increased dramatically in the fourth century, but this was due to Alexander's invasion of Asia, since he was fighting battles and besieging cities practically every year—and sometimes several times a year—when he was over there.

The standard Greek infantrymen were the hoplites, who wore body armor such as a bronze cuirass, greaves, and a bronze helmet with a visor cut into it. They also carried a round, heavy shield (*hoplon*), battling the enemy in fierce hand-to-hand fighting, supported by cavalry. There were also other types of troops depending on the terrain, for the close combat skills of a hoplite were not necessarily suited to a mountain pass but more to a wider, level plain. In an engagement both sides marched against each other at a brisk pace, and on a prearranged signal the hoplites would charge the enemy line while the cavalry attacked its flanks to wheel around them, trapping the foe between two offensive lines. The weight of armor and heat of the Greek summer probably meant that the infantry fight was a cumbersome and exhausting thing and did not last for very long, although sometimes both sides might retreat to regroup and recuperate before fighting again.[15] Any neat formation that the hoplites had at the start of the conflict quickly dissolved into a furious, "down-and-dirty" fight for survival as they were pushed back and forth when both lines were crushed together. Their vision was limited by the narrowness of the visor, so for a lot of the time they must have been slashing away left and right with their swords, killing and dismembering opponents. There was little if any opportunity for the almost choreographed personal combat with plenty of space around each soldier as in the days of Homeric heroes or movie versions of battles. It was kill or be killed—and kill any way you could. Some reactions of individuals to battle are traced later in the book (pp. 283–288).

Before the rise of full-time professional soldiers battles usually took place in the spring, since the bulk of hoplite soldiers were farmers, who were busy on their farms at other crucial times.[16] Occasionally warring cities might discuss the "terms" of the battle in advance, such as a time limit, perhaps to avoid wholesale slaughter, and at the end of the fighting a herald from the losing side was allowed to negotiate a truce and claim the wounded and dead for burial. Religion and warfare were closely linked.[17] The Greeks consulted the Oracle of Apollo at Delphi on the pros and cons of going to war. They piously made vows and sacrificed to gods such as Ares (the god of war), Zeus, and Athena for success in battle, even singing a paean or battle song as they charged (and the victor commonly dedicated spoils in the temples of gods); they returned soldiers killed in battle to their home cities for proper burial, and in the case of Apollo at Delphi they waged "sacred wars" for his protection. When in 355 the state of Phocis sacrilegiously seized Delphi, sparking off the decade-long Third Sacred War, Philip at one stage had his men wear crowns of laurel to symbolize that Apollo was fighting with them, which caused some of the enemy to flee from guilt.

Philip would turn the traditional method of combat on its head by creating an army and introducing new tactics the likes of which the Greeks had never seen. His enemies were no match for him. Nor, as events would prove, were the Persians, Bactrians, and Indians a match for Alexander, thanks to the army he inherited from his father.

PHILIP'S MILITARY REFORMS

The strength of Macedonia's army before Philip had lain in its cavalry, provided by the nobles who alone could bear the costs of horses and armor. The infantry by contrast consisted mostly of peasant farmers, who were hastily conscripted when danger threatened. They were poorly, if at all, trained and armed. When called to fight they had to leave their farms, bringing with them their oxen and wagons, which in turn adversely affected their crop outputs and livelihood. No match for the aggressive tribes on the kingdom's borders or the trained hoplite Greek armies, the

Macedonian army had a torpid track record. Philip changed all that by implementing reforms as soon as he became king to create a professional, full-time fighting force.[18]

Like the Greek cities, Philip relied on mercenaries throughout his reign. However, to attract his own people as well as those whom he conquered to military service, he introduced regular pay and a promotion pathway; he also provided arms and armor to the infantry, although the wealthy cavalrymen still had to pay for their own horses. The elite hypaspist (shield bearer) infantryman was paid one drachma a day, and a cavalryman, three drachmas. These rates were higher than the daily five obols for a Greek hoplite soldier (six obols = one drachma) and two (possibly three) drachmas for a Greek cavalryman. In addition, cash bonuses and even grants of land in conquered territories were awarded to his men in recognition of their service and as an incentive to fight all the more. These simple acts dispensed with the need for conscription and also benefited the economy, as the farmers no longer had to leave their lands to fight.

Philip never considered adopting the Greek hoplite style of hand-to-hand fighting at close quarters. Instead, thanks to the tactical influence of Pammenes and Epaminondas of Thebes, he taught his infantry new skills and grouped them together in various battalions (led by battalion commanders) that together comprised the phalanx, over which he had ultimate control. He may have done so because he lacked money and time to make the armor and train his men in hoplite tactics.[19] On the other hand, given the 4,000 losses under Perdiccas, Philip must have had to hire some mercenaries at the start of his reign, which indicates that he had money. Further, these mercenaries would have been versed in hoplite tactics, affording him the time to train his own men accordingly. Therefore a more plausible reason for fashioning the phalanx as he did is that he wanted it to be utterly different from anything the Greeks had ever been confronted by in battle. To cope with different terrains and enemy formations and numbers Philip varied the depth of the phalanx formation from eight to 32 ranks (he and Alexander preferred 16), thereby affording it weight and power as well as maneuverability in the field.

Philip (or possibly Alexander II) may also have created a contingent of infantry known as *pezhetairoi*, "foot companions," as a sort of "special forces" unit. Later, *pezhetairoi* became the name for all the infantry, perhaps as a "balance" to the Companion Cavalry,[20] and this specialist unit was called the hypaspists (shield bearers), who would prove invaluable to Alexander in Asia. Philip also introduced new weaponry, including the *sarissa*, a 14- to 18-foot-long pike made of local cornel wood, with a pointed iron head, altogether weighing around 14 pounds—the modern reconstructions of them at Thessaloníki show how intimidating these weapons must have been (Figure 9).

The sarissa required both hands to wield it, but since it came in two parts it could easily be carried and then quickly fitted together before engaging an enemy.[21] The infantryman would then carry the weapon upright (in "close order," *pyknosis*), and as the phalanx approached the

FIGURE 9
Sarissas (Thessaloníki). Photo: Ian Worthington.

enemy line the first five ranks of the battalions would lower their sarissas to charge (Figure 10).

The sheer length of the sarissa allowed the Macedonian troops to impale their enemies, whose short swords came nowhere near them, thereby thwarting the close-formation hoplite fighting. Even when the two lines actually did meet the Macedonians' armor of a cuirass, leg greaves, small shield over one shoulder, a short sword, and an iron,

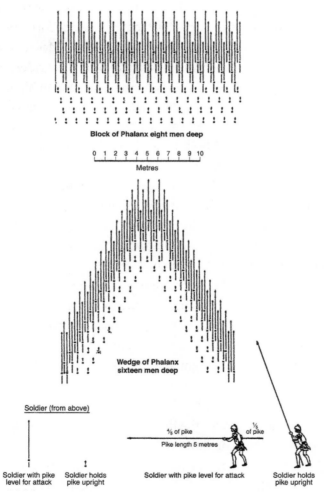

FIGURE 10

Macedonian phalanx formation carrying *sarissas*. From N. G. L. Hammond, *Alexander the Great: King, Commander and Statesman*, 2nd ed. (Bristol: 1989), p. 84.

hoplite-style helmet weighed less than that of the Greek hoplite, again giving them an advantage.

Most of Philip's innovations involved the infantry, but he did not neglect the cavalry and viewed both divisions of his army as equally important. He arranged the cavalry in various divisions (*ilai*), each of about 200 men, which were based on the regions from which the troops came. A special royal squadron of cavalry (*ile basilike*) comprised 300 men. He may even have created the fast, mounted cavalry scouts (*prodromoi*), on whom Alexander relied so heavily in Asia. Instead of a frontal cavalry assault, Philip trained his cavalry to attack in a wedge formation, and its principal role was to disrupt the opposite line. The Macedonian horses pushed and shoved the enemy combatants, while their riders, brandishing spears and short swords, slashed and stabbed from on high. There was also a cavalry squadron named the *sarissophoroi*, who therefore carried sarissas. These must have been shorter than the infantry sarissas, as the riders could not have used both hands to wield a long sarissa and at the same time control their horses. To wreak havoc among enemy ranks even more, Philip reversed the standard Greek tactic of infantry engaging the enemy before the cavalry. His army was unique in Greece for having its cavalry advance against the adversary's flanks at the outset of an engagement and wheel behind it while the massed phalanx bore down on the center and poured through gaps opened up by the cavalry. In this way, his opponents were trapped between two offensive fronts.

Philip kept his men in constant training to help prepare them for any type of engagement. The infantry especially had to learn to use their sarissas effortlessly, especially if marching across rivers and rocky terrain, and to run with them in upright and lowered positions. We learn about aspects of the training and drills from a campaign in Illyria that Alexander waged in 335, shortly after he became king (pp. 129–130). Philip would also have arranged for the infantry and cavalry to work seamlessly together, perhaps charging dummy lines of differing lengths and depths to hone their shock-and-awe tactics. The king also intended his new army to be self-sufficient. To this end, the men were taught to forage for provisions and to carry all their equipment, food, and drink. The "hangers-on" who normally accompanied Greek and Persian armies, from wives and families to various attendants and even prostitutes, were banned from traveling with Macedonian troops. The slow-moving carts carrying provisions and equipment that oxen had previously pulled were also abandoned and replaced by faster-moving pack animals such as mules and horses. The end result was an army that could march quickly and effortlessly regardless of terrain or weather conditions.

Philip's military reforms did not happen overnight but, rather, continued throughout his reign. In about 350 he formed an engineering corps, headed by Polyeides (or Polyidus) of Thessaly, who was designing new siege machinery, including the torsion catapult. This was akin to a spring-loaded crossbow that fired arrows farther and faster than the traditional mechanically drawn catapult (Figure 11).[22] Philip first used the torsion catapult at his siege of Byzantium in 340, and the weapon enabled Alexander to take many walled cities and force others into capitulation. In fact two of Polyidus's students, Diades and Charias, accompanied Alexander on his campaigns.

Philip also integrated regular and specialist troops from the areas he conquered into his army. For example, after his campaign in Illyria in 358

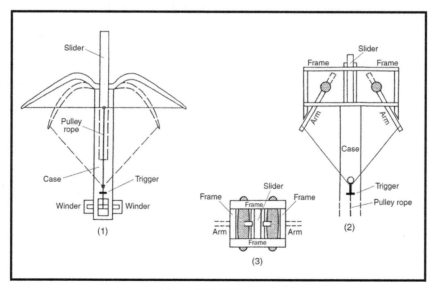

FIGURE 11
Mechanical bow and torsion catapult.

Agrianian javelin men (who lived above the Strymon River) joined his ranks, as did Thracian javelin men and Scythian archers after his conquest of Thrace in 342–341. Some of the individual regiments of the phalanx had special functions or were held in particular esteem, such as the elite hypaspists, who were lighter-armed and marched at faster speeds and whose number included the royal *agema* or guard. Competition to be in these units was fierce, and membership meant everything—as Philip intended. Here, the political nature of his military reforms becomes evident. Former opponents who were made to join the army and who were deliberately kept in territorial divisions fought all the harder to prove that their divisions were the best, while outstanding commanders could be rewarded with membership in Philip's senior staff (like his general Parmenion). In turn they came to owe loyalty to their general and king and maintain a united Macedonia.

To this end Philip may also have introduced the school of royal pages, young noble boys who lived at court from 14 to 18 years of age and received a military training, accompanying the king on campaign in their last year and serving as his personal attendants.[23] This innovation was really a form of hostage-taking and was perhaps inspired by Persian practice. The families of these boys had little say in their sons being taken to court, where their well-being depended on the loyalty of their fathers.

Diodorus grossly overstated that Philip left so vast and powerful an army that Alexander never needed to ask for reinforcements when campaigning against the Persians.[24] Nevertheless, Philip increased the army's size from only about 10,000 infantry and 600 cavalry in 359 to 24,000 infantry and 3,000 cavalry by the end of his reign in 336.[25] He created an offensive army such as Macedonia had never seen before and in doing so enabled his kingdom to become an imperial power.

UNITING MACEDONIA

In 358, only one year after he assumed the throne, Philip resolved to end the threats to his borders once and for all. That spring he led as many as 10,000 infantry and 500 cavalry against the Paeonians, whose king had recently died and who represented less of a challenge for his new army, and defeated them. The details are obscure, but evidently the fate of the Paeonians hung on a pitched battle, which they lost. Paeonia became part of Macedonia and in doing so also opened up the trade route along the Axius Valley to Dardania in the north. Hardly pausing for breath Philip next turned to deal with Bardylis of the Illyrians. At Lake Lychnitis (Ochrid), possibly close to Heraclea Lyncestis (Monastir), the two sides met in battle. The Illyrians had formed themselves into a hollow rectangle to fight their enemy on all sides, but the Macedonians' lethal cavalry and infantry charge opened up gaps in the enemy rectangle, through which they poured into its hollow middle. That allowed them to fight the Illyrians front and behind, and in the ensuing rout 7,000 Illyrians were killed.[26] Philip thus avenged the deaths of Perdiccas III and 4,000 solders at Bardylis's hands the previous year. Bardylis survived the battle and offered to negotiate terms, but Philip refused: he wanted no less than the total end of Illyrian influence in Upper Macedonia.

His stunning victory allowed Philip to unite Upper and Lower Macedonia for the first time in its history and generated a ripple effect whereby he centralized Pella as capital of the kingdom and introduced much-needed economic reforms.[27] He began with the exploitation of the rich gold and silver mines in this region at Damastium, and as his reign progressed mining became the backbone of the Macedonian economy, creating abundant wealth for the kingdom—and king—as never before. Thanks to the induction of Paeonians and Illyrians into his army his manpower reserves were considerably increased, and although Upper Macedonia continued to give him trouble during his reign, his northern and northwestern frontiers were now as secure as they ever would be.[28]

Philip next turned to his southern border with Thessaly (Map 2). He had recently received an appeal for assistance from the ruling Aleuadae family in the city of Larissa, which headed a Thessalian League of sorts, centered in the cities of the rich and fertile inland plain. For some time Larissa had faced opposition from Pherae (Velestinon), whose harbor Pagasae (Volos) allowed it to exercise influence over the coastal states. Enmity between the two cities stretched back to the late 370s, when the Larissans had allied with Alexander II and the Thebans against the ambitious Jason of Pherae's attempts to overcome them.[29] By 358 Jason was long dead, but his sons harbored hopes of dominating all of Thessaly, and the Aleuadae felt suitably threatened. Philip was quick to respond because an alliance with powerful Larissa would protect his southern border and provide him with renowned Thessalian horses for his cavalry. To cement the accord he married a Larissan lady named Philinna (his third wife), who bore him a son, Arrhidaeus, the following year (357).[30] Thessaly, however, was a thorn in Philip's flesh over the years, and since it was a vital buffer state between Macedonia and Greece he attached special importance to it throughout his reign.[31]

In the following year, 357, Philip turned to his southwest border with the tribal kingdom of Epirus (Map 2). He concluded an alliance with its king, Arybbas, and married his niece (the daughter of the recently deceased king), Olympias (Figure 12).[32] She quickly established herself as a forceful personality who was not afraid of Philip or averse to interfering in political affairs. One year later (356) she gave birth to a son, Alexander. This was the future Alexander the Great, but he was not yet the heir, since in Macedonia firstborn sons automatically succeeded to the throne.[33] Relations with Epirus were also problematic for Philip, and later in his reign he was forced to intervene decisively in its affairs.[34]

Philip was not overly concerned at this time about his eastern border with Thrace, because of dissension among the three Thracian kings. In 359 (a little before Philip was acclaimed king) Cotys, the king of Thrace, had died, and his three sons had divided up the kingdom among themselves. Berisades ruled over Western Thrace (from the Strymon River to Maroneia); Amadocus, Central Thrace (Maroneia to the river Hebrus); and Cersebleptes, Eastern Thrace (from the Hebrus to the Chersonese).[35] The aspirations of Cersebleptes to defeat his brothers and unite Thrace under his own rule prompted Philip to intervene in Thrace a number of times, but for now he was convinced that the three separate kingdoms posed no immediate threat to him.[36]

Thus in 357, merely two years after becoming king, Philip had unified Macedonia, centralized Pella, and secured his kingdom's borders from incursions. He had also embarked on ambitious military reforms and stimulated Macedonia's economy as never before. His growth in power,

FIGURE 12
Olympias. Alfredo Dagli Orti/The Art Archive at Art Resource, New York.

however, brought him into conflict with two powers that had a history of interfering in Macedonia's internal politics: Athens and the Chalcidian League. They were next on his list.

FROM MACEDONIA TO GREECE

In 359 Philip had hoodwinked the Athenians into withdrawing their support for Argaeus the pretender by removing the Macedonian garrison from Amphipolis. Now, in 357, it finally hit home that this was merely a ploy. Philip could never permit an Athenian presence so close to his eastern border and on such vital trade and communication routes. Moreover, he had designs on the rich mines at Crenides, which lay 40 miles east of Amphipolis, and had no wish to have an Athenian enclave standing between him and the mines. Nor could he allow the people of Amphipolis their independence, as they presumably expected when he withdrew the garrison. Therefore, in the spring of 357 he turned to besiege the city, an action that he knew would generate alarm in both cities.

The Amphipolitans immediately sent two men, Hierax and Stratocles, to Athens seeking help. Philip neatly countered any Athenian response by dispatching a letter to the Athenians assuring them that Amphipolis was theirs once it capitulated. The people again took him at his word; again their hopes were dashed. By the late summer of 357 the Macedonian battering rams and siege engines had breached Amphipolis's walls, allowing the attackers entry into the city, while more of their comrades used scaling ladders to climb the walls and attack the defenders from above.[37] Thus Amphipolis fell. Philip deserves praise because taking walled cities in the ancient world was no mean feat—in 340 he unsuccessfully besieged Perinthus and Byzantium (p. 78), and in 332 Tyre resisted Alexander for six months before it finally capitulated (pp. 173–178).

Almost immediately Philip besieged and captured Pydna (on the coast of Pieria), an ally of Athens. His action was the start of a concerted campaign to win control of his entire coastline. At last the naive Athenians recognized the reality of the situation and declared war on Philip, calling it "the war for Amphipolis."[38] To their credit, they attempted a union with Grabus, the king of the Grabaei of Illyria, the Thracian kings, the Paeonian king Lyppeius, and the powerful Olynthians. Their efforts proved fruitless thanks to Philip's speed and combination of diplomacy and military skill. He brought about a treaty with the Olynthians by offering to wrest Potidaea (an Athenian cleruchy on the neck of the Pallene Peninsula, only a mile from Olynthus) from Athenian control and hand it over to them. For once he lived up to his word: after a short, successful siege he turned the city over to Olynthus, but he did sell the native Potidaeans into slavery, yet allowed Athenian cleruchs to depart unharmed. Next followed three fleeting and successful offensives against the Illyrians, the Paeonians, and the Thracians, waged by Philip and his general Parmenion. Against this background, incidentally, Plutarch (writing in the first–second century A.D.) relates the story that at the same time as Potidaea capitulated Philip received word that Parmenion had defeated the Illyrian threat, that his horse had won first place in the Olympic Games, and that Olympias had borne him a son, Alexander.[39]

Athens was isolated. To make matters worse, several of its allies had revolted in 356 in the Social War. Possibly even Philip played a behind-the-scenes role in the allied revolt to distract Athens from his siege of Potidaea. When the Social War ended the following year Athenian finances were so severely depleted that the city could not mount large-scale military expeditions against anyone, let alone Philip, for several years.[40]

The next decade witnessed Macedonia's rise as an economic and military power and Philip's slow and steady push into Greece. Before his siege of Potidaea he had assisted the people of Crenides, which was in the Mount Pangaeum region of Western Thrace. After Potidaea, Philip returned to Crenides and assumed control of the region, renaming it Philippi after himself—so was founded his first colony. The gold and silver mines there generated the enormous annual revenue of 1,000 talents, much of which was used for coinage (including the gold staters or "Philips," named after him), which became the mainstay of the Macedonian economy. He also drained and cultivated the marshy plain of Crenides, part of a land-reclamation policy that again was geared to boosting the Macedonian economy.

Philip had already begun to reduce foreign, especially Athenian, influence in the towns of his coastline. He continued to do so with vigor, so that by the winter of 355 only Methone (where the Athenians had landed Argaeus in 359) was left. He began to besiege Methone in the winter of 355, but because of its thick, defensive walls and its people's tenacity in resisting him it held out until the following spring.[41] Also delaying the inevitable was the fact that at some point in the siege one of the defenders on the ramparts shot Philip in the eye with an arrow.[42] His doctor Critobulus saved his life but was forced to remove at least some of the eyeball and, in similar fashion to soldiers so terribly wounded during World War I, for example, probably sew the eye shut. Nevertheless, Philip soldiered on at Methone, and once the city capitulated its walls and buildings were leveled. The inhabitants were spared but were required to leave and allowed to take with them only one item of clothing.

The trauma to Philip's eye helps to identify the small, carved ivory head found in what is purported to be his tomb at Vergina (Figure 8). Some

ancient writers delighted in using the eye wound as an example of his sacrilegious nature. Plutarch, for example, claimed that because Philip spied
on Zeus when the god was disguised as a snake having sex with Olympias
(who became pregnant with Alexander), he suffered the later blinding
as punishment.[43] This story, along with others, belongs to a tradition to
emphasize Alexander's superhuman status even at the time of conception
(pp. 91–92).

Philip's entire coastline—apart from the Chalcidic Peninsula—was now
his, thereby further strengthening Macedonian border security. Any other
king might now have paused, if only to rest after such a horrendous eye
wound, but not Philip. In 353 he made a quick foray into Thrace, seizing
the towns of Pagae, Abdera, Maroneia, and Neapolis. Then events in
Greece sharply redirected his attention, where another clash between Larissa and Pherae sent him again to the former's aid. However, his unblem-
ished record of success was about to change.

As soon as news broke that Philip was advancing to Thessaly Lycophron
of Pherae appealed for help to his new ally, the state of Phocis, which was
embroiled in a sacred war over its seizure of Delphi. The Phocian general
Onomarchus, then occupying Delphi, dispatched his brother Phayllus to
assist Pherae, but Philip's troops easily defeated him. Onomarchus himself
at once marched north into Thessaly with 20,000 infantry and 500 cavalry
and in a series of brilliant tactical maneuvers decisively defeated Philip.[44]
By pretending to fall back before the Macedonian army, Onomarchus lured
Philip into a crescent-shaped valley, in which he had cunningly hidden infantry and stone-throwing catapults on the surrounding hillsides. As Philip's men charged into the valley, expecting another easy fight before the
retreating Phocians, their opponents unexpectedly turned to attack them.
As they did so the catapults bombarded them from above. Utter confusion
reigned as the Macedonians, trapped in the narrow defile, tried either to
fight or to turn around and retreat, only to find their passage blocked by the
men behind them. Eventually they scrambled out but were forced to leave
behind a number of their comrades either dead or dying. Rather than collecting together at the mouth of the valley to await orders from Philip, they
kept running—all the way back to Pella in fact. Philip had no choice but to

follow them, ominously throwing out the comment that he was leaving "like a ram, which next time would butt harder."[45]

Onomarchus deserves great credit for his tactics and skillful use of the terrain. More than that, the Greeks viewed his victory as the beginning of the end for Philip. The Illyrians, Paeonians, and Arybbas of Epirus took steps to reassert their independence, while Cersebleptes of Thrace and the Olynthians, despite their recent diplomatic ties to Macedonia, entered into negotiations with the Athenians. Philip's survival as king was very suddenly in doubt.

3.

THE NEW PLAYER IN GREEK POLITICS

O NOMARCHUS OF PHOCIS'S STARTLING defeat of Philip in 353 was a
major morale boost for the small state of Phocis, which bordered
northwest Boeotia and comprised 22 cities (Map 1). The Phocians had
seized the Oracle of Apollo at Delphi and were then embroiled in a sacred
war, which broke out in 355 and lasted until 346. This sacred war—the
third in Greek history—was ostensibly fought by various Greek states to
liberate Delphi, but it was quickly exploited for political reasons.[1] The
Spartans and the Athenians intended the war to block the growing influence of the Thebans in the Peloponnese and central Greece, while Philip
used it to boost his influence south of Mount Olympus.

THE WAR FOR APOLLO

In the spring of 356 the council that presided over the Amphictyonic
League, a union of some 24 Greek states (including Athens, Thebes, and
Thessaly) that administered and protected the venerable Oracle of Apollo
at Delphi, held its regular biannual meeting.[2] At some point during it the
Thebans angrily denounced the Phocians and the Spartans for not paying
fines imposed on them by the council and demanded that they be doubled. The Phocians had probably been fined for cultivating part of the
plain below Delphi, on which the god's sacrificial animals were kept, and
the Spartans for seizing the Theban Cadmea in 382 and despoiling sanctuaries there. Most likely, the Thebans wanted to counter the Spartans'
attempts to reassert their authority in the Peloponnese, which would

decrease the growing influence of Thebes in southern Greece, and were trying to mask their hidden agenda by using the Phocians as pawns. However, the Spartans and the Phocians met the Thebans' castigation with defiance, and their general Philomelus took the radical step of seizing Delphi in protest.[3] The council called for troops from its members, but thanks to financial support from Sparta Philomelus hired 5,000 mercenaries and throughout the winter of 356–355 thwarted attempts to dislodge him. As a result, the council declared a sacred war on Phocis in the spring of 355.

Philomelus by then had doubled the number of mercenaries by sacrilegiously embezzling from Delphi's sacred treasuries, which held money and valuables such as jewelry and votive offerings belonging to various Greek states. He had scored a number of military victories against his opponents in 355 and 354, but his good luck ended at Neon (by the Cephissus Valley) in 354 when he was defeated by Amphictyonic troops under Pammenes of Thebes (with whom Philip had stayed as a hostage). To avoid capture Philomelus committed suicide by jumping off Mount Parnassus. He was succeeded by Onomarchus, who bribed the Thessalians to shun involvement in the war, invaded Boeotia to curb Theban influence there, and made an alliance with Lycophron of Pherae. It was this pact that prompted Onomarchus in 353 to send his brother Phayllus to Pherae, when threatened by Philip; after Philip sent Phayllus packing, Onomarchus marched to Thessaly, where he attacked and defeated Philip.

The repercussions of Philip's defeat were widespread, as we have noted. The king resolved to deal with them, but first he had to restore the morale of the army. That was why in 352 he stormed back into Greece, this time with 20,000 infantry and 3,000 cavalry, including a contingent from Thessaly, and did battle with Onomarchus, who had roughly the same number of infantry but only 500 cavalry, at the Krokion Plain or Crocus Field, near the coast of Magnesia. This time Philip routed the Phocians. His phalanx kept the enemy line at bay, while his cavalry attacked and wheeled behind it, trapping the Phocian soldiers between Macedonian cavalry and infantry. With no means of escape, 6,000 of them were killed, including Onomarchus, and 3,000 were captured and put to death on the spot.

Despite losing as much as half of their army in the battle the Phocians refused to admit defeat. They immediately appointed Onomarchus's brother Phayllus as general, but later that year he died "of a wasting disease, after a long illness, suffering great pain as befitted his impious life."[4] Phalaecus (Onomarchus's son) succeeded him, and for the next several years the Third Sacred War degenerated into mostly skirmishes between Phocian and Boeotian troops.

PHILIP AND GREECE

The Battle of the Crocus Field both restored the morale of the Macedonian army and reestablished Philip's authority over it. It also led to Pherae, which now lost its powerful Phocian ally, surrendering to him. Philip seized its harbor town of Pagasae but permitted the tyrant rulers Lycophron and Peitholaus, together with 2,000 mercenaries, to depart unharmed. Further, in hopes of securing the long-term amity of Pherae, he married a Pheraean lady, Nicesipolis (his fifth marriage), and later named their daughter Thessalonice ("Thessalian Victory").[5] His good intentions were never realized. Lycophron and Peitholaus quickly joined the Phocian side, and the Pheraeans continued to resent him. For Philip the real coup was that Larissa, on behalf of its Thessalian League, elected him archon of Thessaly in perpetuity.[6] This was a constitutional office that gave him three important benefits: the power to levy Thessalian troops, the receipt of income from Thessaly's harbor and market taxes (a further stimulus to his economy), and the ability to serve with Thessaly's official deputation on the Amphictyonic Council. The "barbarian" king now held a Greek constitutional office, an omen of the influence he would come to wield over all Greece.

The manner of Philip's return to Greece in 352 pointed to a significant change in his attitude to the Greeks and aspirations for his kingdom. When the "ram" marched back into Thessaly he ordered his troops to wear crowns of laurel—"as though the god were going before"[7]—and the psychological effect of these crowns was said to have caused some of the enemy to turn tail and flee out of guilt. After the Battle of the Crocus Field he executed the 3,000 captives by drowning them and crucified the corpse of Onomarchus, both of which were punishments for temple robbery. Macedonia was not a member of the Amphictyonic Council and had played no part in the Third Sacred War. That had suddenly changed— intent on disrupting Pherae's alliance with Phocis because of the threat it posed to Thessalian stability, Philip had involved himself in that war as a pious defender of Apollo. His actions would not have been lost on the Greeks.

Philip's move put pressure on the Athenians, who had earlier sent a squadron of ships commanded by Chares up the Thessalian coast to land at Pagasae and support Onomarchus. Philip had moved so fast that he had seized Pagasae before Chares arrived, so all the Athenian fleet could do was sail by the battlefield. Its presence spurred a number of Phocians to try to swim out to it for safety, but they drowned under the weight of their armor. Until now, Philip had been concerned with protecting and strengthening Macedonia's borders and putting a series of economic reforms into effect to benefit his kingdom. He wanted Macedonia to be secure from enemy invasions, prosperous, and a pow- erhouse in northern Greece. The reaction of his defeated army in 353, followed as it was by various defections and other threats to his king- ship, brought with it a realization that his power was still precarious. Further, the sacred war endangered Thessalian stability, and hence his southern border, and afforded the states fighting against Phocis the pos- sibility of rallying under Athens against him. He had therefore to move Macedonia from a role in just northern Greek affairs to one in central and even southern Greece as well.

Philip was aware that he would be seen as an invader for leading an army into Greece whose sole purpose was revenge on Onomarchus.[8] Therefore he neatly exploited the sacred war to appear as Apollo's savior, in which guise he was prepared to do battle against the sacrilegious Pho- cians. The Amphictyonic Council had little choice but to welcome him, given its dismal track record in dislodging the Phocians from Delphi, but Philip could exploit its authority in Greece to increase his own influence there. Thus came his switch from addressing the needs of his kingdom to creating an empire.[9]

It was now August 352, and after Crocus Field Philip had the opportunity to end the sacred war by marching on Phocis. The quickest route to Delphi and Phocis was through the strategically important pass of Thermopylae (site of the famous stand of the "300 Spartans" against the Persians in 480), which afforded direct access from northern to central Greece. However, the Athenians grew alarmed that once through Thermopylae Philip would ignore Phocis and march directly through Boeotia to Athens and besiege the city. Since there was little love lost between the Athenians and the Thebans, there was the additional worry that Thebes might ally with Philip or at least permit him passage through Boeotia to Attica. For once the politician Eubulus abandoned his pacifist policy and scrambled 5,000 men and 400 cavalry under the command of Nausicles to block the king at the pass. The cost of this expedition was 200 talents, a substantial amount that shows the fear that Philip was causing in Athenian minds. Philip arrived at Thermopylae, but Nausicles stood fast against him, placing the king in a dilemma. He could force his way through the pass or travel a different, more circuitous, route, both of which would take time and leave him vulnerable to attack. In the end, taking into account the pressing need to reassert his influence over those who had shown their disloyalty after his defeat the previous year, he turned around and returned to Pella.

ATHENIAN DEMOCRACY AND THE RISE OF DEMOSTHENES

Nausicles returned in justified triumph to Athens, where Eubulus immediately disbanded his force for the cost savings. However, his action and Nausicles's success paved the way for the rise to political power of Philip's most bitter and vocal opponent: Demosthenes (Figure 13). His surviving political and forensic speeches testify to his reputation as ancient Greece's most outstanding orator, and he has also been praised as its greatest patriot because of his steadfast opposition to Philip.[10]

From the middle of the fifth century Athens was a direct or radical democracy, meaning that the people were sovereign in the state, unlike the representative democracy of today.[11] When citizen males reached the age

FIGURE 13
Statue of Demosthenes. Vanni/Art Resource, New York.

of 18 they were able to discuss all domestic and foreign policy issues in the public forum of the Assembly and vote on them.[12] Although women were citizens, they were denied the franchise. Assemblies were convened four times a month and were held on a rocky outcrop called the Pnyx, close to the Acropolis. Meetings lasted from dawn to dusk and were attended by several thousand citizens. Any citizen was permitted to air his views at the meetings; speakers mounted a rostrum or bema, from which they addressed the people, who sat by tribes in a semicircular auditorium area of the Pnyx, facing the bema, with the Acropolis to their left and the Agora or marketplace behind them (Figure 14).

There were elected officials in the democracy, but political power lay in the hands of speakers (orators or *rhetores*), who more often than not won favor with the people by their rhetorical skills rather than the actual content of speeches and validity of proposals. Rhetoric therefore flourished in Athens as it afforded ambitious men the means to political ascendancy.[13]

FIGURE 14
(a–c) The Pnyx at Athens. Photos: Ian Worthington.

FIGURE 14
(a–c) Continued.

Since Athenian political life revolved around personal relationships with powerful people, an aspiring politician courted such a person until he became his own man in public life and, through speaking in the Assembly, built up a political following.

Demosthenes was one of these speakers. Born in 384 or 383, he first embarked on a highly successful and profitable career writing forensic speeches for clients in the law courts before crossing over to the political arena of the Assembly. His early speeches that dealt with foreign and financial matters failed, however.[14] His political career seemed over by 350, but then came the game changer: the threat Philip posed to Greece. Demosthenes began to shape an anti-Macedonian policy that was anchored in the Athenians taking the war to Philip before he became unstoppable, and he spent the next decade delivering a series of fiery speeches to rouse the Athenians to fight the king. His speeches portrayed Philip as conspiring to crush Athens and take over Greece and all too often embellished the truth or misrepresented the king's intentions. However, by the 340s Demosthenes was the most politically powerful man in the city.

At the start of his political career Demosthenes aligned himself with the influential Eubulus. The two men shared similar views about rebuilding Athens's finances, but Demosthenes came to question Eubulus's pacifist approach to Athens's role in Greece and in the war with Philip, which he felt was not in the city's best interests and allowed Philip to remain unchecked. He was particularly critical of Eubulus's decision to stand down Nausicles and his troops in 352. He believed that military force was necessary to stop the growth of Philip's power before it was too late. Realistically speaking, it was already too late to halt Philip's steady advance because the Athenians had underestimated him. A clear indication of this is that they had declared war on him in 357, yet Demosthenes first mentioned the king only en passant in a forensic speech of 352 (*Against Aristocrates*), in which he dismissed him as a distant threat to Athens.

A year later Demosthenes had changed his tune when he delivered another speech in a series to do with Athenian foreign policy. Instead of discussing Persia or Thrace as he had done in some of his previous speeches, however, he made the subject of this one Macedonia. The first *Philippic*, as it is called (the title is a modern one), applauded Eubulus's rigid fiscal conservatism, which had rescued the city from its dire financial straits.[15] However, Demosthenes went on to urge the people to put together a standing army, in which they should personally serve, to fight Philip wherever he might be, as well as a strike force that would be based in the north to shadow the king and engage him until the standing army arrived. By taking the war to Philip, Demosthenes was convinced he could be beaten.

In the first *Philippic* Demosthenes criticized the people for allowing Philip to grow so strong but stressed that they could still overcome him as long as they themselves fought and did not give in to their usual apathy and feelings of powerlessness. In one memorable passage he compared their reaction to Philip with a "barbarian" boxer who never attacks but uses his hands to cover where he has just been hit:

> You wage war on Philip in the same way that a foreigner boxes. For when one of them is struck, he always moves his hands to that spot, and if he is struck on the other side, his hands go to that place: he has neither the knowledge nor the will to put up his guard or watch for the next blow. It is the same with you. If you hear that Philip is in the Chersonese, you vote to send a relief force there, and likewise if you hear that he is at Thermopylae. And if you hear that he is somewhere else, you run up and down at his heels and are at his command; you have no plan to turn the war to your advantage, and fail to anticipate any eventuality until you learn that it has happened or is happening.[16]

His speech failed because of the enormous cost that his military proposals would require and the people's reluctance to fight personally. Still, Demosthenes was fast making a name for himself in Athenian politics, and Philip would soon find him a daunting adversary.

RECOVERING THE STATUS QUO

Shortly after Philip returned to Pella in 352 he marched into Thrace to deal with the scheming Cersebleptes, who was still intent on resurrecting a single kingdom of Thrace (Map 3). In spring or summer of the previous year (353) the Athenians had sent Chares and 20 ships to the Thracian Chersonese (Gallipoli Peninsula). He had captured Sestus, an important port city on the grain route from the Black Sea to Athens, and as a warning to Cersebleptes he killed all of its male citizens and sold all of its women and children as slaves—one of the more gruesome punishments that civilians suffered in warfare.[17] The grain route was a vital supply line for the Athenians, who were reliant on grain from the Black Sea (specifically the lands of the Ukraine and Crimea) to help feed their population.[18] They therefore regarded the Chersonese region as vital to their interests and were always ready to send troops there if they believed that it was threatened.[19] At this time, their presence in the Chersonese depended on the goodwill of Cersebleptes, whose lands included the Chersonese and bordered on the Hellespont. If Philip were to win him over, then the Athenians feared the worst. Chares's action had the desired effect on Cersebleptes, who recognized Athens's rights over the Chersonese, apart from the town of Cardia on the isthmus, and even went so far as to support the city in its attempts to regain Amphipolis.

Philip had no desire to see Athens control the Thracian coastline, nor could he allow Cersebleptes to unite all of Thrace under his rule and challenge him. He therefore joined a coalition of Byzantium, Perinthus (both cities in Cersebleptes's kingdom), and Amadocus (the king of Central Thrace) and by November 352 was besieging Cersebleptes at Heraion Teichos ("Hera's Wall"), one of his eastern fortresses on the coast of the Sea of Marmara, close to Perinthus (Marmaraeregli). Despite suffering some type of illness, Philip forced Cersebleptes to surrender in 351 and took his son to Pella as a hostage to ensure his loyalty.

On his way back to Pella, Philip stopped off at Olynthus, which had reneged on its treaty of 357 with him by seeking an alliance with Athens when news of Onomarchus's victory over Philip broke. He told the Olynthians an apocryphal story about war and arrogance (*hybris*) that frightened them sufficiently into ending their negotiations with Athens. As a further effort to get back into Philip's good books they expelled a prominent anti-Macedonian, Apollonides, and elected two pro-Macedonians, Lasthenes and Euthycrates, as commanders of their cavalry (hipparchs).

With Cersebleptes and the Chalcidian League duly cowed, Philip turned to the Paeonians, Illyrians, and Arybbas of Epirus. There are references in the ancient sources to operations against the Paeonians and Illyrians, but their details are shadowy. Then in 350 Philip invaded Epirus. He allowed Arybbas to remain on the throne, but he did away with the Molossian bronze coinage in favor of Macedonian. Moreover, he took Arybbas's 12-year-old nephew and heir, Alexander (Olympias's younger brother, so Philip's brother-in-law), to Pella, intending to install him as king of Epirus when he came of age.[20]

In just three years after a military defeat that threatened to displace him as king and potentially unravel his achievements to date for Macedonia, Philip had reestablished his power and prestige. His speed in doing so was breathtaking, as even his enemy Demosthenes recognized in one of his speeches:

> Does any of you observe or reflect on the means by which Philip, who was weak, has become strong? First he took Amphipolis, then Pydna, and then Potidaea, next Methone, then he attacked Thessaly, and after that, Pherae, Pagasae and Magnesia. After winning over the whole country in the way he wanted, he invaded Thrace. Then, after expelling some of the kings there and installing others, he fell sick. When he recovered his health, he did not sink into idleness but immediately made an attempt on the Olynthians. And I pass over his campaigns against the Illyrians and Paeonians and Arybbas and wherever else one might mention.[21]

Philip's speed and decisiveness were ultimately to the Greeks' detriment. Had he been an Athenian, he could not have been a member of the Boule or served on a jury until he was 30 and would always have been held back by the democracy—yet by 30 he had secured all of Macedonia's borders and extended his influence in Thrace and central Greece.[22] However, it is not just the lumbering popular Assembly or the apathy of the people to blame: the inefficiencies inherent in the polis system meant that it could never respond effectively to the threat from Macedonia.

THE INVASION OF THE CHALCIDICE

The Olynthians had professed their loyalty to Philip in 351, but they continued to be untrustworthy. At some point, possibly in 349, they had offered refuge to the king's two stepbrothers (Menelaus and Arrhidaeus) from his father's marriage to Gygaea—the third stepbrother had been executed in 359. Philip believed that they were potential claimants to the throne and demanded their surrender.[23] When the Olynthians refused he invaded the Chalcidice in the autumn of 349.[24]

Philip's strategy was psychological, a talent that Alexander inherited and used to great effect in Asia. Intending to isolate Olynthus from the rest of the Chalcidice, Philip attacked and won over several Chalcidian towns. These included Stageira, the birthplace of Aristotle, which he razed to the ground as a warning to any cities bent on resisting him. The Olynthians sent an embassy to Athens in September or October requesting help. The Athenians debated the appeal, with Demosthenes delivering two speeches (*Olynthiacs*) urging them to deploy troops and combat Philip in the north before he marched on Athens, when, he assured them, he would also join forces with Thebes.[25] The first *Olynthiac* was unsuccessful, but the second, in which he falsely represented Philip as unpopular among his Macedonians, his army as weak, and his kingdom as about to collapse around him, persuaded the Athenians to ally with Olynthus.

Straightaway, Chares and 2,000 Thracian mercenaries on 30 triremes were sent north to Olynthus, but when he arrived he found no Philip. The king had suddenly left the Chalcidice for Thessaly to deal with a rebellious Pherae, which had welcomed back Peitholaus. Philip quickly overcame Peitholaus, but with the campaigning season all but over he decided to spend the winter of 349–348 in Pella. Chares had no choice but to return home with his troops.

In March 348 Philip returned to the Chalcidice. The Olynthians again beseeched the Athenians for help, and the people ordered their general Charidemus (who was based in the Chersonese) to take 4,000 mercenary soldiers and 150 cavalry to Olynthus. Bolstered by Olynthian military support of 1,000 cavalry and 10,000 infantry Charidemus recaptured some Chalcidian cities. It would not be enough. In the early summer

Philip seized the port of Mecyberna, five miles from Olynthus, where he paused to deliver an ultimatum to its people: "there were two alternatives—either they should stop living in Olynthus or he should stop living in Macedonia."[26] He then besieged Olynthus in earnest, and in desperation the people implored the Athenians for more military help, which Demosthenes supported in his third *Olynthiac*.

Demosthenes was again successful, and the Athenians mobilized Chares with 2,000 citizen infantry and 300 cavalry. Unfortunately, his force could not sail for 40 days because of the northerly Etesian winds (the Meltemi), which blow on and off between May and September. As a result the Athenian troops arrived too late to save Olynthus, which capitulated in August or perhaps early September. Possibly there was some truth to Demosthenes's claim that Philip had bribed Euthycrates and Lasthenes (the pro-Macedonian cavalry commanders) to betray the city to him. The king routinely used bribes throughout his reign, and he would not have wanted to be conducting the siege when the large Athenian force arrived.

Many Olynthians were slaughtered when the city surrendered, as presumably were Philip's two stepbrothers, and the captives (including some Athenian troops) were presumably sent to Macedonia to work as slaves in the mines and fields. The Chalcidice was absorbed into Philip's rapidly growing empire, and the revenue from its timber and mineral resources (especially the gold and silver mines at Stratonici) was yet another boost to his economy. In a speech delivered in 341, Demosthenes maintained that Philip destroyed all the cities of the Chalcidian League—"I don't say anything about Olynthus and Methone and Apollonia and 32 cities on the coast of Thrace [the Chalcidice], all of which he destroyed with such cruelty that a visitor would be hard pressed to say whether they had ever been lived in."[27] His exaggerated claim was intended to increase the Athenians' fear of how Philip might (in 341) treat them, but his vivid picture testifies to the strategic execution, speed, and uncompromising nature of Philip's military operations. He may have punished Olynthus in the manner he did as a warning to any city that harbored potential claimants to the throne, something later writers compared with Alexander the Great's razing of Thebes in 335 (pp. 134–135).

Criticism has been leveled against the Athenians for not doing more to help Olynthus and stop Philip, but that is unfair.[28] They had sent three substantial forces to Olynthus and also had had to contend with Philip's speed and unpredictability. At the same time they had been forced to send troops to the island of Euboea to prevent Callias, the tyrant ruler of the town of Chalcis, from creating a league of Euboean cities and defecting from Athens. This scenario was a grave security threat to the Athenians, given the island's close proximity to Attica's eastern coastline, not to mention it was a source for some of their grain. Ultimately the troops they sent to Euboea—who included Demosthenes—were unsuccessful, and apart from the town of Carystus the whole island became independent of Athens. It is even possible that Philip was encouraging Callias to divert Athens's attention from his Chalcidian campaign.

Given their support of Olynthus, the Athenians steeled themselves for reprisals from Philip. None came. Instead, he surprisingly communicated to them that he was their friend and, further, that he wanted to end his war with them. In fact, he wanted not only a peace with them but also an alliance (*symmachia*), by which both parties would be on an equal footing and agree not to attack the other and to go to its aid if it were ever in danger.

THE PEACE OF PHILOCRATES AND THE END
OF THE THIRD SACRED WAR

Why Philip sought peace at this time is not known.[29] Possibly he had concerns about Athens and Thebes uniting against him and so decided to court the Athenians at the expense of Thebes. He also had no desire to see the Thebans regain power in central Greece, which was likely when the Third Sacred War drew to its inevitable close, and in fact during the war when the Thebans were hard pressed he was "pleased to see their discomfiture and disposed to humble the Boeotians' pride after Leuctra."[30] Simply put: he did not like the Thebans, perhaps because of his hostage years with them, and certainly dealt differently with them than with the Athenians throughout his reign.[31] Philip therefore set out to curtail

Thebes's influence, but at the same time he needed to maintain that of Athens as a counter against Thebes in the future. He could not, however, alert the Thebans to his plans, otherwise they might well side with the Athenians. Accordingly he lulled the Thebans into believing that they had his support with an adroit mixture of diplomacy and deceit while he worked to end the sacred war and procure a settlement of Greece that would weaken Thebes and impose some stability on the region.

The Athenians in 348 were at first receptive to Philip's overtures, and Philocrates of Hagnus proposed sending an embassy to Pella to hear Philip's terms. Nothing came of that because their attention was diverted sharply by the fall of Olynthus and the sudden dramatic events in the Third Sacred War. In some haste, Eubulus convinced the people to dispatch an embassy to the various Greek states calling them to war against Philip. A former actor and now an up-and-coming orator named Aeschines, who was destined to become Demosthenes's chief political adversary, supported him.[32] Thus, the final years of the sacred war and the negotiations leading to peace between Athens and Philip became intertwined.[33]

In the sacred war the Phocian general Phalaecus had aggressively maintained pressure on the Thebans by his military operations in Boeotia. Yet in the summer of 347 his command was surprisingly taken from him (why is a mystery) and entrusted to three individuals, Deinocrates, Callias, and Sophanes. They immediately invaded Boeotia, forcing the struggling Thebans to appeal for help to Philip. Their plea presented the king with a golden opportunity to return with troops to Greece, but if he supported them with all his might, he would alarm the Athenians and so wreck his plans to end his war with them peacefully and settle Greece. In the end, he sent only his general Parmenion with a small contingent of troops to help the Thebans, which irked them greatly.

In response, the Phocians enlisted Athenian and Spartan help by surrendering to them the three key towns of Alponus, Thronium, and Nicaea that controlled Thermopylae. The Spartans sent 1,000 men, and the Athenians, 50 ships, manned by all fit males up to the age of 40, under the command of Proxenus, to secure Thermopylae. This bold move impeded Philip's access to central Greece, as had Nausicles's force in 352, and at this point or in the beginning of 346 the Athenians sent another embassy to the Greek cities urging them to join in war against Philip under Athenian leadership. Later, possibly on Demosthenes's urging, they sent troops to the aid of Halus in Thessaly, which was under pressure from Pharsalus, a prominent member of the Thessalian League. To counter this disruption in Thessaly, Philip was forced to divert Parmenion to besiege Halus. To make matters worse for the king, Demosthenes was now demanding the release of the Athenian prisoners seized at Olynthus in 348, which Philip was reluctant to grant because they were a valuable asset to him in peace deliberations.

Still Philip maintained his wish for peace, and in 346 the Athenians sent an embassy of 10 men, including Demosthenes, to Pella to hear his terms. It arrived in the Macedonian capital in March, and the envoys discussed various matters with Philip, including the Athenians' interests in Thrace and the Chersonese, their relations with Cersebleptes, their involvement in Halus, and the need to protect Phocis when the sacred war ended. The Athenians wanted to include at least Phocis and Cersebleptes among their allies, even though they had played no role in the war over Amphipolis, but Philip refused to agree. He insisted only on a bilateral treaty between him and his allies and the Athenians and their allies, with (significantly) each party recognizing the places held by the other at that time. The Athenians were told to abandon their aid to Halus immediately, but Philip did intimate that he would do everything he could to protect the Phocians, and he promised to return the Athenian prisoners from Olynthus once peace had been concluded.

The embassy returned to Athens and reported to the Assembly on April 6. Shortly after it had left Pella Philip sent a Macedonian embassy, led by his generals Antipater, Parmenion, and Eurylochus, to Athens to reconfirm his terms and receive the Athenians' oaths to the peace. At the same time—and unknown to the Athenians—he headed to Thrace, intending to campaign against Cersebleptes. In Athens a major debate was held at an extraordinary two-day Assembly meeting on April 15 and 16, in which some politicians—Philocrates being one—wanted to accept Philip's terms and welcomed the fact that he wanted a peace and alliance with no time limits. Others, however, abhorred the idea of excluding Phocis and especially Cersebleptes, given the importance of Thrace to Athens, and even rejected the notion of a bilateral peace. The first day ended with the people voting for peace but not alliance and to include Phocis and Cersebleptes as allies. Overnight there was a change of heart, and on the second day they sensibly reversed their decision, helped by a blunt warning from Antipater that Philip would not accept their terms. At the end of the debate they swore their oaths to the Macedonian envoys.[34]

After some delay, a second embassy consisting of the same 10 men as the first one left Athens for Pella to receive the king's oath. Philip was not there, as he was still busy in Thrace. In a two-month campaign he successfully besieged Cersebleptes's fortress at Heraion Orus and reduced several other coastal Thracian forts to extend Macedonia's eastern frontier to the Nestus River. Demosthenes urged his colleagues to leave Pella and try to find the king in Thrace because he realized that Philip intended to take over as many places there as he could—which would become his allies—before swearing his oath to peace. They ignored him and waited at Pella, along with embassies from Sparta, Thebes, Thessaly, and Phocis, for the king to return, which he finally did on June 18.

The other embassies clearly wanted to know what Philip was planning to do in Greece. For example, the Thebans and Thessalians probably called on him to punish the Phocians without mercy and curb Athens's influence in Greek politics. The Spartans wanted him to support their moves to reassert their influence in the Peloponnese and counter that of Thebes there, and the Phocians presumably pleaded for his help and protection when the sacred war ended.[35] The number and mission of these embassies illustrate the very real influence that Philip now exerted in Greek affairs.

Philip heard the Athenian embassy last. Demosthenes again pressured him about the Athenian prisoners, dramatically producing a silver talent of his own money to help meet the ransom. Philip promised to release them by the time of the festival of the Panathenaea (in honor of Athens's patron deity, Athena) in two months' time—in other words, after he had returned to Greece with an army to intervene in the sacred war. Then he swore his oath to the peace and with army in tow moved southward ostensibly to deal with the Phocians. At Pherae, a mere two or three days' march from Thermopylae, his allies swore their oaths, and so the Peace of Philocrates came into being, thereby ending the war between Athens and Philip. It did not include Cersebleptes, Phocis, and Halus, and the Athenians finally had to face the fact that they were never going to get Amphipolis back.

The second embassy reported back to the Athenian Assembly, which decided to send a third embassy to Philip, sycophantically extending the peace to his descendants. The Athenians also debated the sacred war and decreed that "Phocians"—not *the* Phocians (significantly distinguishing the Phocians who held Delphi from the entire Phocian state)—should surrender Delphi to the Amphictyonic Council and that they would march against anyone who prevented this. The people clearly hoped that the Phocian state would escape punishment and so continue to be a valuable ally against Thebes. The third embassy left the city in mid-July but never reached Philip. At Chalcis on Euboea the envoys heard the shocking news that the Phocians had reinstated Phalaecus, that he had sent the Athenian and Spartan troops at Thermopylae packing, and—even worse—that he had handed over control of the pass to Philip and formally surrendered to him and not to the Amphictyonic Council. Unsure what to do, the third embassy returned to Athens.

The key to this surprising turn of events in the sacred war has to be Philip, a clue being revealed by Justin's comment that the Phocians as "victims of necessity, struck a bargain for their lives and capitulated."[36] No Greek would have been party to any such pact, so probably the king had persuaded the Phocian embassy at Pella to have its government restore Phalaecus, give him Thermopylae, and surrender to him in return for his promise to moderate their punishment. Shortly after, the Amphictyonic Council met to debate the Phocian punishment. The Athenians and the Spartans did not send a formal delegation to the meeting, but Athens did dispatch a fourth and final embassy to Philip, which attended the council meeting in a nonofficial capacity. Philip treated the embassy with due respect and, as promised, released the Athenian prisoners from Olynthus in time for the Panathenaea festival.

There were some members of the Amphictyonic Council that wanted to inflict the maximum legal penalty on the Phocians of executing all the men by throwing them from the top of the towering Phaedriades cliffs. However, Philip insisted on moderation, apparently supported in this by Aeschines, and he got his way. Among other things, Phocis lost its membership in the council, and the Phocian state was required to repay the amount of money stolen from the sacred treasuries and could not own horses and arms again until it had done so.[37] All of the towns in Phocis except Abae in the east (which had condemned the seizure of Delphi) were razed, and their populations relocated to new villages about 200 yards apart; each one was to comprise no more than 50 houses. Phocian supporters were also punished—the Athenians, for example, lost their right of *promanteia* (priority in consulting the Delphic Oracle), which was given to Philip. As a further reward for his settlement of the war, Philip received the two Phocian votes on the Amphictyonic Council and was elected President of the Pythian Games at Delphi, part of the Olympic cycle of games, which had not been held in the dozen years that the Phocians had occupied Delphi.

A mere 13 years ago, in 359, Philip had been desperately fighting to rescue his kingdom from threats that would have defeated a lesser man. Now, in 346, he was archon of Thessaly, a member of the venerable Amphictyonic Council, President of an Olympic festival, and king of a powerful, wealthy, and expanding country, which had made significant inroads into Greece and even as far afield as Thrace. To celebrate the role he played in liberating Apollo, he minted a gold stater coin with the head of Apollo and a laurel wreath on the obverse and a two-horse chariot with a charioteer under which is the inscription "Philippou" ("of Philip") on the reverse. However, if he thought that he had settled Greece to his liking, he was sadly mistaken, as events quickly proved.

4.

THE GATHERING WAR CLOUDS

Philip's settlement of Greece in 346 was far from what he had intended. The Thebans were furious that he had misled them about the Athenians and that they could no longer use the Amphictyonic Council for their own political ends because of Philip's presence on it. The Athenians were enraged that he had done nothing to reduce Thebes's power in Greece and, further, that he was receiving Phocis's two votes on the council and going to be President of the Pythian Games. They were also incensed that while the punishment meted out to the Phocians could have been far worse, Philip had not protected them better—a feeling that had nothing to do with the Phocians' well-being; rather, the breakup of Phocis as a state robbed Athens of an important ally against Thebes. Defiantly, the Athenians snubbed Philip by refusing to send their official delegation to the games. The Peace of Philocrates was suddenly under threat within weeks of both sides swearing to it.

"BARBARIAN" PHILIP AND THE GREEKS IN 346

Philip was not prepared to overlook the Athenian cold shoulder. He sent a Macedonian embassy to Athens, which included Amphictyonic Council members, ordering the city to send an official delegation to the games. The inclusion of council representatives was a master stroke on his part, for if the Athenians defied the embassy's demand, they would also be rebuffing the council and opening the door to a sacred war against them. The embassy was discussed in an Assembly, at which Demosthenes delivered his speech *On the*

Peace. Sensibly, he exhorted the people not to be disheartened by the unpopular terms of the peace and persuaded them to attend the games—otherwise they might well face Philip leading Amphictyonic troops against them.

What is significant about Demosthenes's speech, however, is the fact that he alluded to a fresh war with Philip over Amphipolis or somewhere else at a future time.[1] The conclusion is inevitable: the Athenians in 346 saw the Peace of Philocrates as nothing but ephemeral. They accepted Demosthenes's argument to keep the peace only while they could build up resources to oppose the king in the future—including a possible alliance with Thebes of all places, to which end Demosthenes now began to work.[2] The Athenians therefore attended the games, after which Philip returned to Pella. Nonetheless, to maintain his hold over Thermopylae, and so his access to Greece, he stationed a Thessalian garrison in Nicaea, just to the east of the pass. The question uppermost on everyone's mind now was how long the peace would last.

Not every Greek state was relieved to see Philip leave, however. Some of the smaller ones, tired of the constant wrangling among large cities such as Athens and Thebes that had contributed to instability on the mainland, welcomed his intervention and wanted him to induce a period of peace and prosperity.[3] Philip even had a number of allies in the Peloponnese, in particular Messene and Arcadia, which looked to him, rather than Athens or Thebes, for support against Sparta. Thus in 344 the Athenians felt the need to send embassies to Messene and Argos in an attempt to dissuade them from accepting military help from Philip. The Messenians and Argives snubbed the Athenians, complaining about their meddling conduct and even setting up bronze statues of the king. Moreover, when Philip was assassinated in 336, many Greek cities remained loyal to the Macedonian hegemony that he had enforced on Greece the previous year.

PHILIP THE "PHILHELLENE" AND ATHENIAN INTELLECTUALS

The male members of the royal family—like other Macedonian noble boys—received a formal education that included studying Greek literature and philosophy.[4] They were philhellenes, people who had a deep regard for Greek culture in all its forms. King Archelaus, for example, had actively promoted Greek culture at his court, while Alexander the Great favored it to the exclusion of all others and attempted to impose it on his subject peoples throughout Asia. Philip also wanted his court to be seen as a cultural center. He invited the great sculptor Lysippus to live and work there and commissioned various artworks, such as the Philippeion, with its statues of him and members of the royal family, which was built at Olympia after the Battle of Chaeronea. Moreover, like Macedonian kings before and after him, he was much attracted to the cultural and intellectual life of Athens and enjoyed personal contacts with leading Athenian orators and philosophers.

Athens was the cultural and intellectual center of the Greek world until eclipsed by Alexandria in the Hellenistic period. Signs of Athens's cultural demise were evident in the fourth century and may be linked to changes in the political fortunes of the city. Tragedy, for example, which in the previous century had reached its zenith with the plays of Aeschylus, Sophocles, and Euripides, had suffered a loss of popularity. Fewer new tragedies were written; instead the focus was on reviving the fifth-century ones, perhaps in an attempt to evoke the heyday of Classical Athenian power.[5] The bawdy genre of Old Comedy, exemplified in the surviving plays of Aristophanes, was likewise changing to Middle and eventually New Comedy, which replaced political satire with gentler plots to do with everyday family and civic life. Philosophy had a far longer life—in the fourth century Athens established itself as the center for philosophy thanks to the work of Socrates and Plato and later Aristotle and Theophrastus. The city would remain the leading philosophical center throughout the Hellenistic period, when Stoicism and Skepticism, with their emphases on virtue and ethics, became the most important philosophies and were embraced by the Romans.

Plato had a special relationship with Macedonian kings, and Perdiccas III even patronized his Academy. Philip was said to have "honored him" when the philosopher died in 347, although what this means is unknown.[6] Aside from admiration of Plato's teachings, Philip may have intended his "honor" to curry favor with the Athenians as he was then seeking a diplomatic resolution to their war with him. In 342 Philip hired Aristotle to tutor his son and heir Alexander when he turned 14 years of age. The king's selection of so preeminent a philosopher perhaps prompted Plato's successor as head of the Academy, Speusippus, to write personally to Philip soliciting his patronage of the Academy. His letter survives among the so-called Socratic letters of the first century A.D. and is important because it gives a very different image of Philip than the one that political warmongers such as Demosthenes depicted in his speeches.[7] As we might expect, there is plenty of sycophantic bluster in the letter, such as praising Philip's good deeds and his predecessors, but Speusippus also made it clear that he saw Philip as an intellectual and a philhellene.

Philip ended Aristotle's instruction of his son after three years in 340, when he appointed Alexander as regent of Macedonia. Exactly what happened to Aristotle between 340 and 335, when he founded his school in Athens, is unknown. However, he may have remained in Philip's employment and acted as his agent in Greece and even northwest Asia Minor.[8] He might have done this only for the pay, but we cannot rule out that part of the reason was respect for Philip and his son.

Speusippus's plea to Philip was unsuccessful, perhaps because he took advantage of his letter to criticize other Athenian intellectuals, especially the rhetorician Isocrates, whom Philip seems to have favored. Athens was also a great center for the study of rhetoric, but a bitter rivalry existed between the Academy and Isocrates's school over rhetoric's function and worth. As a king who preferred diplomacy over military action Philip was attracted to the advances in rhetoric over the fourth century, and Isocrates was its most famous teacher. Isocrates treated the Macedonian king with respect, not least because he saw in him the person who could bring about a venture to end disunity in Greece that he had first advocated in his *Panegyricus* of 380: the invasion of Persia. In 346 he wrote his *To Philip*, urging Philip to unite the Greeks and lead a panhellenic army to Asia. His call at the time was impractical, but after Chaeronea in 338, at the grand old age of 98, he pitched the idea of an Asian campaign to Philip's general Antipater. The following year Philip announced plans for this offensive, and Isocrates may well have sown its seeds in the king's mind.

PHILIP MEETS DEMOSTHENES

Both Demosthenes and Aeschines had radically different views about Philip's policy to Athens and Greece, which polarized Athenian politics from the mid- to late 340s. By then Demosthenes was intent on distancing himself from his role in the peace negotiations of 346 and on persuading the Athenians to overturn the peace and fight Philip before he conquered Greece. Aeschines, on the other hand, believed that the peace had to survive because, albeit imperfect, it was the only way Athens could maintain Philip's friendship and be treated as an equal by him. However, the feud between the two men went beyond political differences. It was personal and had its origins in the first embassy to Philip in 346, which was when Philip and Demosthenes initially met each other at Pella. Philip would have known of Demosthenes's stance toward him, as evidenced in his first *Philippic* of 351, but if the king expected a rhetorical tirade, he was surely disappointed.

Demosthenes was the youngest of the 10 ambassadors who appeared before Philip, and in order of age he spoke last. When it was his turn Aeschines later stated that he lost his nerve: "with all listening so intently, this creature offered an obscene prologue in a voice dead with fright, and after a brief narration of earlier events suddenly fell silent and was at a loss for words, and finally abandoned his speech. Seeing the state he was in, Philip encouraged him to take heart and not to suppose that he had suffered a complete catastrophe.... But Demosthenes... was now unable to recover; he tried once more to speak, and the same thing happened. In the ensuing silence the herald asked us to withdraw."[9]

Aeschines's story is likely exaggerated to portray his adversary in a weak light and, conversely, Philip's compassion, given his later attitude to him. On the other hand, Demosthenes had suffered from shortness of breath and speech impediments in his youth. He was said to have overcome these handicaps by speaking with pebbles in his mouth and shaving one side of his head to force himself to stay indoors and work on his elocution and delivery.[10] When he appeared before Philip he may well have stuttered or fallen victim to stage fright, which Aeschines pounced on to embarrass his opponent. Demosthenes clearly shrugged off the incident, as his political career proves, but he never forgot how Aeschines ridiculed him.

ESCALATING TENSIONS

Philip was preoccupied with matters in Macedonia for the rest of 346 and 345. In the latter year he may have been involved in a campaign—the details are obscure—against Pleuratus, the chieftain of the powerful Illyrian tribe of the Ardiaioi, located in northern Albania. In fierce fighting Philip broke his right collarbone but still won victory and returned with a great deal of booty. He then founded a series of defensive military outposts along his northwest border with Illyria, at places such as Astraea, Dobera, Kellion, and Melitousa, which additionally promoted urbanization and so further stimulated the economy.[11] The king settled these new towns with people from different parts of his kingdom, but they were clearly loathe to go, for they "looked wistfully now at the tombs of their forefathers, now at their ancient family deities, now at the houses in which they had been born and had themselves produced children, sorrowing at one moment for their own fate for having lived to see that day, and at the next for that of their children, for not having been born after it."[12] The people's reaction affords an interesting glimpse into the power Philip wielded over his subjects, at least at this time—by the time he died in 336 they fully appreciated the rise to prominence of Macedonia in Greek affairs (pp. 105–109).

Thessaly caused Philip concerns in 344, when Simus, one of Larissa's rulers, unexpectedly struck his own coinage. Philip decided that it was time to settle Thessaly to his satisfaction once and for all. He expelled the Aleuadae from Larissa; established a governing board of 10 men (decadarchy), supported by garrisons in various cities (including Larissa); and brought back the original four administrative districts or tetrarchies of Thessaly, personally appointing a governor over each one who was answerable only to him.[13] Northern Greece, no matter how grudgingly, was now wholly part of the growing Macedonian Empire. In addition, Philip's administrative arrangements impacted the entire Macedonian kingship, which necessarily had to deal with regions beyond its original domain.

In the same year Philip offered money and men to Messene and Argos in the Peloponnese to use against Sparta. To counteract his growing interest in southern Greece the Athenians sent an embassy to the Peloponnese, while Demosthenes lambasted him for actually enslaving the

Thessalians.[14] Once again Philip took the Athenians by surprise: he sent his friend Python of Byzantium to the city assuring them of his friendship and offering to turn the Peace of Philocrates into a Common Peace, which their allies (and even Demosthenes initially) had wanted and which Philip had steadfastly resisted.

Why Philip changed his mind is not known, but he was not a person to act impulsively. He may have been alarmed at the presence of a Persian embassy in Athens at this time seeking assistance to help the Great King, Artaxerxes III Ochus, recover a rebellious Egypt. Philip knew that if the Athenians were to make an alliance with Artaxerxes against Macedonia, Persian resources and manpower could cripple him, and he may have sent Python to distract them. The Athenians refused Artaxerxes's request, but they did proclaim their friendship to Persia. Another explanation is that the proposed change to the peace substantially increased Philip's power, something Demosthenes recognized. At a meeting of the Assembly to discuss Philip's proposal the orator delivered his second *Philippic*, in which he explained that if the Athenians adopted the change, their hegemony of their confederacy would suffer because allies would be free to make their own pacts with Philip. Demosthenes resorted to his usual brand of scare-tactic rhetoric to present Philip focused only on harming Athens:

Think about it: he wishes to rule and regards you as his only rivals in this. He has been acting unjustly for a long time now and is himself fully conscious of doing so, since his secure control of everything else depends on his keeping hold of your possessions. He thinks that if he were to abandon Amphipolis and Potidaea, he would not even be safe at home. He is therefore deliberately plotting against you and knows that you are aware of this. He believes that you are intelligent, and that you justifiably hate him, and is spurred on by the expectation that he will suffer some reverse at your hands, if you seize the opportunity to do so, unless he anticipates you by acting first. For these reasons, he is alert; he stands against you; he courts certain people—the Thebans and those of the Peloponnesians who agree with them—who he thinks will be satisfied with the present situation because of their greed, and will foresee none of the consequences because of their stupidity.[15]

Demosthenes was followed in the debate by the equally militant Hegesippus, and the two of them cajoled the people into forming a controversial resolution: any changes to the peace should reflect, first, that each side control its own possessions and, second, that any party excluded from the peace in 346 be declared independent but receive military aid from the signatories if ever attacked. Aeschines, who had argued that the modifications to the peace were in the better interests of Athens, gained no ground, yet the Athenians were well aware that Philip would never agree to the terms Demosthenes and Hegesippus had put forward. The first one allowed Athens to reassert its claim to Amphipolis, Pydna, Potidaea, Methone, and places in Thrace. The second prevented Philip making any further inroads into Thrace and threatening Athenian influence in the Chersonese.

It is no surprise that when Hegesippus conveyed the Athenians' amendments to Philip he threw him out of the palace in disgust, even going so far as to banish his host, Xenocleides, an Athenian poet who lived at Pella. Demosthenes can be condemned for deliberately wrecking the peace negotiations, but then again, it was Philip who had made the first move to alter the peace, and he was well aware of what his proposed change entailed. Since he had duped the Athenians before, Demosthenes had every right to be suspicious of him.

The following year, 343, the young Alexander of Epirus, whom Philip had removed to Pella in 350, came of age. Philip had always intended to install this Alexander as king when he became old enough, so he now invaded Epirus, expelled Arybbas from the throne, and established Alexander as king. Arybbas, who held Athenian citizenship, fled to the city, where there was some talk of restoring him, but fortunately cooler heads prevailed. Still, Philip did not abandon his courtship of the Athenians. Some time previously he had expelled pirates from Halonnesus, a small and insignificant island possibly off the coast of Thessaly between Lemnos and Scyros. Halonnesus belonged to Athens, but the people had condoned Philip's action since piracy was a rampant problem for Greek and Macedonian merchant vessels in the Aegean. Now he offered to give them the island, but Demosthenes promptly assailed him because the island was not his to give—he could only give it *back*, the orator smirked, for which Aeschines later ridiculed him for "arguing about syllables."[16]

Perhaps nothing better exemplifies the downward spiral of the Peace of Philocrates than its architect, Philocrates, being indicted in 343 for not acting in the city's best interests—in other words, for proposing peace with Philip in the first place. The anti-Macedonian politician Hyperides was set to prosecute him. Demosthenes, a previous supporter of Philocrates, now stood well clear of him. It was a different Athens from 348 or even 346, and Philocrates fled into exile; he was condemned to death in absentia. That autumn Demosthenes returned to a previous impeachment of Aeschines for misconduct (*parapresbeia*) on the second embassy to Philip in 346 and for misleading the Athenians in the Assemblies debating peace with Philip. He had brought this charge against Aeschines in 345, intending to remove him from political life.[17] Initially, Aeschines had been as resistant to peace as Demosthenes, but after his return from Pella he had changed his tune dramatically. Demosthenes reasoned that Aeschines's volte-face could only have been the result of bribery to lull the people into a false sense of security about the king's intentions toward them. Aeschines was able to prevent his trial at this time by successfully charging Timarchus of Sphettus, Demosthenes's co-prosecutor, with male prostitution, an offense that carried with it loss of citizenship. The resulting discredit forced Demosthenes to abandon his case, though not forget it. Now Aeschines could not escape his adversary. Demosthenes's prosecution and Aeschines's defense speeches from this famous "false embassy" trial (so named because of the titles of their speeches) have survived, a rare occurrence in Greek forensic oratory, which testifies to the importance of the case. Demosthenes, with only circumstantial evidence and mostly mudslinging, lost his suit, although only by a narrow margin of 30 votes out of 1,501 jurors.

Philip finally had had enough. He may have now orchestrated an attempt to burn the dockyards at the port of the Piraeus, home to the powerful Athenian navy.[18] A former Athenian citizen named Antiphon was caught red-handed trying to set them on fire, apparently bribed by Philip to do so. Thanks to Demosthenes, Antiphon was brought to trial and executed. If this story is credible, Philip may have tried to check the power of the Athenians' navy before he embarked on his next operation, which he knew would be the final straw in his relations with Athens: the conquest of Thrace.

BREAKDOWN OF THE PEACE

Before Philip left for Thrace in June 342 he made arrangements for Aristotle to tutor his now 14-year-old son and heir, Alexander, not at Pella but at Mieza, where he would be beyond his mother Olympias's grasping clutches (pp. 95–97). Philip's reason for leading an army once more into Thrace was to assist a number of cities on the Hellespont that the still-troublesome Cersebleptes had recently attacked. Eleven months later Philip had defeated Cersebleptes and absorbed Thrace into the Macedonian Empire. Details of this important campaign are surprisingly brief; Diodorus, for example, merely records that Philip overcame the Thracians in several battles and imposed a tithe tax on them as well as garrisons in a number of key towns including his own foundations, Beroe (Stara Zagora) and Philippopolis (Plovdiv in Bulgaria), to keep them under control.[19] Thrace was turned into a satrapy of sorts, especially when Philip created the administrative position of general (*strategos*) to administer it. He followed up his successes by concluding an alliance with the seminomadic Getae peoples, who lived between Thrace and the Danube Basin by the Schipka Pass. The terms included his marriage to their king Cothelas's daughter Meda.[20] This was his sixth marriage, after a gap of 10 years, but it was in keeping with his policy of political marriages, for it marked the extension of Macedonian influence as far north as the Istrus (Danube) River.

The conquest of Thrace doubled the size of the kingdom Philip had inherited in 359 (Map 3). It is small wonder that the last remaining independent Greek cities to his east, Perinthus (Marmaraereglisi), Selymbria (Silivri), and Byzantium on the Hellespont, wondered when he would deal with them. Equally alarmed were the Athenians, who were surely right to believe that Philip would take steps to reduce their presence in the Chersonese, especially when one of the Greek towns there, Apollonia, entered into a pact with him. In an effort to prevent other towns following Apollonia's lead and to counter Philip's increasing encroachment on their territory, the Athenians settled more cleruchs in the area and deployed the general and politician Diopeithes of Sunium with a contingent of troops to the region.

Philip clearly had his sights set on curtailing Athenian power, for while he was still in Thrace he sent troops to Euboea to assist rebels in various towns and win support for Macedonia. The Athenians considered recalling Diopeithes from the Chersonese, as Philip had hoped, but on Demosthenes's advice they abandoned this notion. Then in 341, after his ally Cardia demanded his help against Diopeithes, Philip sent the Athenians a letter formally protesting Diopeithes's actions in preying on Macedonian merchant ships and looting Thracian towns and demanded his recall.

The Athenians called an Assembly to debate Philip's missive. Aeschines was all for withdrawing Diopeithes to maintain peace with Philip, but Demosthenes seized the opportunity to denigrate the king and terrify the people about his aims. In his speech *On the Chersonese* he scorned pacifist politicians such as Aeschines, calling them "philippizers," and claimed that Philip had already broken the peace, exaggeratedly warning the people that after the Chersonese he would march on Greece and destroy Athens. He was, postulated Demosthenes, the enemy of democracy, and because the Athenians had the only constitution that could resist him, they had to fight him. The people concurred and did not withdraw Diopeithes. A short time later, when Philip had sent soldiers to assist Cardia, another Assembly was held at which Demosthenes delivered his third and most aggressive *Philippic*. The speech repeated much of the scare-tactic rhetoric of *On the Chersonese*, with Demosthenes referring to Philip as a wretched Macedonian. He successfully persuaded the Athenians to dispatch embassies to the Greek states and even Persia to drum up support for a war against Philip. Artaxerxes of Persia, no doubt remembering his rebuff at Athenian hands in 344, was quick to say no, but Byzantium, Chios, Cos, and Rhodes made alliances with the city. A fourth (and final) *Philippic*, probably delivered after the embassies returned, reinforced the Athenian resolve to resist Philip and called for an alliance with Persia.[21]

The Peace of Philocrates had all but collapsed by now, so Philip marched to the assistance of his beleaguered ally Cardia. He did not fight the Athenians in the Chersonese because his influence in Euboea suffered a sudden reversal, which the Athenians eagerly exploited. Callias, the former ruler of Chalcis on the island, unexpectedly sought Athenian aid to expel those rulers whom the Macedonians had recently installed. He intended to unite all of Euboea under his hegemony, motivating Demosthenes to persuade the Athenians to throw their weight behind him. Athenian soldiers successfully routed pro-Macedonian rulers in several cities, while Callias seized Macedonian ships and sent embassies to Peloponnesian cities calling on them to defy Philip. His actions forced Philip back to Pella. Callias's subsequent Euboean League did not make an alliance with Athens, but nevertheless Attic security was no longer compromised.

In the meantime Diopeithes died in the Chersonese and was succeeded by Chares. With his influence in Euboea now eroded, Philip marched with 30,000 infantry to the Hellespont to besiege Perinthus, Selymbria, and Byzantium in the early summer of 340. He left behind the 16-year-old Alexander as regent of his kingdom. Philip invested Perinthus first. Because the city was built in a series of terraces running up a steep hillside, 160 feet high, every time Philip's siege engines breached the walls of one terrace the defenders simply retreated up to the next one, piling rubble behind them as makeshift defense walls to hinder the attackers.[22] Further adding to Philip's woes was the fact that the Perinthians received supplies and military assistance from Byzantium and Persia, while Persian troops raided Thrace, and the nearby Athenian fleet at Elaious was too strong for the king to risk deploying his own small navy.

In August or early September Philip cut his losses at Perinthus. He left half of his force to continue its siege and led the remainder against Selymbria and Byzantium.[23] What happened at Selymbria is unknown, but he certainly failed to take Byzantium, thanks to its huge and enormously thick fortification walls. Even his new torsion catapults, which made their appearance for the first time here, could not breach the walls, and supplies and troop reinforcements from Chios, Cos, Rhodes, and Persia further shored up the defenders. Even though Philip was getting nowhere at Byzantium, his attack directly threatened the grain route through the Hellespont, forcing the Athenians to jump to its defense. Chares took the Athenian fleet to Byzantium, where Cephisophon and Phocion, with more vessels and troops from Athens, joined him. The inevitable war that

Demosthenes had forecast in his *On the Peace* of 346 was about to erupt. Earlier in 340 Demosthenes had been crowned for his services to the people in the Theater of Dionysus, during the annual festival to that god. Now it remained to be seen whether his unwavering anti-Macedonian policy would be worthy of that award.

THE SECOND WAR WITH PHILIP

Philip decided to send another (and final) letter to the Athenians, criticizing them for their attitude to him and the peace over the previous years and for their actions that, he argued, were intended to wreck it. Demosthenes responded with his *To Philip's Letter*—the last of his political speeches that have survived. In it he called on the people to make war on Philip and claimed that Philip had been waging war on Athens for a considerable time already and that he had not lived up to his promises or oaths to them and so had broken the peace. A passage in Philip's letter in which he threatened to deal with the Athenians because of their actions has been taken to mean that Philip had actually declared war on the Athenians, which they failed to realize.[24] Supporting the view that he had opaquely declared war in his letter is the fact that when he captured the Athenian grain fleet he referred to its ships as "prizes of war."[25] Ultimately, however, the technical aggressor is a moot point.

Philip bided his time at Byzantium while the Athenian grain fleet, with its precious cargo, was assembling at Hieron, an island near the Asiatic coast close to the mouth of the Propontis (Sea of Marmara). From there Chares would sail along the coast to protect the cargo from pirates and see it safely to Athens. The fleet consisted of 230 vessels, of which 180 were Athenian and the rest belonged to Byzantium, Rhodes, and Chios. Loading this number of ships was a long process, so while their crews were ashore at Hieron Chares attended a meeting of Persian satraps about the Macedonian sieges of Perinthus and Byzantium. His departure presented Philip with a golden opportunity to strike. He ordered his admiral, Demetrius, to seize the grain ships, while he himself captured their crews. The operation was swiftly accomplished. The king released the 50 ships belonging to the other cities, but he destroyed the Athenian ones, using their timber for his siege engines, and sold their grain for the huge sum of 700 talents.

Chares rushed back when he heard the news, but he was too late. He did manage to attack and blockade the Macedonian fleet in the Propontis, which placed Philip in a bind. He did not want to return home and leave his own ships behind, nor did he want to risk a land battle with so few men. Therefore the master of deception arranged for a letter ostensibly written to his general Antipater to fall into Chares's hands. Its contents spoke of a sudden revolt of Thrace and summoned Antipater to meet Philip there at once. Chares fell for the trick. Thinking that the king was getting ready to leave Chares left at once for Thrace to beat Philip there and encourage the Thracian rebels. His hasty departure allowed Demetrius to take his ships safely out of the Propontis and join Philip for the return to Pella.

While en route home Philip mounted a swift offensive in Scythia, capturing 20,000 horses and the same number of children and women. His good luck ran out when he encountered the Triballi, a group of independent Thracian tribes in the Danube area. They demanded that he pay them for the right of passage through their territory, but he was in no mood to bow to their demand and ordered his men to attack. In the ensuing fight his upper leg or thigh was accidentally speared by the sarissa of one of his men, which in the process killed his horse under him. Losing much blood, he was carried from the battlefield. He spent the winter of 340–339 recovering but limped for the rest of his life.[26] The Triballi made off with the spoils from his Scythian campaign, which was a major loss as Philip practiced a "rolling economy," using money and booty from one campaign to fund the next. The treasury was still in deficit three years later when Alexander became king.

When news of the grain fleet's fate reached Athens, Demosthenes had little problem persuading the Athenians to smash the stele (stone) on which was recorded the terms of the Peace of Philocrates, thereby showing that the city was at war. This second war between Athens and Philip ended in battle at Chaeronea in 338, where the stakes were far higher than simply one side being the loser and recovering to fight another day: mastery of Greece was the victor's prize.

5.

THE DOWNFALL OF GREECE

IN 339 PHILIP MARCHED into Greece, not as invader but as commander of the Amphictyonic forces in yet another sacred war (the fourth), which had been declared the previous year against the people of Amphissa, a city of west Locris (Map 1). His command gave him the means to lead an army legitimately into Greece. Once there he intended to end his war with Athens and bring Greece firmly under Macedonian control once and for all. The time for diplomacy was well past.[1]

THE FOURTH SACRED WAR

At the spring meeting of the Amphictyonic Council in 340 the Amphissans had charged the Athenians with impiety for rededicating in the newly built temple to Apollo at Delphi some Persian and Theban shields seized after the Battle of Plataea in 479.[2] The temple had not yet been reconsecrated, so the Athenians were technically guilty of sacrilege. The Amphissans urged the council to fine them 50 talents and deny them access to the Oracle. Politics rather than impiety was again at the heart of the charge: the Amphissans as allies of the Thebans were reacting to the inscription that the Athenians had added to these shields—"The Athenians from the Medes and the Thebans, when they fought on the opposite side to the Greeks."[3] Anyone viewing this dedication would be reminded that during the Persian Wars the Thebans had contemptibly joined ranks with the Persians and fought with them against Greek troops at Plataea, the final battle on the mainland in the wars.

The members of the Athenian delegation to the council made ex-
cuses not to address the Amphissan accusation—except for Aeschines.
Rather than trying to explain the Athenians' action, which clearly em-
barrassed the Thebans, he turned the tables on the Amphissans, boldly
censuring them for sacrilegiously cultivating part of the sacred Plain
of Cirrha below Delphi and constructing buildings on it. The council
sent a contingent of troops to investigate Aeschines's allegations; finding them credible, they were in the process of destroying the buildings
when Amphissan troops attacked and beat them back. After diplomatic demands on the part of the council were rebuffed, a sacred war
was declared against Amphissa later in 339, and at the behest of its
Thessalian members Philip was appointed commander of its army.
This Fourth Sacred War was a lackluster affair that ended the following year.

The Amphissan charge of sacrilege against Athens never again materi-
alized. Demosthenes later claimed that Aeschines had worked in tandem
with Philip to provoke this sacred war so that the king could march back
into Greece.[4] That cannot be true, because Philip was far away fighting
the Scythians when the council met and—like the Athenians—had no
idea what the Amphissans planned to do, so he was not part of a conspiracy with them.[5] The opportunity to command Amphictyonic troops
was a welcome one for the king, but he did not immediately march into
Greece, because of the onset of winter and because he was still recuperat-
ing from the wound he had suffered in the clash with the Triballi. In the
following spring he had recovered enough to lead his troops southward
and established a camp at Cytinium, six miles north of the Gravia Pass,
through which lay Amphissa.

Then, as often in his reign, Philip defied expectations to achieve his
personal goals. In this case, he left Cytinium but bypassed Amphissa
and turned southeast, down the Cephissus Valley, through Phocis, to
the Boeotian border, and there captured the town of Elatea, only two to
three days' march from Athens. He had clearly decided to leave Amphissa be for the moment while he dealt with the Athenians as well as
the Thebans, who in the same year had expelled the garrison he had
installed in 346 in Nicaea, which controlled access to Thermopylae. He

sent an embassy to the Thebans demanding that they return Nicaea to him and either join him in attacking Athens, keeping whatever Athenian spoils they seized when the city fell, or allow his army passage through Boeotia to Attica.

With the renowned Macedonian army encamped on the Boeotian border the Thebans' mood must have been grim indeed. Philip had treated them leniently in 346, but they had no reason to assume continued benevolence on his part now. The Athenians likewise feared the worst. An emergency Assembly was summoned, at which Demosthenes urged the people to put aside their enmity for the Thebans and join with them in a last-ditch effort to save themselves and Greece from Philip. Demosthenes had been working to this end since 346, when he realized that only an effective union of Athens and Thebes had the chance to stop Philip.[6] His planning now paid off: the people accepted his arguments and sent him at the head of an embassy to petition the Thebans for alliance. He left with a contingent of troops, which held fast at Eleusis while the Thebans debated the issue.

The Theban Assembly was packed. The Macedonians spoke first and bluntly pointed out that if the Thebans refused Philip's demand, his men would plunder Boeotia mercilessly. Demosthenes then gave his speech. After it the Thebans voted—in favor of allying with Athens and so going to war with Macedonia. What Demosthenes said is unknown—Plutarch claimed that his oratory "stirred [the Thebans'] courage, kindled their desire to win glory and threw every other consideration into the shades. As if transported by his words, they cast off all fear, self-interest or thought of obligation towards Macedonia and chose the path of honor."[7] The Thebans' decision was certainly courageous, but they are unlikely to have been swayed for these reasons, not least because they exacted significant concessions from Demosthenes: the Athenians were to recognize Thebes's hegemony of the Boeotian League, pay for one-third of the costs of land operations and the entire bill for naval engagements, and agree to the Thebans being in sole command of the army and sharing in the command of the combined fleet. Still, on the motion of his cousin Demomeles and the orator Hyperides, a jubilant Demosthenes was rewarded on his return to Athens with a gold crown (his second) at the Dionysia festival in March.

To prevent Philip from marching into Boeotia and Attica the Thebans developed a two-stage defensive position. A force of their infantry and 10,000 Athenian-hired mercenaries commanded by the Athenian Chares and the Theban Proxenus was deployed to the Gravia Pass, while another joint force was posted 20 miles away at Parapotamii, on the Boeotian border, close to Phocis. These positions were good, defensive ones, and the Thebans deserve praise for their strategy. When Philip learned that all the passes from Mount Parnassus to Lake Copais were under Athenian–Theban control he knew that he had only two choices: either force his way through or—with winter fast approaching—return home (as the Thebans were banking on him to do). At this point both sides dispatched embassies to the other Greeks for support. Few responded—only Megara, Corinth, Achaea, Euboea, Acarnania, and some islands supported the Greek cause, and just the Thessalians, Phocians, and Achaeans (in the Peloponnese) marched to join Philip. The reason for this lackluster response was probably the same as for the lack of enthusiasm for the Fourth Sacred War: the Greeks were tired of fighting and expected Philip to settle matters anyway.

Later in the same year, 338, Philip and the Greeks clashed in some minor skirmishes in and around the Cephissus Valley before he decided that it was time to act more aggressively. He targeted the enemy troops at the Gravia Pass since he could not use his cavalry in the narrower pass at Parapotamii. Resorting to his tried and tested trick of a Thracian revolt, Philip arranged for a letter to his generals to be intercepted by Chares and Proxenus with his plans to leave for Thrace immediately. As "proof" he directed some of his men at Cytinium to break camp. Chares was just as gullible as he had been at Byzantium in 340 and believed the letter's content. He allowed his guards to relax their vigil, and Philip struck fast and decisively. He ordered his general Parmenion to attack Chares and his men, who were caught unprepared. Parmenion's troops massacred many of the mercenaries and seized the pass; three hours later Parmenion reached Amphissa, which promptly surrendered to him, thereby ending the Fourth Sacred War.

In the meantime, Philip bore down on the other Greek allies at Parapotamii, who could not hold him back and fled to the plain of Chaeronea (not far from Thebes). The Thebans had deliberately chosen this plain as a fallback position because it was merely two miles wide and had hills on its northern and southern sides and several rivers dissecting it, hence Philip would find it difficult to deploy his cavalry effectively. There the Greeks prepared to make their last-ditch stand against the invader.

THE BATTLE OF CHAERONEA

The Greek coalition troops numbered 30,000 infantry and 3,800 cavalry and were commanded by the Athenian generals Chares, Lysicles, and Stratocles and the Theban general Theagenes. Boeotia provided 12,000 hoplites, including the elite Sacred Band, and the Athenians, 6,000 citizen soldiers (to age 50) and 2,000 mercenaries. Demosthenes, who had the phrase "good luck" emblazoned in gold letters on his shield, was one of the infantrymen in the Athenian contingent. Philip commanded 30,000 infantry and 2,000 cavalry, composed of 24,000 Macedonians and the rest from Thessaly and Phocis.[8] The Greeks set up camp on the western side of the plain of Chaeronea, and the Macedonians, on its eastern—in his biography of Alexander Plutarch states that Alexander pitched his tent next to an oak tree by the Cephissus River, "which was known as Alexander's oak" even in the biographer's lifetime.[9] The Cephissus flowed from the northwest to the southeast, forming the plain's eastern border, so Plutarch's anecdote helps to fix Alexander's location in the Macedonian battle line.

Philip was in no rush to fight and waited for the Greek forces to assemble their battle line before he drew up his own. The Greek right flank was stationed by the Cephissus River and had the Boeotians with the Sacred Band on the far right. The Athenians and 5,000 light-armed infantry under Stratocles were stationed on the left flank by the Haemon (Lykuressi) stream. The other Greek allies were in the center of that line. On the enemy front, Philip put himself on his right flank, along with his hypaspists, facing the Athenians. On his left flank, facing the Boeotians,

were the Companion Cavalry. Although it was under Alexander's command, he was most likely supported by Parmenion and Antipater because
Diodorus stated that he was stationed next to Philip's "most seasoned
generals."[10] The various battalions that made up the Macedonian phalanx
were in the center. The Greeks had deliberately strung out their line to
cover almost the entire two miles of the plain's width, forcing Philip to
match it rather than risk being outflanked. That meant that he had to decrease the depth of his phalanx, thereby reducing its mass and the force of
its charge. Further, the narrowness of the plain and its marshy areas impeded his usual cavalry attack. The Greeks were risking everything on a
frontal charge with their right flank, which would then pivot to push the
Macedonian left onto the boggy ground, even into the Cephissus. Philip
therefore had to break up the opposing line and have his infantry carry
the day. To this end, his strategy was to open gaps in the enemy line
through which his men would pour while neutralizing the threat posed
by the fearsome Sacred Band as quickly as possible.

Although the troop numbers of both sides were roughly the same, and
the Greek strategy was by no means flawed, there was a considerable difference in battle experience between the two sides. The Macedonian army
had fought virtually every year since 358 against a variety of foes, from
Greeks to Thracians to Scythians. Apart from reversals against Onomarchus
of Phocis in 353 and the Triballi in 339, it had never been beaten—in fact,
Philip may well have overcome the Triballi had he not been unexpectedly
and severely wounded. By contrast, the Greeks had fought rarely in the
previous two decades and had never faced the massed Macedonian army.
The Boeotians had seen the most action, but only from their involvement
in the Third Sacred War, and the Athenians' hardest battles had been relatively minor ones on Euboea.

The Battle of Chaeronea took place in early August (either the seventh
or ninth of Metageitnion).[11] Philip planned a three-phase operation to
upset the allied strategy. For the first phase he directed his entire line to
march toward the Greeks at an acute angle, not face on, with his right
flank closer to the Greek line than the left. When the Macedonian right
under Philip came into contact with the Athenians on the Greek left, he
put the second phase of his strategy into operation. Rather than engaging

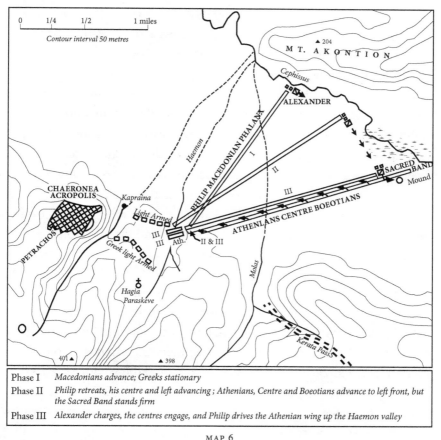

Phase I	Macedonians advance; Greeks stationary
Phase II	Philip retreats, his centre and left advancing ; Athenians, Centre and Boeotians advance to left front, but the Sacred Band stands firm
Phase III	Alexander charges, the centres engage, and Philip drives the Athenian wing up the Haemon valley

MAP 6
Battle of Chaeronea.

the Athenians in hand-to-hand fighting as they expected, he began to lead his wing sideways to the right, and the rest of his line followed suit. The Athenian left moved to stay with him, but as it did so it opened a gap toward the Greek center. The troops posted there and up to the right flank scrambled to plug it, while the Sacred Band on the extreme right followed orders and stood fast. Thinking that Philip was actually retreating, Stratocles allegedly exhorted his men to attack and shut him up in Macedonia. His impetuosity proved fatal.

Philip's retreat was a feigned one. He continued for about 100 feet and then stopped by the Haemon to bring his third phase into play. Alexander and the cavalry on the Macedonian left now rushed to the gap that still remained open between the immobile Sacred Band and the rest of the Greek line. Once through it, they wheeled round at speed to encircle the band, cutting it down to the last man, and then quickly re-formed to assault the other Boeotian soldiers.[12] In the meantime, Philip's men turned back and charged the startled Athenians, forcing them into the river valley. The king had deliberately taken up a position opposite the inexperienced Athenians, anticipating that they would quickly buckle. He was right. The Athenians stood no chance as the Macedonians mowed them down and then broke the allied center apart. The fighting turned into a massacre as 1,000 Athenians were slain and 2,000 were taken prisoner. The other allies also lost substantial numbers, and the Haemon was said to have run red with blood. Perhaps as much as half of the Greek army was killed or captured. In complete shock and disarray the survivors (including Demosthenes) managed to struggle over the Kerata Pass to Lebadea (Levadhia) in Boeotia and thence to their homes.

Philip ordered the bodies of his men to be cremated as was the custom with those killed in battle. Then he buried their ashes under a large burial mound (*polyandreion*), 23 feet high, and honored them with a procession and sacrifice. The mound on the plain today, in which archaeologists discovered bones, teeth, and long spearheads from sarissas, is probably this mass grave. Two contradictory ancient accounts detail Philip's actions following these solemn arrangements. The first is that while walking the battlefield he stumbled across the corpses of the 300 members of the Sacred Band, who had fought to the last man, and burst into tears. His reaction must have stemmed from his memory of watching the band train while he was hostage in Thebes and his admiration of their courage. To memorialize their bravery he ordered a statue of a lion to be set up on the spot (Figure 15).

The second account is that he got so drunk after his victory that he began to mock the prisoners and Demosthenes, sneeringly chanting the opening words of the latter's decrees before the Assembly: "Demosthenes, son of Demosthenes, of Paeania moved this."[13] One of the Athenian captives, an orator named Demades, grew so incensed at his conduct that he contemptuously asked him, "O King, when Fortune has

FIGURE 15
Lion of Chaeronea. Photo: Archimedes Nikolakis.

cast you in the role of Agamemnon, are you not ashamed to act the part
of Thersites?" Philip was said to have sobered up instantly at the reference to Agamemnon, the leader of the Greeks in the Trojan War, and
Thersites, who was slapped down for not knowing his place. Whether
either story is true is not known, although the restored monument of
the lion that stands at Chaeronea today (the original was broken in the
Greek War of Independence) lends credence to the first one; Theopompus, in his critical history of Philip, may have been responsible for the
second anecdote.[14]

Philip's victory at Chaeronea changed the face of Greek politics forever. Gone were the Greeks' cherished ideals of *autonomia* and *eleutheria* (pp. 11–13), and even though the polis as an entity continued to exist, the Greeks now had to contend with the practical rule of Macedonia.[15] The contemporary Athenian orator Lycurgus remarked of the battle, "with the corpses of those who died here the freedom of the Greeks was also buried,"[16] and some centuries later Justin's comment was equally sober: "for the whole of Greece [Chaeronea] marked the end of its glorious supremacy and of its ancient independence."[17] But while Philip had won the battle, could he now establish peace? An even greater challenge for him now was to reconcile the Greeks to Macedonian rule. At the same time he had to contend with the worrying prophecy he had received before the battle:

> Let me fly far from the battle at Thermodon (Chaeronea), let me take refuge
> Watching from high in the clouds, as I soar with the wings of an eagle.
> Tears are for the loser, but death for the victor.[18]

As events the following year proved, he should have heeded that closing line more closely.

Philip must also have been delighted at the role that the 18-year-old Alexander had played in the battle. His father had entrusted him with a key command, and he had not failed him. His routs of the allied right flank and the Sacred Band were portents of his future military successes in Asia. So, too, were aspects of his life before the battle and even the manner of his conception and birth, all of which were said to have signaled future greatness.

THE YOUNG ALEXANDER

It should not be forgotten that it was Philip who carefully crafted plans to invade Asia and would have personally undertaken that campaign had he not been assassinated in 336. Alexander's spectacular exploits in Asia tend to overshadow these details as well as his father's achievements for Macedonia, which provided Alexander with the means and opportunity to build an empire that stretched from Greece to India and come to be dubbed "the Great." There is no question that Alexander's strategic brilliance and military successes must be lauded. However, those very successes were later embellished, and legends were developed about his superhuman status that make it difficult to know the real Alexander. These legends are even connected to his conception and birth.

There are three common myths that explain Alexander's conception.[19] The first involves Olympias dreaming one night that during a thunderstorm a blinding flash of lightning spawned a thunderbolt that fell from the sky into her womb, impregnating her. Second, Philip was said to have dreamed that he sealed his wife's womb with a tablet of wax on which was an impression of a lion. Finally, Philip one night saw Olympias having sex with a huge snake in their bed, and not long after she became pregnant with Alexander. The snake was Zeus Ammon in disguise, and the thunderbolt was commonly associated with that god, which is why Alexander later said that Zeus was his real father and Philip was merely his "mortal" one. Macedonian kings traditionally traced their ancestry back to Zeus and, through Temenus of Argos, to the hero Heracles, and Alexander's mother was a descendant of Achilles. However, common descent was one thing; god on earth, quite another. As his reign progressed Alexander identified himself with Zeus in a very uncommon manner, causing resentment among his troops and eventually mutiny.

On the day of Alexander's birth in 356 the Temple of Artemis at Ephesus burned down. Because of this "Hegesias of Magnesia made such a chilling claim that it could have put out the fire. What he said was that it was no surprise that the temple of Artemis had burned down because the goddess was busy delivering Alexander into the world. However, all the Magi who were at Ephesus at the time interpreted the temple's destruction as a sign of further disaster; they ran around slapping their faces and lamenting aloud that on this day had been born only sorrow and great calamity for Asia."[20] Alexander did indeed bring Achaemenid rule in Persia to an end, but it is highly improbable that this achievement was forecast from his birth. He likely spread these and other stories later to broadcast that he was always destined for greatness.[21] As such, they quickly became part of the Alexander legend.

Alexander was a short man—after the Battle of Issus in 331 one of the captured Persian noblewomen mistook the taller Hephaestion for Alexander, and when he sat on the royal throne in the palace of Susa his feet did not reach the ground. His actual appearance is controversial, depending on which ancient account is read. He was said to have a lopsided face because his neck inclined to the left; a round chin; a long, thin nose; a bulging forehead above watery eyes, one of which was apparently light blue and the other brown; very sharp, pointed teeth; a high-pitched voice; and a thick, tousled mane of blond hair. If he really did look like this, then his later portraits were deliberately softened to make him more handsome.[22] These busts also depict Alexander with his blond hair in ringlets, with a central parting, and—against the tradition of the times—beardless (Figure 2). Roman images of him, like the one on the Alexander mosaic (Figure 16), were likewise idealized, as they feature Alexander with dark curly hair and sideburns.

FIGURE 16
The Alexander mosaic. Scala/Art Resource, New York.

Perhaps the closest to what he actually looked like is the image of him on the so-called Porus medallions, struck after his great victory over that Indian prince at the Battle of the Hydaspes River in 326 (Figure 17). He is also most likely represented on the small, carved ivory head that was found next to that of his father in what is believed to be Philip's tomb at Vergina (Figure 18).

Despite Alexander's military life and reputation, little is known of his youth and upbringing until he turned 14.[23] Philip's constant campaigning meant that he and his son spent little time together, and a number of tutors and instructors were responsible for Alexander's physical and

FIGURE 17
Alexander on the Porus medallion. The Art Archive at Art Resource, New York.

FIGURE 18
Ivory head of Alexander from Tomb II, Vergina. Gianni Dagli Orti/The Art Archive
at Art Resource, New York.

intellectual training. His earliest teacher was one of his mother's relatives from Epirus, Leonidas, who was responsible for his early physical education, teaching him to fight, march, ride, and hunt. Alexander supposedly said that Leonidas fed him a night's march for breakfast and a light meal for dinner. The less-than-close relationship Alexander enjoyed with his father is shown by his calling Leonidas his foster father. Other men must have instructed him in other martial arts, including swordsmanship and javelin throwing. A later tutor, Lysimachus of Acarnania (south of Epirus), taught him how to play the lyre and to read and write. Possibly it was Lysimachus who instilled in him his admiration of Greek tragedy (especially Euripides) and Homer. Alexander's love of reading never abated— even in Asia he requested that his imperial treasurer, Harpalus, send him books by the historian Philistus; tragedies by Aeschylus, Sophocles, and Euripides; and poems by Telestes and Philoxenus.[24] He regularly held literary contests in Asia and enjoyed the company of poets, actors (including the leading tragic actor of the day, Thessalus), and artists such as Apelles and Pyrgoteles—the same Apelles who would sharply rebuke Alexander for his lack of artistic appreciation at Ephesus in 334 (p. 151).

Perhaps the most famous story of the young Alexander is his taming of the horse Bucephalas ("Ox-head"). Alexander may have been no more than 10 or 11 years old when one day a Thessalian horse trader visited Pella. Among the fine horses he brought with him was a large black stallion with an asking price of 13 talents—a small fortune. None of the men was interested because every time anyone approached the horse he reared up violently and no one could ride him. The young Alexander pestered Philip to let him try to mount the horse, and his father reluctantly agreed. Alexander had noticed that the animal was spooked when his shadow fell in front of him. He calmed him by turning him to face the sun so that his shadow fell behind him, jumped on him, and rode off. A tearful Philip at once bought Bucephalas for his son, predicting that Macedonia would never be big enough for someone like Alexander.

We are again dealing with the stuff of legend to depict a superhuman Alexander even as a boy. Alexander's horse was indeed called Bucephalas, and he rode it until 326, when it died from battle wounds suffered in India.[25] However, it is hard to believe that a seasoned Thessalian horse trader, not to mention Philip and his cavalry squadrons, failed to perceive what startled Bucephalas and could not pacify him.

In 342 Philip decided that Alexander, now aged 14, needed a formal intellectual education. He turned to the greatest philosopher of the day, Aristotle, and invited him to be his son's personal tutor. Aristotle was the son of Amyntas III's court physician and already had contacts with the Macedonian court. He was then living in Mytilene on the island of Lesbos at the invitation of the philosopher and botanist Theophrastus. At first Aristotle may have declined, because Philip had to promise to rebuild the philosopher's native city of Stageira in the Chalcidice, which he had razed in 349 during his Chalcidian campaign. Perhaps because of Olympias's influence over Alexander, which Philip likely resented, Aristotle taught

Alexander not in Pella but in the Precinct of the Nymphs at Mieza, part of the Gardens of Midas on the eastern slopes of Mount Vermion. Here, tutor instructed student about biology, ethics, literature, mathematics, medicine, philosophy, politics, rhetoric, and zoology while sitting on stone benches or walking among the orchards and vineyards that are still there today. Alexander was clearly attracted to philosophy because he made a special point of meeting the Cynic philosopher Diogenes in 336. He also took with him to Asia the philosopher Anaxarchus of Abdera, Pyrrho of Elis (the father of Skepticism and student of Anaxarchus), and Aristotle's nephew, Callisthenes of Olynthus.

Aristotle's unwavering assertion that only experimentation and observation could advance scientific thought and understanding explains Alexander's thirst for knowledge and why he took civilian naturalists with him as well as *bematistai* (surveyors), who recorded all manner of information about the botany, biology, geography, and zoology of the areas through which they marched. Their accounts, which were supposedly sent back to Aristotle along with samples of animal life and flora, likely enabled the philosopher to write his famous *Historia Animalium*. Alexander's opening up of intellectual contacts between East and West led to the explosion of Greek science and mathematics in the Hellenistic period.[26]

On the other hand, Alexander's deliberate use of foreigners in his army and administration suggests that he was not swayed by Aristotle's argument "to treat the Greeks as if he were their leader and other people as if he were their master; to have regard for the Greeks as for friends and family, but to conduct himself towards other peoples as though they were plants or animals." To Aristotle all barbarians were slaves, who were nothing more than animate tools, and Greeks were meant to rule them.[27] Admittedly, Alexander's treatment of his foreign subjects was not idealistic but, rather, pragmatic—to help maintain Macedonian rule. Nevertheless, Aristotle would not have approved, and later in Alexander's reign their relationship cooled considerably. The root cause may have been that Aristotle circulated details of what he had taught Alexander, as Plutarch professed, or more likely Alexander's attitude to foreigners.[28] Perhaps that is why Aristotle does not even mention Alexander in the *Nichomachean Ethics* or *Politics*, which he wrote after he left Pella for Athens. Still, the deterioration in relations surely was not enough for the old philosopher to try to persuade Antipater to kill the young king as Plutarch claimed.[29]

For three years Aristotle taught Alexander at Mieza. Then in 340 Philip recalled Alexander to Pella, appointing him regent of Macedonia while he led an army into Thrace to besiege Perinthus, Selymbria, and Byzantium. As a parting gift Aristotle presented Alexander with his own, annotated copy of Homer's *Iliad*, which he took with him to Asia, famously keeping it next to a dagger under his pillow when he went to bed.

As regent Alexander was empowered to use the royal seal on state documents and perform the daily religious sacrifices to Heracles Patrous (Heracles the father), the ancestor of the Temenids, the original dynasty of the Macedonian ruling house. Alexander took his duties as regent seriously. When the Maedians, a tribe in the upper Strymon Valley close to Thrace, revolted from Macedonian rule, Alexander led a contingent of troops north and defeated them. He followed his victory by founding a city, probably nothing more than a garrison post, populated by people from Macedonia, Greece, and Thrace, to keep the Maedians in check, and boldly named it after himself: Alexandropolis. Possibly his action indicates the competitive streak he had with his father, who by then had founded two cities (Philippi and Philippopolis), a streak that grew into an infatuation to outdo his father in everything, no matter the cost. Evidently Philip was pleased with Alexander's success against the Maedians, because two years later, in 338, he gave him command of the Companion Cavalry at Chaeronea. While that battle marked Philip's triumph over the Greeks, it was also the beginning of deteriorating relations between him and his son, which may have led to his assassination.

THE AFTERMATH OF CHAERONEA

Before turning to the larger issue of settling Greece Philip needed to impose terms on the coalition states that had faced him at Chaeronea as well as end his war with Athens.[30] He dealt with the Thebans first since he was still in Boeotia, and he showed no mercy. Among other things he abolished their hegemony of the Boeotian League, installed a pro-Macedonian oligarchy of 300 men supported by a garrison in Thebes, demanded a ransom for the Theban soldiers killed at Chaeronea (excluding the Sacred Band), sold the survivors as slaves, and returned the border town of Oropus, seized by Thebes in 366 and long a bone of contention between Athens and Thebes, to Athenian control.

Next were the Athenians. In his inflammatory speeches Demosthenes had consistently warned that Philip intended to destroy Athens, so he and Hyperides hurriedly introduced a series of emergency measures, which included evacuating the Attic countryside; sending the women, children, and sacred objects to the Piraeus; and promising citizenship to metics (resident aliens) and freedom to slaves if they defended the city if besieged. None of these desperate actions was necessary. Philip sent Demades to Athens to assure the people that he intended no harm to them or their democracy and asked that they send him an embassy to hear his terms. Then he appointed Alexander to lead an official Macedonian delegation to Athens to return the ashes of the Athenian dead from Chaeronea and the 2,000 captives without ransom as well as obtain the Athenians' surrender in their war against Philip.

The Athenians were quick to send an embassy, comprising Demades, Aeschines, and Phocion, to the king. Demosthenes clearly was not a person to serve on it, but in any case he had left Athens ostensibly to acquire grain supplies from elsewhere. Philip's terms were that the Athenians disband their confederacy (although he allowed them to retain their navy), recall their cleruchs from the Chersonese, and sever all their contacts in that area. No moves were taken against the anti-Macedonian politicians, and the king returned Oropus to them, as noted, and allowed them to retain their "traditional" islands of Lemnos, Imbros, Scyros, and Salamis, as well as Delos and Samos. Philip's attitude to the Athenians was clearly different from his stance toward the other Greeks throughout his reign, despite the many years he was at war with them. Why he treated them differently cannot be answered, but it was probably a combination of wanting to curtail Theban power, a genuine appreciation of Athenian culture, and desiring the use of their navy for his invasion of Asia.

Greatly relieved, the Athenians made a treaty with Philip on his terms, not that they had any say in the matter, which ended their second war with him.[31] They also commissioned an expensive equestrian statue of Philip for the Agora and bestowed citizenship on him and Alexander. These actions were unashamedly hypocritical—at the same time they offered refuge to any Greek fleeing from Philip's purges, including Thebans, and, toward the end of 338, appointed Demosthenes, Philip's archenemy, to deliver the solemn public eulogy or funeral oration (*epitaphios*) to honor the Athenians killed at Chaeronea.[32] Philip would have been quite aware of their actions but could hardly have been surprised by them.

The king's next stop was Corinth. He had several allies in the Peloponnese that had not responded to his call to arms before Chaeronea; now he made his displeasure evident. Without delay, the Corinthians and Megarians sent deputations to him, cap in hand, but he still established pro-Macedonian oligarchies and garrisons in Corinth, Chalcis, Ambracia, and probably Megara. He was especially careful to isolate the Spartans, whose attempts to regain their influence in the Peloponnese had been causing instability there. Now they found themselves encircled by a number of pro-Macedonian states. Finally, Philip could deal with all of Greece.

THE LEAGUE OF CORINTH

From Corinth Philip issued a directive to all mainland Greek cities to send deputations to him.[33] Only the Spartans refused him, on the grounds that "what was imposed by a conqueror was not peace but servitude."[34] Philip had learned from the breakdown of the Peace of Philocrates that any voluntary settlement of Greece was ephemeral. He knew that he could not rule Greece as king, as he did Macedonia, and that if he simply imposed garrisons in major cities, the adverse reaction would eventually prompt factions in those cities to topple them and defy Macedonian power. Either scenario boded ill for a passive Greece, which Philip needed while he was away fighting in Asia. Therefore he decided to exploit the rivalries among the Greeks and their xenophobia regarding one another by enforcing a different Common Peace from those of the past: this one would be anchored in his military power yet put the onus on the Greeks to maintain it.[35]

Philip treated the Greek embassies hospitably and then announced his terms for the new Common Peace, which included the standard provisos of member states swearing an oath of allegiance to each other and pledging not to harm any other member, interfere in another's domestic or foreign policy, or conclude an alliance with a potential enemy and to assist anyone under attack. Then he outlined some revolutionary differences from previous Common Peaces: each Greek city would swear a personal oath of allegiance to Philip and his descendants, and there was to be a council (*synedrion*) of the Greeks, presided over by a hegemon or leader, meeting regularly, to which each city was to send envoys (*synedroi*). The council's purpose was to discuss and vote on military, domestic, and foreign issues affecting the Greeks, and its decisions were binding on all members. Macedonia would not be a member of this *synedrion*, thereby allowing the Greeks some autonomy in conducting their affairs.

After his announcement Philip sent the emissaries home and required them to bring their cities' responses to him at Corinth in the following spring. Although the Spartans continued to decry Philip, the other Greeks knew that they had little choice but to accept his terms. In the spring of 337, therefore, Philip received the oaths of allegiance from the Greek envoys and was elected—as he had anticipated—hegemon of the council, even though Macedonia was not a formal member of it. The Greeks referred to this organization as the Community of the Greeks (to Koinon ton Hellenon),[36] but it is more commonly called by its modern name, the League of Corinth.

Philip's Common Peace was brilliant and revolutionary. For one thing, it was an enforced one thanks to Macedonia's military might. For another, Philip knew that one of a Greek city's greatest fears was a union of other cities against it and that, given the opportunity, the Greeks would not hold back from uniting against one of their own. One of the common threads of Greek history was the constant warfare between the poleis, and this Philip neatly exploited. No Greek city would want to break the Common Peace and so face a hostile coalition of cities—this was the deterrent that allowed Macedonia to rule Greece. The League of Corinth forever altered the face of Greek politics and brought to an end the centuries-long period of Greek autonomy. Not until after the Greek War of Independence (1821–1829), in 1832, did the independent and free Greek nation come into being.

6.

PHILIP'S ASSASSINATION AND LEGACY

A T THE FIRST OFFICIAL meeting of the League of Corinth, in spring 337, Philip announced his grand plan to invade Asia. The Greeks were already familiar with Persia and its vast empire from the Aegean to the Indus and from Samarkand to Egypt, the creation of Cyrus II (559–530). Cyrus the Great, as he came to be called, was from the area around Pasargadae and founded the Achaemenid dynasty (taking its name from an ancestor, Achaemenes), which Alexander the Great brought to an end in 330.[1] The Greeks had already enjoyed cultural interactions with the Persians, and there were even similarities between Macedonia and Persia when it came to their development, kingship, and even internal troubles.[2] At the same time the Greeks still held thoughts of revenge for what the Persians had inflicted on them, especially Athens, during the Persian invasion of Greece in the early fifth century. Now thanks to Philip their sufferings were to be avenged.

THE INVASION OF ASIA

The Persians had not undertaken any further attacks on Greece after their defeat in the Persian Wars in 479. In 449 (the year is controversial) the Athenians and the Great King Artaxerxes had concluded a treaty, the Peace of Callias, with the Persians swearing to stay out of Greece. However, Artaxerxes's successor, Darius II, supported Sparta against Athens in the Peloponnesian War (431–404), and in the fourth century the Greeks viewed the Persians with increasing alarm. In 354 some Athenians even advocated war when they thought that Artaxerxes III Ochus had raised a fleet against them—actually it was part of his effort to recover Egypt. The Athenians were in financial ruin after the Social War and were at war with Philip over Amphipolis, so they were in no position to take on Persia; fortunately Demosthenes persuaded them to scrap the idea. Still, their fearful attitude that Persia might have been scrambling warships is akin to that of the West toward the Soviet Union during the Cold War. Because of that attitude Philip and later Alexander were able to win Greek support for their Asian campaigns.

When Philip decided to invade Asia is unknown. The Athenian orator Isocrates had written him a letter, the *To Philip*, in 346 calling on him to unite Athens, Thebes, Sparta, and Argos and lead a Greek army against Persia. His plea was unrealistic, and Philip dismissed it. However, with Greece finally cowed and Thrace conquered (thereby protecting his rear), Philip was free to set his sights on Asia. He may also have been influenced by the murder of Artaxerxes III at the hands of the eunuch Bagoas (not Alexander's later lover), the Persian chiliarch (second-in-command) in 338. Bagoas had then arranged the succession of the Great King's son Arses as Artaxerxes IV. This dynastic chaos played into Philip's hands and may have spurred him to act.

Exactly why Philip targeted Asia is also unknown. He may have simply wanted revenge on Persia for the assistance it gave to Perinthus and Byzantium when he was besieging them in 340—in 333 Alexander supposedly admonished the Great King for Persian aid "to the people of Perinthus, who wronged my father, and Ochus sent troops into Thrace, which we controlled."[3] Possibly Philip sought revenge for what his own kingdom had suffered under Persian rule from the late sixth century to the end of the Persian Wars, when the kings were mere vassals of Persian rulers. He may have intended to bring down Achaemenid rule in Asia to help him establish an absolute monarchy and even his own deification.[4] Perhaps closer to the truth, however, is the fact that he needed money. He practiced a rolling economy, using spoils from one campaign to finance the next. The loss of the Scythian booty to the Triballi in 339, on the eve of his full-scale involvement in Greece, placed a strain on his treasury, especially as he gave out an enormous amount of money in bribes during his reign, which prompted Diodorus's comment that Philip used gold more than arms to enlarge his kingdom.[5] When Alexander became king in 336 he found a mere 70 talents in the treasury and supplies for only 30 days and had to borrow 800 talents—something he brought up when he addressed his rebellious troops at Opis in 324, comparing his wealth then with the situation at his accession.[6] Philip may have turned to Persia because of its wealth; if so, he may have intended to operate only in Asia Minor to increase his finances.[7]

Philip pitched the invasion as a panhellenic (all-Greek) enterprise: to liberate the Greek cities in Asia Minor from the Persian rule forced on them by Sparta in 386 as part of the terms of the unpopular King's Peace and to punish the Persians for what the Greeks, especially the Athenians, had suffered in the Persian Wars.[8] That Philip earmarked the Athenians for special mention probably explains his lenient treatment of them after Chaeronea: he could hardly punish them the same way as he had the Thebans and then a few months later champion them. The Greeks were in no position to refuse the leader of Greece and endorsed his planned invasion.

THE IMPACT OF EMPIRE ON THE MACEDONIANS AND THE KINGSHIP

After their years of hard fighting, including an enforced movement of peoples to the dangerous northwest frontier in 345, how were Macedonians affected by their hegemony of Greece, and what did they make of their kingdom's expansion in power? These are important questions, but they are largely unanswerable because we have no journals or letters written by Macedonians talking about them. Yet certain events and their impact provide glimpses of the people's reactions to their kingdom's imperial successes.

To begin with, in the summer of 336 Philip held celebratory athletic games at Aegae as part of the marriage of his daughter to Alexander of Epirus, discussed below. Both marriage and games formed a "media event" of sorts to commemorate the League of Corinth and upcoming invasion of Persia. The games began with a grand procession including statues of the 12 Olympian gods, one of Philip, and finally Philip himself, to the shouts and applause of all present. The Macedonians' enthusiastic response was probably not only for Philip's benefit but also aimed at the various dignitaries from the Greek states who had attended the royal wedding. The Greeks, after all, had always looked down their noses at the Macedonians for their political system and social customs.

Then there is the speech that Alexander supposedly gave to his mutinous troops at Opis in Mesopotamia in 324, in which he praised his father:

> Philip took you over when you were helpless vagabonds, mostly clothed in skins, feeding a few animals on the mountains and engaged in their defence in unsuccessful fighting with Illyrians, Triballians and the neighboring Thracians. He gave you cloaks to wear instead of skins, he brought you down from the mountains to the plains; he made you a match in battle for the barbarians on your borders, so that you no longer trusted for your safety to the strength of your position so much as to your natural courage. He made you city dwellers and established the order that comes from good laws and customs. It was due to him that you became masters and not slaves and subjects of those very barbarians who used previously to plunder your possessions and carry off your persons. He annexed the greater part of Thrace to Macedonia and, by capturing the best placed positions by the sea, he opened up the country to trade; he enabled you to work the mines in safety; he made you the rulers of the Thessalians, who in the old days made you dead with terror; he humbled the Phocian people and gave you access into Greece that was broad and easy instead of being narrow and hard. The Athenians and the Thebans were always lying in wait to attack Macedonia; Philip reduced them so low, at a time when we were actually sharing in his exertions, that instead of our paying tribute to the Athenians and taking orders from the Thebans it was we in our turn who gave them security. He entered the Peloponnese and there too he settled affairs, and his recognition as leader with full powers over the whole of the rest of Greece in the expedition against the Persians did not perhaps confer more glory on himself than on the commonwealth of the Macedonians.[9]

Alexander acknowledges his father's important achievements that had made the Macedonians "masters" over so many states and peoples and that Philip had conferred more prestige on the Macedonians than on himself. At this point in his Asian campaign Alexander was trying to defuse a mutiny so that he could move to invading Arabia. He goes on to laud his own achievements and put himself above Philip because of his exploits in the East (quoted on pp. 278–279). However, he could not say anything to his men that might enhance their discontent; he was clearly trying to shame them into submission by appealing to their pride in the Macedonian Empire that his father had established in the West. If the Macedonians in 324 appreciated what Philip had done for them and took pride in it, then they surely felt the same a little more than a decade earlier in 337—as their jubilant reaction to his presence at the games of Aegae in 336 demonstrates.

Apart from the rhetoric there is the explicit memorialization of Macedonian power and, I suggest, pride in the Philippeion ("Philip's building") at Olympia, work on which started after Chaeronea. Philip chose Olympia deliberately because it was home to the panhellenic Olympic Games and because in its sanctuary (*altis*) was the great statue of Zeus, one of the wonders of the ancient world, which Phidias of Athens had carved in the 430s. Both of these things made Olympia a major attraction for pilgrims and visitors. The Philippeion was a large, eye-catching, circular building (tholos), a shape commonly reserved for sacred buildings, but there was nothing religious about Philip's monument. It had an open, external row of 18 Ionic columns and an internal row of nine Doric columns. Inside it but in plain view were statues of Philip, his mother and father (Eurydice and Amyntas), his son and heir Alexander, and Olympias (Figure 19).[10]

Philip's statue in the center of the group emphasized his importance. One of the period's preeminent artists, Leochares of Athens (who had worked on another of the ancient world's wonders, the Mausoleum at Halicarnassus), was commissioned to design the building. The Philippeion was built in the temenos, the area of the sanctuary housing statues and buildings in honor of the gods, and this combination of sacred and secular in one setting was startling and deliberate: next to the statue of Zeus, the supreme god of Greece, stood that of the supreme secular ruler

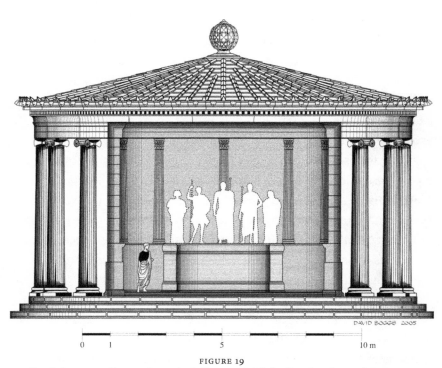

FIGURE 19

The Philippeion at Olympia. Drawn by D. Boggs, in P. Schultz, "Leochares' Argead Portraits in the Philippeion," in P. Schultz and R. von den Hoff (eds.), *Early Hellenistic Portraiture: Image, Style, Context* (Cambridge: 2007), p. 207, fig. 32.

of Greece. Just as the Lion of Chaeronea memorialized the Theban Sacred Band, so the Philippeion memorialized Philip—and Macedonia. We can imagine the grating effect that the building in this religious setting would have on Greeks, with the corollary of empowerment and self-esteem on the part of Macedonians.

Philip's successful campaigns beyond his borders affected the nature of Macedonian kingship. Before Philip the duties and responsibilities of kings were clearly defined but pertained only to the rule of Macedonia. He and kings after him would necessarily have to deal with new issues, from different customs of subject peoples to the administration and stability of newly conquered areas. Philip had already begun to adapt with his measures to control Thessaly (the restoration of the tetrarchy), Epirus (the installation of Alexander as a type of puppet ruler), Thrace (the appointment of a governor answerable only to him), and Greece (the League of Corinth).

He did not have time to acquire more experience since he died the following year, thereby catapulting Alexander to the throne. The new king had precious little time to gain much experience of ruling at home because two years later he invaded Asia. Like Philip he had to learn as he went along because of new demands that became part of the kingship.

The Macedonians recognized their new status in the Greek world, a far cry from a mere two decades earlier, when they were prey to foreign invasions, looked down upon by Greeks south of Mount Olympus, and largely ignored because of their peripheral location. Now from afar they ruled a burgeoning empire that stretched east to the Hellespont and south to the Peloponnese (Map 3), and they were ready to embrace their position in this new Greek world. However, they never had the time to enjoy their hegemony of Greece under Philip—the following year he was assassinated.

PHILIP'S SEVENTH MARRIAGE AND MURDER

In the summer of 337 Philip married again. His seventh wife was a teenage noblewoman, Cleopatra, who had been adopted by Attalus, a powerful Macedonian baron who was married to one of Parmenion's daughters.[11] Philip's previous six marriages had been for political and military reasons, but according to an ancient biographer he married Cleopatra out of love.[12] Olympias, who wasted "no opportunity criticizing [Philip] to her son," disliked the new bride intensely.[13] That aversion was heightened at the wedding banquet, when Attalus stood up, toasted the newlyweds, and then prayed that they might produce a legitimate heir. The racial barb was clearly aimed at Olympias and Alexander since Cleopatra in all likelihood came from Lower Macedonia, whereas Olympias hailed from Epirus.[14]

Attalus was not going to get away with his taunt, however. Alexander threw his drinking cup at him and demanded that he apologize. He was met with a blank refusal, so he turned to his father for support. Philip, who may have found Attalus's comment amusing given he had little time for Olympias, took his new father-in-law's side and ordered Alexander to beg Attalus's pardon. The amount of alcohol that had been drunk by now did not help matters—when Alexander angrily defied his father, Philip drew his sword and rushed him, stumbling and falling over a table, which caused Alexander to remark contemptuously: "here is the man who was making ready to cross from Europe to Asia, and who cannot even cross from one table to another without losing his balance."[15] Then Alexander and Olympias left Pella for the court of her brother, Alexander of Epirus.

At some later point Alexander moved on to Illyria, Macedonia's traditional enemy, possibly because he and his mother intended to provoke trouble for Philip.[16] The king evidently thought the same, for he recalled Alexander to Pella and, to nullify any hostile action from Alexander of Epirus, offered him the princess Cleopatra in marriage. Since this Cleopatra was Olympias's daughter, that made her Alexander of Epirus's niece, but he was quick to accept Philip's offer, and the wedding was set for summer 336.

In the meantime Alexander (Philip's son) returned to Pella in a sullen mood, which hardly abated when his father aligned himself more closely with Parmenion, Antipater, and, even worse, Attalus.[17] Alexander's feelings of marginalization added to the rapidly growing estrangement between father and son and to his resentment toward Philip's Old Guard generals, such as Parmenion, whom he removed when he was in Asia.[18] In 336, after Philip's assassination, the loyalty of Antipater and Parmenion played no small role in ensuring Alexander's succession; later, he did not have the same need of them.

Late in 337 relations between father and son deteriorated further. Pixodarus, the ruler of Caria in Asia Minor, had made plans to free himself from Persian control and to this end sought an alliance with Philip. As an incentive Pixodarus offered the hand of his daughter in marriage. Philip was quick to agree because Pixodarus would provide him with a valuable base in Asia Minor. He selected his eldest son, Arrhidaeus, as the lucky husband. Alexander, aggrieved at his father's decision, sent his friend Thessalus to Pixodarus offering Alexander in marriage instead. Why Alexander did this is unknown. His motive may have stemmed from antagonism between Olympias and Arrhidaeus's mother, Philinna. Both women were witches who practiced different religions, and Olympias did not take kindly to Philinna for her beliefs.[19]

Pixodarus of course was delighted to have his daughter marry the heir to the powerful Macedonian throne. However, when Parmenion's son Philotas discovered the plan he promptly informed Philip, not least because only Macedonian kings had the constitutional right to arrange marriages of family members. Furious, Philip and Philotas "angrily reproached [Alexander] for behaving so ignobly and so unworthily of his position as to wish to marry the daughter of a mere Carian, who was no more than a slave of a barbarian king."[20] The proposed marital tie with Pixodarus's house evaporated.

Philip took no formal action against Alexander, although he exiled several of his close friends—Harpalus, Ptolemy, Erigyius and his brother Laomedon of Mytilene, and Nearchus of Crete—and ordered the arrest of the unfortunate Thessalus, who had fled to Corinth. Alexander had a long memory: when he was king he treated all of these men well for their loyalty and friendship to him as well as to make up for their treatment at Philip's hands. His generosity was one of his more appealing character traits.[21]

In 336 Philip sent 10,000 Macedonian and mercenary soldiers commanded by Parmenion, Attalus, and Amyntas (the son of Arrhabaeus of Lyncestis) to Asia Minor to win over some of the Greek cities there and prepare the way for the main army under Philip after the wedding of Cleopatra to Alexander of Epirus at Aegae that summer. The advance troops scored successes along the Ionian coastline, with at least Chios and Erythrae defying Persia, while the people of Ephesus even set up a statue of Philip in their temple to Artemis. Things were going well, so much so that Philip decided to turn the royal wedding into a media event, attended by dignitaries and ambassadors from all over Greece and intended to mark the one-year anniversary of the League of Corinth and the forthcoming invasion of Asia. Who could blame him? In just 23 years he had led Macedonia from a dismal northern backwater to a superpower, laying the foundations of its empire under Alexander. He had fashioned a new era in Greek history and now, at 46 years old, could look ahead to untold successes in Asia.

The wedding itself went off without a hitch. But it would be the last joyous occasion for some time. The following day celebratory athletic games were held in the theater at Aegae, one of the largest in Greece (Figure 20).

FIGURE 20
Theater at Aegae. Photo: Timothy Johnson.

The spectators began cramming into the theater at dawn and settled down in excitement over the day's events. They were soon greeted by a grand procession, in which first appeared statues of the 12 Olympian gods and then a splendid one of Philip, as if he were "enthroned among the 12 gods."[22] Then Philip, Alexander the heir, and his new son-in-law Alexander of Epirus strode into the theater's *orchestra* (performance area). The two Alexanders dutifully removed themselves to their seats so that Philip, dressed all in white, occupied center stage, to the shouts and applause of all present. The king turned to his personal bodyguards and told them to fall back so that he could "show publicly that he was protected by the goodwill of the Greeks, and had no need of a guard of spearmen. Such was the pinnacle of success that he had attained."[23]

Suddenly, as Philip stood alone basking in all the glory, one of his bodyguards, Pausanias of Orestis, rushed from his position and before the horrified stares of the people, stabbed the king in his chest and fled. Rousing themselves from their shock, some of the other bodyguards tore after him, while others hastened to where Philip had collapsed. In his rush to get away Pausanias fell over a vine, and three of the pursuing guards without hesitation speared him to death with their javelins. By the time they returned carrying Pausanias's bloody corpse, Philip II was dead, his white attire crimson with his blood. The theater dissolved into pandemonium, as Alexander's friends grabbed their weapons to protect him in case he too was a target for assassination.

CONSPIRACY THEORY

How Pausanias killed Philip is certain enough. Why he did so is a different matter because the ancient accounts offer conflicting motives, so there is no irrefutable evidence.[24] Alexander himself put out the official explanation that Pausanias acted from feelings of spite and jealous rage because some time previously Philip had ended a homoerotic relationship with him and taken up with another man. This personal motive is at odds, however, with statements by Plutarch, that "it was Olympias who was chiefly blamed for the assassination, because she was believed to have encouraged the young man [Pausanias] and incited him to take his revenge, but a certain amount of accusation was also attached to Alexander,"[25] and Justin: "it was also believed that Pausanias had been suborned by Olympias, mother of Alexander, and that Alexander was not unaware of the plot to murder his father."[26] Justin's account continues with the detail that both Olympias and Alexander were afraid that the status of a son born of Philip and Cleopatra posed a threat to Alexander. Plutarch and Justin thus give us a political conspiracy to end Philip's life that involved Olympias and Alexander.[27]

Pausanias was certainly a jilted lover, but Philip had ended their affair some time ago. After falling from the king's favor Pausanias had complained to Attalus, who, we are told, had no time for him and even allowed his servants to gang rape him, further adding to his insult and injury. It is odd that Pausanias would not have reacted at once to either of these personal upsets rather than waiting many months after them to murder Philip—indeed after Attalus had left for Asia with the advance force—and that he would choose to do so in such a public place where everyone would know what he did.

It has been suggested that a group of disenchanted barons from the more remote regions of Macedonia plotted the assassination in order to maintain their influence at court in light of the new situation that Philip's marriage created.[28] However, the comments of Plutarch and Justin point to a political conspiracy closer to home. Attalus's taunt at the wedding banquet may well have provoked Olympias's concerns about the status of a son born to Cleopatra, as Justin claims, and she certainly took measures to propel Alexander forward—Plutarch relates the story that she poisoned Arrhidaeus so that Alexander would become the preferred heir.[29] Arrhidaeus did have a mental incapacity that forced Philip to set him aside, although whether this was the result of Olympias's action is unknown.[30] Possibly, then, Olympias cynically took advantage of Pausanias's hurt and anger over Philip's treatment of him and convinced him to kill her husband, knowing that Philip's bodyguard would kill Pausanias and hence prevent him from disclosing details of the plot.

Yet why the paranoia? Philip had clearly designated Alexander as his successor, and at the time of the wedding in 337 he was 19 years old. Were Cleopatra to bear Philip another son he would not come of age for at least 16 years. Still, Attalus clearly did not want to see Alexander succeed his father; if he and other barons threw their weight behind an infant boy of Macedonian blood, then Alexander might well have had to fight for the throne. Then again, perhaps too much has been made of Attalus's drunken comment; he may have simply wanted to take Alexander, who was perhaps boastful of his military exploits, down a peg or two.[31] Nevertheless, Alexander had grounds for resenting his father, and to make matters worse he must have been devastated when Philip told him that he would not be going with him to Asia but would remain behind in Macedonia as regent and deputy hegemon of the League of Corinth. Alexander had twice tasted battle by now and was hungry for more, but as he told his friends, the more Philip conquered, the less would be left for him.

It is perhaps significant that the three members of the bodyguard who so quickly dispatched Pausanias—Perdiccas, Leonnatus, and Attalus, son of Andromenes—were friends of Alexander and later served with him in Asia. Equally significant is Alexander's question to the priest of the Oracle of Zeus Ammon in Egypt, which he visited in 330, about whether all of the murderers of his father had been punished (p. 182). This exchange took place a full six years after Philip's assassination, suggesting that there was still a lingering suspicion that he had played a role in his father's demise and that only a god's word would exculpate him.

We can only imagine the mayhem in the theater immediately after Philip was stabbed. Nevertheless, Antipater kept a cool head and loudly proclaimed Alexander king. His rapid thinking helped to calm the people, who at once rallied to Alexander. Shortly afterward, Alexander convened an Assembly, where he was officially recognized as king. There, he swore the customary oath that he would rule according to the laws, and the people swore their oath of allegiance to him. He also remitted the people's taxes (perhaps only for a selected period), which helped garner their support. The speedy acclamation of Philip's successor maintained stability in Macedonia. However, as Philip's body lay on the floor of the theater, what must have been uppermost in people's minds was what was going to happen to Macedonia.

LEGACY

Philip did not enjoy anything like the fame of his son Alexander. There was no marvelous account of his exploits, like the *Alexander Romance*, to which authors frequently added throughout the ancient and medieval periods (see p. 303). No major motion picture has chronicled his life and career. Yet, when we consider the life that Philip led, his accomplishments for Macedonia, and especially what he left Alexander, he is thoroughly deserving of similar treatment: he has lived too long in Alexander's shadow.

Even a cursory comparison of Macedonia at the time Philip came to power in 359 to its strength and position in the Greek world when he was assassinated in 336 proves his greatness as its king.[32] From a backwater located on the periphery of the Greek world Philip fashioned Macedonia into a military and economic powerhouse in a reign of only 24 years. His union of Upper and Lower Macedonia and the centralization of the monarchy at Pella so early in his reign were arguably his greatest accomplishments, allowing him to introduce all of his other reforms and extend his kingdom's territory and power. Not content with doubling Macedonia's size and population by conquering the entire Greek mainland and all points east to the Hellespont (Map 3), Philip was all set to invade Asia and had taken the first step toward this goal when he dispatched an advance contingent of troops to Asia Minor in the early summer of 336.

Although the kingdom's treasury was not overflowing on his death, Philip had exploited Macedonia's natural resources and promoted its trade and economy more than any other king before him. His policies included land-reclamation and irrigation practices, the building of new roads and towns, fresh revenues from the areas he conquered as well as his kingdom's own mines, the revision of its weights, and new coinage minted at Pella (the main mint), Amphipolis, and Philippi.

Then there was the army that Philip created—not refashioned or updated but created almost from scratch—which provided Alexander with the means to win all of his spectacular victories. Thanks to Philip, the ineffectual conscript force was a thing of the past. Instead, there was now a professional fighting force, well trained, well equipped, boasting new weaponry such as the sarissa and new battle tactics that gave it superiority over its enemies and a fearsome reputation. Innovations in siegecraft thanks to the introduction of an engineering corps led to the appearance of the torsion catapult, which helped Alexander succeed in his own sieges (Figure 11, p. 37). In 353, after suffering defeat at the hands of Onomarchus in Thessaly, Philip's army lost heart and fled back to Macedonia. Within a matter of months Philip had restored its confidence and inflicted a crushing defeat on Onomarchus at the Battle of the Crocus Field. From then on, his generalship of his army was never challenged, no matter how hard he pushed it or where he ordered it to march and fight.

When Philip died he left Alexander none of the problems and threats that had faced him when he became king. The neighboring tribes of the Illyrians and Paeonians had long been cowed into submission, as had cities and states, such as Athens, Thebes, Olynthus, Epirus, and Thrace, that had meddled in Macedonia's domestic politics before. The Macedonian coastline was entirely free from foreign influence. A stable dynasty ensured the smooth succession of his son Alexander. The Macedonias of 359 and 336 were worlds apart.

As a king and statesman Philip combined diplomacy and military action to vanquish his enemies, although he preferred the former.[33] Included in his diplomacy were his unashamed recourse to bribery, although Theopompus and Demosthenes wrongly attributed all of his successes to his use of bribery,[34] and his exploitation of political marriages. He had a mastery of meshing diplomacy with unashamed deceit to play off one Greek city against another or to buy himself time. Against his enemies he moved quickly and resolutely, something that the Greeks, with their cumbersome democracies, could never do and fell victim to.[35] In Athens, Demosthenes tirelessly urged the people to fight Philip before he grew too powerful and conquered Greece. His policy was the right and only one to advocate, but it was doomed to failure because of Philip's speed, decisiveness, and autocratic power and the apathy of the Greeks.

In 324 Alexander the Great faced a mutiny at Opis. In a speech, quoted above (p. 106), he praised his father for transforming Macedonia and bringing about Macedonian mastery over the peoples who used to attack and interfere in it. Likewise, ancient writers also lauded Philip for his achievements—and legacy. In concluding his narrative of Philip's reign, Diodorus wrote:

> Such was the end of Philip, who had made himself the greatest of the kings in Europe in his time, and because of the extent of his kingdom had made himself a throned companion of the twelve gods. He had ruled twenty-four years. He is known to fame as one who with but the slenderest resources to support his claim to a throne won for himself the greatest empire in the Greek world, while the growth of his position was not due so much to his prowess in arms as to his adroitness and cordiality in diplomacy. Philip himself is said to have been prouder of his grasp of strategy and his diplomatic successes than of his valor in actual battle. Every member of his army shared in the successes which were won in the field, but he alone got credit for victories won through negotiations.[36]

Justin was even more verbose. He compared Philip with Alexander in a long necrology (unique in Alexander literature) in which he criticized both of their personal traits but may be said to elevate Philip over his son:

(1) Philip...was a king with more enthusiasm for the military than the convivial sphere; (5) in his view his greatest treasures were the tools of warfare. (6) He had a greater talent for acquiring wealth than keeping it, and thus despite his daily pillaging he was always short of funds. (7) His compassion and his duplicity were qualities which he prized equally, and no means of gaining a victory would he consider dishonorable. (8) He was charming and treacherous at the same time, the type to promise more in conversation than he would deliver, and whether the discussion was serious or lighthearted he was an artful performer. (9) He cultivated friendships with a view to expediency rather than from genuine feelings. His usual practice was to feign warm feelings when he hated someone, to sow discord between parties that were in agreement and then try to win the favor of both. (10) Besides this he was possessed of eloquence and a remarkable oratorical talent, full of subtlety and ingenuity, so that his elegant style was not lacking fluency, nor his fluency lacking stylistic elegance. (11) Philip was succeeded by his son Alexander, who surpassed his father both in good qualities and bad. (12) Each had his own method of gaining victory, Alexander making war openly and Philip using trickery; the latter took pleasure in duping the enemy, the former in putting them to flight in the open. (13) Philip was the more prudent strategist, Alexander had the greater vision. (14) The father could hide, and sometimes even suppress, his anger; when Alexander's had flared up, his retaliation could be neither delayed nor kept in check. (15) Both were excessively fond of drink, but intoxication brought out different shortcomings. It was the father's habit to rush from the dinner party straight at the enemy, engage him in combat and recklessly expose himself to danger; Alexander's violence was directed not against the enemy but against his own comrades. (16) As a result Philip was often brought back from his battles wounded while the other often left a dinner with his friends' blood on his hands. (17) Philip was unwilling to share the royal power with his friends; Alexander wielded it over his. The father preferred to be loved, the son to be feared. (18) They had a comparable interest in literature. The father had greater shrewdness, the son was truer to his word. (19) Philip was more restrained in his language and discourse, Alexander in his actions. (20) When it came to showing mercy to the defeated, the son was temperamentally more amenable and

more magnanimous. The father was more disposed to thrift, the son to extravagance. (21) With such qualities did the father lay the basis for a worldwide empire and the son bring to completion the glorious enterprise.[37]

These ancient writers recognized character flaws in both kings but preferred Philip over Alexander when it came to the way they ruled. In other words, they recognized Alexander's brilliance as a general and the extent of his conquests, but how he and Philip ruled and who was the better king for Macedonia drove their evaluations. These passages will be revisited in the concluding discussion of Alexander's reign, when I will also compare him with his father (p. 308).

Philip certainly had his personal faults, but his achievements outweighed them, and he remained the traditional warrior king to the end of his life. His military exploits did not shine as brightly as those of Alexander, but there is more to being a king than just generalship. As the architect of the Macedonian Empire (something to which Justin called special attention) and the king who provided Alexander with the means to be its master builder, Philip can justly take his place as one of the ancient world's greatest rulers. As we move now to the reign of Alexander the Great, we need to assess Alexander not as just a great general (which he undoubtedly was) but as a king. Whether he was a better ruler for his kingdom than Philip remains to be seen.

7.

ALEXANDER'S EARLY

KINGSHIP—AND PERSIA

THE PAUCITY OF THE ancient evidence for Philip stands in contrast to the abundance for Alexander, but all too often its nature causes only frustration (see the appendix). Contemporary accounts of Alexander's reign are no longer extant, although fragments of them survive in later, narrative accounts of his reign from the first century B.C. to the fourth century A.D. These were written against a Roman background in which Alexander was adapted and manipulated for various literary, political, and even philosophical ends. All of these later accounts are often inconsistent because of how they present Alexander and their use of the earlier ancient writers, some of whom were sensationalists or were focused only on unromantic military affairs. As Arrian remarked: "different authors have given different accounts of Alexander's exploits, and there is no one about whom more have written, or more at variance with each other."[1] Trying to reach the historical Alexander is not really possible. The Alexander I present in the following pages was certainly a brilliant general and a strategic genius, but he was also a flawed king and man, caveats that must be taken into account when considering his "greatness."

SECURING THE THRONE

Philip's assassination set off a chain of events that threatened Macedonian stability and security. The Illyrians, Paeonians, Thracians, and other tribes expected to regain their liberty, while many of the Greeks revolted from the League of Corinth. The Ambracians and the Thebans even expelled the Macedonian garrisons and oligarchies that Philip had set up in their cities after Chaeronea. In Athens, Demosthenes rejoiced openly at the news of Philip's death and proposed a public sacrifice of thanksgiving and a posthumous congratulatory crown for Pausanias the assassin. He even "appeared in public dressed in magnificent attire and wearing a garland on his head, although his daughter had died only 6 days before."[2] His daughter, on whom he doted, was about 10 years old. His ignoring the traditional mourning period of one month and dressing as if going to a festival show the depth of his hatred for Philip.

Fortunately for Macedonia Alexander inherited a stable kingdom, a first-class army, loyal generals, and his father's characteristic speed, focus, and brilliant strategic and tactical planning. The Greeks might be hailing the end of Macedonian hegemony, but they would have been better off heeding the Athenian general Phocion's blunt warning that the army that had defeated the Athenians at Chaeronea was merely now one man short.

Alexander's reign continued as it began: bloody. Under Macedonian law a traitor's family was executed, therefore Alexander ordered the deaths of the three sons of his father's assassin, Pausanias, even though they were not implicated in the murder. Concerned that his kingship faced threats, for "all Macedonia was seething with discontent, looking to Amyntas and the sons of Aeropus,"[3] the new king took prompt steps to eliminate opposition, and within a year of coming to power he had purged himself of likely—and suspect—rivals to the throne.[4]

Amyntas was Perdiccas III's son, the proper heir when Philip was acclaimed king in 359. He may have been attempting to enlist Theban help to seize the throne for himself, given his claim to it, but in 335 he was executed.[5] The sons of Aeropus (of Lyncestis in Upper Macedonia) were Arrhabaeus, Heromenes, and Alexander. Philip had exiled their father when he suspected him of treason, and Alexander now ordered the sons to be killed.[6] Alexander, son of Aeropus, however, had prudently thrown in his lot with the new king. That his father-in-law, Antipater, had led Alexander before the people in the aftermath of Philip's assassination may have prompted him to act as he did. He did not stay loyal for long; even though he served as Alexander's general in Thrace in 336, and in Asia was given a cavalry command, in 334 he was implicated in a plot to assassinate the king and, in 330, was executed.

Alexander was not concerned about his senior generals. Antipater had quickly proclaimed his support, and Parmenion followed suit from Asia Minor. Their actions, not to mention their personal factions, went a long way to persuading other factions to throw their weight behind Alexander.[7] There was little doubt about Attalus's attitude to Alexander, and Demosthenes had sent letters to Parmenion and Attalus calling on them to oust Alexander and claiming that Athens would support their insurrection. Parmenion would have none of it—when in 335 Alexander sent him orders to execute Attalus, he did not miss a beat in carrying them out. Thus Alexander finally had his revenge for Attalus's racial slur at the wedding feast of his father and Cleopatra in 337. Alexander's purges were understandable, but one set of murders was gruesomely personal. His mother, Olympias, engineered the deaths of her husband's last wife, Cleopatra, and their baby daughter, Europa, by burning them alive.

One man who did not fall victim to Alexander's purge was his older half-brother Arrhidaeus, the son of Philip and Philinna of Larissa. Why Alexander allowed him to live is unknown. Possibly he did not think Arrhidaeus and his diminished mental abilities presented a threat. Then again, both boys had grown up together in Pella, and at only one year apart they would have shared many first-time experiences and bonded. Alexander may therefore have had a soft spot for him, especially if he suspected that Olympias had poisoned him to advance Alexander as heir. Arrhidaeus's life was a tragic one: after Alexander's death in 323, a group of generals proclaimed him king as Philip III, but in 317 Olympias arranged his execution and that of his wife, Eurydice.

BURYING PHILIP

In his first days as king Alexander had to attend to the funeral of his father, which took place at Aegae. Philip's body, together with his arms and armor, was placed on a large pyre, around which the Macedonian army solemnly marched. Arrhabaeus and Heromenes (the sons of Aeropus), along with the horses to which Pausanias the assassin had fled, were put to death next to the pyre, and when it was set alight their corpses were tossed into the flames. When the fire had died down attendants carefully removed Philip's bones, washed them in wine, wrapped them in purple cloth, and placed them inside a gold *larnax* or box. On its lid was emblazoned the Macedonian starburst (a 16-rayed star)—the emblem of the royal house—and rosettes. The *larnax* was placed inside a stone sarcophagus and interred in a simple, barrel-vaulted tomb along with gold and silver vessels, some of Philip's arms and armor, and a set of small, carved ivory heads of the royal family, which were placed on a chryselephantine (gold and ivory) wooden couch. Alexander had to bury his father in a hurry because of the pressing problems he was facing from the Greeks and neighboring tribes. He later claimed that he would build a proper tomb to his father that would rival the pyramids, but he never did. Much later, in the mid-270s, marauding Galatians invaded Macedonia, and for protection against them Philip's tomb was covered by earth to form a large tumulus, 13 meters high and 100 meters in diameter.

More than 2,000 years later, in 1977, a team of archaeologists led by Manolis Andronikos excavated a tumulus in the small village of Vergina, ancient Aegae (Figure 21). It contained four tombs, one of which (Tomb II)

FIGURE 21
Tumulus at Vergina (ancient Aegae). Photo: Ian Worthington.

had a main chamber and a smaller antechamber.[8] Unlike the other tombs, Tomb II had not been plundered. Among other things, its main chamber contained expensive personal artifacts, arms and armor, a stone sarcophagus, and some carved ivory heads, which were lying on the floor as the wood of their original stand had perished over the centuries. The stone sarcophagus housed a gold *larnax* with a starburst and rosettes on its lid; when opened, it was seen to contain bones with strands of purple cloth wrapped around them.

Forensic testing demonstrated that the bones were those of a middle-aged man and that they had been fired and washed in wine, as had happened to the corpse of the 46-year-old Philip. Then the skull fragments were assembled, and the face was rebuilt to reveal severe damage in and around the right eye (Figure 1).[9] This trauma is consistent with the blinding wound Philip received at the siege of Methone in 355/4. On top of that, one of the ivory heads depicts a bearded adult male with a disfigured right eye (Figure 8). The others appear to be members of the immediate royal family, including Alexander (Figure 18).

The antechamber contained a similar sarcophagus with the skeletal remains of a woman in her twenties, as well as weaponry, including a magnificent gilded *gorytus* (quiver). The occupant may well have been Philip's sixth wife, Meda, the daughter of Cothelas of the Getae, a warrior society in which women were fighters, hence the *gorytus*. She may have committed ritual suicide (*suttee*) sometime after her husband was assassinated and was buried close to him.

Philip's tomb appeared to have been found, but there are skeptics who claim that the remains are those of Philip III Arrhidaeus and his wife, Eurydice, who were buried at Aegae in 316, and that some of the grave goods, such as pottery, appear to postdate Philip's death. Yet the antechamber was clearly added after the main chamber was completed, whereas Philip III and Eurydice were buried at the same time. The main chamber surprisingly has no paintings on its walls but only rough stucco and seems to have been constructed and sealed quickly. That also is in keeping with the chaotic aftermath of Philip's assassination, when Alexander had several major problems on his plate and had to give his father a hasty burial. More important, there has never been a compelling refutation of the forensic evidence.[10] On balance, Tomb II must be the final resting place of Philip II.

THE REVOLT OF GREECE

The Greek revolt had expanded from Thessaly to the Peloponnese. Alexander marched south to reassert Macedonian hegemony, winning over "some cities by diplomacy, others by striking fear into them, and others by the actual use of force."[11] He would have advanced from Pella along his coastline via Methone and Pydna into Thessaly, well aware, like his father, of Thessaly's strategic importance to his borders. A force of Thessalians obstructed him at the Tempe Pass (between Mounts Olympus and Ossa), but rather than fight them he climbed the seaward slopes of Mount Ossa and descended on them from their rear. They surrendered at once. He assured them—and all Thessalians—that he would treat them no differently than his father had, and he was duly elected archon of Thessaly and received Philip's two votes on the Amphictyonic Council. Just as important, he received money to help pay his men and a cavalry contingent to boost his numbers.

By now news had spread that Alexander had pacified Thessaly and arrived at Thermopylae. There a number of cities followed the lead of Ambracia (southern Epirus) and sent him embassies seeking his favor. He responded politely to all of them and continued his push southward, through Thermopylae, to Thebes. The Thebans had expelled the Macedonian garrison installed by Philip after Chaeronea, and they may have been supporting Amyntas in a bid for the throne. Alexander could not tolerate their meddlesome involvement in Macedonian politics; when he arrived before the gates of Thebes he ordered his men to wear full armor. He promised leniency if the Thebans submitted to him as hegemon of the League of Corinth; duly intimidated by his army, they surrendered. However, he took the precaution of setting up a Macedonian-backed oligarchy and garrison in the city.

The Athenians had sent a hurried and apologetic embassy to Alexander at Thebes. The king bypassed their city and moved directly to Corinth, intent on resurrecting his father's league. Once there he summoned envoys from all the Greek states to come to him with their cities' oaths of allegiance. In this way the League of Corinth was again constituted, with the same terms and provisions as under Philip, and with it Macedonian hegemony of Greece. Only the Spartans remained defiant, asserting that they would bow to no one and that Alexander was hardly master of Greece. The king also received the league's approval of the panhellenic invasion of Asia for the same reasons as Philip had put forward the previous year.[12]

Alexander next traveled to Delphi, where initially the priestess of Apollo refused to see him because of the onset of winter when the Oracle was "closed." According to tradition, Alexander forced his way into her inner sanctum and grabbed her, prompting her to exclaim, "You are invincible, my son!" and Alexander to say that he "wanted no other prophecy but had obtained from her the oracle he was seeking."[13] In other words, he would never be defeated. Then it was back to Pella, where he spent the winter fine-tuning plans for a campaign in Thrace and Illyria the following spring. He wanted to strengthen his borders and give the army the experience of fighting under its new king before invading Asia.

A postscript to Alexander's stay in Corinth was his meeting with Diogenes, the Cynic philosopher, famous for his penchant of walking city streets by day with a lighted lamp looking for a "good man." Diogenes was born in Sinope, a Greek colony on the southern coast of the Black Sea, but moved to Athens and from there to Corinth, where he died in 323. He had famously abandoned any pretense of a regular life and believed that poverty was a virtue, even forsaking clothing and living in a barrel. For his animal-like lifestyle, which included urinating and defecating in public, he was nicknamed the dog, *kuon*, and described as *kynikos*, "doglike," from which hails the word *cynic*. Alexander admired Diogenes and came upon the philosopher as he was sunbathing. He asked him what he could do for him. Diogenes, who was never at a loss for words, stonily told him that he could move as he was blocking his sun. His rebuff angered Alexander's men, but the king famously stated that if he were not Alexander, he would want to be Diogenes.[14]

ALEXANDER'S EARLY CAMPAIGNS

In the spring of 335 Alexander marched with 15,000 infantry and 5,000 cavalry to Amphipolis. From there he moved to Neapolis (Kavala), crossed the Nestus (Mesta) River, and traveled north to Philippopolis (Plovdiv). At a narrow pass over Mount Haemus (probably the modern Shipka Pass), he encountered some unknown Thracian tribes, who blocked him. The tribes lined up wagons (perhaps nothing more than carts) on the heights of the pass; they intended to roll them down on the Macedonian line as it entered the defile and then, in the ensuing disarray, attack the invaders in force. Against any other general their tactic might have worked, but Alexander was not any general. When the wagons began to thunder down he shouted to men at various intervals in the battalions in the wider part of the pass to move to one side and so open up gaps that the wagons could pass through harmlessly—he employed a similar tactic against Persian scythed chariots at the Battle of Gaugamela in 331. At the same time, he ordered those men in the narrower parts of the pass, who could not move far enough to the sides, to kneel or lie down and lock their shields over their heads so that the wagons rolled over them. With the danger from the wagons neutralized, the entire line regrouped and stormed the enemy. This brilliant countertactic overawed the attackers, and in the ensuing fight 1,500 of them were killed, and the remainder fled back to their homes. Their wives and children, who had traveled with them, were too slow to escape: they were caught and sent back to Macedonia as slaves.

After this engagement Alexander marched without incident to the Danube. There he clashed with the Triballi and in a pitched battle killed 3,000 of them to a loss of only 11 cavalry and 41 infantry. As so often with the figures in our sources for troop numbers, and especially for those killed and injured on both sides, there is distortion to exaggerate the extent of Alexander's victories, but even so Alexander had avenged his father's loss to them in 339.

Down but not out, the remnants of the Triballi collected together on an island called Peuce on the main stream of the Danube and were quickly reinforced by other Thracians. Alexander decided to starve them into surrender since his ships could not safely cross the fast-flowing current and were easily beaten back by the defenders. Unfortunately for him, 4,000 cavalry and at least 8,000 infantry of the Getae tribe of the northern Danube plain arrived to relieve the blockaded men. Alexander suddenly found himself in a vulnerable position, but for him retreat was never an option. Reacting with his customary speed and unpredictability, he decided to invade the lands of the Getae. With a flotilla of hastily made rafts, really only tent covers stuffed with hay, he led 1,500 cavalry and 4,000 infantry across the Danube one dark night and laid waste to their crops and lands. They capitulated immediately. When the defenders on Peuce realized that they were now isolated they surrendered—exactly as Alexander had intended.

In these two months of hard fighting Alexander had proved his fighting prowess and tactical genius. He probably intended to allow his men some respite and so marched south into the lands of his ally Langarus the Agrianian. However, when news reached him that Cleitus, king of the Illyrian tribe of the Dardani (and the son of the Bardylis whom Philip had resoundingly defeated in 358), had allied with Glaucias of the Taulantii tribe (around Tirana) and the Autariatae tribe (in modern Bosnia) and planned to attack Macedonia, Alexander had no choice but to deal with the threat to his northwest frontier immediately. Adopting a similar strategy as Philip had used to nullify the developing multiple alliances among the Athenians, Olynthians, Illyrians, Paeonians, and Thracians in 357, he ordered Langarus to attack the Autariatae, while he rapidly crossed the Axius River at Stobi and besieged Cleitus in Pelium, on the western border of Macedonia.

Glaucias took up position behind Alexander's camp in the heights opposite Pelium, which was surrounded on three sides by dense forest. In doing so he encouraged Cleitus to attack Alexander as well, so that he would be trapped between both enemy positions. To gain the upper hand over his foes Alexander turned to psychological pressure, something for which he would become famous. He decided to put on what appeared to be military maneuvers, arranging his entire phalanx into a single block 150 ranks deep with cavalry squadrons of 200 or so on either side of it. The men were ordered to march back and forth with their sarissas up, lowered as if for a charge, and then pointing to the right and left before forming into their standard wedge formation. All of these moves were carried out in total silence except for the sharp commands to the men to change directions and angle their weapons.

Thinking that Alexander was simply drilling his troops Glaucias and his men began to move forward, more to get a better look at the rigorous and disciplined training of Macedonian infantry than anything else. In doing so, they played into Alexander's hands. The king waited till they were close enough and then gave a prearranged signal. At once the men turned to face the enemy and shattered the silence as they clashed their swords against their armor and at the tops of their voices roared out their battle cry, "Alalalalai!" over and over again. The Taulantii practically jumped out of their skins and in panic turned tail and fled.

Nevertheless, Glaucias was able to rally his men before they had gone too far and return to keep Alexander trapped between his own forces and those of Cleitus. Then complacency set in: when Alexander was informed that they had reduced the guards around their camps he struck, pouncing on the camp of the Taulantii one night. Caught unawares, the enemy was cut down and had no recourse but to flee. With no reinforcements Cleitus set fire to Pelium so that he could slip away under cover of the smoke and confusion. The Macedonians were readying to pursue him when Alexander received word that out of the blue the Thebans had again defied Macedonian rule and were urging the Greeks to war. The news was surprising, but then again it would have been more of a shock if no Greek city had risked revolt while Alexander was away fighting, especially as a rumor was currently circulating in Greece that he had been killed. Alexander had no choice except to march straightaway to Thebes to nip the revolt in the bud, and fortunately Cleitus did not bother him again.

Alexander's first campaigns as king were successful, but there had been some hard-fought and even worrying moments. Nevertheless, they proved his generalship and decisiveness as well as the superb training and battle skills of his army: in all, they were the shape of things to come.

THE REVOLT OF THEBES

Democrats forced into exile from Thebes when Philip installed a pro-Macedonian oligarchy there in 338 had always planned to return and wrest control from the oligarchic rulers. In September of 335 they exploited a rumor that Alexander had been killed in Illyria to convince the Thebans to topple the oligarchy, besiege the Macedonian garrison on the Cadmea, and, in keeping with the Greek ideals of *eleutheria* and *isonomia* (pp. 11–13), call the other Greeks to arms "against the Macedonian tyrant."[15] They may even have supported Amyntas, who had been next in line to the throne in 359 and who was perhaps planning a coup.[16] There is also a tradition that the Persian king sent 300 talents to Athens to support Thebes and encourage the other Greeks to rebel but that Demosthenes kept all of it and so allowed Thebes to be destroyed. That is almost certainly without foundation.[17]

No wonder, then, that Alexander marched immediately to Thebes with 30,000 infantry and 300 cavalry. He marched so quickly that he had reached Thermopylae before the Greeks knew that he was back in Greece. His men had covered 250 miles in a mere 13 days, averaging 18–20 miles a day over both flat and rugged terrain via Mount Grammus, Mount Pindus, and Mount Cambunia, and had had only one day of rest at Pelinna in Thessaly. Once again the superb stamina and pace of the army were proved. In fact, when Alexander appeared before Thebes the people did not believe that anyone could move so fast and thought that he was Antipater, who—on Alexander's written orders from Illyria—had advanced on them from Macedonia! Alexander ordered the Thebans to surrender the ringleaders of the revolt or suffer a siege. He was impatient to invade Asia and perhaps expected that the Thebans would capitulate when they saw his numbers, which were swelled by Phocian, Plataean, and other Boeotian troops, who were seeking revenge for the Thebans' previous harsh treatment of their cities.[18] Expecting other Greeks to come to their support, the Thebans called Alexander a tyrant and resolved to fight to the end.[19]

The defenders had to prevent the garrison on the Cadmea from fighting its way out and opening the city's gates to the soldiers outside, and they also had to block Alexander from liberating his garrison troops. They boosted their numbers with slaves and metics (resident aliens) and built a double palisade to reinforce the southern section of their wall, which formed part of the Cadmea. Given the strength of Thebes's walls and the resolution of its people to fight, the siege was not going to be easy. They pluckily decided to take the fight to Alexander by making sallies to disrupt his siege preparations, which allowed time—they hoped—for other Greeks to come to their rescue. Although the Theban cause was widely discussed on the mainland, only the Arcadians (for reasons unknown) sent a contingent of troops, although they held fast at the isthmus awaiting events. The Thebans thus found themselves facing a merciless Alexander alone.

The ancient sources contradict one another on aspects of the siege, including how it even began. Some say that after offering the Thebans one chance to surrender Alexander gave orders to breach the palisade. However, his general Ptolemy claimed in his account that one of the commanders, Perdiccas, jumped the gun and rushed the palisade.[20] Ptolemy and Perdiccas were not the best of friends, and after Alexander's death Perdiccas had unsuccessfully invaded Egypt to topple Ptolemy's power there. Ptolemy may well have falsely accused Perdiccas of recklessness at Thebes to denigrate him and exonerate Alexander for the atrocities that befell the Thebans.

Regardless of the veracity of the sources, the Macedonians' initial assault on the city was unsuccessful. They fought their way through the first palisade but became trapped in the space between it and the second one. Their predicament spurred a force of Theban infantry to attack them, badly wounding 70 Macedonians including Perdiccas. Alexander rushed to their rescue and managed to overcome the Theban soldiers and push them back onto the city gates. The numbers involved must have been substantial because they jammed open the gates as they tried to get back into the city. Alexander seized this sudden opportunity to break into the city, ordering a contingent of his men to rush to the Cadmea and free the garrison there.

As more Macedonians poured into Thebes and were joined by the liberated garrison troops, brutal street fighting ensued in which Alexander's men wreaked havoc. They killed defenders in hand-to-hand combat and, ignoring religious conventions, dragged suppliants, including women and the elderly, from their sanctuaries and murdered them. Alexander would show a similar disregard for the civilian populations of cities he besieged in Asia, a grim reminder that in the taking of a city, the rape and murder of women and children were par for the course.[21]

At some point the Theban cavalry fled, and the infantry prepared for a last stand against the attackers at the Temple of Amphion. Alexander did not give an actual "take no prisoners" order, but he may as well have done, for in the systematic massacre that followed 6,000 Thebans fell, and 30,000 were taken prisoner and sold into slavery—to the loss of 500 Macedonians and allies. The king spared only the priests and priestesses and the descendants of the fifth-century lyric poet Pindar, who had written an encomium to a former king of Macedonia, Alexander I (the Philhellene). The sale of the Theban captives and the appropriation of the city's treasury netted Alexander about 440 talents—not a fortune, but if he was strapped for cash, every bit helped.

Worse was to follow. Alexander summoned the Phocians, Plataeans, and other Boeotians who were with him and convened a makeshift meeting of the League of Corinth to decide Thebes's fate. In so doing, he cynically presented himself as acting on behalf of the league against a recalcitrant city. They bade him burn the city to the ground, ostensibly because the Thebans had medized (turned pro-Persian) during the Persian Wars. The king ruthlessly executed the grim order, leaving only the temples and houses belonging to Pindar and his descendants standing. Thebes would not be rebuilt until 316.

On the one hand, Alexander needed to make clear that resistance to Macedonian rule was futile. His action therefore "presented possible rebels among the Greeks with a terrible warning," according to Diodorus, and Plutarch claimed that "Alexander's principal object in permitting the sack of Thebes was to frighten the rest of the Greeks into submission by making a terrible example. But he also put forward the excuse that he was redressing the wrongs done to his allies."[22] On the other hand, there was a personal element in the demolition of Thebes that casts a dim light on Alexander's character. The Thebans had personally insulted Alexander by calling him a tyrant; as he showed time and again throughout his reign, once he had been crossed redemption was impossible. The Greeks had a word for the enslavement of a city's entire population: *andrapodismos*. It was meant to underscore the severity of this frightful punishment. However, Alexander's razing of Thebes went beyond shocking because of how he had exploited the animosity that the league members with him had for the city and so neatly sidestepped personal blame. He knew that they were eager for payback, just as they knew that he wanted blood.

Thebes's destruction was one of the darkest episodes in Alexander's early reign; it set a pattern that grew increasingly bloody as he marched through Central Asia and India. Yet even in the midst of these horrors an incident took place that displayed his regard for bravery and dignity on the part of his enemies. During the sacking of Thebes a Macedonian soldier was said to have raped Timocleia, a noblewoman who was the sister of Theagenes, the Theban commander at Chaeronea. In response to her rapist's demands for her money and precious items, Timocleia told him that she had thrown her silver bowls, gold, and money down a well and led him to it. When the man climbed down the well she pelted him with stones and other debris and killed him. She was captured and brought before Alexander but showed no remorse, proudly declaring: "Theagenes was my brother—he was a general at Chaeronea. He died fighting against you while defending the freedom of Greece so that we might not be subject to outrages like these. I am ready to die now because I have been shamed in a way unworthy of my status. I would prefer to die than to experience another night like the previous one, which is what will happen to me unless you forbid it."[23] Alexander spared her life because of her courage and bearing, characteristics he likewise held important and strove to live by and look for in his men.[24]

The sacking of Thebes became a topos in contemporary Greek oratory and in later written accounts of the period.[25] For example, the late fourth-century rhetorician Hegesias of Magnesia likened Alexander's action to removing one of the "eyes" of Greece and compared it with Zeus removing the moon from the sky. Striking is Hegesias's coupling of

Thebes's destruction at the hands of Alexander with that of Olynthus by Philip in 348—and how both actions "horrified and greatly alarmed many Greeks."[26] Philip arguably destroyed Olynthus because the city had been harboring his two stepbrothers as a warning to anyone who proved disloyal. Likewise, Alexander borrowed a page from his father's book and destroyed Thebes, which may well have been offering asylum to a power-hungry Amyntas.

Apart from an abortive attempt by Sparta in 331 to incite war against Macedonia (p. 207), the Greeks remained passive until Alexander died in 323. Yet their spirit was far from broken—for one thing, his order that no city was to receive Theban fugitives was disregarded by at least the Athenians. At the same time, the Athenians hypocritically sent an embassy headed by Demades to Alexander to reassure him that their favorable attitude to Thebes meant nothing and to congratulate him for the way he had punished the city. Alexander responded by demanding the surrender of several Athenian politicians (including Demosthenes) and the general Charidemus, and at an Assembly Phocion advised the people to do so.[27] A panicked Demosthenes "compared himself and his allies to sheepdogs who fought to defend the people, referring to Alexander as the lone wolf of Macedonia"[28]—in other words, if the Athenians surrendered him and the other men, they would be like sheep surrendering their sheepdogs to wolves. In the end, Demades was able to persuade Alexander to change his mind, and only Charidemus was expelled from Athens. The scare that Demosthenes suffered arguably explains his low profile in Athenian politics during Alexander's reign.[29]

ALEXANDER AND PERSIA

From Thebes Alexander returned to Pella via Dium, the Macedonian religious center in the foothills of Mount Olympus. During the winter of 335–334 he undertook final preparations for the invasion of Asia. Alexander had been fascinated by the Persian Empire since the age of seven, when he had bombarded visiting Persian ambassadors at Pella with questions about the size of their army and communications routes within their empire. Like his father he knew about Persia from Herodotus's *Histories*, the *Persica* of Ctesias of Cnidus (a doctor to Artaxerxes II), and especially Xenophon's *Anabasis* or *March of the Ten Thousand*—the famous account of an ill-fated expedition of Greek mercenaries in Persian employ. This story began when Darius II died in 403 and his two sons Artaxerxes and Cyrus fought over the throne. Cyrus hired 11,000 Greek mercenaries, mustered troops from Lydia to Mesopotamia, and at Cunaxa, near Babylon, did battle with Artaxerxes. Cyrus's strategy was to kill or capture his brother, but his army lost heart when a javelin killed him. The Greek mercenaries then marched from deep within Persia through Armenia to the Greek towns that had been founded centuries before in the Black Sea area—when they made it there they excitedly yelled, "thalatta, thalatta"—"the sea, the sea."

Xenophon's *Anabasis* influenced Alexander greatly—writing in the early fifth century A.D. the Roman historian Eunapius claimed that "Alexander the Great would not have become great had Xenophon never been."[30] Xenophon's account showed Alexander that a foreign army could survive, albeit with difficulty, in hostile territory, and Cyrus's attempt to kill or capture the enemy leader revealed to Alexander the value of this psychological strategy. Of course the Persian Empire was more formidable than Xenophon presented, at least in the early fourth century, but it was not invincible, as Alexander proved.

In 334 Alexander appointed Antipater as guardian (*epitropos*) of Greece and deputy hegemon of the League of Corinth in his absence, entrusting him with a force of 12,000 infantry and 1,500 cavalry.[31] He was anxious to invade Asia to take advantage of a fresh disruption to the Persian court caused by the chiliarch Bagoas murdering Artaxerxes IV (whom he had brought to the throne two years earlier by killing the previous Persian king) and setting up Artasata, a cousin of Artaxerxes III, as Darius III. One of Darius's first actions—wisely—was to poison Bagoas to make sure that he did not become another of his victims.

Alexander's desire to launch his invasion without further ado perhaps explains why he disregarded the advice of Antipater and Parmenion to marry at this time so that he could have an heir.[32] In some respects there was no obvious lady to marry or at least no one who would not ruffle the feathers of the noble factions that competed at court. In hindsight, however, his refusal was his costliest mistake ever: the lack of an undisputed heir contributed the most to the Macedonian Empire's dismemberment on his death in 323.

On the other hand, there is a tradition that Alexander was not interested in the opposite sex and even sexless. Philip and Olympias were apparently so concerned that their son showed little interest in women when he was growing up that they hired a Thessalian prostitute named Callixeina to seduce him.[33] She was evidently unsuccessful, if there is truth to the story that Alexander only lost his virginity in 333 to Barsine in Asia Minor.[34] However, what Alexander did not indulge in during his youth he certainly made up for after his first time with Barsine. He lived with her in a de facto relationship, later married the Bactrian princess Roxane in 327 and two royal princesses in 324, and enjoyed numerous dalliances with both men (the most famous being his close friend Hephaestion and the eunuch Bagoas) and women, including (reputedly) the Amazon Queen. In fact he is made out to have had more encounters with women than any other Macedonian king, perhaps to explode the notion, found in some ancient and modern writers, that he was effeminate or sexless.[35]

In the spring of 334 Alexander set off to march the 300 miles from Pella to Sestus on the Hellespont (Dardanelles), which separated Europe from Asia (Map 3). His journey took him 20 days. Along the way he gathered Balkan troops at Amphaxatis and Greek forces at Amphipolis, where his fleet had assembled. From Sestus he would sail across the Hellespont to set foot on Asian soil and prepare to bring down the mighty Persian Empire. The Greek world was never going to be the same again.

8.

FROM EUROPE TO ASIA

For DETAILS OF ALEXANDER in Asia and of the Persian Empire generally we have to draw mainly on Greek sources.[1] However, increasing numbers of documents from the East have been emerging in recent years. These include Babylonian astronomical tablets, contemporary documents written in cuneiform, which throw light on chronology, events in Babylonia, and military affairs, and Aramaic documents from Bactria. Alexander certainly intended for the Greeks back on the mainland to know of his exploits as they happened, and to this end he took with him Aristotle's nephew, Callisthenes, as his court historian—an embedded reporter in effect—who sent home his accounts in embellished installments.[2]

THE INVADING ARMY

Alexander commanded a mixture of Macedonian and allied general and specialist troops, including Macedonian hypaspists (the elite "shield bearers") and Companion (Hetairoi) Cavalry, Thessalian cavalry, Thracian and Agrianian javelin men, and general mercenaries.[3] The actual size of his invading army is unknown because of variations in the ancient sources, which put it anywhere from 30,000 infantry and 5,000 cavalry to 43,000 infantry and 5,500 cavalry.[4] The Macedonian infantry probably numbered 12,000, based on Diodorus's statement that Alexander left Antipater with the same number of Macedonian troops in Greece.[5] We also need to take into account the nonmilitary personnel needed to maintain, equip, and feed his army—cooks, doctors, engineers, black-smiths, carpenters, priests, and even artists and entertainers. In addition, there was a fleet of more than 160 warships (half of which were Macedonian, crewed by men from the Chalcidice) and transport vessels. Finally, the vanguard force that Philip had sent to Asia in 336 was still there and comprised as many as 10,000 troops under Parmenion.[6]

The Macedonian infantry was broken up into six battalions, each of 1,500 men, under the respective commands of Craterus, Perdiccas, Coenus, Amyntas, Meleager, and Philip, son of Amyntas, as well as three battalions of hypaspists under Nicanor, son of Parmenion. The allied contingent of 18,000 infantry consisted of 7,000 citizen troops commanded by Antigonus and 5,000 mercenaries led by Menander; the remaining 6,000 were Agrianian javelin men (under Attalus), Thracian peltasts (under Sitalces), and Cretan archers (under Cleitarchus). The cavalry consisted of 2,000 Companions led by Philotas, another of Parmenion's sons; 2,000 Thessalians led by Calas; and 1,000 Thracians, Paeonians, and Greeks commanded by Agathon, Ariston, Amyntas of Lyncestis, and Philip, son of Machatas.

SPEAR-WON TERRITORY

Alexander's large army would have taken some time to cross the mile-wide Hellespont from Sestus to Abydus (where he would rendezvous with Parmenion). Never one to waste time, Alexander visited Elaeus (the "Place of Olives"), on the southern tip of the Thracian Chersonese (Gallipoli Peninsula), while his troops slowly made their way across the Hellespont. At Elaeus Alexander sacrificed at the tomb of Protesilaus, who had commanded the Thessalian troops in Agamemnon's great army, which had sailed from Greece eight centuries earlier to rescue Helen, wife of Agamemnon's brother Menelaus of Sparta, from the clutches of the Trojans. Protesilaus had been the first man to leap onto foreign soil and the first man killed in the Trojan War, hence his name, which means "First-jumper." Alexander paid his respects to the heroes of old, at the same time praying that he would not suffer Protesilaus's fate, before returning to Sestus and embarking on his ship.

Halfway across the Hellespont Alexander sacrificed a bull to Poseidon and poured libations to the Nereids (the nymphs of the sea). When his ship ground to shore he threw a spear into the foreign soil before disembarking. His action was believed to signify that he claimed all of Asia as his spear-won territory.[7] His father had expanded Macedonia's frontiers by the sword, and Alexander intended to do the same thing in Asia—and by the sword as well. But there was a difference. Philip might have planned to campaign only in Asia Minor, liberating the Greek cities there and acquiring new sources of revenue. Alexander intended to expand on his father's plan to bring down the entire Achaemenid Empire and march eastward to the end of the "civilized world":[8] see Map 5.

Once the army had fully disembarked in Asia Alexander and some of his men detoured to Troy (Hisarlik) to sacrifice at the tombs of Achilles (a maternal ancestor) and Ajax. They poured libations of oil, and then he and his boyhood friend Hephaestion ran naked around the tomb of Achilles before laying wreaths on it, evoking the funeral games for Patroclus in the twenty-third book of the *Iliad*. Then, in a neat combination of religion and politics, Alexander also sacrificed to the Trojan king Priam at the same Altar of Zeus that (it was said) Priam had fled to for sanctuary as Troy fell, only to be sacrilegiously cut down by Neoptolemus. Alexander was descended from Neoptolemus, so his sacrifice to Priam was also an attempt to appease the spirit of the dead king and grant the Macedonians good fortune. The sacrifices to Priam and Achilles symbolized Alexander's heroic piety.

In the Temple to Athena in Troy hung the arms believed to be those of Achilles. After solemnly sacrificing to the goddess Alexander swapped his own shield for that of Achilles, a move that went beyond mere familial piety to identifying himself with his ancestor and Homeric hero. Alexander was already seeing himself as a young Achilles and intended his invasion to put him on a par with the Homeric warriors—a desire that underscored many of his personally risky actions in Asia.

The army traveled southward from Abydus, winning over some towns perhaps because Philip's advance force had prepared their way, before making camp in Hellespontine Phrygia. From there Alexander planned to march eastward to the capital Dascylium (Eskili). He was intent on forcing the Persians onto the battlefield, perhaps because he did not want to be a financial burden on the Greek cities he was attempting to champion. At the same time, his rapid move prevented Darius III, Great King of Persia, from marching from Babylon in time to confront him. At the Granicus River a Persian army was establishing a position that had every chance of blocking Alexander's advance, but Darius did not have time to lead a larger army to meet his enemy personally.

THE GREAT KING

The sheer size of the Persian Empire—from modern Bulgaria to Pakistan and as far south as Egypt—made it impossible for one ruler to administer it effectively. In 513 Darius I had divided it into 20 satrapies or regions, each one under the direct control of a satrap or governor. The satrap was subservient to the King (the capitalized K is a modern practice to denote the Great King of Persia as opposed to kings elsewhere); his principal duties were to levy troops from his satrapy when so ordered and collect annual taxes, which were paid to the King. The size and resources of the satrapy dictated troop numbers and the amount of taxation. Beyond that, satraps were free to rule their satrapies as they wished, and they became wealthy and powerful.

There was a very close connection between the satraps and the King, who often corresponded with them in Old Persian rather than the official administrative language of the empire, Aramaic. More than that, the connection was religious in nature. The "Great King, king of kings, king of lands," as was the full official title, ruled thanks to the grace of the Zoroastrian god of light, Ahura Mazda ("Wise Lord"), whom the Greeks identified with Zeus. The cult of Ahura Mazda was of utmost importance in Persian religion, and it was the means by which the King exerted his authority over his satraps and his people as a whole. In return, they accepted and honored his rule over them by means of the cult. This relationship was something that Alexander—who ruled not by anyone's graces but only by conquest—never fully comprehended.

The Great King ruled from not one royal capital but several, which also were religious centers. The most important were Pasargadae (built by Cyrus II the Great and home to his tomb), Susa, Persepolis (with its great palace of Darius and Xerxes), and Ecbatana (Hamadan), which was used as a summer palace. Many of these capitals were connected by an excellent system of purpose-built roadways, including the famed "Royal Road," which ran 1,600 miles from Sardis (the most western capital) to Susa. These roads aided communication and allowed armies to travel large distances quickly and relatively effortlessly, helped by plentiful supplies from towns and cities along their way. Alexander was always careful to make use of the same supply routes to provision his army.

The wealth of the Persian court was legendary, as was the King's harem of 365 women. The Macedonians had never seen such splendor before and were much influenced by it—"so this is what it's like to be a king," Alexander remarked when he entered Darius's giant tent after the Battle of Issus in 333 and saw its luxurious contents. In addition to his administrative and diplomatic duties the Great King was the commander in chief of the Persian army and was expected to fight in battle. His usual position was in the center of his line for reasons of safety and to help communicate efficiently with both flanks.[9] His personal bodyguard, which included the famous 10,000 Immortals and the 1,000 apple-bearers (*melophoroi*), so called because their spear butts were in the shape of golden apples, surrounded him for added protection.

The Great King was a diplomatic and military leader and was expected to prove himself in both areas. The Greek sources tend to depict Darius as a coward in battle and a weak ruler, but that is far from the truth.[10] He most likely put down a revolt in Egypt in the same year he came to power, and although he was not the great general Alexander was, he still outfoxed him before Issus in 333 by marching around his rear, forcing an astonished Alexander to change his plans. It has often been thought that Darius initially believed Alexander's troops posed little threat to his kingdom and that by underestimating the invader he became easy prey for Alexander. Not so. Darius proved a worthy opponent of Alexander.

THE BATTLE OF THE GRANICUS RIVER

Arsites, satrap of Hellespontine Phrygia, had hastily summoned various generals to the town of Zelea (Sarikoy), about 20 miles from the Macedonian camp. Everyone present had an opinion about how to defeat the Macedonians, but the most prudent advice came from Memnon of Rhodes, the leader of a contingent of Greek mercenaries in the employ of the Persians. Memnon had once visited Pella and had experience of Macedonian military tactics. He knew that once Alexander ran out of the provisions he had brought with him he would have to forage for more. Therefore Memnon proposed to devastate the area by burning the crops and demolishing towns if need be, which would severely impede Alexander's ability to feed his men and force them back to Macedonia.

Arsites naturally had no desire to bless Memnon's scorched earth policy in his satrapy, nor did he take too kindly to his blunt warning that the Persians should not do battle against Alexander because their infantry was nowhere near as well trained and was outnumbered by the enemy. Alexander had perhaps 40,000 infantry to the Persians' 30,000 or less. However, the Persians had 20,000 highly trained, tough Greek mercenaries, and they could also field 16,000 or so cavalry, compared with the Macedonians' 6,000.[11] Taking these factors into consideration Arsites decided that he had the edge over the invaders, especially as his men would be fighting on familiar terrain. Ignoring Memnon's counterarguments, perhaps even because he looked down on Memnon as a Greek, Arsites gave the order to do battle.

The Persians took up a position west of Zelea, above the plain of Adrasteia, through which ran the Granicus River. Probably this was near the modern Dimetoka. There they encamped on the river's east bank. Alexander took 13,000 infantry and 5,100 cavalry and marched to the west bank of the river either later in the afternoon or as dusk fell. The Granicus River was fast flowing and about three feet deep, but the entire riverbed was 80 feet wide. The topography of the area has changed little since Alexander's time, so the river's western and eastern banks were very steep and around 12 feet high, most likely covered in the same woodland and scrub as today. Crossing the river would have been a struggle at the best of times, let alone when an enemy army was ranged along the opposite bank, ready to take advantage of any Macedonian slips. That was why Parmenion tried to persuade Alexander to wait until he found another way around the enemy line. Parmenion's advice was sound, but it was not what Alexander wanted to hear: he sarcastically retorted that he would never be able to live down the shame of halting at a stream like the Granicus after crossing the Hellespont.

At this point our major ancient writers for the battle disagree.[12] Arrian states that Alexander engaged the Persians the same evening as he arrived at the river, while Diodorus has it that he waited until the next morning when he could lead the army across undetected. Most likely Arrian is correct because Alexander characteristically took an enemy by surprise. Besides, it is highly unlikely that the Persians would not have seen thousands of Macedonians making their way across the river as day broke. Diodorus further says that Arsites positioned his cavalry slightly back from the water's edge and stationed his infantry on the hill above them, whereas Arrian puts the cavalry right on the water's edge with the infantry behind. Diodorus's account is more likely to be correct because the Persian infantrymen atop the riverbank would be able to bombard the attackers with missiles and disrupt their line rather than trying to charge it from behind their cavalry.[13]

The odds of the Persians preventing Alexander's advance were therefore excellent. He had to lead his army down the western bank and across the river, neutralize the enemy cavalry, and force his way up the opposite bank while at the mercy of spears and arrows launched from its heights. A stumble by any part of the phalanx would cause instant disruption to his line, and the ensuing chaos would practically hand victory to the Persians. On the other hand, Alexander was well used to rivers thanks to growing up in Macedonia, and he may well have been eager to fight the enemy here rather than somewhere else as Parmenion had suggested.[14] He saw that the various bends of the river gave rise to bluffs that had more gentle slopes of gravel running down to the water, which were virtually opposite one another, and decided to take advantage of these natural ramps. His strategy was to lead his men down one of the gravel slopes to the riverbed. Then, with the cavalry protecting both flanks of the phalanx,

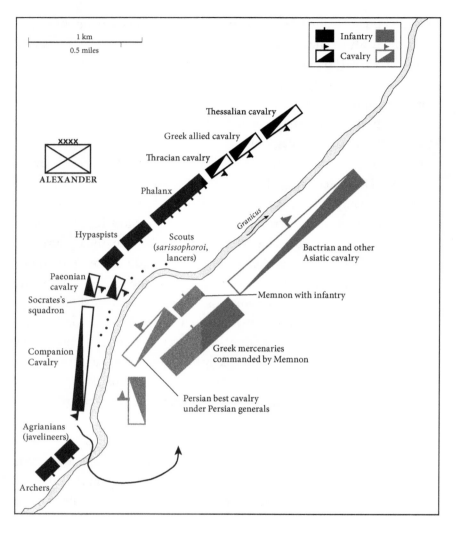

MAP 7
Battle of the Granicus River.

the men would cross the river in a diagonal line, no doubt because of the current, to the nearest gravel bed on the opposite side to attack the Persian army (Map 7). From Philip's time the Macedonian phalanx had been trained to cross all manner of terrain, including flowing water, and Alexander was banking on it not missing a beat now.

Alexander's line stretched for a little over a mile. He stationed the Thracian, Thessalian, and other Greek cavalry on his left flank, commanded by

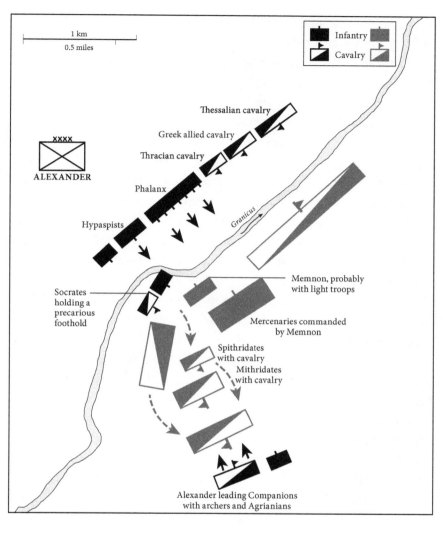

MAP 7
Continued.

Parmenion. The right flank comprised the Macedonian cavalry, which Alexander formed into two groups, one under the command of Philotas on the extreme right and the other, immediately next to the massed phalanx at the center, under Amyntas. Next to him Alexander took up his own position. The cavalry was arranged 10 horses deep, and the infantry line, eight men deep.

The Battle of the Granicus River witnessed Alexander's introduction of the stratagem of a pawn sacrifice.[15] He ordered Amyntas and a small strike force of fast cavalry (*prodromoi*) to cross the river ahead of the main army, thereby drawing the enemy's fire. As Alexander had anticipated, the Persian cavalry charged Amyntas's soldiers and even forced them back. In the meantime Alexander and the right wing began their move across the river, followed by the center and left flank, in a planned left-to-right diagonal line toward the opposite gravel beds. At that point the Persians realized that Amyntas's brave action had merely been a distraction. Unable to regroup in time, the Persian cavalry fell victim to Alexander's massed counterstrike, and as more of the Persian commanders were killed in the fighting when the two sides met, the cavalry lost heart and fled.

Now the battle became an infantry one. Parmenion had brought his left flank successfully across the river and regrouped into one continuous line that easily made its way up the west bank of the river to face the Persian infantry and Greek mercenaries. The Persian line became a bloodbath as the sarissas tore into the Persian troops, who were armed only with light javelins that were no match for the enemy's long, deadly weapons. Thoroughly demoralized, and in an effort to cut their losses, they made their getaway after the cavalry. Alexander expected the Greek mercenaries under Memnon, who had not yet taken part in the fighting, to offer tougher resistance. Memnon at first sought terms, but Alexander was in no mood for leniency—he was also angry that Greek mercenaries were prepared to fight other Greeks. Without delay the king regrouped his line into its usual wedge formation and with the cavalry on the wings attacked the mercenaries head-on. It was said that Alexander's men fought harder against Memnon and his men than against the Persians, and in one clash Alexander's horse (evidently not Bucephalas) was killed under him. Eventually the king's shock-and-awe tactics paid off, and 18,000 of the mercenaries were cut to pieces. Memnon managed to escape, but the surviving 2,000 mercenaries, including a contingent of Athenians, were captured and sent back to Macedonia to work in chains in the mines. Arsites, who had fled into Phrygia, took responsibility for the entire defeat and committed suicide.

"Of the Barbarians, we are told, 20,000 infantry fell and 2,500 cavalry. But on Alexander's side, Aristobulus says there were 34 dead in all, of whom 9 were infantry":[16] These numbers were very likely exaggerated to magnify the Macedonian victory, but nevertheless the battle was a triumph of Alexander's strategic planning, bold tactics, and daredevil courage.[17] It was his first victory on Asian soil, and he had proved the fighting superiority of his army against a numerically greater enemy. Granicus began sounding the death knell of the Achaemenid dynasty.

ALEXANDER'S CLOSE CALL

The battle, however, exposed a worrying aspect of Alexander's personality and by extension his regard for his kingship. At one point in the hand-to-hand fighting Mithridates, son-in-law of Darius III, spotted the bright red plume on Alexander's helmet and galloped straight toward him. He threw a javelin with such force that it penetrated Alexander's shield and lodged in his breastplate. Alexander immediately caught Mithridates with his spear and dislodged him from his horse. He was about to go in for the kill when another Persian, Rhoesaces, rode up behind him and smashed his sword against Alexander's helmet with such force that it broke off and probably cut his head. Despite his wound Alexander instantly reacted, wheeling his horse and running Rhoesaces through with his sword. Even then he was not out of danger, because yet another Persian, Spithridates (the satrap of Ionia), was aiming his sword at Alexander's bare head. As he was about to strike him down Cleitus the Black, commander of the Royal Squadron of Companion Cavalry, slashed off his arm, saving Alexander in the nick of time.

This stirring episode illustrates the intensity of the fighting as well as Alexander's lightning-fast reaction time, but could he really have survived this ferocious attack with what seems like nothing more than some cuts and scrapes? Probably the sycophantic court historian Callisthenes was the ultimate source for this battle and embellished Alexander's fight for his life because he was bent on depicting a heroic king.[18] Certainly the Alexander propaganda machine was in full swing during the reign, but to deny the historicity of the engagement in question is going too far. What the scene does demonstrate is Alexander's dangerous impetuosity and how cavalierly he took himself as king. Had he died, the entire invasion of

Asia would have ended with him. Moreover, since he was unmarried and childless, who would have succeeded him as king, and what would have happened to Macedonia? Yet, as the army continued its relentless march eastward, Alexander continued to take risks with his life just for the sake of a fight. His generalship skills were indeed peerless, and Diodorus makes it clear that his men always recognized his bravery in battle,[19] but Alexander was also a king, something he attached less importance to than a good fight.

After the battle, Alexander buried the dead and—another example of his generalship—patiently visited all of the wounded men individually to listen to their battle stories. He also sent 300 Persian panoplies (suits of armor) to Athens as a dedication to its patron goddess, Athena, together with a short dedication: "Alexander son of Philip and all the Greeks except the Spartans won these spoils of war from the barbarians living in Asia."[20] It is significant that he sent the panoplies to the Athenians, since both he and Philip had singled them out for their suffering in the Persian Wars. But even more meaningful is the dedication's wording, which made it plain that the Spartans, who had refused to join the league, had no share in the panhellenic invasion or its spoils. Perhaps a further rub to Sparta is the fact that Alexander sent back 300 panoplies. This was the number of the famed Spartan band that had bravely confronted Xerxes's army at Thermopylae in 480 and was annihilated. The Sparta of 334 was very different from that of 480, and the number of panoplies underscored the state's military impotence and isolation.

FROM THE GRANICUS TO MILETUS

After the dust of the battle had settled Alexander dispatched Parmenion to Dascylium, which opened its gates to him. On Alexander's orders he installed his own man, Calas, as the new satrap of Hellespontine Phrygia, who was to collect the tribute of the satrapy and ensure that it was paid no longer to Darius but to Alexander. All of the cities of Asia Minor were to pay money to Alexander, but he altered its name from *phoros* (tribute) to *syntaxeis* (contributions) in a thinly disguised attempt to distinguish it from what they had paid the Great King.[21] From the Granicus Alexander marched the 200 miles to Sardis, capital of Lydia. As always in Asia he followed known routes and supply lines to ensure that his men had regular provisions.[22] He was 10 miles from Sardis when its commander, Mithrenes, met him to surrender the city—and especially useful at this time, its treasury—to him. Mithrenes joined Alexander's camp, and the king declared the Lydians free from Persian rule. However, to govern Lydia he chose Asander (perhaps Parmenion's brother), installed a garrison on the citadel under the command of the Companion Pausanias, and tasked a Greek named Nicias to collect the taxes. Alexander's actions were part of a general administrative strategy of keeping the Persian satrapal system but limiting the power of the individual satraps, which becomes more evident after the capture of Babylon in 331.

From Sardis Alexander marched the 60 miles to Ephesus, one of the cities taken by Philip's advance force, arriving there four days later. The Ephesians had earlier set up a statue to Philip in the Temple of Artemis but had smashed it when Memnon and some Persian sympathizers had retaken the city and established a pro-Persian oligarchy. Alexander discovered that the mercenary garrison had fled, so he expelled the ruling oligarchs, recalled those men exiled under the regime (hence Macedonian supporters), and established a democracy. When some of the democrats began to murder the Persian sympathizers, presumably to get into Alexander's good books, he personally intervened to halt further bloodshed. Nevertheless, the people refused his offer to rebuild the Temple of Artemis, which was said to have burned to the ground the same day as he was born.

While at Ephesus Alexander decided to commission a portrait of himself sitting on top of Bucephalas by one of the leading artists of the day, Apelles. Alexander was far from happy with the painting and insisted on another, bringing in the actual horse this time for Apelles to paint. Apparently Bucephalas caught sight of the original portrait and neighed, prompting Apelles to remark sarcastically that the horse knew art better than his master. Still, Alexander was unmoved, and Apelles—probably because he wanted to be paid—painted a portrait of Alexander as Zeus holding a thunderbolt. What Bucephalas thought of this one is unknown.

In the meantime embassies arrived from Magnesia and Tralles offering their surrender. Alexander sent Parmenion east to secure Magnesia and Tralles and Alcimachus north to liberate the cities in Aeolia and Ionia, the northern portion of the Asia Minor coastline. He himself went to Priene, where he finally got his wish to dedicate a temple, in this case to Athena Polias. A simple inscription—"King Alexander dedicated this temple to Athena Polias"—survives today. Unfortunately for Alexander the run of good fortune was about to expire. The massive Persian fleet of 400 ships (double that of the Macedonian) was racing down the coastline to the powerful coastal city of Miletus, where the city's garrison commander, Hegesistratus, was preparing to resist Alexander. Miletus was surrounded on three sides by the sea; if the Persian fleet reached it, then Alexander's rear and entire system of communication would be compromised, torpedoing further inroads into Persia.

THE SIEGE OF MILETUS

Alexander rushed to Miletus by land, while his admiral Nicanor sailed there as fast as he could with ships that had probably been docked at Ephesus. His fleet was to stand by at the island of Lade, just off the harbor mouth of Miletus. The Macedonian vessels made such good time that they arrived three days before the Persians. Although they were inferior in numbers, Nicanor's defensive position gave him the advantage; the Persians were unable to sail into the harbor and had no choice but to carry on sailing another 10 miles to Cape Mycale. Parmenion now urged Alexander to give Nicanor the order to attack the enemy fleet, especially as an eagle had landed on the shore, which the old general took as an omen that the gods were on their side. Alexander was unmoved. A defensive position was one thing, but open combat at sea was quite another, especially given the training and expertise of the Phoenician and Cyprian contingents in the Persian fleet—eagle or not, he could not afford a Macedonian loss.

In any case Alexander needed to focus all his energies on the siege of Miletus. The Milesians had asked for their independence and offered to allow him free access to their city, but he wanted total control. The Macedonians easily gained entry to the city when Hegesistratus and his men fell back to the citadel. When an initial assault to dislodge them failed Alexander brought his siege engines into play—high towers manned with archers on their tops, protected by reinforced low walls, who rained down their arrows mercilessly on the defenders. In tandem with this onslaught Macedonian battering rams smashed into the citadel walls, breaching parts of them. Unable to resist the onslaught Hegesistratus and his troops surrendered. The king spared the city's civilian population; however, he ordered the execution of the military personnel who had not been fortunate enough to escape south to Halicarnassus (Bodrum) in Caria to block Alexander there. He also installed a Macedonian garrison in Miletus. His action was perhaps a warning to any city planning to defy him, which continued a pattern beginning with Thebes in 335.

After the fall of Miletus some 300 Greek mercenaries on the losing side had managed to evade Alexander by swimming to a nearby island. Well aware of the fate of their fellows at the Granicus River they prepared to fight to the death. However, Alexander spared them and incorporated them into his ranks. His decision was inconsistent because he had shown no mercy to the mercenaries at the Granicus. Possibly their number reminded him of the 300 Spartans at Thermopylae, but it is more likely that he needed to increase the number of men with him. It thus made more sense to absorb ex-mercenaries into his army than to kill them or ship them back to Macedonia.

Alexander next visited Didyma, home to the Oracle of Apollo. During the Persian Wars its priests, the Branchidae, had treacherously allied with the Great King, which had caused the Oracle to fall silent and the sacred spring to run dry. When Alexander arrived at Didyma in the autumn of 334 the spring water began flowing again, and Apollo found his voice—or so the story went. Alexander appointed a new priestess to administer the Oracle, and perhaps not unexpectedly she prophesied that he was destined to achieve great things and would bring down the Persian Empire.

Alexander's strategy so far had been to win over Asia Minor in order to secure his rear and lines of communication before he marched deeper into Persia. Now, however, he compromised both by disbanding his fleet.[23] The Persian ships' impotence at Miletus, the fact that the numerically smaller Greek fleet would never be able to confront the Persian one at sea, and the sheer cost of maintaining a fleet influenced his decision. Even though the Persian ships were now sailing to Halicarnassus to join rebels there, Alexander boldly—and paradoxically—told Parmenion that he had no need of ships because he would defeat the Persian fleet by land. He kept about 20 Athenian triremes and some transport vessels and sent the rest home. To neutralize the Persian navy—by land—he intended to capture all of the cities on the coast of Asia Minor, Syria, and the Levant and all the way down to Egypt, thereby denying the Persians a port in which to anchor. Within a year, though, he realized his error because the Persian fleet launched a counteroffensive that took him by surprise and could have abruptly ended his Asian plans. For now, he had to deal with the siege of Halicarnassus, his most difficult to date.

THE SIEGE OF HALICARNASSUS

Halicarnassus was famous as the birthplace of the "father of history," Herodotus, and home to one of the Seven Wonders of the Ancient World, the Mausoleum—the tomb of Mausolus, satrap of Caria, who had died in 353, and which was eventually completed by his widow (and sister), Artemisia. Halicarnassus was built on a hillside and was seemingly impregnable, with enormous, six-foot-thick defensive walls, on top of which were fortified battlements and a series of high towers for protection. In front of the walls was a deep moat, at least 40 feet wide, and behind them were the main city and its two citadels, which the people could retreat to and fight on if necessary. The city's harbor was well shielded from attack, and the Persian fleet was now riding at anchor in it. Because Alexander had dismissed his own fleet the defenders could ferry in supplies or even escape unhindered if need be, whereas his own supplies were starting to run out and had to be ferried in from Miletus, at least two days away.

Halicarnassus was in the hands of the satrap Orontobates, but the Great King had personally ordered the experienced Memnon, who commanded several thousand Greek mercenaries, to defend the city when Alexander besieged it.[24] The king first ordered a frontal attack on the northeast part of the wall, but his men were pelted with stones and other missiles from the ramparts and driven back, suffering more casualties thanks to a lightning-swift sally by some of Memnon's soldiers. Alexander therefore decided to wait for his transport vessels to bring his siege engines from Miletus. When they arrived he fixed stone-throwing catapults on their tops and ordered the archers at the top of the towers to shoot the sentinels on the battlements while the catapults bombarded the walls. His plan was to use the catapults to breach the walls and protect a contingent of troops as they filled in the moat so that he could attack the walls from the bottom with his battering rams. However, the defenders repaired the breaches of the walls with makeshift bricks and one night bravely attacked the siege engines with burning torches and set them on fire. In bitter hand-to-hand fighting 300 of Alexander's men were wounded before they overcame the onslaught.

On another night, so the story goes, two drunken members of Perdiccas's battalion tried to scale Halicarnassus's walls and were soon joined by their comrades. They were shot at with burning arrows and sobered up quickly enough to retreat. Even so, a number of them were killed, and Alexander was forced to make a truce with the enemy so that he could recover their bodies and bury them. He resolved that he would never again be put in this position, although in 330 he suffered an initial reversal at the Persian Gates where he was forced to leave his dead behind.

For two more weeks Halicarnassus held out against Alexander's non-stop bombardment. In some desperation Memnon approved a plan put forward by Ephialtes, an Athenian mercenary commander, to take the fight to Alexander rather than continuing a defensive strategy. They handpicked 2,000 troops and sent them out against the Macedonians in two waves. The first wave was to set fire to the new siege engines, and the second was to lie in wait by the city's west gate and ambush the troops Alexander sent out to deal with the fires. This daring plan was actually working, and the Macedonian casualty figures were rising, until their comrades rushed to their assistance. In extremely bloody fighting they decimated Memnon's troops and killed Ephialtes. The panicked defenders closed the gates, trapping the men outside.

Fearing that all was lost Memnon and Orontobates set fire to the city, and under cover of the smoke they and their men stole down to the Persian ships in the harbor and sailed off to the island of Cos. There was nothing Alexander could do to stop them because he had no fleet. The fires in the city were not extinguished until the following day, at which time Alexander officially declared that he had taken Halicarnassus. Still, a contingent of diehard Persians continued to occupy the citadels and control the harbor, so Alexander installed a garrison of 3,000 infantry and 200 cavalry in the city under Ptolemy and ordered him to capture the Persians.

The king now entrusted the satrapy of Caria to Ada, the younger sister of Mausolus and current ruler of the satrapy. She was the sister of the Pixodarus who had sought an alliance with Philip in 337 (pp. 110–111). As Alexander had approached Halicarnassus Ada had come to meet him, and he had allowed her to adopt him. They remained close long after he left, for she would send him various baked goodies and pastries and even some of her personal chefs. Ada, however, was given only civilian power and had no control over the troops in the satrapy, which Alexander placed in Ptolemy's hands to be on the safe side. His willingness to allow Ada to adopt him was a variation on his father's policy of political marriage, but the end result was the same: he had won Carian support should the Persians attempt to retake Asia Minor, and ultimately he controlled Caria.

It was now almost midwinter of 334–333, and in keeping with his new plan to control the coastline, Alexander could embark on the next leg of his march southward to Lycia and Pamphylia. Before he set off he gave leave to his men who had married shortly before the army had left Greece to return home and spend time with their wives. They were to rejoin him at Gordium (near Ankara) in the summer of 333, bringing with them fresh troops from the Greek mainland. He also sent Parmenion with the Thessalian cavalry, Thracian cavalry (under Alexander of Lyncestis), and allied troops north to Sardis to conduct some mop-up operations there, after which they too were to rendezvous with Alexander at Gordium.

GAINING ASIA MINOR

Little is known of Alexander's movements in Lycia except that he succeeded in winning over all the cities in the satrapy. Some of them he had to overcome, such as the coastal town of Telmessus, which was in the hands of a Persian garrison. Here, one of Alexander's boyhood friends, Nearchus, persuaded courtesans to dance for the garrison troops, get them drunk, and then kill them, which they carried out with zeal, so that Telmessus fell to Alexander without a fight. From Telmessus Alexander marched to Phaselis, where Parmenion sent him a Persian messenger named Sisines. The man claimed that Darius had offered Alexander of Lyncestis 1,000 talents to murder Alexander and promised to support his bid for the Macedonian throne.[25] This is the first of at least four conspiracies against the king. Alexander of Lyncestis had been a possible rival for the throne in 336, but he had come out in favor of the new king and been spared, whereas his two brothers were put to death. Whether Alexander believed Sisines's information is unknown, but to be on the safe side Alexander sent one of his senor staff, Amphoterus, to Parmenion with orders to arrest the Lyncestian. Possibly Parmenion had prompted Sisines to accuse Alexander of Lyncestis, anticipating that after his demise he would be given command of his cavalry contingent. If so, he was mistaken, for Alexander entrusted that command to his boyhood friend Erigyius of Mytilene, perhaps because he suspected Parmenion's motives.

Satisfied with his arrangements in Lycia, Alexander departed for Pamphylia. He sent most of his men on a path they had carved over Mount Climax, while he took a small force with him along the shoreline of the Pamphylian Sea under the mountain. Here an event took place that the court historian Callisthenes zealously exploited for propaganda purposes. As the men made their way over the shore they were buffeted by large waves, but Alexander refused to turn around. All of a sudden the wind changed direction, from south to north, calming the waves and revealing a narrow path along the rocks that brought them safely out beyond the beach and into Pamphylia. Callisthenes proclaimed that the sea itself was performing *proskynesis* (genuflection)—it was bowing to Alexander.[26] The similarity with Xenophon's account in his *Anabasis* of

Cyrus's crossing of the Euphrates at Thapsacus because the water receded for him is obvious.[27] The Asian custom of *proskynesis* resurfaced in Bactria in 327 when Alexander unsuccessfully attempted to enforce it on his own men.

In Pamphylia an attack on Alexander's men by the inhabitants of Pisidia wounded and killed a number of them. In retaliation he besieged their fortress, but to prevent capture 600 of the defenders burned their families alive in their houses and stole through the Macedonian position one dark night. The towns of Perge and Aspendus surrendered as Alexander approached them, but the people of Aspendus changed their minds when he demanded money and the horses they bred for Darius (and paid as their tribute). His insistence on horses may indicate that his own were wearying from campaign exhaustion and needed replacing. The Aspendians refused and barricaded themselves in their town's citadel. When Alexander threatened them with a siege they capitulated, handing over their horses and paying double the indemnity he had first stipulated. To ensure their passivity he took some of the citizens as hostages, installed a garrison, and returned stolen lands to their neighbors.

Alexander's harsh actions may have been motivated by news of the Persian fleet's activities in the Aegean thanks to Memnon and of the Great King calling up large numbers of troops to him at Babylon, 600 miles to the east, as a precursor to battling the invader. Alexander could not afford for the towns he had subjugated to revolt as he marched first to Gordium and then to meet Darius, and his treatment of Aspendus, like that of Thebes and Miletus, was intended to send out a warning message.

From Aspendus Alexander made his way back to Perge and then to the inland town of Termessus. Its residents blocked his entry to the Maeander Valley and then withdrew to their high, fortified citadel. Rather than waste time besieging them, especially as the rugged terrain prevented him from properly using his siege engines, he made an alliance with the people of another mountain town, Selge, who were enemies of the Termessians. They were to attack them and treat them in whatever way they wanted. By the middle of spring 333, thanks to the Macedonians' ability to march and fight throughout winter, all of Pisidia was his.

The army had been fighting hard for the past several months, but Alexander was not prepared to give the men any respite. A week after leaving Pisidia he had arrived at Celaenae, capital of Phrygia, a city of great strategic importance on the Royal Road from Sardis to Susa. Celaenae refused to yield to him, but after a 10-day siege Alexander agreed to the people's terms that they would surrender in two months if Darius did not send them any help, and he appointed his general Antigonus (Monophthalmus or "the One-eyed") with 1,500 mercenaries to oversee operations there. He was eager to press on to Gordium, which he reached in the early summer of 333. There he rendezvoused with Parmenion as well as the troops he had sent back to Macedonia the previous winter, who had brought back with them 3,000 infantry and 650 Macedonian and Greek cavalry reinforcements. He also heard an Athenian embassy pleading for the release of the Athenians captured after the Battle of the Granicus River, but he was not yet prepared to grant its request.

Alexander's reason for visiting Gordium was part of a psychological plan to unsettle the Persians and involved the famed Gordian knot. In the eighth century a man named Gordius had set out from Macedonia and at Gordium had founded the Phrygian dynasty. His son Midas (mythologically famous for anything he touched turning to gold) had dedicated Gordius's wagon to Zeus on the Acropolis. The wagon was famous because the knot that fastened its yoke was made of cornel wood and tied in such an intricate manner that the ends were hidden. There was a tradition that whoever untied the cord of the yoke was destined to rule Asia.[28] The reason for Alexander's determination to reach Gordium was obvious: he needed to undo the knot and be heralded as the next ruler of Asia. In the presence of his own men and no doubt many of the locals, he did just that—either by cutting it with his sword or by pulling the wooden pin out of the wagon pole that held the cord together.[29]

Whichever of these versions is true does not matter: Alexander had undone the knot when everyone before him had failed. The symbolism of his act, as he planned, was obvious, and a sudden storm that night had his seers proclaiming that Zeus himself was greeting Asia's new master.

PERSIA RETALIATES AT SEA

While Alexander was in Cilicia and Pamphylia, Memnon, to whom the Great King had entrusted command of his fleet, was slowly but surely undoing Macedonian gains in the northern Aegean.[30] In the early summer of 333 he used the sheer size of his fleet to intimidate the island of Chios and the towns of Antissa, Methymna, and Eresus on Lesbos into returning to the Persian fold. However, Mytilene in eastern Lesbos resisted him thanks to Macedonian reinforcements sent by Alexander. Memnon besieged Mytilene but at some point died of sickness or was killed, and his nephew Pharnabazus succeeded him. Mytilene capitulated later that summer, and the whole of Lesbos returned to Persian control. At that point Miletus, sensing Alexander's increasing vulnerability to his rear, revolted. To add to Alexander's troubles the Persians were also active in the vital Hellespont region. There, Pharnabazus established a base at Callipolis and sailed to Siphnos in the western Cyclades from where he could threaten Euboea and even Macedonia. He also gave money and naval support to the Spartan king Agis III, who was planning to reassert Sparta's influence in the Peloponnese and who, in 331, would even call Greece to arms against the Macedonian hegemony.

Alexander now realized that disbanding his fleet had been a grave error. Since Pharnabazus was fast closing all of the Macedonians' exit routes from Asia, the king was left with no other option but to assemble another fleet. With his customary speed and planning he dispatched Amphoterus to the Hellespont to counter the Persian presence there while ordering Hegelochus to recapture the islands that Pharnabazus had won over to his side. He also sent Menes with 3,000 silver talents to Macedonia so that Antipater could hire mercenaries to deal with Agis's threat. In this way, Alexander restored his lines of communication across the Aegean: the invasion of Asia could continue.

A major contributing factor to the success of the Macedonians in undoing the damage caused by Memnon and Pharnabazus was Darius's call to his satraps and commanders to send him all the troops they had. The Great King, probably shaken by the undoing of the Gordian knot, was assembling an enormous army at Babylon and intended to defeat Alexander in pitched battle. His satraps and officers scrambled to obey his orders, which meant cannibalizing the Persian navy of the mercenaries who provided its manpower. Now a fraction of its former self, the fleet was thus no match for the Macedonians, which was lucky for Alexander.

ALEXANDER AND THE GREEKS OF ASIA MINOR AND THE EASTERN AEGEAN

The Macedonians had achieved one of the aims of the panhellenic invasion by liberating the Greek cities of Asia Minor and the adjoining islands from Persian rule. Alexander set up democracies in them, brought back exiles (hence Macedonian supporters) who had been forced to leave during Persian control, and arranged for the tribute previously paid to the Great King to come to him. This last move immediately addressed his need of money. Although the vast majority of these cities probably joined the League of Corinth, a handful of others, Mytilene on Lesbos and Tenedos, for example, made separate alliances with him.[31]

Alexander dealt with individual cities on a case-by-case basis, which explains his overall political pattern of setting up democracies, exiling pro-Persians, and recalling democratic exiles and his occasional interference in other aspects of city life. For example, he allowed a popular court at Eresus on Lesbos to try the city's recent tyrants and execute them and their families, but at Mytilene he issued a personal directive to reconcile the returned exiles and the general population. Neither city appears to have become a member of the League of Corinth. However, Chios, which was a member of the Common Peace in 334 but was forced by Memnon to ally with Persia the following year, joined the league in 332, when Hegelochus brought down the Persian oligarchy. Alexander sent a letter to the Chians ordering them to draw up a new set of laws that he would vet as well as submit to his personal ruling in any disputes arising from the return of exiles.[32]

One measure that seemingly flew in the face of the panhellenic war of liberation was the installation of Macedonian garrisons in a number of cities during 334 and 333, specifically Halicarnassus, Side, Soli, Ephesus,

Aspendus, Priene, Mytilene, Chios, and Rhodes. These garrisons were set up when the threat from the Persian fleet was at its greatest and perhaps were meant to prevent civil strife (*stasis*) occurring over the return of exiles.[33] However, there is no evidence for garrisons in other cities of western Asia Minor apart from Halicarnassus, Ephesus, and probably Priene, when we would expect more, and by 331 all garrisons had been withdrawn except at Ephesus and Rhodes, when the Persian fleet was no longer a danger. Because Alexander knew that garrisons offended a city's population and were an infringement on its freedom, he was careful to install them only in select towns to secure his rear and remove them as soon as he could.

It is important to realize that Alexander's proclamation of the freedom of these cities was only for propaganda reasons. In reality they were simply liberated from Persian rule but were not independent because they now had to pay their tribute to Alexander and he had been the one who had set up garrisons in them in the first place. However, his dealings with them allow interesting insights into how he was envisioning his empire. For one thing, that he made separate treaties with some of them rather than enrolling all of them in the League of Corinth shows that he viewed them as part of his Asian kingdom, so ultimately under his personal control. This attitude toward conquered cities does not change the farther east he marched, which implies that he had drawn a clear line between the European and Asian halves of his empire. Second, his arrangements show his intention to maintain the Persian satrapal system of government and even continue with the tradition of appointing native aristocrats to these posts—a measure that eventually backfired on him.

9.

ALEXANDER: MASTER STRATEGIST

AND EMERGING GOD

DARIUS'S MOVEMENTS HAD FORCED Alexander to switch his attention from the sea to the land. Leaving Gordium later in the summer of 333 he marched via Cappadocia and Paphlagonia, receiving their submissions, and assigned responsibility for both to Calas, the new satrap of Hellespontine Phrygia. Alexander's route took him through the Cilician Gates, the narrow, main pass on the Golek-Boghaz hills through the Taurus mountain range. Here a token resistance on the part of Arsames, the Persian governor of Cilicia, quickly crumbled away, and the king entered the city of Tarsus in September. His stay there almost cost him his life.

A BRUSH WITH DEATH

The Macedonian army had performed magnificently in overcoming enemies, coping with new terrain, and marching through scorching summer temperatures in full armor. At Tarsus the inviting waters of the river Cydnus, which flowed through the city, persuaded Alexander to swim in them. Still wearing his armor he dived off a bridge into the water. The locals had tried to warn him that the river was fed by the melting snows of the Taurus range and was ice cold, but he ignored them. He suffered cramps and had to be dragged, shaking with cold, out of the water. Within the day he had fallen victim to a full-blown tropical fever, possibly malaria, which threatened his life.

A week went by, and his condition did not improve. At that point the royal doctor, Philip of Acarnania, a man Alexander had known since his childhood, prepared a potion. As Philip was about to administer it a letter from Parmenion arrived, warning Alexander to be wary of the doctor because Darius was still offering 1,000 talents and now his own sister in marriage to anyone who killed the king. Whether Philip was plotting against Alexander is unknown, but it is doubtful, not least because Alexander gave the letter to him while he calmly drank his medicine—which saved his life. Three days later he was strong enough to appear before his troops and restore any declining morale on their part.

News of his illness had reached Darius, who had increased his marching speed in an effort to force Alexander into battle before he was fully recovered. Thus the consternation in the Macedonian camp over Alexander's illness, and especially what his death would have meant for the men so far from home, switched to the upcoming battle against the Persians. Darius was a skilled general, and his army was far larger than the Macedonian. He is portrayed in the ancient sources as weak and ineffectual, lacking in leadership skills, but that depiction was meant to downplay him in comparison with Alexander. The Macedonians' gloomy mood is possibly manifested in the sudden flight to Greece of Harpalus, the finance officer, one of the king's boyhood friends. Some form of physical deformity had precluded him from military service, so Alexander had awarded him a financial post. Harpalus may have been caught embezzling money, given that he fled with a shady character named Tauriscus, and decided to leave to escape Alexander's wrath. Equally possible is the idea that he feared that Darius would overcome Alexander in battle and wanted to get back to Greece before it was too late. For now Alexander let him go and replaced him with two finance officers, Philoxenus and Coeranus.

Alexander had planned to do battle with Darius on a narrow coastal plain between the Amanus (Nur) mountain range and the sea. He deliberately chose this area because he was aware that the Persian cavalry matched or even bettered his own and the plain would hinder the effective deployment of both sides' cavalry. The battle would be mostly an infantry one, and here Alexander knew that his phalanx had the upper hand over the enemy. However, Darius foiled Alexander's plan because he remained east of the Amanus Mountains, about 100 miles away, where he hoped to lure the invading army onto the spacious northern Syria plains and so force a cavalry battle after all.

Parmenion, who was shadowing the Great King, sent news of his movements to Alexander, who left Tarsus in September and marched south along the coast toward the Behlen Pass. For their protection he sent his sick and stragglers to Issus (Iskenderun), on the Gulf of Issus, which Parmenion had earlier taken. Darius was not going to allow Alexander an easy passage, though. As the Macedonians approached the pass Darius outflanked them by suddenly leading his men through the mountains via the Bahce Pass to the coast at Issus. There he came across the Macedonian sick and wounded, who were too feeble to defend themselves. Nevertheless he cut off their hands, cauterized the bloody stumps with pitch, and sent some of these men to report his arrival to Alexander. Finally, he made his camp on a narrow coastal plain south of the Pinarus River— either the modern Payas River or the Kuru Çay (the Kuru Çay is only a stream today but may have been larger in antiquity).

Alexander did not initially believe this grim news. Only after he sent a ship along the coastline that confirmed the report did the ramifications of this new situation dawn on him. Darius's unpredicted move had severed Macedonian lines of communication through Cilicia. It was also unknown whether Darius had stationed Persian troops to attack the Macedonian rear from the southern passes, from which direction Alexander had anticipated Darius would march. Alexander was consequently forced to deploy some troops to these passes before he could head north to deal with the Persians.

THE BATTLE OF ISSUS

The battlefield was probably on the two-mile-wide plain between the Mediterranean Sea and the Amanus range, most likely around the Kuru Çay. Both sides would have positioned themselves on either side of the river. Alexander could field 40,000 troops, including 5,800 cavalry. Darius's army easily outnumbered him, although the figures in the ancient writers of 600,000 (Arrian and Plutarch), 400,000 (Diodorus and Justin), and 250,000 infantry and 62,200 cavalry (Curtius) are clearly exaggerated to magnify the Macedonian victory.[1] A more plausible number for the Persian army is 100,000 to 150,000, since it included all the manpower reserves of Persis and Media as well as 30,000 Greek mercenaries.

The night before the battle Alexander and his men occupied a vantage point by the Pillar of Jonah (the Syrian or Assyrian Gates) from where they could see the Persian campfires on the plain below. It was an uneasy time for all of them, and Alexander took great care to sacrifice to the local deities in an attempt to calm his men. At dawn he led his army the several miles onto the plain, a task that took a number of hours because of the difficult and narrow terrain, and prepared to do battle.[2]

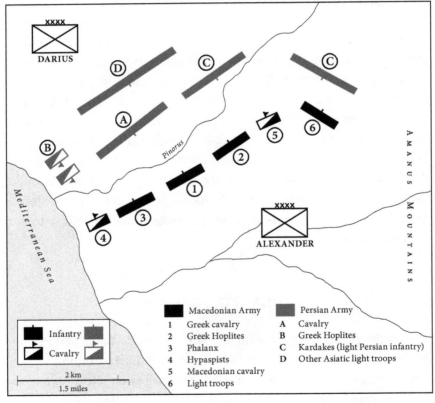

MAP 8
Battle of Issus.

Darius deployed the bulk of his cavalry on his right flank, by the gulf, next to which he stationed a contingent of Persian archers. In actuality he did not move his cavalry to this position until the last possible moment to keep Alexander guessing about his battle tactics. In the center of his line were the Greek mercenaries, another force of Persian archers, and the Persian infantry, who merged into the remainder of the cavalry on the Persian left flank. Darius, in his high, decorated chariot, surrounded by his Royal Bodyguard, was customarily positioned in the center behind the Greek mercenaries. The Persian line stretched from almost the shore of the gulf on the right to the foothills of the Amanus range on the left and took up an excellent defensive position. Further, the Persian cavalry was not going to be Alexander's greatest challenge because the Great King had angled his left wing into a dog-leg shape that outflanked the Macedonian right and he had built a palisade across the river to disrupt a full-scale Macedonian charge.

Alexander's line had the Thessalian and allied cavalry, commanded by Parmenion, on its left flank, next to the gulf. In the center were the various battalions of the phalanx, each under its own commander, and on the right flank, by the Amanus mountains, were the Macedonian and remainder of the allied cavalry, together with a force of archers and mercenaries. They had the unenviable task of preventing the Persian left wing (which outflanked them) from overcoming them and wheeling behind their line. Alexander with his tried and trusted hypaspists took up a position behind his center, together with more Macedonian cavalry and allied and mercenary infantry.

Alexander knew that he stood little chance against the huge Persian army in actual fighting, but he was not panicked. Instead, he resorted to overcoming his foe psychologically, something that became his trademark. Specifically, he decided to capture or kill Darius, which he calculated would demoralize the Persian troops and bring the battle to an abrupt end before many of them even joined in the fighting. As they rushed from the field in disarray they would become easier targets for the Macedonians. His strategy was not as far-fetched as it seemed and was how Cyrus planned to overcome his opponent at the Battle of Cunaxa in 403. For Alexander's strategy to work he had to penetrate the Persian line and focus his attention solely on Darius. With this in mind he gave the order to march slowly forward; when the Great King held fast rather than attacking him, Alexander gave the order for his line to engage the enemy. Then on the prearranged signal of a shrill trumpet blast he and his cavalry jumped over the palisade and charged through the Persian center toward Darius.

Alexander's cavalry was performing superbly, as he expected, but elsewhere his line was in trouble. The steepness of the river's banks, the rockiness of its bed, the palisade, and the boggy ground around the river all combined to slow his infantry down, hampered by the length of their heavy sarissas. As a result a large gap opened up between the infantry and cavalry. The Greek mercenaries in the Persian line quickly took advantage of the Macedonian soldiers' hardships and attacked them side-on because their sarissas could point only forward. They killed 120 troops (including Seleucus's son Ptolemy) before some of the Macedonian cavalry doubled back to save them. In the meantime the Persian cavalry under Nabarzanes on the right flank had charged the Thessalian cavalry on the Macedonian left and was pushing it back.

Relying on Parmenion's skill and experience to hold his left wing as long as he could, Alexander continued bearing down on Darius. Although the Royal Bodyguard fought valiantly to protect the Great King, Alexander and the men with him wreaked havoc among them. As more of them fell and presumably the horses that pulled Darius's chariot were killed or at least maimed, Darius suddenly jumped from his chariot into a smaller one and fled, followed by the remainder of his bodyguard and 4,000 mercenaries, toward Thapsacus. Alexander chased him for a little while but then returned out of concern for the hard-pressed Parmenion on the right flank. As it turned out, his help was not needed.

Darius's flight was swiftly communicated among the Persian ranks, as Alexander expected, which caused disillusionment and uncertainty in the enemy left flank. Parmenion seized his chance: he rallied his men and attacked the enemy. Faced by the Macedonian onslaught the Persians lost heart and raced off the battlefield in the same direction as their King. The rest of their line followed suit. Alexander, now assured of victory, gave the order to pursue the retreating Persians and show no mercy. Many of the enemy infantry had already been mown down and killed by their own cavalry, which had fled after the infantry and ridden over them. Those of the infantrymen who survived found that they were nothing more than sitting ducks because their sheer number prevented them from moving quickly across the plain to safety. More Persians were killed in the horrific pursuit than in the actual battle—in his later account of Alexander's reign the general Ptolemy claimed that the Macedonians "in the pursuit of Darius, coming to a ravine, passed over it upon the corpses."[3]

A combination of his brilliant generalship skills, use of psychological tactics, audacity, bravery, and luck came together to give Alexander victory. Had Darius not fled but, rather, forced Alexander's cavalry into the gulf, the outcome of the battle would have been far different. The sources scorn Darius for fleeing the battlefield, but they are Greek and so bound to be biased. His getaway was not the sign of a coward but, rather, of a king who knew that he needed to regroup to fight the invader another day. That he was putting his kingdom ahead of himself is shown by his decision, no matter how emotionally painful, to leave behind his wife and other family members who had traveled with him. He certainly did not abandon them, because he repeatedly offered Alexander huge sums of money for their return; however, the fate of the Persian Empire took priority over his family.[4]

Alexander now held a military procession to commemorate his men who had fallen in the fighting, after which he visited the wounded to hear their stories and commend their courage. According to some accounts the Persians lost 100,000 infantry and over 10,000 cavalry to Alexander's 500. These figures are exaggerated, but even so, at only 23 years old Alexander had defeated a numerically superior army on its home terrain and had forced the Great King from the battlefield. In triumph, he issued a special gold coin with the head of Athena on the obverse and Nike, goddess of victory, on the reverse. Even more significantly, he began to develop a new title for himself, King of Asia, which he alluded to in a letter sent to Darius shortly after that battle.[5] He would never call himself Great King. To do so would have provoked a hostile reaction from his own men as well as the Persian ruling aristocracy, whose support was essential in ruling Asia, though Alexander never enjoyed the religious bond they had shared with the Achaemenid rulers.[6] "King of Asia" summed up the influence he now wielded, although as time continued he came to see himself as an absolute monarch.[7]

Darius was still at large, and in some respects Alexander would have been better off hunting him down at this time rather than allowing him the means and opportunity to regroup and, with the support of his eastern satraps, do battle two years later at Gaugamela. Then again, Alexander still had to contend with the Persian navy threatening the coastline and his lines of communication. In order to neutralize Persian naval power he had little choice but to leave Darius to his own devices and concentrate on reducing the entire western coastline.

It is no surprise that all manner of stories associated with the Battle of Issus quickly circulated as part of Alexander's propaganda machine. Alexander and Darius never fought each other, but the Macedonian king was supposed to have sent a letter to Antipater in Greece describing "with all sincerity" how Darius had wounded him in his thigh with a sword.[8] More famous is the "Alexander mosaic," which was discovered in the House of the Faun at Pompeii in 1831 (Figure 16).[9] The mosaic depicts Alexander on a rearing Bucephalas rushing Darius in his chariot while

FIGURE 22
The Alexander sarcophagus. Erich Lessing/Art Resource, New York.

members of his bodyguard lie dead and dying around him. Darius is surrounded by sarissas, and the eyes of both kings are locked on each other.
The mosaic may have imitated a contemporary painting, perhaps by
Philoxenus of Eretria, which in turn was based on eyewitness accounts of
the battle. The image quickly established its own tradition and may have
influenced another portrayal of the battle on the so-called Alexander sarcophagus. This was commissioned for Abdalonymus of Sidon, possibly in
333 soon after Alexander had made him king, and was discovered there in
1887. On one side is a carving of Alexander riding Bucephalas attacking
the Persian army (Figure 22).

BECOMING KING OF ASIA

After the battle the Macedonians overran Darius's base camp, where they
found his gigantic personal tent with its expensive, elaborately carved
chairs and tables, gold plate, and clothing. The splendor of a Great King's
camp was in marked contrast to the military functionality of a Macedonian one. Alexander changed into some of the King's robes and treated
himself and his senior staff to a celebratory banquet, where amid all the
rich trappings he is supposed to have said, "So this is what it's like to be a
king." At some point during the banquet Alexander heard the crying and
lamenting of women. Darius had left Babylon with his sister-wife, mother,
and two daughters and a baggage train loaded with treasure. He had sent
most of the treasure to Damascus, 200 miles to the south; however, in
keeping with Persian custom, the royal family had remained with him.
They had been captured when the Persian army abandoned the battlefield
and now supposed that Darius was dead and their fate was sealed.

Alexander sent Leonnatus to assure them that Darius was very much
alive. He treated them with dignity as befitted their status and wanted them
to know that his war was against Darius, not his family. He promised that
he would find husbands for the princesses and arranged for them to learn
Greek and receive a Greek education. Although the common version is that
Alexander visited Sisygambis, the queen mother, there is a story that she
visited him in his tent to thank him personally for his lenient treatment of

them. She mistook Hephaestion for Alexander because he was taller and curtsied to him. The men present laughed, and when she looked bewildered Hephaestion told her of her mistake. She grew alarmed, but Alexander put her at ease by telling her that Hephaestion was as much an Alexander as he was. Alexander's treatment of the royal ladies had a political purpose. In arranging their education and especially overseeing who the princesses were to marry he was assuming Darius's role as the father and protector of the family. His action was designed to help legitimize his claim as King of Asia and further discredit Darius's power, which would have had an effect on the Persians. Sisygambis and Alexander may even have had a physical relationship, for when she heard that he had died, in 323, she starved herself to death.[10]

In the meantime Alexander sent Parmenion to seize the baggage train in Damascus. The old general also captured a Persian noblewoman named Barsine, the daughter of the satrap of Hellespontine Phrygia, Artabazus, who in the 350s had revolted from Artaxerxes II and lived with his family for some years at Pella. Barsine played a role in Alexander's sex life, which casts an interesting light on his personality. During her time as an exile at Pella, she would have met and even befriended a young Alexander (who was born in 356). When her father, Artabazus, was recalled to Asia in 343 she had left with him and later married Mentor of Rhodes, the brother of Memnon. When Mentor died, she married Memnon, who was killed during the siege of Mytilene in 333. Now, at least in her thirties, she was sent to Alexander. According to one source Alexander lost his virginity to her, for he "did not have sex with any woman before he married apart from Barsine." This may well be true, as Alexander showed little sexual interest in women up to this time; he and Barsine subsequently lived together in an open relationship.[11]

Alexander continued with his conquest of the entire eastern Mediterranean seaboard. Leaving behind two of his Companions, Balacrus and Menon, to administer Cilicia and northern Syria, he marched south into Syria, accepting the submission of towns along his route. At Marathus ('Amrit), which surrendered to him, Alexander supposedly received a letter from Darius. The Great King protested the invasion of his empire but offered to recognize Alexander as his friend and ally, offered his daughter in marriage and a ransom of 20,000 talents for his family, and proposed to cede him all territory west of the Halys River. Alexander refused to bargain with Darius but insisted that he defer to his power—if he did not, Alexander promised, he would hunt him down wherever he might flee. Needless to say Darius, then safely ensconced in Babylon, would have none of that, and he began to make plans for the next battle with Alexander.

THE SIEGE OF TYRE

The close of winter 333–332 saw Alexander in Phoenicia (now Lebanon). The towns of Aradus, Marathus, and Byblos surrendered to him without incident, and at Sidon the people even deposed their king, Straton II, because of his ties to Darius. Hephaestion, on Alexander's orders, picked his replacement, a poor member of the royal family named Abdalonymus— the same man who later commissioned the Alexander sarcophagus. The most important port city commercially and militarily between Cilicia and Egypt was Tyre, which in antiquity was an island about half a mile offshore. Tyre had two natural harbors, one to its north facing Sidon and the other to its south facing Egypt. The Persian navy could anchor in either or both of these and so disrupt Alexander's lines of communication, making it too risky for him to move into Egypt or farther inland into Persia. It was not just Alexander's control of the coastline of Asia Minor that was at risk if he allowed Tyre its independence and a safe haven for the fleet—there was a possibility that enemy ships could ferry troops across the Aegean to mainland Greece and join with Agis of Sparta, who was already planning an offensive against Macedonia. For these strategic reasons control of Tyre was essential, no matter the cost.

As Alexander approached the city its king, Azemilk, met him with gifts at Old Tyre (Palaeotyrus), which was on the mainland facing the island. He pledged his allegiance to the invader. Azemilk may have intended for his diplomacy to buy time for the Persian fleet, based at Cyprus, to sail to Tyre. However, when Alexander announced his intention to sacrifice to the god Melqart, a local equivalent of Heracles, in Tyre's main temple, the

Tyrians politely suggested that he do so in the temple in Old Tyre. Possibly they thought that his action in their temple would be sacrilegious since they were about to celebrate the main festival of Melqart and insisted on closing their city to Persians as well as Macedonians for its duration.[12]

Alexander was not swayed by politeness. He felt personally affronted, and as so often in his reign, once anyone crossed him forgiveness was out of the question. He sent messengers to the Tyrians formally demanding their surrender, at which point they abandoned diplomacy, killing the envoys and throwing their corpses from the battlements in full view of the Macedonians. Alexander immediately ordered the siege of the city.[13] His men understood the need to seek revenge for their murdered comrades, but they must have been daunted by what they faced. Tyre was a fortress, with fortification walls rising 200 feet high straight up out of the water. Anyone sailing across the windswept straits to attack it would be vulnerable to the showers of arrows from the Tyrian archers high atop the battlements. Since the population numbered about 50,000, there would always be a ready supply of archers to keep the invaders at bay. On top of all that, there was the constant worry that the Persian navy would arrive to reinforce the Tyrians. To ensure that he had his troops' committed support Alexander fell back to exploiting religion for his own ends, claiming that he dreamed that Heracles was stretching out his hand to him from the ramparts and calling him.

The Tyrians presumably assumed that they were safe because of their city's natural defenses, but Alexander had noticed that the straits from the mainland to the island were quite shallow, reaching a depth of 15 to 20 feet by Tyre's walls. He therefore ordered his military engineer, Diades of Thessaly, to design a mole or causeway, initially some 20 feet wide, which his men would build. On it he would set up siege engines to bombard the walls while his men crossed over under their protection. In this way, the Macedonians would not suffer the same losses as if they tried to sail across the straits, and once across the mole they would smash their way into the city and overcome the defenders. It was an audacious plan but perfectly in keeping with Alexander's character, and while the siege of Tyre proved to be his longest and most costly, it nevertheless demonstrated his brilliance at siege warfare.

The Macedonians destroyed Old Tyre to use its earth and stones for the mole and also brought in wood—especially cedar—from Lebanon. Since the area around Tyre could not support such a large force for a protracted siege, the same men who brought back the timber came with provisions, but to be on the safe side Alexander even wrote to the high priest in Jerusalem for supplies. The workmen began the mole by sinking piles into the mud at the bottom of the straits and rocks in between the piles to reinforce them and provide a stable foundation. When they began to lay the actual wooden causeway the Tyrian archers launched an offensive. To protect the workmen Alexander stationed two enormous siege towers, each one 160 feet high, at the end of the causeway. Archers on top of the siege engines fired arrows at their Tyrian counterparts, while torsion-powered catapults bombarded the defensive walls with huge boulders, allowing the workers to move the makeshift roadway slowly forward.

The Tyrians changed their tactics and decided to destroy the siege towers. They packed a large transport ship with wood, pitch, and anything else that burned; attached two long masts to its bows so that they protruded well beyond the prow; and hung two containers of bitumen and sulfur on each one. Then they loaded heavy rocks in the ship's stern to lift the prow out of the water. When one of the regular strong winds blew up volunteers sailed the floating firebomb toward the closer end of the Macedonian pier. The sources are at odds regarding how this part of the operation was conducted: either volunteers rowed the ship out, set fire to its contents, and jumped overboard to escape or two triremes (one to either side of it) guided it until their crews set it alight, scrambled for safety onto the triremes, and beat a hasty retreat back to Tyre. The wind carried the burning fireship the remaining distance. It smashed into the wooden end of the mole, setting fire to it, but when the two protruding masts snapped off and dumped their fiery contents all over the place the siege towers and the entire wooden causeway went up in a huge ball of flame. The Macedonians fought desperately to extinguish the blaze but were hampered by archers shooting at them from other Tyrian boats that had sailed alongside the mole. The result was complete devastation.

Furious, Alexander immediately ordered the construction of a new mole, as wide as 200 feet, to accommodate more siege towers. Not content with these fixed towers, which could still fall victim to another Tyrian fire attack, he mounted siege towers on ships, which sailed up and down the mole protecting the workmen. Work thus continued into the summer, when the Macedonians were buoyed by the arrival of 80 Phoenician ships that had defected from the Persian fleet and 120 ships from Cyprus. Alexander used them to blockade Tyre's two harbors so as to prevent the Tyrian fleet from attacking his siege vessels and deny the Persian fleet—if it arrived—safe anchorage. His determination to force Tyre to capitulate infected his men, who bravely finished the mole by the middle of the summer.

The Tyrians now prepared for the inevitable Macedonian attack by sea and from across the mole. To obstruct the former they dropped massive rocks and slabs of stone into the water at the foot of their walls and prepared burning arrows or fire darts to shoot at the enemy ships. To hamper the latter they filled cauldrons with burning sand to empty on Alexander's men—the sand would work its way through any gaps, no matter how tiny, in the men's armor and clothing and once trapped would severely burn their skin. They also strengthened their walls by attaching skins stuffed with seaweed to them and installed revolving wheels on the ramparts to deflect enemy arrows. Their efforts were impressive but were to no avail. Alexander had decided to breach a southern section of the wall, away from the causeway, and fixed battering rams to the ships—the first known instance of this floating weapon in the history of siegecraft. As the floating battering rams smashed part of the wall, Alexander ordered his fleet to attack the Tyrian fleet in the south harbor while the Cyprian ships captured the north harbor and attacked the city from that side. The Tyrians rushed to reinforce the vulnerable south wall, but just as all seemed lost for them the region's strong winds blew up and turned the tide in favor of the defenders. As some of his ships were sunk Alexander could not risk losing more, so he called off his planned frontal assault.

For two days the Macedonians could do nothing. On the third day the winds abated, and Alexander renewed his onslaught. First and foremost he needed to remove the stones and other debris that the Tyrians had dropped into the sea to keep the battering ram ships at bay. For this operation he installed winches in ships that would be anchored off the walls.

The winches would retrieve the rocks, and catapults would fling them far away into deep water. Undaunted, the Tyrians sliced the ropes that secured the ships to their anchors so that the winches could not be used. In frustration Alexander replaced the anchor ropes with chains, which the defenders could not cut through, and finally cleared a route to the walls. The battering rams on his ships resumed their pounding, while other ships ferried across troops, who began to clamber up the walls on scaling ladders. Some of them must have been killed by the grappling hooks and sharp poles that the Tyrians used against them, but a sufficient number of them held on stubbornly enough to make it to the top and overpower the defenders. During this turmoil Alexander led a contingent of hypaspists over the causeway and entered the city through the gate and the holes in the wall. The six-month-long siege was about to end in a bloodbath.

Alexander gave his men permission to run amok—more out of exasperation at the length of the siege and the people's staunch resistance than anything else. They massacred anywhere between 6,000 and 8,000 Tyrians and enslaved 30,000. The Macedonian casualty number of only 400 that Arrian claimed is clearly rhetorical.[14] Those Tyrians who had fled for sanctuary to the Temple of Melqart (including Azemilk, the king) were spared. When the slaughter was over, the Macedonians processed through the city in full armor before Alexander finally sacrificed to Melqart. He cynically dedicated to Heracles the Tyrians' sacred ship and the first battering ram that had breached the city walls. As a further sign of his victory, and to send out a warning message to other towns that he would next encounter as he marched south, he had 2,000 Tyrian survivors crucified and their corpses displayed along the Syrian coast.

A postscript to the siege of Tyre is Alexander's capture of 30 envoys from Carthage (a colony of Tyre founded in the late ninth century, now near modern Tunis) who were in the city to celebrate the festival to Melqart and who may have offered assistance to the defenders. The king spared their lives only so that they could take a message back to the Carthaginian government that he now regarded Carthage as his enemy and would deal with it in the future. The Carthaginians probably thought little of Alexander's threat at this time, but in 323 Carthage was one of several cities that sent an embassy to Alexander at Babylon congratulating him on his successes to date and safe return from India. The embassy indicates that the Carthaginian government was treating his threat of a decade earlier more seriously, as he had just planned to invade Arabia and may have set his sights on the western Mediterranean after that.

The siege of Tyre was a costly one for Alexander, but it demonstrated his genius and boldness in siege warfare. Control of the city not only denied the Persian fleet a safe anchorage but also gave Alexander mastery of the Levant. He replenished Tyre's population with settlers from the surrounding areas and installed a garrison in the city. Then he left Tyre, bound for Egypt. Close to the Egyptian border stood the old and wealthy Philistine city of Gaza, which was built on a hill (*tel*) 250 feet high and was surrounded by a fortified wall. Its garrison commander, an Arab eunuch named Batis, evidently thought little of the message of the crucified Tyrians, because he refused to yield to Alexander.

THE SIEGE OF GAZA

Alexander entrusted Hephaestion with command of the fleet, which was to sail southward along the coastline presumably gathering provisions in advance of the land army. The Macedonians reached Gaza in September 332. Alexander was in no mood for diplomacy and immediately invested the city.[15] The height of Gaza posed a problem for the besiegers, as Batis had anticipated, but Alexander simply built a matching mound, on top of which he set up the siege towers that Hephaestion had transported from Tyre. Since Gaza's walls were built on soft sand Alexander ordered his men to dig under them while his siege engines blasted away at them with huge boulders. The defenders were hardly intimidated, and in fact they resisted three attacks on the city, wounding Alexander in the leg during one of them and forcing him to retreat. They also made a daring sally in which a catapult bolt penetrated Alexander's shield and cuirass and lodged itself in his shoulder. He was forced to give the order to withdraw so that his doctor could stop the bleeding.

Eventually, however, the walls gave way to the siege engines and sappers. The Macedonians rushed through a section of collapsed wall and wreaked havoc in the city. They massacred 10,000 men and enslaved the women and children. Batis survived, remaining defiant of the king to the end. Perhaps because of his wound Alexander decided on a harsh reprisal. He ordered Batis's heels pierced, ran a rope through the holes and attached it to the back of a chariot, and, while he and his men looked on and laughed, had him dragged naked and screaming around the walls of Gaza until he died.[16] Batis's death was meant to evoke the similar treatment that Achilles inflicted on the Trojan prince Hector at Troy—except that Hector was already dead when Achilles dragged him around Troy's walls.

EGYPT: FROM MAN TO GOD

From Gaza to the Egyptian border town of Pelusium (Port Said) was 130 miles across the Sinai Desert, which Alexander covered in a week with a series of forced marches. Egypt was home to 4,000,000 people, who paid high levels of taxes, and boasted abundant supplies of grain and easily defensible natural borders. The Greeks had had contacts with the Egyptians since the sixth century, when Amasis II allowed them to settle in the town of Naucratis, about 50 miles south of the later Alexandria, and turn it into a trading colony with the West. Most likely at Pelusium the Persian satrap, Mazaces, greeted the Macedonian king and surrendered Egypt to him. Mazaces was well aware that there was little point in resistance because the Egyptians despised being ruled by Persia. Since their conquest by Cambyses II, son of Cyrus the Great, in 525, and the subsequent moves to curtail the power of the venerable Egyptian priests, they had revolted a number of times. There would be no native support if Mazaces opposed Alexander.

From Pelusium Alexander traveled along the Nile to Memphis, Egypt's 3,000-year-old capital, and held a thanksgiving sacrifice with games and musical contests. Partly in response to the Egyptians' warm welcome, and because of his desire to show that they were not swapping one despotic king for another, he sacrificed a bull to the native god Apis. His action, which especially appealed to the priests, was a deliberate contrast to previous Persian rulers, such as Cambyses, who had killed the Egyptian sacred bulls. In fact, he was also active in initiating restoration projects on some of Egypt's most ancient temples, including part of the Temple of Amun-Re at Thebes (including the sanctuary of Akhmenu) and the great Temple of Thoth at Hermopolis.[17] His actions further endeared him to the Egyptian people, and Egyptian royalty are even known at his court.[18] It is a pity that as Alexander marched farther eastward he did not show the same respect for the religious beliefs and social customs of other peoples.

Egypt now belonged to Alexander. He received the titles previously reserved for the pharaohs: King of Upper and Lower Egypt, Son of Ra (the supreme god), and Beloved of Ammon (Amun). He was also Horus, god on earth. Alexander was never formally crowned pharaoh, even though the *Alexander Romance*—a fantastic later account of his reign—has it that he was. Not that that mattered, for the titles meant that he alone performed the ritual sacrifices for the well-being of the country and its people. He was to all intents and purposes pharaoh, as the carving on the temple at Luxor depicting him as pharaoh performing homage to Min attests.[19] His example was followed by the Ptolemies, Macedonian rulers of Egypt after Alexander's death, although during the reign of Ptolemy V (203–181) social turmoil forced that ruler to be crowned Ptolemy V Theos Epiphanes in the traditional capital of Memphis, not Alexandria.

The wealth of Egypt and its trading network were obvious reasons for Alexander's determination to conquer the country. Another was personal. He was still only 25 years old, yet his exploits to date surely placed him on a par with his Homeric heroes. As pharaoh Alexander was identified with Horus and Osiris and so worshiped by the Egyptians as a god on earth. During his visit to Didyma in Asia Minor in 334 he had supposedly received the first indication that he was no ordinary man, and the events connected to his superhuman status since then clearly had an effect on him. Therefore he decided to visit the Oracle of Zeus Ammon (a Greek form of the Egyptian Amen-Ra, whom the Greeks equated with their Zeus) at Siwah in the Libyan Desert to find out from the god whether he really was divine.[20] This Oracle was one of the most important to Greeks and on a par with that of Apollo at Delphi and Zeus at Dodona. Ancient writers now begin writing about Alexander's *pothos* or "personal longing" to visit the Oracle—it was often this *pothos* rather than strategic reasons that motivated him to continue marching eastward.

With a handpicked body of troops Alexander sailed off from Memphis down the Nile. He was presumably bound for Naucratis, perhaps to enlarge it as a commercial center, but instead he stopped off at coastal Lake Mareotis. There, a narrow isthmus connected the lake to the sea, opposite the island of Pharos. Alexander immediately saw the potential of the area for a new city, which he would connect to the Nile by a canal, thereby providing it with two natural deep harbors and facilitating trade with the entire Mediterranean Basin. Thus was born Alexandria, the second city Alexander named after himself—the first being Alexandropolis, after he had defeated the Maedians in 340 (p. 97). Arrian and Plutarch claim that he drew up the plans for Alexandria at this time, while Diodorus and Curtius put this after his return from Siwah.[21]

The journey to Siwah was a horrific one for the Macedonians. From Lake Mareotis the men marched 180 miles westward (passing through what is today El Alamein) to the coastal border town of Paraetonium (Mersa Matruh) without encountering any problems. From there the 150-mile trek southward through the desert to the oasis was a different story thanks to the searing heat and harsh natural conditions. Instead of the regular single week that the local Bedouins took to make the trip, the Macedonians struggled for two weeks. They lost their way several times because of sudden sandstorms and even torrential downpours that obliterated landmarks and tracks. After about a week they had exhausted their supplies (carried by camels, a first for the Macedonians) and were savaged by hunger and thirst. Finally, perhaps more by luck than anything else because they followed birds flying to it, they found the oasis.

Alexander knew about the hazards of the desert before he began the trek. The contemporary writer Aristobulus described the effects of the region's south wind, which "piles up sand on the route in every direction, which makes the outline of the road invisible. As a result travelers are at a total loss as to what path to take across the sand, just like if they were at sea, because there are no landmarks along the way, no visible mountains, no trees, no unshifting hills, the sorts of things that would enable them to determine the right route, as sailors do by the stars."[22] However, ancient writers embellished these common desert occurrences of sandstorms, rainfalls, zero visibility, and even crows flying to and from oases to lend a divine element to the grueling journey. For example, when Alexander got lost Callisthenes talked of crows that rescued him by guiding him to the oasis.[23] Ptolemy, however, claimed that it was not birds but two snakes, speaking in a human voice, that showed them the way to the Oracle and back again.[24]

The actual Oracle was inside a mud-brick fortress in the center of the oasis. Visitors met the priest in a small room, about 10 by 20 feet, inside the fortress, where they put their questions to the god. The priest then moved to an inner sanctum to communicate with the god. Rather than a verbal response, as at Apollo's Oracle at Delphi, Zeus Ammon moved his answer—80 priests carried aloft a golden boat in which was set the god's statue, which induced them to move one way or another and even shake the boat, movements that the priest interpreted and so came up with an answer for the visitors.

Alexander's sudden appearance at the oasis evidently startled the Egyptian priest because it was said that instead of uttering the standard greeting (in Greek), "O paidion," meaning "My boy," he slipped in his pronunciation and greeted Alexander as "O pai Dios," meaning "Son of Zeus." Alexander must have been well aware that this was a slip on the part of a nonnative Greek speaker, but he took it seriously. He moved into the room with the priest, and they had a lengthy meeting, during which he allegedly asked several questions—who his father really was, whether he was fated to rule the world, and whether all the murderers of his father had been avenged, to which the priest answered yes. The implication of this last question, almost six years after Philip was assassinated, is that a belief still lingered that Alexander was involved in a plot against his father and needed the god to exculpate him.

At the end of the audience an excited Alexander emerged from the sanctum and reported to his men that the god had said that his real father was Zeus and that Philip was only his mortal father. Only Alexander and the priest met privately so that no witness could corroborate anything about the exchange. Ptolemy later asserted that Alexander "heard what he found agreeable to his desires,"[25] but the priest may have said something entirely different, which Alexander would not have repeated. After all, Aristobulus claimed that Alexander went to Siwah to discover exactly what his origin was—"or at least be able to say that he had learned it."[26] Regardless, Alexander, a descendant of Zeus, now openly began to call himself Son of Zeus, a major difference. This nomenclature and the overall psychological effect of visiting Siwah make the episode a major turning point in his pretensions to personal divinity.[27] Possibly he now began to circulate the stories of his divine conception and birth to help legitimize his claims to godhead.

His pretensions to personal divinity caused resentment among not only the Greeks, given their religious belief that no living man was immortal, but also his own men, and they will be discussed at length later (pp. 265–269). Alexander also wrote to his mother, Olympias, telling her that he had learned all sorts of secret affairs from the priest but could tell her only in person when he returned home. These he was never able to share with her because he died in Babylon in 323.

ALEXANDRIA

From Siwah the Macedonians returned to Lake Mareotis, experiencing few if any of the problems they had encountered on their outward march. Alexander had clearly been thinking about the future Alexandria because he tasked the leading architect of the day, Deinocrates of Rhodes, to design the city and supervise its construction. He insisted that the island of Pharos be joined to the mainland by a mole so as to protect the natural harbors and, in an effort to appease the natives, that a splendid temple to Isis be built in the city.

The official foundation date of Alexandria was April 7, 331. From the outset Alexander intended it to be a Greek city, complete with all the trappings of city life—an Agora, gymnasium, odeum for music, and theater and sanctuaries for Greek gods. It was therefore meant to be a cultural center as well as a means of promoting Hellenic civilization in his empire. Alexander died long before the city was completed; it did not become the official capital of Egypt until the reign of Ptolemy I (323–283), who, with his son Ptolemy II (283–246), steered the city to be the greatest intellectual center of the Hellenistic and Roman periods.[28]

From his fledgling Alexandria the king moved back to Memphis and sacrificed to Zeus for his safe return. To control Egypt, given its size and diversity, Alexander combined military power with tradition, somewhat reminiscent of his settlement of Caria. An Egyptian named Doloaspis was put in charge of all civilian administration; garrisons were installed in Pelusium and Memphis (in all about 4,000 troops), each under the command of a handpicked Macedonian commander, and other Macedonians commanded the troops of Upper and Lower Egypt. Alexander also made an innovation to the administrative structure in the shape of a Greek named Cleomenes from Naucratis, who collected the taxes from all of Egypt and ensured that they were paid to the king.[29] Although Cleomenes quickly exploited his position to amass considerable personal wealth, the native Egyptians gave him little trouble as the bulk of administration remained in their hands. As a reward for Cleomenes's efforts, in 325 Alexander made him the actual satrap of Egypt.

Even though Alexander had spent less than a year in Egypt, it was time to leave the country and refocus attention on Darius. For some time the Great King had been building up manpower in the East thanks to the support of Bessus, the satrap of Bactria and Sogdiana (between the Hindu Kush and the Oxus River, now in parts of northern Afghanistan, Tajikistan, and Uzbekistan). The next battle would decide the fate of the Persian Empire.

10.

THE FALL OF THE PERSIAN EMPIRE

I N THE LATE SPRING of 331 Alexander left Egypt and made his way across the Sinai and Phoenicia to Tyre. Various foreign embassies were waiting for him there, complimenting him on his successes to date and putting forward petitions, which he granted. For example, he agreed to take measures to curb the activities of the garrisons in Chios and Rhodes, a clear sign that he recognized the need to conciliate the Greeks in the vital coastal Asia Minor and eastern Aegean regions. He also released the captured Athenian captives from the Battle of the Granicus River, who were working as slaves in Macedonia. There was also an embassy from Darius, although the sources may have confused it with the one at Marathus before the siege of Tyre.[1] Darius was still willing to be Alexander's friend and ally, pay him a ransom—raised to 30,000 talents—for his family, and give him his daughter Stateira in marriage and would now yield to him all lands west of the Euphrates. He won Parmenion over, who told Alexander to accept his concessions. Intent only on Darius's unconditional surrender, Alexander supposedly replied that if he were Parmenion, he would.[2]

ALEXANDER AND HELLENISM—*ARS GRATIA ARTIS*?

While at Tyre Alexander celebrated a festival in honor of Heracles, which included athletic games and performances of Greek tragedies, all judged by his generals. Eager to show their goodwill to Alexander, the kings of Salamis and Soli on Cyprus contributed to the festivities. Appearing were the preeminent actors of the time, Thessalus and Athenodorus—the same

Thessalus who in 337 had acted as Alexander's intermediary when the young heir had offered himself in marriage to Pixodarus's daughter. Athenodorus was so keen to perform before Alexander that he broke his contract to appear at the Athenian Great Dionysia festival (in honor of the god Dionysus), which included the foremost tragic competitions in the Greek world. He was heavily fined, but Alexander came to his rescue and paid it.

Alexander was a genuine philhellene, or lover of Greek culture and learning, from the time he was a boy. He had spared the house of the lyric poet Pindar when he razed Thebes in 335, and one of his most prized possessions was Aristotle's personal copy of the *Iliad*, which he supposedly slipped under his pillow when he went to bed. When his foreign subjects received a Greek education it included the Greek language (which thanks to him would replace Aramaic and Old Persian to become the lingua franca of the empire), Homer, and the fifth-century Athenian tragedians, Aeschylus, Sophocles, and Euripides. Alexander's predilection for their plays ensured their reception and longevity in the eastern half of his empire. The cities he founded from Egypt to India were established for strategic and economic reasons, but Greek cultural events were still part and parcel of life in them. Arrian tells us that he regularly held literary contests as well as music and athletic competitions (which included armed combat) in Asia and patronized building projects in the Greek style.[3] Alexandria in Egypt was a Greek city to all intents and purposes, as was—thousands of miles to the east—Ai-Khanoum in Afghanistan, which began life as one of Alexander's garrison outposts. Excavation of the Hellenistic Ai-Khanoum, when it had grown into a flourishing city, has yielded Greek temples, a theater, and even an odeum for music performances.

Alexander's athletic, literary, and philosophical retinue comprised some of the best artists, writers, and philosophers of the era—including Pyrrho of Elis, who went on to found the Skeptic school—and was obviously for his own physical and intellectual gratification. Yet the various artists and intellectuals had a self-serving purpose, realizing that their association with the most powerful man of the time elevated their own reputation, social status, and income.[4]

That Alexander deeply loved Greek culture is beyond doubt, and Plutarch exaggeratedly praised him as the bringer of civilization to foreign peoples.[5] Greek culture did spread like a spider's web throughout the empire, but how Alexander introduced it to his subject peoples had adverse side effects. His festivals and competitions deliberately featured Greek cultural and athletic performances to the exclusion of native ones. In doing so they set the invading army apart from the local people by actively promoting a cultural gap that only increased native resentment of Alexander and stiffened resistance to his attempts to govern Persia.[6]

THE MARCH TO GAUGAMELA

Darius had left Babylon in the summer of 331. He had lost almost all of his support in the western satrapies after Issus, but Bessus had supplied him with infantry and in particular superb cavalry from the eastern and northeastern parts of the Persian Empire. The Persian army marched north through Mesopotamia, crossing the Tigris one week later, thence through Assyria (northern Iraq) to Arbela (Irbil). Finally, 70 miles later, it arrived in the village of Gaugamela (Tell Gomel), probably close to the modern Mosul, between the Khazir River and the ruins of Nineveh, capital of the Neo-Assyrian Empire and one of the oldest cities in the world.

Darius was well aware that the Persian infantry was less well trained than the Macedonian and had inferior weapons. Most Persian infantrymen were equipped with merely bows and arrows and javelins, and the spears of the famous Immortals could not compete with sarissas. However Bessus's cavalry was certainly on a par with the Macedonian. On the cavalry and a corps of 200 scythed chariots, with razor-sharp scythes attached to the wheels, chassis, and yoke poles, Darius pinned his hopes of victory. To deploy them effectively he selected a wide plain between the river Bumelus (Gomel) and the Jabel Maqlub hills, between the Tigris and the foothills of the Zagros Mountains. There he awaited Alexander's arrival.

In the meantime the Macedonian army moved north through Syria and crossed the Euphrates, near Jerablus, in probably July. The satrap of

Cilicia and Syria, Mazaeus, had been ordered to prevent Alexander from crossing the river, but he and his force of 3,000 cavalry and 2,000 mercenaries scattered as soon as the invaders arrived. Alexander marched the 275 miles through northern Mesopotamia to the Tigris River, a little northwest of Mosul. He crossed the river on the evening of September 20, a date known from a lunar eclipse on September 20–21 recorded in the Babylonian astronomical tablets.[7] Alexander's personal seer, Aristander, quickly proclaimed that the eclipse showed that the gods were on the Macedonians' side.

From the Tigris Alexander marched due east, through areas that offered him abundant provisions to feed his army. Scouts had already reported the Persian position to him, so he allowed his men a four-day rest period before moving to Gaugamela toward the end of September. Under cover of darkness he set up a camp behind a row of small hills about seven miles from the Persian troops. With a select contingent of his Companion Cavalry he moved carefully through the hills to study the plain and the Persian line. However, the moon must have come out because some Persians spotted them and told Darius. The Persian king suspected an imminent attack and gave orders to form his line. When no attack came he kept his men at their posts in full armor for the rest of the night just to be on the safe side. That was a blunder, as it allowed Alexander to see his deployments and arrange his own battle strategy and tactics. Even worse was the fact that the Persian troops became exhausted and worried, which gave Alexander a tremendous psychological advantage over their vast numbers when he decided to do battle the next day.

THE BATTLE OF GAUGAMELA

The battle was fought on either the last day of September or the first day of October 331.[8] Arrian put the size of the Persian army at 40,000 cavalry and 1,000,000 infantry; Diodorus and Plutarch claimed that it numbered 1,000,000, with Diodorus breaking it down into 200,000 cavalry and 800,000 infantry, while Curtius has 45,000 cavalry and 200,000 infantry.[9] These are absurdly high numbers to show how hopelessly outnumbered

Alexander's army was at 7,000 cavalry and 40,000 infantry.[10] A more plausible figure for the Persian army is 100,000, which is still double that of the Macedonian.

Darius arranged his line in ethnic units (Map 9). Mazaeus was appointed commander of the right flank with troops from Syria, Mesopotamia, and the central satrapies of the Persian Gulf region. In front of them were

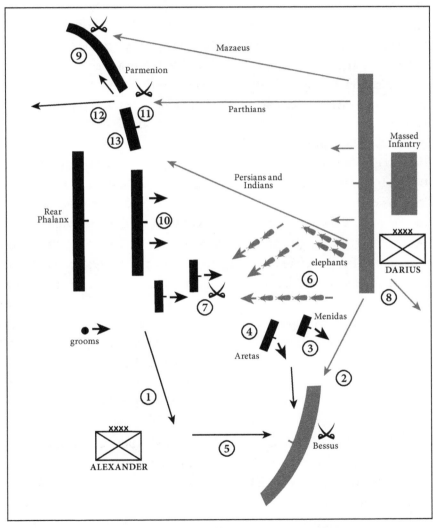

MAP 9
Battle of Gaugamela.

posted 50 scythed chariots and cavalry from Armenia and Cappadocia. In the center were Darius and the Immortals, flanked by contingents of Greek mercenaries who were still in Persian employ, and in front of them 50 scythed chariots and 15 war elephants from India. Behind him was the bulk of his infantry, mostly from Mesopotamia. Bessus commanded the left flank of cavalry from Bactria, Armenia, Arachosia, Persis, and the Sacae, Dahae, and Massagetae peoples. Before them stood another cavalry detachment along with 100 scythed chariots (in two groups of 50). Darius's enormous line easily outflanked the Macedonian, and he expected that his left flank would cause the earliest and greatest damage to the enemy line.

To meet the threat from the Persian left Alexander stationed the hypaspists on his right flank under Hephaestion—his first significant command in Alexander's army. The king and his infantry phalanx and Companion Cavalry took up position in the center. The left flank (facing Mazaeus) was commanded by Parmenion and comprised the cavalry of the Greek allies including the Thessalians. A row of infantry, mostly troops from the League of Corinth, was set up behind the front line. Its job was either to press forward with the front line or to turn and fight the Persians if they got behind them. On each flank more infantry and cavalry plugged the gap between the front and rear lines, thereby preventing the Persians from pouring into it. The right "plug" consisted of infantry, archers, and the Agrianians; the left, of Thracian infantry and mercenary cavalry.

Temperatures in the plain at that time of the year would have been over 100 degrees Fahrenheit, and Darius's men were already tired, hot, and anxious from their nightlong vigil. Nevertheless, the Great King's cavalry and scythed chariots, each one pulled by four horses, could still wreak havoc in the Macedonian line. There was also the danger from the elephants, from whose backs soldiers in wooden towers would rain down javelins on the men below while the massive animals trampled others underfoot. Moreover, Alexander had seen the Persians dig spikes (caltrops) in the plain to wound the Macedonian horses as they charged the enemy and walk back and forth over parts of the plain smoothing out bumps and getting rid of any obstacles that might topple the chariots. Alexander understood that Darius had built his entire battle strategy on his chariots cutting viciously through the Macedonian line to open up gaps in it, through which the Persian cavalry would ride and wheel around to encircle it. He took measures to combat these dangers, but ultimately he staked his battle strategy once more on the demoralizing psychological effect of killing or capturing Darius. That was why he deliberately stationed himself and his cavalry in the center to face Darius.

Before the battle Alexander rode up and down the entire length of his line exhorting his men. He called some of them by name and recounted various exploits they had experienced and hardships they had faced together. He made himself appear as no different from any of the rank and file about to face the vast Persian horde. Then Alexander lifted his right hand and prayed that if he were really a son of Zeus, the gods would defend and strengthen the Greeks. At that moment an eagle flying overhead swooped down on the Persian line, which Alexander interpreted as a portent that Zeus was with them. He might have simply taken advantage of the bird's flight, but his interpretation exhorted his men to face the tens of thousands of enemy troops.

Many of the details of the actual battle are unknown because the large number of horses kicked up thick dust clouds that reduced visibility and caused confusion in eyewitnesses' versions of events. That has led to the ancient writers presenting conflicting accounts of many aspects of the battle. It appears that both sides slowly advanced toward each other, neither one anxious to initiate the first charge. This standoff dragged on, and eventually an impatient Darius sent word to Bessus on his left to attack the Macedonian right wing, which had advanced at a 45-degree angle to the right as if it was trying to evade the line of chariots. This evasion was a hoax. Alexander wanted Darius to deploy his left wing so that it would open a gap in the Persian line; when it did, he intended to halt his feigned advance to the right, turn his men, and tear through the opening to rush Darius. Unfortunately for him the gap was too narrow. When Darius realized what Alexander was up to he immediately brought in contingents of Bactrian and Sacae cavalry to block his enemy. Nevertheless, Alexander's failed tactic was still to his advantage because Darius had had to delay his scythed chariot charge.

Alexander kept the pressure on the powerful Persian left flank. He ordered Menidas on the right wing to launch his mercenary cavalry against the

Bactrians and Sacae people. As their casualty numbers grew he continued to reinforce Menidas to keep the Bactrian cavalry bogged down in fighting there. Robbed of deploying his valuable cavalry elsewhere in his line, Darius could only fall back on his chariots, but his earlier delay now proved fatal to his battle strategy. As soon as the fearsome chariots tore toward the Macedonians a trumpet blast rang out loudly above the noise of the battle. This was the prearranged signal to the Agrianian archers and javelin men to open fire on the horses pulling the chariots, which caused the vehicles to veer off course onto the rougher, bumpier terrain and overturn. The same signal alerted the Macedonian infantrymen to move quickly to their left or right so that any chariots that survived the initial attack could be ridden only through these gaps. Those charioteers now had their backs exposed to the Macedonians and fell victim to a deadly onslaught of arrows. The whole episode was an example of Alexander's cunning and his men's precision and split-second timing.

In the meantime Alexander finally managed to break through the Persian line when he lured Bessus and his Bactrians to move too quickly for their comrades on the left to follow. That was the turning point in the battle. Alexander now plunged through the gap, followed by some of his Companions and slower-moving infantry, and rode hell-bent after Darius. A last-minute rally on the part of the Great King might have saved the day for the Persians, but none came: Gaugamela now became a repeat of Issus. As Alexander bore down on him Darius abandoned all hope; he and his bodyguard fled the battlefield to Arbela, about 70 miles away, pursued by Alexander. The news of his flight spread like wildfire through the Persian line and broke the soldiers' spirits. Although Bessus intended to carry on fighting, he and his men had no choice but to flee after Darius when the Macedonians broke the left flank and began to surround them.

There was, however, still fierce fighting on the right, where Mazaeus had actually pushed back the Macedonians under Parmenion, who was fighting huge numbers of enemy infantry in front of him and Parthyaean and Indian cavalry to his rear. Parmenion had sent an urgent appeal to Alexander for help but to no avail, possibly because the messenger could not find the king, given the dense, swirling dust clouds, or because Alexander had already left the field in pursuit of Darius. He chased him as far as Arbela, but the Great King was too far ahead, so he returned to the battlefield. As he did so he fell in with retreating Persian, Parthyaean, and Indian cavalry from the Persian left. The two sides clashed head-on, and in fierce fighting 60 of Alexander's Companions were killed.

At that point Mazaeus realized that all was lost. Parmenion quickly rallied his men, and the Thessalian cavalry charged the Persians, scattering them even as Mazaeus yelled the retreat. The battle was finally over. Curtius claimed, perhaps rightly, that the Persians lost 40,000 men to the Macedonians' 100 to 1,200.[11] Callisthenes later defamed Parmenion as "lazy and ineffectual because either his courage was now marred to an extent by old age or he was jealous and resented the arrogance and display...of Alexander's power."[12] His criticism is completely unjust, given the old general's valiant fighting on the left flank, and was no doubt meant to belittle his achievement compared with Alexander's actions on the field.

The battle that Darius had needed to win after the debacle at Issus was over, and so too was the Achaemenid Empire, founded by Cyrus the Great 200 years earlier. The battle was a spectacular triumph for Alexander and excited the imaginations of artists throughout the centuries, as LeBrun's eighteenth-century masterpiece the *Battle of Arbela* attests (Figure 23).

Darius and Bessus fled eastward toward the Zagros Mountains, while Mazaeus escaped south to Babylon. Believing that Darius was a spent force, Alexander prepared to march the 300 miles southward along the Royal Road, with its proximity to supplies, through Babylonia to Babylon and thence to Susa (Shush) and Parsa—what the Greeks called Persepolis, the symbolic heart of the Persian Empire in Persis.[13] Capture of those palace capitals would give him all of Persia and would truly be revenge for what the Greeks had suffered in the Persian Wars. Yet, while Darius was down, he was not completely defeated and was still alive to fight another day.

BABYLON

Three weeks later, on October 24 or 25, Alexander's army reached Babylon, on the junction of the Tigris and Euphrates rivers. En route he passed through Mennis (close to Kirkuk), where the people literally lit up one of the roads by setting fire to a flammable substance he had never come

FIGURE 23

Charles LeBrun, *Battle of Arbela*. Photo: Daniel Arnaudet/Gérard Blot. © RMN-Grand Palais/Art Resource, New York.

across before. It was petroleum or naphtha, whose fierce burning power and ignition speed fascinated Alexander.

Mazaeus traveled out from Babylon to greet the new King of Asia and formally escort him into the city, an attempt no doubt to protect his life and possibly save the city from any destruction that the conqueror was planning. Alexander accepted his gesture, well aware what lay behind it, and entered Babylon through the Ishtar Gate—in similar fashion to Cyrus II after his victory at Opis, whose liberating action Alexander may have been emulating. It is even possible that the type of supreme kingship and world empire Cyrus had envisaged, and which had been taken up by subsequent Great Kings, had had a profound influence on Alexander, who in turn set out to outdo his greatness.[14]

The people of Babylonia turned out in force to greet their new master. The Babylonians were not Persians, and they had had enough of oppressive Persian rule and (like the Egyptians) welcomed Alexander as their savior. Some of them threw rose petals across his path, while others burned incense. Alexander took up residence in the 600-room palace of Nebuchadnezzar overlooking the fabled Hanging Gardens. From Babylon's enormous treasury he paid his valiant troops a special bonus: 600 drachmas for each Macedonian cavalryman, 500 drachmas for each Greek cavalryman, 200 drachmas for each Macedonian infantryman, and two months' pay (roughly 60 drachmas) for the rest. At the same time he was careful to respect local religious customs. The previous Persian rulers had torn down the temple of the city's patron deity, Marduk, which was known as Egasila and stood atop a 300-foot ziggurat, and melted down the god's gold statue. Alexander promised to rebuild the temple in an effort to endear himself to the Babylonians.

The Macedonians spent one month in Babylon, where they consumed all manner of fine food and wines and were lavishly entertained by courtesans, striptease artists, and numerous prostitutes. Not everything that happened in Babylon stayed in Babylon, though. Diodorus informs us that Alexander began to wear select items of Persian clothing, in particular a white robe, a girdle, and the purple-and-white headband that Darius had preferred. Probably he did so because he now received one of the royal titles, "king of lands," which still falls short of Great King.[15] He did not wear the Persian striped trousers and long-sleeved upper garment, probably because the Greeks viewed them as distinctly barbarian. Nevertheless, his adoption of Persian dress and practices—such as using the Persian royal seal and keeping a harem of 365 women (the same number as the Great Kings)—did not endear him to the Persians, nor did it sit well with his men. Curtius and Plutarch talk of the men's shame and embarrassment over Alexander's growing orientalism and that he was becoming more like one of the conquered than the conqueror.[16]

Alexander's personal changes in Babylon were bad enough, but the men were further upset when he appointed Mazaeus satrap of Babylonia—the first appointment of a native satrap, but still with Macedonians in charge of the treasury and army. If anything flew in the face of the panhellenic reason for invading Asia, it was this action. Mazaeus was his former enemy and the general who almost overcame Parmenion at Gaugamela—it was as "if King George VI had appointed Rommel after the Battle of El Alamein to be his Viceroy in India."[17] Alexander's action was a pragmatic attempt to reconcile the Persians to Macedonian rule and conformed to a pattern that began as early as his arrangements for Lydia in 334, when he took political, military, and financial obligations from the hands of just one man. Nevertheless, the native satraps were hardly won over by their new ruler, as their frequent opposition to him testifies.

ADMINISTERING A MULTICULTURAL EMPIRE

Alexander never proclaimed himself Great King, yet in calling himself King of Asia he was as much an absolute monarch as any Persia ruler.[18] That did not mean that the subject peoples automatically accepted his rule. In addition to ensuring his military superiority in Asia, Alexander had to attend to the actual governance of his realm, no easy task given its geographical size and multicultural diversity. Moreover, his empire was continually shifting its frontiers and absorbing new peoples because he never stopped conquering. That meant that he faced opposition throughout his reign, from Persia to India, from his subjects as well as his own men who wanted to return home. These inherent problems and challenges impeded efficient administration and uniting the different peoples, challenges that exist in the West today when it comes to "nation-building" or trying to construct a united and national identity.[19]

Alexander has been criticized for the way he administered his empire because he could not bring about a structure that was efficacious and maintained stability in the areas he had conquered.[20] In truth, any empire this size posed problems and had major handicaps, as even Persian rulers recognized, which is why Darius I introduced the satrapal system. The satraps had supreme authority in their satrapies, controlling their treasury and army, and had only to ensure that they paid the satrapy's taxes to the Great King and provide troops for him when needed. Alexander knew of the satrapal system well before he invaded Asia and had no intention of dismantling it, but by necessity he had to introduce some significant modifications to it the farther east he marched.

In keeping with the apparent symbolism of "spear-won territory," Alexander appointed satraps from among his own men to govern the western satrapies, men such as Calas of Hellespontine Phrygia and Asander of Lydia. As he marched eastward he sometimes added a conquered area to an existing satrapy, such as Paphlagonia, which he made part of Hellespontine Phrygia in 333. Not every appointee was a general. In 332 he made one of his royal bodyguards, Balacrus, satrap of Cilicia. These initial military appointments were to be expected because Alexander had to protect his rear and lines of communication with the West. He deviated slightly from this policy in Caria, appointing his adopted mother, Ada, as satrap, presumably because of their relationship. To be on the safe side, though, he entrusted Ptolemy with all the military forces of the satrapy, so Ada was clearly given only civilian power.

After Gaugamela and throughout his campaigns in Central Asia and India Alexander tapped local aristocrats as satraps in earnest at least until 329. The first was Mazaeus in 330, the former satrap of Cilicia and Syria, to whom he assigned Babylonia. Later we find Abulites of Susiana, Phrasaortes of Persis, Astaspes of Carmania, Oxydates of Media, Satibarzanes and Arsaces of Areia, and Artabazus of Bactria, to name but a few.[21] Involving foreigners in his administration provided continuity of rule because they had enjoyed influential positions before; further, they had the same social and religious customs and spoke the same language and local dialects as the ordinary people. Since their power would be dependent on Alexander's favor, he expected that they would be loyal to him and help the people grow accustomed to Macedonian rule.

On the other hand, he could not allow them to continue to wield the same authority, especially in financial and military affairs. In Lydia he had diluted satrapal power by dividing civil, financial, and military affairs among three men, and in Caria and Egypt he had likewise kept military power in Macedonian hands. He continued with this structure, whereby native satraps had responsibility only in civil affairs while his own men controlled the troops and later the treasuries. Thus Mazaeus had the title satrap of Babylonia, but Apollodorus of Amphipolis and Agathon of Pydna were in charge of the manpower and garrison, and Asclepiodorus (who was either Macedonian or Greek) was in charge of collecting the tribute. In this way Alexander integrated foreigners into his administration while protecting his money and manpower. This practical innovation made perfect sense, but it is not a surprise that the native satraps, who were no more than titular figureheads, bitterly resented the curtailment of their power.

To streamline taxation collection and management Alexander introduced the new position of imperial treasurer in his administrative hierarchy. As he accumulated more money and treasure from the satrapal cities, it made sense to have an official who would have oversight over all imperial finances and liaise directly with the satraps and financial officers. Philoxenus and Coeranus seem to have shared this new position, but after 331 only one man held it, Alexander's boyhood friend Harpalus. This was the same man who had fled before Issus in 333 to Greece, but by 331 Alexander had forgiven him, and he returned to the court. At first Harpalus was headquartered at Ecbatana (where he oversaw the massive sum of 180,000 talents of gold), but eventually he moved to Babylon.

Another measure that cut across administration, security, and trade and communication was Alexander's foundation of cities, which also facilitated the spread of Greek culture in his empire. Although Plutarch credited him with 70 cities, "which helped to repress the barbarian and brutal way of life" throughout Asia, probably no more than half a dozen were actual poleis with civic buildings, a regional marketplace where people would buy and sell their wares, a theater, and a gymnasium.[22] Of these the most famous and influential was Alexandria in Egypt, founded in 331. The vast majority were military outposts, with garrison troops that could be deployed to trouble spots at a moment's notice or populated by veteran soldiers and locals who kept the peace and Macedonian influence in their areas. Here Alexander was likely following his father's practice of establishing defensive settlements in problem areas—in Philip's case along his northwest frontier in 345 to check the Illyrians. Alexander's cities also indicate that he did not think that his satrapal arrangements would be enough to maintain his authority and ensure passivity. It is no coincidence that after Alexandria his next foundations were in the most troublesome spots of his empire, Bactria and Sogdiana (Afghanistan), or that they were mostly garrison settlements.[23] The first was Alexandria in Areia (near Herat), founded in the aftermath of a revolt by Satibarzanes in 330; later ones included Alexandria in Arachosia (Kandahar), Alexandria in Caucaso (Begram), Alexandria Eschate (Khujand, formerly Leninabad), and Alexandria on the Oxus (Ai-Khanoum).

Alexander called himself King of Asia, but he was a conqueror, with no legitimate claim to the Persian throne. He allowed all Persians their religion but never understood the intimate bond that tied the satraps to the Great King via their common worship of the Zoroastrian god of light, Ahura Mazda, the supreme deity in the Persian pantheon. There was no similar connection between Alexander and the native satraps he appointed, nor could there ever have been unless he converted to the native religion—as anathema to him as it would have been to his men. He came to disregard his subjects' religious beliefs, as when he ordered the quenching of all sacred fires on the death of Hephaestion in 324, which caused outrage, for this solemn act was reserved only for the passing of a Great King. Far from reconciling the people to his rule, Alexander was alienating them.

Thus the Persians—and later the Bactrians and Indians—always perceived Alexander as the invader and strove to resist him at every opportunity they could.[24] They resented his policy of founding cities in their areas, with their influx of Greek and Macedonian populations. They even hated the coins that were struck at mints in Asia after Issus that exploited Greek and Persian religion. In particular was the silver tetradrachm, which had on its obverse a youthful Heracles head and on its reverse Zeus sitting on a throne with a scepter in his left hand and an eagle on his right hand. The young Heracles, one of Alexander's ancestors and a god worshiped in Asia, evoked the young Alexander, just as the seated Zeus identified the king with the seated figure of the Persian god Ba'al. In some places—Sidon, Cilicia, and Babylonia, for example—the locals had to discontinue minting their own coins for those of Alexander or at least remove any local identification from them—they thus became anonymous.[25]

On his return from India in 325 Alexander was forced to remove and even execute a number of disloyal satraps and in their place appoint his own men. Ultimately, although he used high-level foreigners in his administration, drafted native troops into his ranks (especially from Central Asia), adopted aspects of Persian dress, and took on some Persian customs to endear himself to his subjects, his measures never appealed to either the natives or his own men. No one wants to be conquered, and in the end his rule was anchored only in military power. In some respects this was not his fault because he had to grapple with the stresses and challenges posed by subject peoples far beyond the Greek mainland. He had to learn as he went along, and his arrangements show a desire to create an effective administrative structure that would last in the long run.

Where Alexander fell down was not in what he tried to do—or achieved—but, rather, how he went about it. He did not fully take into account or properly understand social customs and religious beliefs, and that cost him dearly. The problems he encountered may shed light on contemporary problems in this or any culturally diverse region of the world striving to be united, and the hard lessons he learned should serve as timely warnings to modern makers of strategy. Here it is worthwhile quoting from a Pentagon study of 2002, which used the Macedonian Empire and imperial Rome as case studies for the ongoing military predominance of the United States and concluded that Alexander "led his army to innumerable tactical and operational victories, but his leadership was based more on a 'cult of personality' than on a sustainable institutional structure."[26]

SUSA

From Babylon the army marched the 200 miles southeast to the next royal capital, Susa, on the border of Iraq and Iran. Their journey took 20 days, and along the way they were joined by 15,000 fresh Macedonian, Thracian, and mercenary troops, taking the total number of the army to about 50,000. After Gaugamela Alexander had sent one of his officers, Philoxenus, to secure Susa, so when the king arrived there, in December 331, the satrap Abulites surrendered without a fight. Susa yielded the largest haul of money to date—40,000 talents of gold and silver bullion and 9,000 talents of Persian gold darics. Alexander eagerly confiscated this money, but his action was a sign that he did not properly understand that royal capitals were not simply repositories of money but part of the Great Kings' administration and were religious centers.

The wealth of the Persian kings was proved also by the vastness of their palaces and their rich trappings and furnishings—at Susa, Alexander found a dining room that also housed 5,000 talents of gold, and atop the King's bed was a fancy golden vine inlaid with precious stones. The wealth and finer things of life affected the Macedonians. Alexander began to wear a combination of Macedonian and purple (the color of the Persian court) clothing, while his Companions wore purple hats and cloaks with a purple border. They used myrrh rather than ordinary oil when bathing, and Hagnon of Teos was said to have worn silver nails in his boots, and Leonnatus to dust himself with Egyptian powder before wrestling.

In a room in the palace Alexander came across the artworks that Xerxes had stolen from Athens during the Persian Wars. Among them was the famous statue of the late sixth-century Athenian tyrannicides Harmodius and Aristogeiton, which was meant to symbolize democracy as the best form of government. Alexander returned them all to Athens. In effect he had achieved the aims of the panhellenic invasion, and his success was brought more sharply into focus when he sat on the throne of Darius under its golden canopy. Great Kings appear to have been tall men, however, and Alexander's feet did not reach the ground. To save him from this embarrassment one of his pages quickly slid a nearby table, from which Darius was said to have eaten, under his dangling feet—thus Darius's dinner table became the King of Asia's footstool.

It was now midwinter, and the passes through the 15,000-foot-high Zagros Mountains would have been covered in snow. Normally, travelers would wait until spring when the temperatures rose above freezing and the snow melted, but with Darius still on the loose this was not the time for normality. Alexander appointed Abulites satrap of Susa, with Macedonians in charge of the army and treasury, and left for Persepolis. Despite the freezing-cold weather and cumbersome snow, the men set off over the mountains. They made good progress until they reached Uxiana, southeast of Susa. Here they routed a force of Uxians that had attempted to block their way. Not long after another Uxian tribe, which lived in the upper region of Uxiana, demanded a fee to allow the Macedonians passage through their territory. That was the last costly mistake they ever made: Alexander's men mowed them down. Since the Uxians did not have a monetary economy, those who survived the carnage had to pay Alexander an annual tribute of 600 horses and mules and 30,000 cattle, goats, and sheep.

BATTLE AT THE PERSIAN GATES

The army's rate of progress must have made Alexander impatient because by the border with Persis—possibly at modern Fahlian—he divided the troops into two groups, one led by Parmenion and the other by himself. His intention was to march at speed over the Zagros Mountains via the Persian Gates to Persepolis while Parmenion with the Thessalians and other troops would take the slower-moving baggage train along an easier but less direct route via Kazerun and Shiraz to Persepolis. By the time Parmenion reached Persepolis, the king predicted, he would have taken the city and so control all Persis. With 20,000 troops, including the Agrianians, Alexander set off, but he found his route blocked at the Persian Gates, a narrow gorge six miles long and passable only by foot, by Ariobarzanes, the satrap of Persis. Ariobarzanes had with him as many as 40,000 infantry and 7,000 cavalry, so he had evidently received word that Alexander had traversed the Zagros Mountains in winter. He posted his troops atop both sides of the gorge to permit Darius the necessary time to raise another army and do battle with the invaders once more, on the plain of Persepolis.[27]

Alexander was in no mood for delays and gave the order to attack, but in doing so he fell into an enemy trap. Ariobarzanes knew the terrain better than the Macedonians; as they entered the gorge they were pelted with missiles, maimed and killed by large boulders, and fired on by archers from the heights. As the bodies began to pile up in the narrow pass Alexander had no choice but to retreat. Unfortunately the troops at the rear of his line, unaware of what was happening ahead of them, kept pushing forward and became entangled with their comrades trying to escape. Some tried to turn around but fell down, while others were pushed over in what must have been total chaos. They became even easier targets for the enemy archers, who shot more of them to death as they struggled to escape from the gorge. Eventually it was all over, but Alexander was forced to leave his dead and dying behind, a major failing on the part of a general.

An entire month went by while Ariobarzanes kept Alexander's men pinned down. The king was anxious that he would not reach Persepolis before Parmenion and might lose the baggage train and its escort to Persian attacks. His luck changed, however, when he captured a local shepherd, who told him of a rocky, 12-mile path over the Boloru Pass that would bring him out behind Ariobarzanes's position. (There is an interesting affinity here with the treacherous Greek who, in 480, informed Xerxes of a path that would take him behind the Greek troops at Thermopylae.) Alexander wasted no time. At nightfall he ordered Philotas (Parmenion's son) to lead 3,000 men along an alternate path to a point about halfway along the enemy line. They were to stay there and wait for Alexander's signal to attack. The king took more troops across the path over the Boloru Pass, which was no easy feat: for the rest of that night, the whole of the next day, and the following night they picked their way over the rocks, forced to go slow because of the arduous terrain and suffering from the heat during the day. Nevertheless, by dawn on the second day they had made it.

Ariobarzanes did not realize what Alexander was up to, perhaps because he had left behind Craterus with the remaining two battalions of infantry and 500 cavalry with orders to burn extra fires at night and raise as much of a din during the day so that it looked—and sounded—as though the entire army was still camped at the mouth of the pass. Ariobarzanes only knew that something was wrong when he heard a shrill trumpet blast early one morning from behind his position that resonated off the rocks all around. That was Alexander's prearranged signal to his other commanders. While he charged the Persians from behind, Craterus attacked from the front, and Philotas from the middle. Ptolemy, bringing up the rear, cut down any Persians who escaped the battle.[28]

Ariobarzanes was completely taken by surprise, and his men were cut to pieces. Alexander's victory was another example of his cunning and swift execution, though had he not been told of the path behind Ariobarzanes's position the standoff at the Persian Gates may have forced him to retreat and find a different route to rendezvous with Parmenion. Exactly what happened to Ariobarzanes is unknown. Either he charged the enemy when he realized all was lost and died heroically, or he escaped but then surrendered, or he broke away with a small force of cavalry and infantry to Persepolis, where he was denied entry by the city's commander, Tiridates, and died fighting Alexander and his approaching troops.

The Macedonians entered Persepolis at the end of January 330. Dubbed "the most hated city in Asia" by Diodorus,[29] Persepolis, the ceremonial religious center and the traditional heart of the Persian Empire, now belonged to Alexander.

"THE MOST HATED CITY IN ASIA"

Alexander made his headquarters in the enormous royal palace, once home to Xerxes, which stood a little distance outside the walls of the city (probably at Istakhr). The palace's elaborate friezes depicting embassies from Ethiopia, India, Central Asia, and Asia Minor, offering their gifts and tribute to the Great King, brought home the fact that he was now to all intents and purposes Great King. Alexander also took control of the city's treasury, which might have housed as many as 120,000 gold talents. He sent the majority of this sum back to Ecbatana on a convoy of 7,000 camels and pack animals and kept the rest with him, in keeping with his father's practice of a rolling economy to help finance his next campaigns.

Tiridates had surrendered Persepolis, but Alexander did not take that into account. On behalf of the League of Corinth he gave orders to his men to do as they wished in the city in revenge for the casualties and looting that the Persians had inflicted on the Greeks 150 years earlier. For a whole day the Macedonians killed military and civilian men indiscriminately and raped the women before enslaving them, together with their children. Some inhabitants even committed suicide to escape the horror, an indication that this type of abuse was known to be the natural corollary of the fall of a city.[30] The invaders pillaged from every house in the city and even at times fought each other over expensive artworks. Persepolis paid a terrible and unprecedented price when it came to Alexander's treatment of the royal cities—and with his blessing.

The Macedonian army spent over three months in Persepolis, during which time Parmenion with the slower-moving baggage train arrived. Alexander also conducted a brief and obscure campaign against the Mardi of southern Persis, probably to keep his men fit and active. In addition, he visited Pasargadae, first capital of the Persian Empire, where its founder, Cyrus the Great, had been buried after his death in battle in Scythia in 530. Then, not long before the Macedonian army left Persepolis, the palace famously burned to the ground.[31] The palace's symbolic importance was so great that at an earlier meeting between Alexander and his senior staff to debate its fate Parmenion was said to have urged him to do nothing in case of a native revolt, especially as Darius and Bessus still posed a threat. What had already happened to the city of Persepolis was bad enough, but if Alexander still wanted to endear himself to the Iranian aristocracy as King of Asia, he could not let anything happen to their ceremonial palace. Whether anything was formally decided is unknown, but one night the palace suddenly caught fire.

The evidence for the burning is contradictory. One explanation, perhaps too fanciful to be credible, is that Alexander and some of his men had been drinking heavily when an Athenian courtesan named Thais (later Ptolemy's wife) urged them to set fire to the palace for the looting and burning of her city in the Persian Wars. The drunken Macedonians grabbed torches and set alight the tapestries on the walls and the wooden furniture and then sat along the eastern wall watching the flames engulf the palace.[32] More likely is that Alexander deliberately ordered the destruction of the palace to proclaim the end of Achaemenid rule and the beginning of the era of a new ruler, one who would not be greeting his subjects in the great halls of Persepolis as was their custom.[33] The palace's destruction was in keeping with a pattern he had begun in 335 when he razed Thebes: out with the old, in with the new. The demolishment of the palace is one reason why Alexander is still held in contempt by the Zoroastrians of Iran today.

The propaganda element to the palace's destruction was obvious and, given the timing, might even be tied to the message it conveyed to mainland Greece, where Agis III of Sparta was attempting to call the Greeks to arms against the Macedonian hegemony. If Alexander could destroy Persepolis, what might he order Antipater to inflict on any mainland city that threw its weight behind Sparta?

EVENTS ON THE GREEK MAINLAND

Alexander had limited contact with the Greeks while he was in Asia and relied on Antipater to maintain Macedonian rule.[34] Under Antipater's stewardship the Greeks remained passive—presumably they had learned from the brutal treatment of Thebes in 335 that resistance was futile, especially after Alexander's game-changing victories at Issus in 333 and Gaugamela in 331. Even the fervently outspoken Demosthenes was a shadow of his former self.[35] He had apparently returned to his earlier career as a speechwriter because several of his private speeches were written in the 320s. He had initially prayed that the Persians would defeat and kill the young king—Aeschines sneeringly remarked that Demosthenes expected "Alexander would be trampled under the hoofs of the Persian cavalry at Issus."[36] The king's victories alerted Demosthenes, as it did the other Greeks, that Macedonian rule was here to stay; their world would be utterly different from the past.

A threat to the Macedonian hegemony did come in 331 from the Spartan king Agis III, who had previously solicited the financial and military assistance of Persian satraps in a bid to reassert Sparta's dominance in the Peloponnese. In that year he took his war to the Greek mainland and called the Greeks to arms against Macedonia.[37] He was taken seriously—in Athens, for example, there was a long debate at an Assembly at which Demosthenes spoke, although his speech has not survived. It appears that he had initially been in favor of Agis's war but then changed his mind, given the tight hold Macedonia exercised over Greece, and he had no desire to see Antipater's wrath descend on Athens as Alexander's had on Thebes. Therefore, with the support of the general Phocion, he convinced the Athenians not to join with Agis. His advice turned out to be right.

In the end, only a handful of Greek states threw their weight behind Agis, perhaps because most read between the lines in Alexander's burning of Persepolis, as he had intended. Agis hired 10,000 mercenaries with money that the satrap Pharnabazus had given him and managed to defeat a Macedonian force under Corragus. His victory brought a furious Antipater at the head of 40,000 troops into the Peloponnese in April or May 330. In a bitter battle at Megalopolis he defeated Agis's army, killing half of its number, including Agis, to the loss of 3,500 of his own men.

The League of Corinth met to decide how to punish Sparta and its supporters. It fined the Spartan allies heavily but decided to refer Sparta's actual fate to Alexander himself. Possibly the council members did so because they thought that Alexander would expect them to raze Sparta, and they had no desire for that. To everyone's astonishment Alexander pardoned the Spartans, insisting only that they pay 120 talents to the people of Megalopolis for besieging their city and surrender 50 noblemen as hostages to him. Sparta most likely now became a member of the league. Possibly Alexander was swayed by a Spartan embassy that begged him for mercy and cannily brought him the news that the Spartans had voted him divine honors.[38] By now, a year after his visit to Siwah, his pretensions to personal divinity were well known, and the Spartans were quick to capitalize on them.

Agis's war was the only spike in the flat line of the Macedonian hegemony of Greece until Alexander's death in 323, when the Greeks again unsuccessfully revolted. However, in 330 Athens was a scene of activity when the famous "Crown trial" took place, in which Aeschines finally got his chance to attack Demosthenes in court.[39] In 336 a man named Ctesiphon had proposed that Demosthenes be awarded a gold crown (his third), among other things for his services to the city. Aeschines had indicted Ctesiphon on various legal grounds as well as for having a flawed rationale for the award: because Philip had defeated the Greeks at Chaeronea, Demosthenes's anti-Macedonian policy had therefore hardly been to Athens's benefit. When Philip was assassinated in the same year Aeschines had let the matter drop, but now, in 330, he rekindled the charge against Ctesiphon, principally because he thought that Demosthenes had mishandled the Athenian response to Agis.

Aeschines's prosecution speech (*Against Ctesiphon*) survives, most of which is a massive attack on Demosthenes's career and anti-Macedonian policy from the Peace of Philocrates to the war of Agis. Ctesiphon responded with a short defense speech, and then, as Athenian law permitted, Demosthenes responded to Aeschines's speech with his famous *On the Crown*, which is widely regarded as his masterpiece. His principal argument was that his policy was justified because, even though it failed, it was the right and only one to put forward against a tyrant like Philip, who wan ted to conquer Greece. Any other policy, such as Aeschines's maintaining peace with Philip, would have been ineffectual and wrong, as Philip's actions proved. Yes, the Greeks were defeated at Chaeronea, but, Demosthenes claimed, they had lost fighting for the noblest of Greek causes: freedom. They were, then, far from being losers and could hold their heads high and compare themselves with their ancestors who fought the Persians for freedom. The jurors overwhelmingly acquitted Demosthenes.

In the meantime Darius was assassinated in Asia. His death rescued Alexander from the problem of either killing or imprisoning the deposed ruler if he had captured him alive, but then Bessus declared himself Great King, forcing Alexander to turn the invasion of Persia in an entirely new direction.

11.

THE WAR IN AFGHANISTAN

D ARIUS WOULD HAVE RECEIVED news of the events in Persepolis in Ecbatana (Hamadan), the capital of Media. The sacking of the city and burning of the palace sounded his personal death knell: gone was his last chance of uniting the people, and he fled eastward with only 3,000 cavalry and 7,000 infantry into Afghanistan. Alexander heard of his flight at Gabae (Isfahan). He ordered Parmenion to take the remainder of his men and the baggage train to Ecbatana and with 20,000 soldiers took off in pursuit of Darius.

THE DEATH OF DARIUS

Alexander intended to capture Darius west of the Caspian Gates. That meant moving fast through ovenlike temperatures and inhospitable terrain, but thanks to a series of forced marches over 10 days he was able to cross 200 miles of the Great Salt Desert to Rhagae (Rey, just south of Tehran), only 50 miles from the Caspian Gates. A number of his men had collapsed from dehydration and heat exhaustion, and horses had even died, but Alexander was not going to allow Darius to escape his clutches again. He pushed on, inspiring his troops to follow him by sharing in their suffering. When they arrived at the Caspian Gates they discovered that Darius had managed to evade them after all; disappointed, Alexander allowed his men a much-needed break of one week.

The brutal march continued. Two days after leaving the Caspian Gates the Macedonians had arrived at Choarene (Khar) on the Great Salt

Desert's shore. Their grueling pace was working in their favor though, as an increasing number of eastern satraps were withdrawing their support for Darius and his own men were deserting him. The Great King would not survive much longer. Late one night at the oasis of Thara (Semnan), two deserters, a Babylonian nobleman named Bagistanes and Antibelus, a son of Mazaeus, told Alexander that Bessus, Nabarzanes (the Persian chiliarch), and Barsaentes, the satrap of Drangiana and Arachosia (the region south of Areia that makes up much of modern Afghanistan), had deposed Darius. Nabarzanes had suggested that Darius should bestow his title on Bessus, who had blood ties to the Achaemenids, because he might have better luck rousing the natives against the Macedonians. If this worked out, then Bessus would renounce his title and restore it to Darius. Needless to say Darius would have none of this plan—but to no avail: he was deposed and put in chains. Bessus then declared himself Great King—taking the name Artaxerxes V—and donned the upright tiara, the symbol of Persian kingship.

Despite the late hour Alexander handpicked 500 of his fittest men and set off across the desolate Dasht-i-Kavir salt desert. The rest of the troops were to follow as quickly as they could. Alexander marched nonstop until noon the next day, when the searing afternoon heat of the desert forced them to rest or suffer further heat stroke and exhaustion. The coolness of the evening saw them on the march again, with no rest breaks throughout the night, and by dawn they were approaching Hecatompylus (Qumis), the capital of Parthia, where Darius and his captors had been sighted.

The news of Alexander's astonishing trek through the desert sufficiently spooked Bessus and Nabarzanes to leave Hecatompylus before he arrived. Bessus retreated into Bactria, and Nabarzanes to Hyrcania. In desperation, Satibarzanes, the satrap of Areia, and Barsaentes stabbed Darius, with either knives or javelins, and fled to their respective areas. There is no question that Bessus and Nabarzanes were aware of what the others had decided to do to Darius, and so they were accomplices to the Great King's murder. We have conflicting versions of Darius's last moments: either he was dead when Alexander came across his body or he was barely alive but managed to ask a Macedonian soldier who found him, Polystratus, for water. Polystratus got him water and summoned Alexander, who found Darius dead. Either way, the assassination of a Great King was a heinous offense, and it is a fitting tribute to Alexander's respect for Darius that he ordered his body transported to Persepolis for ceremonial burial.

The Macedonian Empire now stretched from Pella to Hecatompylus and included Syria and Egypt. Bessus's usurpation of royal power posed an obvious threat to its security, so Alexander had no choice but to hunt him down in Bactria. However, all his men wanted to do was to return home—some of them even had expectantly packed up their belongings. At what must have been a tense meeting in Hecatompylus they put their objections about pursuing Bessus to Alexander. In response, he spoke of the danger from Bessus, sensationally declaring that if they returned home now, the rebel satrap could raise an army to invade Greece, thereby undoing everything that he and even Philip had achieved. In the end, Alexander won over his troops, helped in part by a cash incentive to each man that totaled over 12,000 talents, paid for out of his own resources.

BACTRIA: A NEW WAR

The Macedonian invasion of Bactria heralded a new phase in the offensive in Asia, for now Alexander would be fighting Bactrians, who had played only a minor role in the Persian Wars.[1] The burning of Persepolis and the death of Darius, the last Achaemenid king, had achieved the aims of the invasion that Philip had first outlined to the League of Corinth in 337. Bessus's threat to the stability of Alexander's empire was not the Greeks' problem, but in taking his army into Bactria Alexander was moving well beyond anything the Greeks or his father had envisaged. The young king's *pothos* (desire or yearning) was to create an empire that was without parallel, to outdo everyone before him including even Cyrus the Great, and to ensure his fame long after his death.[2] Even at this time Alexander may have intended to travel to the Southern (Indian) Ocean to determine whether his old teacher Aristotle was right when he described India as a small triangular promontory on this ocean. These motives explain why he discharged some of the soldiers provided by the League of Corinth, who went home with a generous bonus; those who remained were now enlisted in his army as mercenaries. The composition of the Macedonian army was also changing. That autumn (of 330) 300 cavalry and 2,600 infantry from Lydia joined the Macedonian army. These were the first of the recruits Alexander had had trained in Macedonian tactics even as early as his campaigns in Asia Minor. The following year 1,000 cavalry and 8,000 infantry arrived from Lycia and Syria. Unfortunately, Alexander's thirst for fighting, relentless march eastward, and integration of foreigners into his army and administration still proved to be his undoing.

With his men doubtless grumbling the army left Hecatompylus and marched north to Zadracarta (Sari), capital of Hyrcania, by the southern shore of the Caspian Sea. While en route Nabarzanes (an assassin of Darius) wrote to Alexander begging for mercy and offering his surrender. This unexpected event gave Alexander and his men cause to assume that Bessus was not as powerful after all, an assumption that received further support when Artabazus (father of Barsine) and other Persian dignitaries came to Zadracarta seeking Alexander's friendship. They had in their armies some 1,500 Greek mercenaries, whom he incorporated into his ranks.

Alexander's troop numbers were increasing, but not so his horses. In the past few months a goodly number of these animals had died from the forced pursuits as well as the intense heat. With this in mind he invaded the territory of the Mardi peoples of the Zagros (not to be confused with the Mardi in southern Persis, against whom he had previously campaigned), who were known for their horses and cavalry skills. In reprisal the Mardi kidnapped Bucephalas, Alexander's horse, but quickly returned him when Alexander vowed to slaughter all of them and lay waste to their lands. They sent envoys to him who would have brought presents, presumably including horses, which replenished Alexander's cavalry numbers.

When Nabarzanes surrendered to Alexander in Zadracarta he gave the king various presents including the eunuch Bagoas. Alexander was so taken with this extraordinarily beautiful man that he entered into a lengthy sexual relationship with him.[3] Zadracarta was also the venue for Alexander's alleged encounter with Thalestris, the Amazon Queen, who wanted to bear his child.[4] She seems to have been more attracted to Alexander by his reputation than anything else, for his short stature surprised her, and she said that it did not live up to his "illustrious record."[5] Her insatiable sexual appetite was said to have been too much for him, and after two weeks he bade her leave.

From Zadracarta the Macedonians marched to Susia in Areia, on the crossroads of Bactria to the north, India to the east, and Drangiana to the south. There, Satibarzanes, another of Darius's murderers, submitted to Alexander. His information that Bessus was levying more troops than Alexander had imagined, including many from the tribes living beyond the river Oxus (Amu Darya), which marked the southern boundary of Bactria, motivated him to chase Bessus as quickly as he could. Leaving behind Satibarzanes as satrap with a small garrison of 40 javelin men at the capital Artacoana, Alexander set off along the Kopet Dag massif. His treatment of Satibarzanes shows that he intended to continue using native satraps when and where he could.[6] He had been marching three or four days and had covered about 70 miles when he received the news that Satibarzanes had thrown his weight behind Bessus after all: he had murdered the Macedonian garrison and engineered the revolt of Areia.

At all costs Alexander had to protect his rear. He immediately took a contingent of troops and in just two days was back at Artacoana. A startled Satibarzanes took flight with 2,000 cavalry into Bactria. The other troops with him were not so lucky. They took refuge on a nearby hill, but an impatient Alexander set it on fire, killing them all. With Areia now his again, Alexander installed Arsaces, another Persian nobleman, as satrap and returned to his main army. It was also at this time that the rebellious Barsaentes (also one of Darius's murderers), satrap of Drangiana and Arachosia, was apprehended as he fled toward the Indus; Alexander wasted no time executing him, thereby removing another potential threat to the Macedonians.

At Phrada (Farah), the capital of Drangiana, Alexander halted and decided to rest his men for the remainder of that winter. Here he was faced with a conspiracy against his life that brought to the surface the critical mood of his men toward his growing orientalism.

ALEXANDER'S ORIENTALISM

The Macedonian troops came to believe that Alexander's whole outlook was tainted with orientalism and that he had little regard for them or their customs. The impact of 30,000 Macedonian-trained native youths (*epigonoi*) joining the army in 324 was the final straw, as Arrian relates:

> They say that the arrival of the *Epigonoi* hurt the Macedonians; it was as though Alexander was doing all he could to make himself less reliant on his own people. Alexander's Median style of clothes also brought them no little anguish, it is said, and the Persian-style weddings were reportedly not to the liking of the majority, either—liked not even by some of the grooms, despite the great honor of being put on the same footing as the king. There was also the case of Peucestas, the satrap of Persis, who adopted both Persian dress and language; that rankled because Alexander was pleased with his playing the barbarian. And then there was the matter of the cavalry of the Bactrians, Sogdianians and Arachotians being enrolled in the Companion cavalry.... That hurt too, as did the addition of a fifth hipparchy [cavalry commander]. This was not entirely composed of barbarians, but when the entire cavalry force was increased there was an enrollment of barbarian troops for it. Barbarian offices were also appointed to the *agema* [royal bodyguard].... All this was offensive to the Macedonians. It looked as if Alexander was developing a completely barbarian mentality, and placing Macedonian culture and the Macedonians themselves at a low level of esteem.[7]

The men's gravest dissatisfaction with Alexander was not with his continual marching with no end in sight or his suspicion and resentment of critics among his senior staff or even his belief in his personal divinity. It was the fact that he was changing from a traditional Macedonian warrior king into more of an oriental potentate before their eyes. True, he continued to perform his political and religious duties and lead from the front in battle, but the men resented the way he adopted Persian customs and favored the conquered.

The most obvious change was Alexander's manner of dress, which he first showed off in Zadracarta. He opted for a mixture of the Persian blue-and-white royal diadem, a purple tunic with white stripes, and a girdle with the Macedonian cloak and *kausia* (the flat, wide-brimmed hat). Possibly the diadem at this time was merely a band of cloth worn around his head or even around his *kausia*. He was trying to find a form of dress that would suit both his Asian subjects and his own men by representing both cultures, just as today, for example, the clothing of Hamid Karzai of Afghanistan combines three different regions of his country: the *chapan* (silk robe), worn by Uzbek and Turkman tribesman in the north; the *peran* (baggy trousers) and *tunban* (tunic), worn in the south; and the *karakul* (lambskin hat), worn in the city of Kabul. However, Alexander's men resented the way their king combined the different forms of cultural attire, just as the Persians felt slighted that he stopped short of wearing the traditional Persian long-sleeved robe and trousers. In the end his compromise in dress pleased neither side.

It seems that Alexander also encouraged his Persian subjects to perform *proskynesis* (genuflection) before him, as they had done before the Great King. This was an act that to Macedonians and Greeks smacked of worship of the living individual, and they believed that it was sacrilege. The king seems not to have been in tune with their scorn, because he would soon attempt to enforce the custom on them, albeit unsuccessfully. Alexander also began to keep a harem of 365 women, one for each day (or night) of the year, which was part of the trappings of a Persian king but again flouted Macedonian tradition. For some time he had been integrating foreign troops into his army and high-level natives in his administration, as either satraps or other officials. He also used two royal seals, the official Macedonian one for business to do with the western or European half of his empire and Darius's signet ring for matters concerning Asia, as well as Persian officers at court such as the royal usher (*eisange-leus*), taster (*edeatros*), and rod-bearers (*rhabdophoroi*).

Two seals (which meant in effect two courts), a proliferation of Persian court officials, foreigners in the army, and the mishmash of two types of dress only served to exaggerate the differences between the two cultures rather than reconcile them. Criticism of his orientalism continued, especially among the "Old Guard," which included Parmenion, Alexander's most senior general; Parmenion's son Philotas, the commander of the

Companion Cavalry; and Cleitus, who had saved Alexander's life at the Granicus River. These and other men had served with Philip and remembered how grounded in tradition that king had been.

Not everyone, though, was against Alexander's new look or the ways he favored his Asian subjects. He tapped his boyhood friend Hephaestion for the majority of his dealings with the Persians, presumably because Hephaestion had a similar attitude. Moreover, some of the Companions wore Persian silver studs on their boots and purple-and-white cloaks, used perfume, and fitted Persian harnesses on their horses. The elements of Persian dress infused with the Macedonian continued to be worn after Alexander's death, as the "Alexander sarcophagus" shows (p. 170 with Figure 22). This sculpture depicts Companions wearing a combination of Macedonian cloaks and Persian long-sleeved tunics with bracelets (which would have been gold) on their wrists.[8]

It is easy to blame Alexander for the anger that his actions generated among his men. At the same time it must be remembered that he was trying to be as practical as possible in dealing with a completely new challenge: ruling a vast multicultural subject population the likes of which no Macedonian king had ever seen. In this regard we have no one to compare him with—either before his reign, for Philip never invaded Asia, or after it, since the Macedonian Empire was torn apart on his death. We can call the manner of his clothing divisive, but he may have believed that he had come up with a genuine form of compromise, even the "standard" dress for a king of Macedonia and King of Asia. Still, he knew that he would face anger from his men. Perhaps that is why he began to hold more drinking parties and encouraged the rank and file of his army to marry the Asian women with whom they had been living for years to lessen the growing tension.[9] Ultimately he was unsuccessful—but perhaps not for want of trying.

THE PHILOTAS AFFAIR

While the Macedonian army was at Phrada in the winter of 330–329 one of the more puzzling events in Alexander's reign took place: the so-called conspiracy of Philotas.[10] A Companion named Dimnus (about whom nothing is known) decided to assassinate Alexander, although why is a mystery. Dimnus told his lover, Nicomachus, of his plan, who in turn told his brother, Cebalinus. Without missing a beat Cebalinus informed Philotas of the plot. Because of his rank Philotas had automatic access to Alexander, who regulated his court carefully and admitted only a select few into his presence without any prior invite.[11] Cebalinus wanted him to take the news to the king at once. Philotas had only recently rejoined the army because he had had to make funeral arrangements for his brother Nicanor (the commander of the hypaspists), who had died during Alexander's operations against Satibarzanes. Perhaps still grieving over the loss of his brother, Philotas may have conducted only a cursory investigation into Cebalinus's claims. At any rate he apparently decided that Dimnus posed little to no threat to the king. After another day of prompting him a frustrated Cebalinus took the matter to one of the royal pages, Metron, who smuggled him into the royal tent, where he finally alerted Alexander that he was at risk.

Alexander immediately gave orders to seize Dimnus (who stabbed himself to death) and the other conspirators. Only one ancient writer (Curtius) gives their names; if he is correct, there were nine other men, including Demetrius, a royal bodyguard no less.[12] There was no evidence against Philotas, but nonetheless Alexander ordered his arrest, not for his failure to warn him but as a co-conspirator. After a brief consultation with his senior staff he ordered the army to convene the next day, where he would formally charge Philotas with treason. That day, as Dimnus's corpse lay dramatically on the ground in front of Philotas, none of the other generals supported him, principally because they had never liked his arrogance or boastfulness. After Cebalinus and Metron gave their testimony, which fell far short of implicating Philotas in any conspiracy, the generals followed their king's lead and accused him of treason. Coenus, Philotas's brother-in-law, got so worked up that he wanted to stone him—the traditional execution for treason—on the spot. Philotas defiantly rebutted all their accusations, noting that no one compellingly accused him of treason, and assured Alexander that he had investigated Cebalinus's claim but found that it lacked foundation.

Alexander, however, had clearly decided on Philotas's demise and at one point even criticized him for not speaking in Macedonian (the dialect that seems to have been used on these occasions). A man so contemptuous of even his native tongue, Alexander said, would surely not think twice of betraying his king! Philotas was found guilty of complicity in the plot. That night Alexander ordered Craterus, Hephaestion, and Coenus to torture Philotas until he confessed to this crime and, significantly, implicated his father, Parmenion, in it. The old general at the time was 800 miles away in Ecbatana, oblivious to what was happening in Phrada. They did their work ruthlessly, especially if they were aware, as Plutarch claimed, that Alexander was listening to the goings-on from behind a curtain.[13] The next day a broken Philotas was carried before the army and, along with the other alleged conspirators, stoned to death.

Parmenion was next. Macedonian law dictated that a traitor's family be executed, but Parmenion was no ordinary person. He headed the most powerful faction at the Macedonian court, was enormously popular with the troops, controlled 12,000 men and the vast treasury at Ecbatana, and would seek revenge for what had happened to his son.[14] Alexander might well suffer a backlash of discontent if he still executed him, which perhaps explains why he needed Philotas to give up his father under torture. In that way, the soldiers would have little choice but to accept Parmenion's demise.

So as not to alert Parmenion that anything was amiss, Alexander disguised a Companion, Polydamas, as an Arab and sent him on a racing camel to Ecbatana. He was to deliver a royal letter containing Parmenion's death sentence to the other generals there, Cleander, Sitalces, and Menidas. Polydamas arrived without incident a little under a fortnight later and gave the fateful letter to Cleander, who set up a time for Parmenion to meet with all of them the next morning. Polydamas greeted the senior general and handed him two letters, one from Alexander and the other allegedly from Philotas, as though they were the purpose of his visit. As an unsuspecting Parmenion opened the letter from his son, Polydamas stabbed him in the throat, and the other generals followed suit, jabbing their swords and daggers into every inch of his body. When news of his murder broke the soldiers were ready to riot, but Cleander quickly read out Alexander's letter containing Philotas's so-called confession and subdued them. Nevertheless, he had to give in to their demand to bury Parmenion with full military honors.

Was Philotas innocent or guilty of conspiracy? Was there even a plot in the first place, or, as has been suggested, did Alexander cook up the entire thing to rid himself of Philotas and Parmenion?[15] Fabricating a conspiracy is unlikely because of the numbers of men involved, including the high-ranking Demetrius. Dimnus therefore had a grievance against the king over which he was prepared to kill him. Certainly the danger he posed to Alexander should have been communicated to the king. Philotas's inaction was, then, a serious error of judgment on his part but hardly deserving of execution. Nor was he party to the plot as is sometimes asserted, otherwise Cebalinus would not have approached him in the first place. Possibly Alexander's other generals, who personally disliked Philotas, seized the opportunity afforded by Dimnus's threat to implicate him. Yet, if so, why would Alexander let himself be swayed by them and go on to arrange the death of Parmenion? More likely the reason for Philotas's fall lies with his father's relationship with the king. As one of Philip's Old Guard, Parmenion was always a "Philippian" rather than an "Alexandrian"[16] and not one to bite his tongue over Alexander's changing personality and his questionable military actions. Alexander had needed the support of all of Philip's powerful generals when he first became king in 336, but as time continued and he became his own man, he dispensed with them when he could.[17]

For some years Parmenion had been crossing swords with his king. He had queried Alexander's decision in 334 to cross the Granicus River against the Persian army as soon as the Macedonians arrived there, and he had argued with him in 331 over Darius's offer of ceding his lands west of the Euphrates to Alexander. Worse, he and Philotas had been openly critical of Alexander's mixture of Macedonian and Asian dress and his adoption of the Persian diadem. Alexander might even have recalled the marginalization he suffered in 337 after his father's seventh marriage when Parmenion became one of an inner circle of advisers. Moreover, in the same year Philip and Philotas had heaped stinging and humiliating criticism on him for putting himself forward as husband to Pixodarus's daughter. Alexander had a long memory: once anyone crossed him redemption was impossible, a character flaw that stood in stark contrast to his proverbial generosity and loyalty.[18] It is even possible that he deliberately ignored Parmenion's plea for help at Gaugamela in 331 in the hope that the Persians would finish him off. Parmenion's criticism of his king and popularity with the army were concerns for Alexander, who decided that it was safer to remove him completely. He exploited the opportunity of Dimnus's plot to rid himself of the powerful Parmenion by charging his son with treason, exploiting his unpopularity with the other generals to achieve his ends.

The killing did not stop there. Alexander of Lyncestis, Antipater's son-in-law and the commander of the Thessalian cavalry, the man whom the king had spared shortly after he came to power in 336 but who had been accused of plotting with Darius against Alexander in 333, was finally put to death after three years of house arrest. At least in his case there was evidence of conspiracy. Alexander next assigned Philotas's position as commander of the Companion Cavalry to two men, Hephaestion and the veteran general Cleitus the Black. Slowly but surely Alexander was promoting his boyhood friends to senior positions so that he could surround himself with people more in tune with his grand aspirations.

HUNTING BESSUS

Alexander's dealings with Philotas and Parmenion had held up his pursuit of Bessus, whose flight is alluded to on a fragmentary Aramaic document calling him "Artaxerxes the King."[19] Even though it was now winter Alexander set off from Drangiana and marched northeast through Arachosia toward the Hindu Kush. In the meantime Satibarzanes, who clearly never refused to give up on anything, again roused Areia to revolt. Its satrap, Arsaces, proved completely ineffectual, so Alexander sent Erigyius, Caranus, and the Persian Artabazus back to Areia. In a clash with the rebels Erigyius at last killed the troublesome Satibarzanes, cutting off his head and sending it in a box to Alexander. Stasanor was installed as the new satrap of Areia, but the satrapy long remained a problem area.

By early 329 Alexander had subdued Arachosia, in the process founding Alexandria in Arachosia (Kandahar) and appointing a Macedonian, Menon, as its satrap. In April the army set out for Drapsaca (Kunduz) via the 11,000-foot-high Khawak Pass over the Hindu Kush—which the Greeks called the Caucasus. For over two weeks the men struggled across the pass in trails deep with snow and in atrocious freezing conditions. Many were smitten by frostbite and snow blindness. To make matters worse, in the second week their food ran out, forcing them to eat their pack animals raw because there was no wood to build fires. Eventually they emerged from the pass into northern Afghanistan.

Alexander had deliberately taken the Khawak Pass despite its hardships because he knew that he would surprise Bessus, who was then at Aornus (Tashkurgan) with 7,000 men. He was right. Bessus was flabbergasted when he first learned that the Macedonians were crossing the Hindu Kush in winter but assumed that they would take one of the lower passes into the Oxus Valley. By taking the highest and most eastern pass, however, Alexander had come out only 80 miles west of him. He and his commanders Spitamenes and Oxyartes promptly fled from Bactria across the river Oxus into Sogdiana (Bokhara and Turkestan), the most northeastern province of the Persian Empire. There they intended to fight Alexander on its plains and deserts, altogether very different terrain from Bactria. With no one to stop him Alexander arrived in Drapsaca and, aware that Bessus was now on the back foot, immediately launched a propaganda campaign: whoever delivered Bessus to him would become the friend of the King of Asia.

In June Alexander departed Drapsaca for the Oxus. The capital of Bactria, Bactra (modern Balkh, sometimes called Zariaspa because of its association with Zoroaster and its Zoroastrian fire temple, Azar-i-Asp), fell to him without a struggle. After installing Artabazus as satrap of Bactria he marched across the burning, waterless desert, with its blistering temperatures of over 100 degrees Fahrenheit by day and a chilly 50–60 by night. The army marched by night to combat the heat, but even so by the time they reached the Oxus, probably at Kelif, the men were exhausted and dehydrated—and decided that enough was enough. The Thessalian soldiers, at least, refused to cross the river and remained defiant despite

Alexander's cajoling. He was forced to grant them honorable discharges, with pay and even bonuses, and replenish his numbers with local troops.

Before he had escaped into Sogdiana Bessus had given orders to destroy every boat in the area to prevent Alexander from crossing the three-quarter-mile-wide Oxus River. His action only slowed down the king, whose men spent one week putting together rafts of skins and grass and anything else that floated. In this manner (the same, incidentally, as the British used in the nineteenth century) the Macedonian army crossed the Oxus, a feat that led directly to the downfall of Bessus. Spitamenes and another Sogdian chieftain, Dataphernes, now responded to Alexander's propaganda appeal. They seized Bessus and offered his surrender to Alexander. Ptolemy, at the head of a substantial force of 4,000 infantry and 1,600 cavalry, was dispatched to retrieve Bessus and escort him back to the king. When Ptolemy reached the agreed rendezvous point he took control of Bessus and, in keeping with Alexander's orders, stripped him of his clothes, bound him in a wooden collar, and led him on the right-hand side of the road so that Alexander could ride up to him in a chariot, an action symbolic of a Great King.[20] Alexander ordered Bessus to be whipped and sent to Bactra, where he had his nose and ears sliced off—a Persian punishment—and the following year he was put to death by ritual impalement in Ecbatana.

Bessus was dead, but the challenges to the invading army did not die with him, as Spitamenes quickly proved. Alexander set off north to Maracanda (Samarkand, in Uzbekistan), Sogdiana's capital, from where he intended to move to the most northeasterly boundary of the Persian Empire, the river Jaxartes (Syr-Darya). Along the way, he installed garrisons in a number of mud-brick forts to maintain control of the region, including the largest, Cyropolis (Kurkath), which Cyrus the Great had founded in 544. On the southern bank of the Jaxartes he founded a new city, Alexander Eschate or Alexander the Farthermost (Kuhjand, the former Leninabad). This new city, like all those that Alexander established in Central Asia, had the twofold function of keeping the region pacified and providing a refuge should the natives decide to attack the conquerors.

Before the Macedonians reached Maracanda they fell into a fight with a local tribe, during which Alexander was shot in the leg by an arrow that shattered part of his fibula. The wound was nothing compared with the news he now received: Spitamenes in tandem with another chieftain, Dataphernes, had called upon all of Bactria and Sogdiana to revolt. Their motive was simple: they had no wish to be conquered by any invading army, let alone a Western one. The same attitude prevails today. Spitamenes besieged Maracanda, while enemy tribes slaughtered the Macedonian garrisons in the forts. Thus began the most grueling years in Asia for the Macedonians.

THE REVOLT OF BACTRIA AND SOGDIANA

Alexander immediately ordered a Lycian named Pharnuches to lead 300 cavalry and more than 2,000 infantry under Andromachus, Caranus, and Menedemus to relieve Maracanda while he stormed the forts. Again resorting to psychological warfare, he ordered Craterus to besiege Cyropolis while he isolated the defenders there by successfully reducing the smaller fortresses. Since much of the resistance in Bactria and Sogdiana came from local rulers who barricaded themselves into what they thought were impregnable mountain forts, Alexander was also gaining invaluable experience that would pay dividends in several later sieges. He rejoined Craterus at Cyropolis, where he noticed a dried-up riverbed that ran under the walls of the fortress into the city. He took a contingent of troops along it and successfully opened the gates to his men. In the ensuing rout 8,000 of the defenders were massacred, while others leapt to their deaths from the battlements to escape capture. Alexander again was severely wounded in the fighting when a stone struck him in the throat, affecting his speech for some days. He had no time to recuperate because as soon as Cyropolis fell to him he learned that the Sacae people, who lived north of the Jaxartes, were massing at the river to defy the invaders.

In similar fashion to his siege of Tyre Alexander set up catapults on some of his boats, which fired missiles at the enemy line on the opposite bank of the Jaxartes. The Sacae had little choice but to take cover, which allowed his troops to cross the river without suffering from enemy missiles. In crossing the river Alexander had traveled farther than Cyrus the

Great, but there was no time to pat himself on the back. Almost as soon as his men regrouped they fell victim to the Sacans' deadly cavalry tactic of galloping around and around their foe while firing off arrows into their midst. As many as 1,000 of the invaders were killed, and Alexander ordered a hasty retreat. He knew that he could not afford more losses, so he gambled on tricking the enemy with a similar tactic as his pawn sacrifice at the Granicus River. He sent a small contingent of cavalry at speed toward the Sacan line. Puzzled by so small a force the Sacae nevertheless galloped out to meet it. They were so focused on encircling this Macedonian force that they only realized it was a trap when Alexander gave a prearranged signal for the rest of his cavalry and a contingent of Agrianians and other infantry to rush them head-on before they could regroup to face the fresh assault. In the ensuing fighting 1,000 Sacans were killed and 150 were captured, to Alexander's 60 cavalry and 100 infantry, with 1,000 troops wounded. The Sacan leader agreed to Alexander's terms, and as a sign of good faith the king returned their prisoners unransomed.

Things were not as good for the Macedonians elsewhere. When news had first reached Spitamenes that Macedonian troops were rushing to Maracanda's aid, he had appeared to turn tail and flee westward along the Zeravshan Valley. Naively, the commanders of the relief force gave pursuit but too late realized their error when Spitamenes, reinforced by groups of Massagetae cavalry, wheeled to attack them. Unable to overcome their opponents, the Macedonians were cut down—2,000 infantry and 300 cavalry were killed. This was the greatest defeat that Alexander's army ever suffered in Asia. Maracanda then opened its gates to Spitamenes, and the people of the Zeravshan Valley voluntarily joined him in defying Alexander—in doing so, they sentenced themselves to death.

Three days of forced marches later a furious Alexander and half of his entire army arrived at Maracanda thirsty for blood. Spitamenes hastily retreated westward for good, and Alexander retook the city with ease. The people paid a terrible price for throwing in their lot with Spitamenes: Alexander spent the rest of the summer of 329 devastating the entire Zeravshan Valley—burning the crops, razing the towns, and slaughtering as many as 120,000 Sogdians. It is really from this point onward that he adopted a far more brutal approach to natives who defied him. For example, shortly after arriving in the region of the Jaxartes he came upon a town populated by the Branchidae. Their ancestors had been the priests of the Oracle of Apollo at Didyma who during the Persian Wars had supported Persia. To safeguard them from future Greek reprisals the Great King had moved the townspeople en masse to the Jaxartes. The Branchidae now surrendered to Alexander, but that did not stop him slaughtering the men and enslaving the women and children. In some respects his action is understandable because of the original revenge mission and the association of the Branchidae with the Persian Wars—even though the present population was many generations past their treacherous ancestors.[21]

Spitamenes stood a very real chance of uniting all of Bactria and Sogdiana against Alexander, so the king had to act fast. He divided his army into four parts, each under its own commander, with orders to operate in different areas of Sogdiana to conquer the province once and for all. For the remainder of 329 and early 328 the troops fought intense guerilla warfare—something completely unfamiliar to them, but they had no choice other than adapt quickly or face dire consequences—and built a series of various fortified garrison posts with standing contingents of troops to pacify the province. Alexander returned to Bactra for the winter. The following spring (of 328) saw him setting off to track down Spitamenes, but the rebel leader was like a phantom, and a frustrated Alexander made his way to Maracanda for the summer. There, the exasperation he was feeling over this long campaign and his inability to capture Spitamenes came terribly together in the murder of Cleitus.

THE MURDER OF CLEITUS

As king Alexander was also chief priest to the Macedonians. One evening in the palace at Maracanda a religious ritual turned into a customary drinking party for him and his commanders. Things quickly grew out of hand. It was common for attendees at a Macedonian symposium to tell stories of their battle exploits, often striving to outdo one another, but at this particular one the tales centered on how Alexander was responsible for all of Macedonia's successes. One person sycophantically compared him with the god Heracles (one of his ancestors), and when Alexander drunkenly and falsely boasted that he and not his father had been responsible for victory at Chaeronea in 338, everyone applauded.

One of the remaining Old Guard present, Cleitus the Black, co-commander of the Companion Cavalry after Philotas's execution in 330 and the man who had saved Alexander's life at the Granicus River in 334, was growing increasingly angry at all the vacuous praise.[22] Cleitus had served under Philip and had known Alexander since he was born—his sister Lanice had been one of his nurses. He was also well aware of Philip's achievements in unifying Macedonia and laying the foundations of its empire, just as he well knew whose strategy was responsible for routing the Greeks at Chaeronea. He also sharply disparaged Alexander's favoring of Asian customs and his refusal to return home. His attitude probably explains why Alexander had appointed him as the new satrap of Bactria and Sogdiana (Artabazus was now too old)—it was a means to rid his court of an especially ardent critic.

Cleitus nevertheless continued drinking while the stories of Alexander's prowess grew more unctuous. Then came the straw that broke the camel's back. Someone present performed a song that seems to have poked fun at the Macedonians who had been so resoundingly defeated by Spitamenes when they had gone to relieve Maracanda.[23] Alexander was said to have laughed at it and called to hear it again. At that point Cleitus rose to his feet and delivered a stinging, alcohol-induced rebuke to everyone for laughing at brave comrades who had fallen in battle, which then turned into a personal attack on Alexander for his orientalism and even his divine pretensions. With caution now completely thrown to the wind Cleitus yelled that it was the army that had won Alexander's successes and finished off by scornfully reminding him that he had saved him from death at the Granicus.

The scene cannot be fully imagined, but Curtius talks of the younger and older soldiers likewise arguing among themselves as to whether Philip deserved accolades like Alexander—arguably evidence for splits in the ranks or "nationalism against the orientalizing policy."[24] Cleitus would have known he had overstepped the mark, but he remained defiant. An enraged Alexander threw an apple at him (presumably the first thing that came to hand) and launched himself at him while shouting—in Macedonian, to show the seriousness of the situation—to the hypaspists outside the palace to seize the old general. A nasty fistfight was averted when Ptolemy bundled Cleitus out of the room. However, Alexander shouted after him that he was a coward for running away rather than facing his king. Cleitus struggled free of his comrades and dashed back into the room, where he and Alexander continued their row. The amount of alcohol that both had consumed made an already ugly situation worse as Alexander was beside himself with anger. He grabbed a weapon, most likely a sword or even a spear by some accounts, from one of his personal bodyguard (the only men allowed to carry arms at symposia) and stabbed the unarmed Cleitus, telling him to go and join Philip, Parmenion, and Attalus. Cleitus died on the spot.

Alexander was immediately horrified at his action. He pulled the weapon out of Cleitus's corpse and tried to turn it onto himself, but his bodyguard wrested it from his hands and carried him to his room. For the next three days he remained in his bedchamber, weeping, tearing at his face with his nails, refusing to eat and drink, all to the consternation of his men. Callisthenes attempted to coax him out but to no avail. Then the other court philosopher, Anaxarchus of Abdera, put it to him simply that the gods had fated Cleitus to die at that time and had used Alexander as their agent. He could not therefore hold himself accountable for what he had done. The king accepted this patent lie and emerged from his quarters, where his men were so overjoyed to have him back that they condemned the unfortunate Cleitus for treason.

The killing of the unarmed Cleitus casts another shadow over Alexander as king and man. Cleitus should not have berated his king publicly, that is true, but even so it is hard to justify his murder. His criticism of the king's plans and orientalism was bad enough, but what had sent Alexander over the edge was his praise of Philip. Alexander's relentless march into the heart of Asia was not merely to satisfy his love of fighting and his *pothos* but to eclipse the exploits of his father, hence Cleitus's belittling him was the last thing he wanted to hear. No one of course would have really believed that Cleitus was guilty of treason; Alexander had merely shown that once anyone had crossed him there was no redemption—and ominously, that he believed that his actions were above the law. His ignoble response here, as everyone could see, was a stark contrast to the personal honor that drove his campaigns and which he expected of others.[25]

Fortunately for Macedonian morale Spitamenes now found his support base fast waning as the Macedonians increased their presence in Sogdiana. In late 328 or early 327 Spitamenes and 3,000 Massagetae cavalry did battle with a Macedonian force under Coenus at Gabae and were all but annihilated. Spitamenes survived the rout, but the Massagetae en masse deserted his cause and declared their loyalty to Alexander. To show that they were serious they killed Spitamenes and sent his head to Alexander. By the end of 328 or possibly early 327, after two–three years of strenuous campaigning, the conquest of Bactria and Sogdiana was in sight. All that remained were some defiant locals who had taken refuge in rock fortresses in the southeast of the province (modern Tajikistan), to which Alexander now turned.[26] They would be the scenes of some of his boldest and most brilliant sieges.

"WINGED SOLDIERS"

A number of local rebels and their families, including (it was said) Oxyartes of Bactria, had fled to a fortress under the command of a nobleman named Ariamazes. It lay atop a high, sheer cliff, commonly referred to as the Sogdian Rock, which afforded them perfect protection. The current icy, wintry conditions would have made climbing up the cliff to launch an assault on Ariamazes's fortress practically impossible, and in any case he had stationed archers along the top to shoot down any climbers. He also had plenty of provisions and if need be could melt snow for water. When Alexander offered terms for the people's surrender Ariamazes felt sufficiently secure to refuse them and even taunted the king that he would need "winged soldiers" to capture him.

Ariamazes had not set up defenders at the rear of the cliff since he believed that Alexander would attack him only from the front. The king pounced on his blunder. Turning to his men, he appealed for volunteers to climb to the summit of the rear rock face, which would bring them out above the defenders. The climb had to be undertaken at night so that Ariamazes would be oblivious to the attempt. The mission was virtually a suicidal one, given the darkness and treacherous weather conditions, but nevertheless enough of his troops showed their willingness for Alexander to select 300 of them, offering to pay the first man who made it to the top the huge sum of 12 talents.

The men began their ascent, roped together as climbers would be today, driving iron tent pegs into the hard, icy rock face to help them inch slowly upward. During the climb 30 of them fell to their deaths. The remainder struggled to the summit, and as dawn broke they signaled the king below with white, linen flags. Alexander had banked on the psychological effect of being hemmed in by enemy forces at the front and rear causing the defenders to lose heart, and as usual he was right. Ariamazes, thinking that there were far more Macedonians to his rear than just the 270, surrendered without a fight, and Alexander now taunted *him* that he had his winged soldiers after all. He crucified many of the defenders and put the remainder to work in the fields of his new cities in the region. The Sogdian Rock episode, incidentally, is perhaps the only time that Alexander did not personally lead his men from the front. Every other encounter with an enemy saw him in the thick of fighting.

The final renegade to defy Alexander was a local ruler named Sisimithres (also called Chorienes), who lived in a rock fortress in Nautaca called the Rock of Chorienes. News of Ariamazes's defeat at the Sogdian Rock must have spread quickly, but Sisimithres clearly believed that Alexander posed no danger to him. His fortress was built on the far side of a deep ravine, was surrounded by dense woods, and had abundant supplies and water. Like Ariamazes, Sisimithres believed that the exceptional location of his fortress would thwart any enemy attack; like Ariamazes, he was wrong.

Alexander gave orders to bridge the ravine, in similar fashion to the mole at Tyre, so that he could lead his troops in an attack on Sisimithres's stronghold. Working day and night, his men drove wooden stakes into the sides of the chasm, on top of which they built an elaborate crisscross foundation of wooden struts, which they then covered with packed earth to form a makeshift causeway. During this time the defenders rained down arrows on them, killing many of them and slowing down progress on the bridge. To combat the enemy onslaught Alexander built large wooden screens, which were lowered to shield the workers from any missiles. In this way the foundations of the bridge were completed. To protect his men as they worked on joining the two parts of the earth roadway Alexander brought up his siege engines on his side of the ravine. The construction of the bridge had already panicked Sisimithres and his men, but once they saw the massive siege engines being rolled into place they lost heart completely and surrendered.

Alexander's boldness and his uncanny ability to use psychological tactics to demoralize and overcome his enemy were again demonstrated in these sieges. Spitamenes's victory over the relief force at Maracanda was really the only blemish on the invasion record to date, and even that was overshadowed by Alexander's tactical genius and leadership skills over the course of the previous years. With Bessus dead and Bactria and Sogdiana finally pacified, Alexander's men were all set to return home, but their hopes were dashed when he announced the next campaign in another new land for all of them—India.

12.

PASSAGE TO INDIA

B EFORE ALEXANDER LEFT FOR India he decided that the time had finally come to marry and produce an heir. Exactly when he met Roxane (Roshanak, "Beautiful Star") is unknown, but it was after his capture of either the Sogdian Rock or the Rock of Chorienes. Roxane was the 16-year-old daughter of the Bactrian noble Oxyartes; she was reputedly the most stunning girl in Asia, and when Alexander saw her he fell immediately in love with her. His marriage in the spring of 327, however, did not endear him to his men.

MARRYING ROXANE

Curtius describes how Alexander met Roxane and even goes so far as to say that the king saw the marriage as a means of helping to unite the disparate parts of his empire:

> Oxyartes had arranged a banquet of typical barbaric extravagance, at which he entertained the king. While he conducted the festivities with warm geniality, Oxyartes had thirty young noblewomen brought in, one of whom was his own daughter Roxane, a woman of remarkable physical beauty with a dignified bearing rarely found in barbarians. Though she was one of a number chosen for their beauty, she nonetheless attracted everybody's attention, especially that of the king, whose control over his appetites was weakening amid the indulgences of Fortune, against whom mankind is insufficiently armed. So it was that the man who had looked with what

were merely paternal feelings on the wife and 2 unmarried daughters of Darius—and with these none but Roxane could be compared in looks—now fell in love with a young girl, of humble pedigree in comparison with royalty, and did so with such abandon as to make a statement that inter-marriage of Persians and Macedonians would serve to consolidate his empire, that only thus could the conquered lose their shame and the conquerors their pride.[1]

The young Bactrian princess had no say in the marriage, and to add insult to injury Barsine, who had been living with Alexander since Issus, was pregnant and soon bore him a son, Heracles. The marriage to Roxane was conducted in Macedonian fashion, with Alexander slicing a loaf of bread with his sword and sharing it with the bride's father, Oxyartes.[2] The custom was obviously alien to the Bactrians, but Alexander may have followed it to appease his men, who were discontented with the union because their king's children would not be full-blooded Macedonians. The Macedonian ruling dynasty was about to change forever. In the process Attalus's taunt about legitimate heirs at the wedding banquet of Alexander's father to Cleopatra in 337 was conveniently forgotten.

Alexander was a born pragmatist like his father, so it is not easy to accept that he simply fell in love with Roxane or decided that now was as good a time as any to settle down. It is more likely that he followed in his father's footsteps by marrying for political reasons, as Curtius indicated in the passage quoted above. In other words his marriage was a means to an end: recruiting a powerful father-in-law, who would help ensure the passivity of Bactria and Sogdiana. Alexander intended Amyntas to succeed the deceased Cleitus as satrap, but the rebellious nature of the local people was something he had to take seriously. Since he intended to march next into what the Greeks called India, today Pakistan and Kashmir, he could not allow a revolt that would compromise his rear. There was no guarantee that a Macedonian satrap would prevent this, but a Bactrian baron acting on behalf of the king was a different matter.[3] As with Alexander's previous use of Iranian noblemen as satraps, Oxyartes was therefore meant to help reconcile the subject peoples to Macedonian rule and maintain stability.

PROSKYNESIS AND THE PAGES' CONSPIRACY

From Maracanda Alexander and his army made their way to Bactra (capital of Bactria), where he tried to introduce *proskynesis*—genuflection—before himself, which turned out to be a major blunder. The Asian custom of *proskynesis* required those entering the presence of the Great King to prostrate themselves before him or perhaps bow before him and blow him a kiss and the King to return their obeisance with a kiss.[4] The Persians dutifully performed *proskynesis* before Alexander, but his men routinely mocked them. One time when Leonnatus, one of the royal bodyguards, guffawed over a Persian who slipped and fell as he was prostrating himself, Alexander punched him to the ground. His men thought that the posture turned free men into slaves, and they also believed that the entire ritual was sacrilegious because it implied worship of a living ruler. Alexander, as pious as the next man, would have been well aware of their religious reservations but ignored them. He now insisted that, if not all of his men, at least his senior entourage perform *proskynesis* before him.[5]

It is possible that Alexander was attempting to establish a common form of greeting for all of his subjects, given that there was a clear divide between his own men, who bowed to him, and his Asian subjects, who prostrated themselves.[6] Yet he must have known that his own people would reject the ritual because of its religious undertones and be outraged that he was not asking the Persians to modify *their* approach before him. The only plausible motive for his action must be that he had come to believe that he was a god on earth and wanted everyone to treat him as one. For one thing, the court philosopher Anaxarchus had argued that since Alexander had already overshadowed every predecessor and the gods Heracles and Dionysus, he ought to be worshiped not when he was dead but while he was alive. Curtius believed that Alexander exploited *proskynesis* to claim divine honors: "the time had come for the depraved idea that Alexander had dreamt up previously, and in wondering how he could accord himself divine honors he gave orders for the Macedonians to follow the Persian custom of prostrating themselves on the ground, and so do him homage," although Justin merely called it "a piece of vanity in keeping with Persian royalty."[7]

The *proskynesis* attempt would soon flounder because of resistance from Callisthenes. At a banquet one night various members of Alexander's retinue performed *proskynesis* before him and received a kiss from him. Not Callisthenes. Alexander had not noticed this, but when one of his Companions, Demetrius, told him about it, Alexander refused to kiss Callisthenes unless he prostrated himself, prompting his famous reply, "I will leave you then, the poorer by a kiss."[8] Callisthenes's defiance encouraged the other attendees to follow suit, forcing Alexander to abandon his attempt. He did not take defeat easily. Callisthenes's days were now numbered, and the opportunity for Alexander to have his revenge presented itself soon enough in the so-called Pages' Conspiracy.

At some point during the stay at Bactra Alexander and some of his men had gone on a hunt. As the king was aiming a spear at a wild boar one of his pages, Hermolaus, struck first and killed the animal. An angry Alexander had Hermolaus publicly caned and his horse confiscated, as the right of first kill lay with the king. Hermolaus was not prepared to accept his punishment. He persuaded another page, Sostratus, who was in love with him, and then possibly as many as seven others to join him in assassinating Alexander while he was asleep one night.[9] One of the duties of the pages was to stand guard over the king while he slept, so their plan was feasible. A whole month went by before they were all together in the royal bedchamber poised to do the deed. Then Alexander unknowingly thwarted the plot. One tradition claims that he stayed drinking at a party until dawn and so did not go to bed, while another states that as he was leaving a party a trusted Syrian prophetess, who "was then being inspired by the god pleaded with him to go back and continue drinking all night."[10] Either way, Alexander lived. The next day a page informed Ptolemy of the plot. No doubt remembering Philotas's fate Ptolemy immediately went to Alexander, who tortured all the pages for information and then had them put to death. He also accused Callisthenes, whose duties at court included the pages' intellectual education, of complicity, although no page gave up his name, and ordered his execution (although there is a tradition that he was imprisoned and died from obesity and lice).

The Pages' Conspiracy was probably the most serious threat to Alexander's life, even though he suffered no harm. Yet it is as controversial as the

Philotas affair. Yes, Hermolaus had acted impetuously in killing the boar, but his extreme punishment was well within legal rights. The Macedonians were a hard people, and Hermolaus was unlikely to have gained much sympathy. Why, then, even if he had wanted revenge for his public humiliation, would several other pages who had done nothing wrong join him in killing their king? Regicide was a heinous crime, and if they had murdered Alexander in his bed, they would have been the only suspects. Curtius ascribes a political motive to the conspiracy, claiming that under torture Hermolaus told Alexander that they plotted to murder him because he no longer acted as a king to his own men but, rather, as a master to his slaves.[11] Possibly there is some truth to this assertion, but it still does not explain why Alexander charged Callisthenes as a conspirator when there was no hard evidence against him.

Yet Callisthenes had crossed Alexander when he blocked his attempt to enforce *proskynesis*. As we have seen, once anyone defied the king there was no redemption. Callisthenes had close contacts with the pages, which made it all the easier for Alexander to accuse him. Possibly also the other court philosopher, Anaxarchus, who disliked Callisthenes, may have exploited the conspiracy to persuade Alexander to remove his adversary.[12] Whether Callisthenes's death caused friction between his uncle Aristotle and Alexander is unknown. What can be said with some certainty is that Alexander's increasingly brutal treatment of critics and his deteriorating relations with his men weigh heavily on his track record.

THE INVASION OF INDIA

In the late spring of 327, with an army of anything up to 70,000 men including nonmilitary personnel, Alexander could finally turn to his next major offensive, the invasion of India.[13] In actuality, he campaigned almost exclusively in the Punjab. He had various reasons for invading. An Indian contingent had fought with Xerxes against the Greeks in 480, and more recently the Indians of the Kabul Valley had sent men and 15 elephants to support Darius III at Gaugamela. Plus the subordinate relationship of the Indian rulers to the Great King meant that Alexander had to bring them under his control.[14] However, personal reasons may have trumped all others. Cyrus the Great had invaded India, and Alexander was keen to emulate some of his actions for propaganda reasons. He also wanted to follow in the footsteps of Dionysus (who had traveled through India on his way to Greece) and Heracles (whose daughter had a son who founded an Indian dynasty). Alexander had long identified himself with Heracles, who was born mortal and apotheosized on death, but in India he paired himself openly with the divinely born Dionysus, and Curtius even stated that he wanted the Indians to accept him as a god.[15] Alexander also wanted to reach the Southern (Indian) Ocean to find out whether Aristotle was right about the country jutting out into the ocean and being connected to Africa. Finally, there was his *pothos*, which made it impossible for him to stop until he reached the edge of the inhabited world— not necessarily to rule it but to see what it was like.[16]

The Greeks knew little about India despite the accounts of Hecataeus in the late sixth century (the first to write of India in Greek literature), Herodotus, and the Greek doctor Ctesias in the fifth century.[17] Darius I had enforced Persian rule over the country in the latter years of the sixth century, but its extreme distance from the major Persian capitals and the independence of the Indian tribes, especially those in the Swat, Bajaur, and Buner regions of the northwest frontier, had eroded the Great Kings' influence. By Alexander's day India was but a nominal part of the Persian Empire; the princes of the various regions held little loyalty to Persian rulers, similar to the relationship of the Upper Macedonians to the monarch at Pella before Philip. There were Greeks in India from the sixth century B.C. to the fifth century A.D., from early traders, explorers, and soldiers with Alexander's army to those who lived and worked with the Buddhist sculptors of the Kabul Valley. Nevertheless, Alexander had to use interpreters in India more than at any other time in his Asian campaign.[18] Each of these different cultures impacted the other in religion, philosophy, and art,[19] but it was Alexander's campaign that led to the explosion of Greek civilization and interactions in the Hellenistic era.

Alexander intended to march first to the Indus River but needed to protect his rear before moving farther into the interior. To this end he split his army in two. One half under Hephaestion and Perdiccas would head there along the Cophen (Kabul) River and through the Khyber Pass, the main road into India. There had already been diplomatic contacts from the towns of this region, so their task was to secure them and establish Macedonian authority there. Alexander and Craterus with the other half of the army would travel along the Choaspes (Kunar) River and the northerly Bajaur and Swat regions. Alexander expected that he would need to overcome resistance because he had not received any diplomatic overtures from the people there. By the time that both halves of the army reunited at the Indus, their rear would be secure, and the next leg of the invasion could take place.

Hephaestion and Perdiccas made good progress and rested at Peucelaotis (Charsadda), whose prince had come out to greet them and offered them his city. As soon as they left, however, Peucelaotis revolted, forcing them to return and besiege it for 30 days. When its prince was killed in the fighting the defenders surrendered, and Peucelaotis again became the property of Macedonia. The remainder of their march to the Indus was uneventful, and as they approached the river they received supplies from Taxiles, the ruler of Taxila (Takshashila), about 20 miles northwest of Islamabad and the largest city between the Indus and Hydaspes rivers.

Alexander and the men had more of a struggle. At the Choes River the local natives withdrew to a number of fortresses and refused to let him pass, forcing him to attack each one individually. They fell to him with relative ease, but as each one did so he ordered the slaughter of its inhabitants or sold them into slavery. As he approached the town of Nysa in the Kunar Valley an embassy came to him from there seeking his friendship on the grounds that the people were descendants of men who had traveled with Dionysus and had named their town after his nurse. They further claimed that their local deity, Indra or Shiva, was identified with Dionysus. When Alexander saw ivy, Dionysus's symbol, growing in the area he accepted their story at face value. In fact the plant was scindapsus, which resembles ivy. Since his growing association with Dionysus was becoming known by now, the Nysans may have made up their association with the god to win him over.[20] Possibly they were a group of isolated

Greeks, perhaps descendants of mercenaries who had served under Darius, and wanted to mask this fact.[21]

Alexander and his men then began a 10-day drunken party, running and screaming through the woods and along the mountainsides with ivy crowns crammed on their heads. As far as Alexander was concerned, he was walking in Dionysus's footsteps, and he allowed Nysa to retain its autonomy. To be on the safe side, though, he took the ruler's son and grandsons as hostages and drafted 300 of the city's cavalrymen into his army.

A far greater challenge for the king lay in the Lower Swat Valley, near the foothills of the Himalayas, where the Assaceni peoples took refuge in several of the area's mud-brick and stone fortresses. The king of the Assaceni had barricaded himself into Massaga at the northern end of the Katgala Pass along with 7,000 Indian mercenaries. Alexander decided to besiege and capture Massaga first in the hope of psychologically demoralizing the rest of the natives. For four days Massaga defied him, but when its king was killed the queen, Cleophis, agreed to terms. Alexander assured her that he would spare the population as long as the Assaceni surrendered to him and the mercenaries joined his army. The latter were to leave the fortress and assemble on a nearby hill to await Alexander's orders. However, as soon as the mercenaries gathered on the hill Alexander had his men kill all of them. Their horrified wives dashed out from the fortress and courageously took their places, fighting with great ferocity, until they too were cut to pieces.

Even ancient writers condemned Alexander's treachery and called it a blot on his career.[22] Possibly he suspected that the mercenaries would flee as soon as they could and join ranks with other natives against the Macedonians, so his offer of assimilating them into the army was merely a ruse to lure them out of the stronghold. What happened now of course was that the Assaceni in the other fortresses saw that there was no hope of escape and prepared to fight to the death. Those at Bazira (Bir-Kot), for example, actually got the upper hand over Coenus's men, who were besieging them, and he had to call on Alexander for help. At that point the defenders escaped via the Shang-la Pass to a fortress set atop a 10,000-foot rocky mountain named Aornus (Bar-sar ib Pir-Sar), a few miles west of the Indus River. Alexander needed to conquer Aornus so as to give him control of the entire Cophen Valley, but aside from this obvious strategic consideration the siege gave him the chance to outdo Heracles, as we will soon see.

SOCIAL CUSTOMS: THE DILEMMA
OF WEST MEETING EAST

Alexander had seemingly tolerated religious beliefs and social traditions that differed from his own for political reasons. In Egypt, for example, he made no attempt to impose the Macedonian pantheon on the native Egyptians and in Memphis even sacrificed a bull to the native god Apis. In Persia he had been likewise careful, even promising the people of Babylon that he would rebuild the Temple of Marduk, the city's patron deity. Although he and his men were disgusted with the Persian practices of brothers marrying sisters and sons marrying mothers, they turned a blind eye. Of course Greeks condemned the Macedonian practice of polygamy, and in later Ptolemaic Egypt ruling brothers married their sisters. However, when Alexander reached Central Asia and India he encountered customs that he regarded as especially abhorrent and attempted to eradicate them.

For example, the contemporary writer Onescritus describes the Bactrians' ritual of having dogs eat their elderly and sick people alive:

> In the distant past the Sogdians and Bactrians were very similar to the nomads as far as their way of life and customs went, although the Bactrians were a little more civilized. However . . . those who cannot care for themselves because of old age or sickness are cast out alive as prey to dogs that are kept only for this purpose—in their native language they are called "undertakers"—and while the land outside the walls of the cities of the Bactrians is clean, most of the land inside the walls is full of human bones. Alexander ended this custom.[23]

Greeks and Macedonians believed that the dead should be buried properly so that their souls would find peace in the afterlife rather than roaming for eternity in limbo. In Athens, for example, a law supposedly attributed to Solon in the early sixth century ordered children to look after elderly parents or be prosecuted. Alexander, as Onescritus claims, put a ban on this Bactrian practice. We may applaud Alexander's action because of our own Western morality, inherited in large part from the Greeks, but we may also judge him as insensitive to local customs. Did Alexander have the power to abolish this Bactrian tradition? As conqueror (so he thought), technically yes. However, his action was no doubt counterproductive to his attempts to maintain rule, as it merely exaggerated the social and cultural differences between the invaders and the invaded. He made no attempt to understand why the Bactrians had this ritual and to try to get them to change it diplomatically. Furthermore, his marriage to Roxane fell short of pacifying Bactria and Sogdiana since it also slighted age-old local customs and sensitivities.

Yet in India Alexander allowed some local traditions, some of which he and his men must have condemned. For example, in a variation of Bactrian custom, the Indians "kill their parents and next of kin, just as they would sacrificial victims, before age or disease eat away at them; then they feast on the entrails of the slain. That is not a crime there but a symbol of piety. There are even people who move to hidden places far from anyone else when they fall sick and wait for death with equanimity."[24] Widows also committed suicide by ritual burning on the deaths of their husbands, and doctors were responsible for deciding whether a baby was weak or deformed in any way, in which case they, and not the parents, would have it killed. The Indians also equated the value of an elephant with that of a woman—they thought "it honorable for women to prostitute themselves for an elephant, and women even claim it an honor if their beauty is on a par with the value of an elephant. When they marry they do not give or receive a dowry but their fathers bring out the girls of marriageable age and stand them in a public place for the man who wins the prize for wrestling."[25] A man's future wife was a prize won in competition, although elsewhere we are told that impoverished fathers had to marry off their young daughters another way, by taking them to the marketplace, blowing trumpets and banging drums to attract a crowd, and then exposing their daughters front and back up to their shoulders in the hope of enticing a would-be husband.[26]

Perhaps the sheer size and population of India daunted Alexander too much to try to curtail these practices, and such a ban would have been impossible to police anyway. The same must have been true for the remote areas of Bactria and Sogdiana. Possibly some Indian customs were not as offensive to the invaders—after all, in Greece parents arranged marriages; the bride-to-be had no say in the matter, and she was often young, in only her early teens, while her husband was in his late twenties or early thirties. In Sparta it was common practice for a tribal elder to examine the health of a newborn baby, and if he decided that it was weak in any way, it was left in a cave to die—with the parents' consent.

The biggest insensitivity that Alexander demonstrated in India was his treatment of the venerated Brahman philosophers, who were a highly respected part of Indian society. The Brahmans were not only philosophers but also political advisers to Indian rulers and soldiers who fought fearlessly next to regular troops. Alexander never seemed to grasp that they were more than intellectuals and failed to understand—or appreciate—how they mixed religion and politics. During a particularly bloodthirsty campaign against various strongholds held by the Mardi people in 325, he massacred a large number of the Brahmans. In revenge, they incited a massive revolt of India, which the Macedonians were never able to put down and which forced them to leave the country.

Alexander's experiences in Bactria, Sogdiana, and India—stemming from an inability to grasp the importance of local rituals to the native populations and the role that religion played in political life, compounded by his naive and cavalier attitude that his customs were better and should be followed—serve as timely lessons to the West in its involvement with other cultures worldwide.

THE ROCK OF AORNUS

Tradition had it that during his Twelve Labors Heracles (whose local equivalent was Krishna) had attempted to take Aornus and failed—admittedly due to an earthquake. Alexander eagerly seized the chance to outdo Heracles, setting the scene for another spectacular siege.[27] Aornus was set atop the mountain's eastern summit. Alexander ordered Ptolemy to take a contingent of troops to the western summit and establish a base there, thus intending to use the same psychological tactics as he had done at Sisimithres's fortress. In case the defenders held out longer than expected he bade Coenus forage for provisions and store them at Ecbolima, the nearest town to Aornus. When Ptolemy signaled that he had made camp, Alexander and more troops joined him and then, with the Agrianians and 200 Companions, climbed a high ridge overlooking the 800-foot Burimar-Kandao ravine, beyond which lay the citadel of Aornus. The climb took two days because the defenders could fire off arrows and other missiles at them and so impede their progress.

As he had done in his attack on Sisimithres at Nautaca, Alexander gave orders to construct a bridge across the ravine. He intended to set up his siege engines on this makeshift bridge, and as they bombarded the citadel with stones, his men would dash across to attack the Assaceni frontally. After four days of hard work, day and night, the bridge had begun to take shape, and the siege engines were trundled into place. As at Nautaca, just the sight of these fearsome machines trained on their walls panicked the defenders, who sent an envoy to Alexander asking for terms. Remembering the massacre of the mercenaries at Massaga, they suspected that Alexander would put them to death no matter what, and so they planned to flee down the mountainside as soon as night fell. Unfortunately for them, Alexander had anticipated their action. As soon as they made their move, he and 700 men crossed the bridge and took the citadel. Some of the Assaceni were able to escape across the Indus and joined the army of Abisares, Prince of Hazara (in what is now Kashmir); the rest were captured and enslaved but not put to death.

Alexander could now boast that he had succeeded where Heracles had failed and moreover he controlled the entire Cophen Valley. From Aornus he marched quickly to rejoin the troops with Hephaestion and Perdiccas, perhaps at Ohind (Udabhandapura), and after celebrating games and sacrifices the entire army traveled to Taxila, arriving there about April 326. Its ruler, Taxiles, had sent his son Omphis to escort Alexander to the city, where several other princes in the surrounding areas (including Abisares) formally surrendered to him.

It was still 326, and in less than a year Alexander, who was not yet 30 years old, had made significant inroads into India. His men were looking forward to a well-deserved period of rest and recreation in Taxila, especially with the onslaught of the drenching monsoon rains, but it was not to be. Not long after came the unwelcome news that a neighboring prince, Porus, who ruled Paurava, the area of the Punjab between the rivers Hydaspes (Jhelum), a tributary of the Indus, and Acesines (Chenab), had led a considerable army to his side of the Hydaspes River, intent on preventing Alexander from penetrating farther into India. His army was substantial, and Abisares, with all of his troops, had decided to join him. Despite the relentless monsoon rains, Alexander left some of his men in Taxila to ensure the Taxiles' loyalty and, with an additional 5,000 Indian troops, marched the 100 miles across the Salt Range to the Nandana Pass, which overlooked the Hydaspes River at Haranpur. From the top of the pass they could see Porus's huge army waiting for them.

THE BATTLE OF THE HYDASPES RIVER

The Hydaspes River was wide and flowing faster and higher thanks to the melting snow of the Himalayas and the monsoons. Haranpur was a logical crossing point, but Porus had stationed the bulk of his troops on the opposite bank there, as well as other detachments to his right and left along the river. For Alexander to attempt the sort of crossing he had undertaken at the Granicus River in 334, for example, was suicidal, and even if his men did successfully struggle across the river, they would be in no shape to resist Porus's troops, especially his war elephants, whose very size would intimidate their horses.

The ancient sources provide differing and expectedly exaggerated figures for Porus's army: 30,000 infantry, 4,000 cavalry, 300 six-man chariots, and 200 elephants (Arrian); the same numbers but only 85 elephants (Curtius); 50,000 infantry, 3,000 cavalry, 1,000 chariots, and 130 elephants (Diodorus); and 20,000 infantry and 2,000 cavalry (Plutarch).[28] The actual infantry number might be 25,000, since Porus stationed his elephants 50 feet apart. That would have made his line anything from three-quarters of a mile to 1.5 miles long, with perhaps 16 men, 8–16 deep, occupying the gaps between the elephants.[29] Alexander had no chariots or war elephants and could field only 34,000 infantry and 7,000 cavalry.

The monsoon rains would only abate in September, but Alexander had no intention of waiting that long, not least because he could not allow Abisares to reinforce Porus.[30] It was time for deception again. He established a base camp at Haranpur and ordered his men to forage for provisions and build up a store of them. He paraded his troops up and down the riverbank and even landed some on nearby islands, as if he were checking how difficult the actual river crossing would be. To all intents and purposes, then, the men were familiarizing themselves with the terrain and keeping themselves occupied while preparing to wait out the monsoons. Porus was careful though and kept his men in line in case Alexander made a surprise attack in the hope of catching him off guard. The days dragged by, and the Macedonians continued their stressful charade, which, as Alexander intended, had a negative psychological effect on the Indians. They began to complain about their continuous standby to Porus and slowly but surely relaxed their vigil—and fell into Alexander's trap.

The wide Hydaspes River had a number of small islands in midstream. Alexander had long ago decided to use one of them as cover during a night crossing, and to find the right one he had sent scouts along the riverbank as far east as Jalalpur. About 18 miles upstream from his base camp they had discovered the perfect spot: a densely wooded headland (of the Great Salt Range) opposite an equally wooded island named Admana. Because of the headland's thick vegetation, the invaders were able to assemble a flotilla of boats, from small rafts made of skins to 30-oared galleys, without Porus suspecting a thing. When the appointed night came Alexander ordered Meleager, Attalus, and Gorgias to move troops up and down the riverbank, but Porus's men paid them little attention because they were used to these nightly maneuvers. In the meantime Alexander left Craterus in charge of the main camp and took 6,000 infantry and 5,000 cavalry under the commands of Hephaestion, Perdiccas, Coenus, and Cleitus the White to the hidden headland. He even used a double at the base camp to make it look as though he were still there. Alexander's plan was to attack Porus from one side and neutralize the threat from his elephants while Craterus crossed the river to charge the Indians head-on. This simple but brilliant strategy trapped Porus between two Macedonian attacking lines: whichever one he faced first would expose his rear to the other (Map 10).

Alexander and his men set off in their makeshift boats. They were soon past the midstream island of Admana, helped also by a sudden thunderstorm

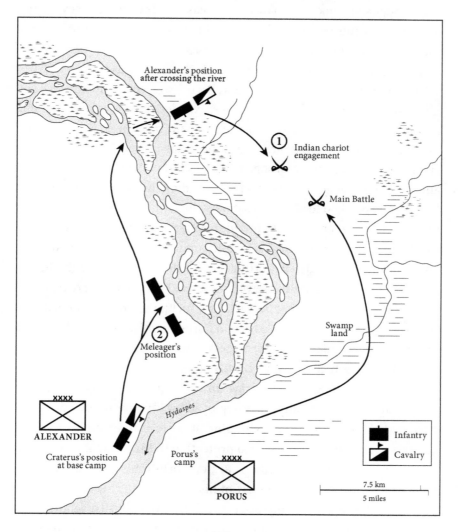

MAP 10
Battle of the Hydaspes River.

that further hid their presence from Porus's troops. Then their luck ran out. For once Alexander had not conducted a proper reconnaissance of that part of the river. What he thought was the opposite bank was actually another island, beyond which was a further channel of the river. To make matters worse the storm ended as abruptly as it had begun, and as it did so the moon sailed into view. The time it took to cross the other channel was longer than Alexander had expected, and his men did not reach the actual opposite bank until dawn was breaking. They were easily visible, and enemy scouts immediately reported their position to a contingent of Indian troops commanded by one of Porus's sons. The element of surprise—on which Alexander had based his strategy—was lost.

There now followed a bitter battle, as Porus's son, with 2,000 cavalry and 120 six-man chariots, dashed to where Alexander's troops were scrambling ashore on a sandy plain. This in itself was no mean feat, for his forces, numbering in the thousands, must have taken considerable time to clamber onto shore and regroup. There was little time to plan any tactics, and Alexander's major worry was probably the exhaustion of his men and horses, who had had to wade at least waist-high through the swirling water of the unforeseen channel. As the Indians arrived Alexander ordered his cavalry to charge them while his infantry under Seleucus tore into the survivors of the cavalry attack. Fortunately for the Macedonians the Indian chariots quickly bogged themselves in the wet ground and were rendered useless. In the ensuing fight 400 Indians, including Porus's son, fell. The survivors managed to scramble back to Porus but mistakenly told him that the entire Macedonian enemy army was now on their side of the river. An astounded Porus had no choice but to engage Alexander.

The two sides had time to draw up their lines, each over one mile long (Map 10). The Indian prince deployed his infantry 10 men deep and stationed the elephants along the line at 50-foot intervals so that the giant animals provided additional protection to his whole line. On each flank were 150 chariots and 2,000 cavalry. Porus himself deliberately sat on top of his elephant in full view of his men to exhort them—this was a great display of generalship because he was five cubits (seven feet) tall and so easily visible to the enemy. Porus intended to use his elephants to panic the Macedonians' horses as they stomped toward them, thereby staving off a cavalry attack, and then crash into the phalanx, trampling the soldiers to death.

Alexander positioned himself with the largest contingent of cavalry on his right flank facing the Indian left. The massed battalions of the phalanx were in the center. He gave Coenus, with 1,000 cavalry, command of the Macedonian left flank facing the Indian right. As at Issus and Gaugamela Alexander based his strategy on killing or capturing his rival. Since Porus's strength lay in his cavalry, which could very well outflank the Macedonian line, Alexander had to neutralize that before anything else. His strategy therefore was to use the bulk of his cavalry to lure Porus into ordering the cavalry on his right flank to change position and gallop across to engage the Macedonians on the left, believing that a rout there would give him the battle. If this happened, then Coenus was to take his cavalry toward the Indian left, as though he were rushing to reinforce his comrades, but then wheel around the Indian position and trap them between the two Macedonian offensive lines. Alexander was also concerned about the danger posed by the elephants to the infantry phalanx if he lavished too much time and attention on the enemy cavalry. Just as he had neutralized the danger posed by the scythed chariots at Gaugamela, so he set about achieving the same end with the elephants now. For that he had a gruesome plan.

Alexander did not wait for Porus to make the first move. He ordered his horse archers on the right flank to engage the Indian left, prompting Porus to make the decision that Alexander had gambled on: he ordered his cavalry on the right flank over to the left. The rest of Alexander's plan then neatly fell into place. The Indians saw Coenus and his troops leaving their position and expected them to join the other cavalry. They were completely taken by surprise when he suddenly broke off from what they thought was going to be a frontal attack and wheeled around their flank. They panicked and began to break rank, forcing Porus to unleash his elephants earlier than he had planned to save his left flank. Although many of the elephants did kill the enemy, trampling some underfoot, impaling others on their tusks, and sweeping up still others with their trunks and pounding them to the ground, Alexander was ready for them. He bade his trumpeters sound out a shrill blast to the infantrymen to move to their left and right and so open up gaps through which the elephants lumbered. As they did so some soldiers used their sarissas to dislodge the mahouts, and others slashed away at the eyes, underbellies, and genitals of the giant beasts, blinding them and inflicting terrible agony on them. Naturally all the elephants wanted to do was escape the brutality. They turned around and with no one to guide them stampeded away to their own line, where they trampled many Indians underfoot.

The Indians now had to contend with the elephants running amok in tandem with a full frontal Macedonian cavalry and infantry charge. They could not. Porus's line gave way as almost all of his cavalry was annihilated, and the battle became another rout. To make matters worse, Craterus had by now crossed the Hydaspes, and he and his men chased down the survivors of the battle as they attempted to flee and killed more of them. The exact number of Indian fatalities is unknown. Arrian claimed that Porus lost 20,000 infantry and 3,000 cavalry to the Macedonians' 280 infantry and 35 cavalry, while Diodorus maintained that the Indians lost 12,000 men to the Macedonians' 700 infantry and 280 cavalry.[31] Abisares now halted his advance and sent Alexander a sycophantic embassy bearing precious gifts and elephants (a sign of the increasing presence of elephants in the Macedonian army).

Unlike Darius, who had twice abandoned his men, Porus resolutely remained on top of his elephant and never stopped encouraging his men to fight. He took a javelin through his shoulder but despite the blood loss refused to leave his position. When the battle was clearly over he rode off on his elephant, oblivious to his fate. His action impressed Alexander, who followed him, and when he caught up with him Porus refused to bow to the conqueror. When Alexander asked Porus—through interpreters, since Porus did not know Greek—how he wished to be treated, he replied laconically, "like a king" (basilikôs).

Porus's bravery in battle, coupled with his present demeanor and refusal to be intimidated—perhaps reminding Alexander of the defiant Timocleia at Thebes in 335—earned him his life. Alexander reconfirmed his position as ruler of Paurava and bestowed further territories east of the Hydaspes on him, probably making him his vassal. The rank and file of the army were not impressed by the king's action, but Alexander was continuing a pattern of treatment displayed toward Persian and Bactrian nobility to help him maintain Macedonian rule in the areas he conquered.

One of the battle's casualties was Alexander's horse Bucephalas, bought for him by his father, Philip, when he was but a boy, which had received fatal wounds to its side and neck. This was a great personal loss for Alexander, as is evidenced by the name of one of the two cities the king now founded to celebrate his victory: Nicaea (Victory City—perhaps Jalalpur), where the battle took place, and Bucephala (modern Jhelum), on the site of his base camp. Alexander later ordered his mint at Babylon to strike two types of commemorative medallions. The first was a tetradrachm (four drachma coin), with an Indian bowman holding the characteristic body-length bow on the obverse and an elephant on the reverse. The second was a decadrachm (10 drachma coin), with what is believed to be Alexander on Bucephalas attacking an Indian (presumably Porus) on an elephant on the obverse and on the reverse the goddess Nike (Victory) crowning Alexander, who is wearing a diadem and clasping a pike and thunderbolt with an ivy wreath (Figure 17, p. 93). The propaganda value of this coinage was enormous as coins circulated widely in the ancient world: Alexander therefore was sending a message to people who would never see an actual Indian army or even an elephant; he had symbolically turned his victory over Porus into one over India.[32] In this we have the first encounter between East and West on record—and the first representation of Alexander on a coin depicting him with a thunderbolt as Son of Zeus.[33]

The outcome of the battle was another testament to Alexander's tactical genius and overall generalship. It was a brilliant example of what in military parlance is called "convergence"—focusing on one point while attacking from another.[34] His initial plan had been to cross the river by night and then signal Craterus to do the same with his troops while Alexander crept up on Porus, thereby trapping the Indian army between two Macedonian attacking lines. That had been foiled by his failure to research his own route. Nonetheless, he had never been at a proper disadvantage, and once his army engaged Porus its superb fighting prowess completely outclassed the enemy. Equally impressive was his feat of leading over

10,000 men across a swollen and fast-flowing river on all manner of boats within a single night.

The Battle of the Hydaspes River was, however, the apogee of Alexander's invasion of India. The same army that had performed brilliantly for him and followed him faithfully for thousands of miles would soon turn on its beloved king.

13.

RETREAT FROM INDIA

THE MEN HAD LITTLE time to rest after battling Porus at the Hydaspes. Word soon reached them that his cousin, coincidentally named Porus, had just fled across the Hydraortes (Ravi) River, even though he had earlier surrendered to Alexander. The king took this as a sign of defiance and set off in pursuit. He met resistance from the town of Sangala (near Lahore) and besieged it, but the monsoon rains hampered the deployment of his siege engines, and the defenders almost escaped one night. The opportune arrival of troops and elephants from Porus the vassal (the defeated prince at the Hydaspes) gave Alexander the advantage; even so it took two days before finally the defenders capitulated. In this unexpectedly tough siege 1,200 Macedonians were wounded, and in retaliation the army massacred 17,000 defenders, took 70,000 as prisoners, and razed Sangala to the ground. Thus the pattern of barbarity continued. Needless to say, Alexander's actions merely stiffened the resolve of the Indians to oppose him, but then out of the blue an event occurred that forced him to leave the country: his men mutinied.

THE MUTINY AT THE HYPHASIS RIVER

Alexander's *pothos* might well have been driving him forever eastward, but his men thought differently. They were exhausted from all the fighting and could not care less about any worldwide empire.[1] Discontent had been brewing since Hecatompylus in 330, when the men had first started to agitate to go home. Still, they had followed their king into Bactria, but their present experiences—from the daunting size of this unexpectedly mammoth country to being permanently soaked from the unyielding monsoon rains—were the final straw.

For 70 more days after the siege of Sangala the army marched farther inland, saturated, probably suffering from dysentery, snake bites, trench foot, exhaustion, and depression. In addition, they were likely demoralized and terrified by the Indians' poison arrows, the likes of which they had never experienced before, which resulted in an agonizing death: the victims convulsed in pain and shivers, vomited uncontrollably, and suffered a black pus oozing from their wound before gangrene spread throughout their bodies, finally bringing death.[2] Finally, in the summer of 326, they reached the river Hyphasis (Beas), the second-to-last river of the Punja, beyond which lay the vast territory of the Nanda dynasty. Its people numbered in the hundreds of thousands—their capital, Pataliputra, located at the confluence of the Son and Ganges rivers (by modern Patna), alone had a population of 400,000. They were all fierce warriors and were reputed to have 4,000 war elephants, animals the rank and file of the army feared the most. Possibly Alexander's information about what lay beyond the Hyphasis was tainted because it came from local inhabitants, who had every reason to mislead the invading army when they could.[3] Nevertheless, Alexander was resolved to cross the river; perhaps he had his sights set on reaching the Ganges, as he had been finding out details about the Gangetic Plain and its population during his operations in the Punjab.[4] His men thought differently: they refused to cross the river.[5]

At first Alexander tried to coax them across and when that failed gave way to openly berating them for letting him down and shaming them to action, but all to no avail. Finally Coenus stepped forward. He went to great pains to impress on Alexander that his men loved and respected him. Nevertheless, he was adamant that their energy was running out, their bodies were weakened from wounds, their clothes were in tatters, their armor was falling apart from age and damage, and they needed to return to their homes and families. His comments provide an interesting glimpse into the adverse psychological effect that their threadbare clothing and deficient equipment were having on them as well as all their hard years of fighting.

Alexander withdrew in disgust into his tent. Two days went by, and still the men refused to budge; king and army had reached a stalemate. Alexander knew that he had been beaten, but he could not admit defeat. Instead, on the third day he took the auspices (how is unknown), as was his daily regnal duty for the well-being of his people, and proclaimed that they were unfavorable. This was a message from the gods, he declared, to abandon further campaigning and turn around. His men were overjoyed and were reconciled to him. All sides knew that his explanation was to save face, but it did not matter—they were going home.[6] Before he left the Hyphasis Alexander set up 12 stone altars dedicated to the Olympian gods, each said to have been 80 feet high, to mark the eastern boundary of his empire. He had been denied the chance to reach the Ganges, but no one could fail to be impressed by how far east he had marched.

A postscript to the Hyphasis mutiny was Coenus's sudden death, apparently from an unknown illness, a few days later. No ancient writer accuses Alexander of engineering the demise of his most vocal opponent at the Hyphasis; however, we have seen that the king did not like his plans or personal intentions to be thwarted and that those who did so met with untimely ends. Coenus had stymied Alexander's desire to march farther into India: the coincidence of his sudden death is too striking to ignore.[7]

THE SIEGE OF MALLI

From the Hyphasis the men marched back to the Hydaspes, where Alexander had his first sight of a massive fleet of 2,000 vessels that he had early ordered Craterus to build. Even though he had not reached the Ganges, he was still adamant about sailing down the Indus into the Southern (Indian) Ocean, to which end he appointed his boyhood friend Nearchus of Crete as admiral of the new fleet and resolved to set out on his epic journey as soon as he could. He also received at this time 30,000 infantry and 6,000 cavalry reinforcements from Greece, Thrace, and Babylon, the last the headquarters of the imperial treasurer, Harpalus, who had recently provided 25,000 new panoplies for the men, presumably on Alexander's orders. They men joyfully burned their old suits of armor and got some psychological boost from the brand new ones.

In November (of 326) Alexander and 8,000 troops set off for the great voyage down the Indus. The rest of the army was to march alongside the fleet, Hephaestion on the left bank of the river and Craterus on the right. This division was not simply to intimidate the natives on both sides of the river but to separate the two commanders because their personal enmity was exploding daily. Hephaestion appears to have thrown his weight around because of his intimate relationship with Alexander, which made him unpopular with all of his comrades. On one occasion he and Craterus had actually fought with each other and drawn their swords until Alexander intervened and rebuked both of them.

The king sacrificed from the prow of his ship to Poseidon, god of the sea; his wife, Amphitrite; the 50 Nereids, or sea nymphs, as well as to the rivers on which he intended to sail (the Hydaspes, Acesines, and Indus); and finally to Heracles and Zeus. Then to the sound of trumpets and the applause of the natives, who would never have seen anything like this before, the fleet slowly departed, perhaps as many as 40 vessels abreast once the river widened in size to over two miles. Unfortunately, the gods were not moved by Alexander's sacrifice. The fast-flowing waters at the confluence of the Indus and Acesines rivers wreaked havoc with the ships, and a number were damaged or sunk.

In some respects his setback was just as well because news was now reaching him that in the lower Punjab region the Oxydracae (Sudracae) and Malli (Malavas) peoples intended to band together with as many as 100,000 men to obstruct his passage. Since the Macedonians were in the territory of the Malli Alexander decided on a blitzkrieg of their lands, relying on information provided by the area locals.[8] He divided his army into a number of separate units, each under an individual commander. With 6,500 infantry and 2,000 cavalry, including half of the Companion Cavalry, the hypaspists, the Agrianians, and the Dahan mounted archers, he marched 50 miles in only one day and night to attack the Malli from the north. In the meantime Craterus and the satrap of northern India, Philip, son of Machatas, were to advance down the river's west bank, and

Hephaestion, down its east, while Nearchus and the fleet were to sail the Acesines to the Mallis' borders. Finally, Ptolemy was to wait three days and then march to rendezvous with the others. Alexander's plan was to crush the Malli by a series of surprise attacks from different directions; any survivors would fall victim to Ptolemy as they tried to escape.

The troops were far from happy at the prospect of another tough fight, and there was talk of mutiny once more. However, Alexander was able to convince them to conduct this campaign, and they reluctantly followed him into enemy territory. In a mere week they had subdued the Mallian towns west of the Hydraortes, massacring all in their wake as had become their custom—in fact the Malli campaign has rightly been described as a "conquest through terror."[9] As news of the devastation spread the remaining Malli retreated to a citadel in a city also named Malli. The Macedonians took the city with ease; however, the high citadel was a different matter.[10] Perhaps because of their tiredness and unwillingness to be fighting in the first place, the men attacked the citadel halfheartedly. To spur them on Alexander grabbed a scaling ladder and scampered up it to the battlements. His bravado had the desired effect, but as they rushed to follow him all the hypaspists tried to climb the ladders at the same time and broke them under their weight. That left Alexander, along with only Peucestas, Leonnatus, and Abreas, suddenly alone and vulnerable atop the citadel wall.

Alexander realized that he was a sitting duck for the expert Mallian archers. Therefore, in typical brash fashion, he jumped down into the citadel, closely followed by his three comrades. If he were going to die, he intended to take as many of the enemy with him as possible. Inside the citadel they faced a horde of the enemy, and in bitter fighting Abreas was killed by an arrow. Alexander was pushed back against a fig tree, which had the advantage of protecting his back, but then he was shot through the chest by an arrow, which came out of his neck.[11] Most likely the barbed point punctured one of his lungs, for "breath and blood came out from the wound."[12] He slumped to the ground bleeding profusely. Peucestas reacted instantly. He threw the Shield of Achilles that Alexander always carried over the king's supine body and turned to face the enemy soldiers, intent on dispatching as many of them as he could before he suffered a deadly blow. It never came. The Macedonians outside had become near hysterical when Alexander vanished from view; with no thought for their own safety they smashed through the citadel gates and rushed in, searching for Alexander. When they saw him lying in a pool of blood they lost control of themselves and slaughtered everyone—men, women, and children. The fate of the population of Malli induced the Oxydracae to surrender immediately; their lands became part of the vast satrapy of northern India under Philip, son of Machatas.

Alexander's personal doctor, Critobulus of Cos (the same man, incidentally, who treated Philip's eye wound at Methone in 354), was able to remove the arrow from Alexander and sew up the holes in his chest and neck. Nevertheless, he had lost a lot of blood and was dreadfully weak. He had to be taken by ship to the main camp at the confluence of the Acesines and Hydraortes, insisting that he be uncovered so that he was visible. Even so he could hardly move, and his men began to panic, thinking that he was dead. He managed to wave a hand weakly as the boat docked, and everyone erupted in loud cheering. Later, with grim determination he was hoisted onto his horse and grittily rode up and down before the army to show that he was very much alive.

Some weeks later, when his strength returned, Alexander marched to the confluence of the Acesines and Indus. The various people along his route offered their submission to him, and he appointed Peithon, son of Agenor, satrap of southern India as far as the Southern Ocean. There followed a brief campaign against a prince named Musicanus, who was swiftly overcome. Alexander permitted him to continue as ruler, but to be on the safe side he installed a garrison in the capital, Alor. Musicanus soon rebelled against Alexander, who in fury sent Peithon to deal with him: on the king's orders he crucified Musicanus and his Brahman counselors. More bloody were a series of minor campaigns that now followed, the first one against a prince named Oxycanus and the second against a certain Sambus, west of the Indus. Both Oxycanus and Sambus—Musicanus too—had been encouraged to defy Alexander by their Brahman advisers. In this campaign the Macedonians put to death as many as 80,000 natives, including many Brahmans, and kept all of the spoils. Their treatment of these holy men proved to be a dreadful miscalculation.

ALEXANDER AND THE BRAHMANS

The Brahman sages were members of a religious sect who were also politically active as advisers to rulers and fought against enemies when needed.[13] This mixture of thinkers, soldiers, and counselors was something Alexander had not encountered before. They lived an ascetic life in which they suffered all manner of endurance tests, including standing, sitting, or lying naked on stones and motionless all day in the boiling-hot sun, as part of their reflections on teachings about knowledge and reality versus appearance. From their nudity the Greeks coined the term *gymnosophistai,* or "naked thinkers," for them. The Brahmans today are the highest order of the four varnas (social classes) in Indian society, which trace their roots to the late Vedic period (ending in 500 B.C.) when the *Vedas,* the oldest Hindu scripture, was written. They were held in equally high regard by the Indians of antiquity, and anyone who wished to converse with them went to visit them at Taxila rather than inviting them elsewhere.

The sources differ on whether Alexander himself met them or not. The contemporary writer Onesicritus claims that he refused to go to them but at the same time he did not want to offend them by forcing them to his court. Therefore he sent Onesicritus to visit a group of 15 of them and learn about their beliefs and way of life. One of the Brahmans, named Calanus, broke into laughter when Onesicritus told him that Alexander had sent him to learn about their philosophy and bade the Macedonian remove his clothes, boots, and *kausia* and sit naked on the same stones if he wanted to understand the Brahman teachings. When Onesicritus hesitated another philosopher, Dandamis, criticized Calanus's arrogance and praised Alexander because "although he was preoccupied with administering a great empire, he wanted to acquire wisdom, for he was the only warrior philosopher he had ever encountered, and thought it more advantageous than anything else if rulers who have the power to persuade the willing and force the unwilling to learn self-control were wise."[14] Dandamis's answer sounds like invention to make Alexander into a philosopher king.

On the other hand, Arrian relates that Alexander did go to meet the Brahmans but when he reached them they

did nothing more than beat with their feet on the ground they stood on. When Alexander enquired through interpreters what their action meant, they replied "King Alexander, each man possesses no more of this earth than the patch we stand on; yet you, though a man like other men, except of course that you are restless and presumptuous, are roaming over so wide an area away from what is your own, giving no rest to yourself or others. And very soon you too will die, and will possess no more of the earth than suffices for the burial of your body." On that occasion Alexander commended their remarks and the speakers, but his actions were different from and contrary to what he commended.[15]

It is well to note Arrian's closing comment. During the Malli campaign Alexander had attacked a city populated by the Brahmans and slaughtered them indiscriminately. His action demonstrated his misunderstanding of the role that Brahmans played in Indian society and the respect in which they were held. His blunder came back to haunt him when the Brahmans orchestrated a massive revolt as he prepared to leave India.

Despite their opposition and scornful comments to him now, Alexander seems to have been attracted to the simplicity of their lifestyle and beliefs, perhaps seeing in them an affinity with the asceticism of the Cynic Diogenes, whom he had visited when in Corinth in 336. In this he was mistaken, not least because of the Brahmans' belief in independence and their political views. Alexander invited them to join him on his campaign when he left Taxila, but Dandamis refused point-blank and even said that none of the others would follow Alexander. However, Calanus took him up on his offer, which earned him criticism for his lack of self-control and for serving a master other than God. Calanus stayed with the king until illness persuaded him to commit suicide at Persepolis in 324. Presumably he did not take part in the Indian revolt that the Brahmans were behind in 325.

SAILING THE INDIAN OCEAN

If Alexander expected that his bloodthirsty reprisals would help stifle opposition, he would soon find out how mistaken he was. For now he again divided his army. Craterus and Polyperchon were to take three battalions of the phalanx, those soldiers unfit to fight, and the elephants and march across Arachosia to Carmania, where Alexander and the rest of the army would join them after he sailed the Indus. He also promoted Hephaestion to the position of chiliarch and commander of the Royal Hipparchy of the Companion Cavalry, making him second only to Alexander himself in the military hierarchy. After that he marched to Patala (perhaps Hyderabad in southern Pakistan), arriving there in July 325, from where he intended to embark on his journey down the Indus into the Southern Ocean. This was not the only voyage of exploration he had in mind. He now tasked Nearchus with sailing along the relatively unknown thousand miles of the Makran coast to the Persian Gulf. Nearchus was to map the entire coastline and find out whether the ocean was an inland sea like the Mediterranean or an open one encircling the entire world as Aristotle believed.

The Indus at Patala was not a single river but, rather, had a western arm and an eastern one. Alexander had decided to sail down the western arm, and all eyes were on his fleet as it began its long journey. Almost immediately the southwest monsoon winds struck, wrecking some ships and forcing him back. Undaunted, as soon as the winds abated he set sail once more, and this time successfully sailed all the way out into the ocean. In celebration he sacrificed bulls and gold cups to Poseidon and on a small island built altars to Ocean and Earth, thereby marking the southern boundary of his empire—just as the altars on the Hyphasis River designated the eastern. Triumphantly he returned up the eastern arm of the Indus to Patala.

Alexander's achievement was a magnificent one. A mere decade earlier he had been fighting the Triballi and the Illyrians and eliminating potential claimants to the throne in only his second year as king. Now he had sailed the Indian Ocean, had vanquished all opposition from Pella to Hyderabad, had fought battles and prosecuted sieges when he was often seemingly hopelessly outnumbered, and was worshiped by some of his subjects—and he was still only 31 years old.

Now, however, Alexander's successes were about to unravel. He had conquered, so he thought, an area roughly stretching from Kashmir to Karachi (Map 5), but for some time Porus the vassal had been prevailing upon the Indians to rebel against the Macedonians. As Alexander sailed back to Patala the Brahman philosophers, whose love of independence would never have allowed them—or their country—to submit to any invader, organized a full-scale revolt.[16] Philip the satrap was murdered, and in the Punjab a young rebel leader named Chandragupta Maurya (Sandrocottus) joined forces with Porus to undo Macedonian influence in India. The revolt also forced Nearchus to leave Patala early, before Alexander returned. In doing so he was forced to take fewer provisions with him than planned and sail down the western, not eastern, arm of the Indus. He also ran full tilt into the escalating monsoon rains, which threatened to capsize his triaconters, light, open boats with 15 oars on each side. He was therefore compelled to put in at a small island for three weeks—where the crews ate oysters for the first time since they had left Greece.

The widespread Indian revolt showed Alexander's flaw in believing that defeated in battle meant conquered. With 30,000 men he marched north to the river Arabis (Hab) to attack the Oreitae people, who lived close to the modern Lasbela in Baluchistan. He devastated the plain of Lasbela and sent out a message to the natives by symbolically renaming Rhambaceia—the most important village of the region—Alexandria. Then he appointed Apollophanes as satrap, providing him with a force of Agrianians, archers, and mercenary infantry and cavalry under the command of Leonnatus. Almost as soon as Alexander left India the Oreitae revolted, and in a pitched battle Leonnatus slew 6,000 of their troops to reestablish Macedonian control. Still, Alexander's departure from India was hardly covered in glory: it was an ignominious end to his campaign not only there but also in the whole of Central Asia.

Alexander had opened up India (Bactria too, for that matter) to the West, and the Seleucids, Macedonian rulers after Alexander's death, followed in his footsteps by expanding their trade with the Indians. Tales of Alexander's exploits in the country would be told for centuries to come—the *Visnu Purana* (second half of the first millennium A.D.), for example, talks of *yavanas* (Greeks) still living in western India, whose ancestors may well have been Alexander's men. Closer to the king's own time, the argument has been made that his intention to unite all of Asia under his single rule influenced the conquests of Chandragupta, who turned the Indian ideal of the chakravartin, or universal king, into reality.[17]

Alexander's original intention had been to march to Carmania along the desolate Gedrosian coastline (Makran, in Baluchistan), digging wells for water and laying in supplies for Nearchus's fleet at regular intervals. He had consciously made use of Persian royal roads and supply routes during his marches rather than simply foraging for supplies, and he was not going to deviate from this method now.[18] Despite his best intentions he had to scotch that plan when the men ate and drank all the food and water on the arduous 80-mile trek southward from the oasis of Turbat to the coastal town of Pasni. If they consumed all of that in just 80 miles, then a march of several hundred was an impossible feat. Alexander was therefore forced to find another passage west so that he could feed his troops, leaving Nearchus and his crews to fend for themselves.

It would have been an easy matter for Alexander to have left India by the same route he had entered it. Instead he sent most of his men, including those unfit for service, to Carmania via the Mulla Pass, while he took some troops—perhaps as many as 30,000—and a baggage train of the men's Asian spouses, families, and belongings and set off via present-day Karachi and the Lasbela plain, over the Kirthar Range, and then through the harsh, bleak Gedrosian Desert.[19] The Gedrosians had supported their eastern neighbors the Oreitae in their earlier revolt, but that was not why Alexander took this route—he wanted to cross the desert, as has been argued, to better the attempts of previous rulers, such as Semiramis, Queen of Assyria, and Cyrus the Great, who had lost almost all of their men because of the frightful natural conditions.[20] Guided by these personal reasons, Alexander committed arguably the biggest military blunder of his reign.[21]

THE MARCH THROUGH THE GEDROSIAN DESERT

From Pasnia Alexander marched for seven days west along the coast to Gwadar before turning north to follow an inland road. The monsoon rains had watered the area well enough for the men to feed themselves and their families. Then came a nightmare trek of 450 miles lasting 60 scorching days and freezing nights from early October to early December (325) across the Dashtiari Plain to the north of the Bampur River and eventually to Pura (perhaps modern Iranshahr), the capital of Gedrosia, with practically no food and water. It was, said Arrian, worse than all the fighting of the previous decade.[22] According to the ancient writers the men had to turn to eating the pack animals when some of them choked to death from eating local plants. Many of them succumbed to the scorching heat and lack of water, either dying from heat stroke or simply falling down, too weak to continue, and never getting up again from the burning sand. Their horses and pack animals likewise suffered because of the depths of the shifting sands. The sudden flash flooding that occurred in the region added to their woes. One dark night the men camped by a dry riverbed, but a torrential downpour turned it into a raging river, which swept away the entire baggage train, including most of the wives and children of the men, never to be seen again. The soldiers managed to escape drowning, but only with their arms and armor: everything else was lost. Another time a sandstorm so blotted out navigational landmarks that the troops exhaustedly marched farther inland than they ought to have done. When Alexander realized this error he took some cavalry southward and eventually made it to the coast. There he was able to dig wells for fresh drinking water and summon the survivors to him. The last week of the journey followed the coastline, but it was still a struggle before the men reached Pura, where they ate and drank nonstop and gradually recovered from their ordeal.

During the march an incident occurred that again demonstrated Alexander's great leadership skills and concern for his men:

> Alexander was suffering terribly from thirst and he was also in great pain
> from leading his men on foot so that they might bear their own difficulties

better because everyone was feeling the same hurt and stress. In the meantime some of the light-armed soldiers went in search of water and found a small pool in a shallow cleft formed by a small, dribbling spring. They collected the water with difficulty and straightway took it to Alexander as if it were a valuable gift. As they approached him they poured it into a helmet and gave it to him. He took it, and praising the men for what they had done, immediately poured it out on the ground in full view of everyone. His action reinvigorated the entire army to such an extent that it was as if everyone had drank the water that Alexander had poured away.[23]

This is certainly a tribute to Alexander. But can it excuse the fact that for his own personal reasons his march resulted in the deaths of possibly a third of the men who had accompanied him and their families as well as the loss of their belongings and spoils of war? He had survived the march with fewer losses than Semiramis and Cyrus, but it is still a massive blot on Alexander's entire Asian campaign, much like Napoleon's disastrous retreat from Moscow in 1812.

ROYAL PUNISHMENTS

During his stay at Pura Alexander received unwelcome reports that about 14 of his 23 satraps and governors had been guilty of corrupt practices and even openly rebellious while he had been in India. Presumably they did not expect him to return alive, but their actions also stemmed from discontent at their loss of power thanks to Alexander's changes to the satrapal system. It was also brought to his attention that some of his senior staff and regular troops had violated local women, some of whom were virgins. In addition, he was smarting from the fact that during the latter stages of his march through the Gedrosian Desert his urgent appeals to the satraps of Gedrosia and Carmania for food and supplies had been ignored. Therefore he embarked on an immediate purge of men he deemed had done him a disservice, sometimes dramatically described as a reign of terror.[24]

A number of satraps, most of whom were Iranians, were deposed or killed, including Astaspes, satrap of Carmania; Orxines of Persis; Abulites of Susiana; and Oxathres of Paraetacene. Alexander replaced them with his own men. He also executed the generals Cleander (Coenus's brother) and Sitalces (both of whom had murdered Parmenion), together with 600 regular soldiers for raping women. Then Alexander issued a royal edict, which is commonly called the Dissolution Decree, instructing all his satraps and generals in Asia to disband their mercenary armies. They had at their disposal tens of thousands of mercenaries, which Alexander saw as a threat to himself if he were ever opposed. He hired those mercenaries who elected to join him, but at least 50,000 of them were transported to Taenarum, the southern tip of the Peloponnese, which had by then become a refuge for mercenaries. The remainder simply roamed the eastern half of the empire, robbing and pillaging to survive. In actuality, his Dissolution Decree created a major military and social problem that he was forced to deal with several months later in Susa.

Alexander's return from India prompted the imperial treasurer, Harpalus, to take flight from Babylon. Harpalus had deserted Alexander's court before, in 333 before the Battle of Issus, but Alexander later forgave his boyhood friend and appointed him treasurer. At Babylon Harpalus had led a life of luxury, enjoying the company (at different times) of two expensive Athenian mistresses, Pythionice and Glycera. Alexander might have been prepared to overlook Harpalus's venality and opulent lifestyle, but not when he began calling Glycera his queen and struck his own coinage at the Babylonian mint. Both actions exceeded his own authority and flouted that of Alexander. Fearing for his life, the treacherous Harpalus made his getaway, taking with him 6,000 mercenaries, 5,000 talents of stolen money, and 30 warships. He sought asylum in Athens, where he worked to incite a revolt against Alexander, which he considered was his only chance of survival (pp. 290–291).

The men's relief at surviving the Gedrosian Desert manifested itself in a week-long drinking binge, arranged by Alexander as a Dionysiac revel, as they marched from Pura across Carmania. Alexander was said to have dressed as Dionysus and danced atop a special chariot. The march, though, was another misjudgment on Alexander's part—as Curtius noted, the Macedonians were so drunk that they would have been "easy prey if the vanquished races had only had the courage to challenge riotous drinkers—why, a mere 1,000 men, if sober, could have captured this group on its triumphal march, weighed down as it was from 7 days of drinking. But it is fortune that allots fame and a price to things, and she turned even this piece of disgraceful soldiering into a glorious achievement!"[25] At the same time Alexander's appearance as Dionysus brought the idea of Alexander the god sharply back into focus.

ALEXANDER'S DIVINITY

Alexander exploited his divine lineage throughout his reign, but after his visit to Siwah in 331 he openly called himself Son of Zeus and referred to Philip as merely his mortal father. Greeks and Macedonians were a deeply pious people who routinely believed that the gods assumed human or animal shape and came down to earth to mix with humans. Even on his deathbed Alexander still performed the daily sacrifices for the well-being of his kingdom so as not to offend the gods. As the Classical period progressed scientific and intellectual thought questioned various events and natural phenomena rather than simply accepting them as the will of the gods, but nevertheless traditional religious orthodoxies still held sway. The story that Zeus had taken on the guise of a snake and impregnated Olympias, for example, would not have raised any eyebrows, nor would Alexander's divine ancestry.

Alexander thus had a claim to divinity, given his background, divine ancestry, and the visit to Siwah, especially at such an early age.[26] At the end of the fifth century the people of Amphipolis established a cult to the deceased Spartan general Brasidas. Then the people of Samos appear to have worshiped another Spartan general, Lysander, celebrating a festival to him while he was still alive. There was a cult of Amyntas III at Pydna, and Philip may have been worshiped in his lifetime if the statue of him set up in the Temple of Artemis at Ephesus and the Altar to Zeus Philippios at Eresus (on Lesbos) are anything to go by, but significantly these places were far from the Greek mainland, and he did not try to make his own people worship him. Compare the early Roman emperors, who were content with their provincial subjects worshiping them but not the people of Rome or Italy. However, Philip—like other Macedonian kings—was most likely deified on death.[27]

Alexander therefore had precedent on his side for the worship of a living man, and he was far from the Greek mainland when he began to tout his divinity. He may well have been behind Anaxarchus's attempt to persuade the army that since he was going to be a god when he died, he may as well be one while alive. Anaxarchus did not peddle this idea to the Greeks and Macedonians back home but only to the army in Asia. To set that up, Alexander most likely enticed Callisthenes into embellishing events even before Siwah to depict his superhuman status all along, including, for example, the apparent obeisance of the Pamphylian Sea under Mount Climax and the thunderstorm from Zeus following Alexander's severing of the Gordian knot. After his crucial visits to Didyma and Siwah Alexander may well have put into circulation the various tales of his divine conception and birth to give himself more of a divine pedigree.

Of course there was a ripple effect to the more conservative mainland, but there the people did not take Alexander the god seriously. After Antipater defeated Agis III of Sparta in 330 the Spartans had sent an embassy to Alexander appealing for mercy and buttering him up by recognizing him as divine. Perhaps because of this Alexander pardoned them—as they had hoped. Then in 323 Demosthenes sarcastically told the Athenians that "if Alexander wants he can be the son of Zeus and of Poseidon."[28] At that time, as we shall see, the Greeks were debating Alexander's godhead not because he had demanded deification but to support their appeals over his recent decree sending exiles back to their native cities.

Did Alexander really believe that he was a god on earth, or did he exploit his pretensions to personal divinity for political and psychological reasons, as did his successors, men such as Ptolemy, Seleucus, and Antigonus Monopthalmus?[29] This is not a question that can be compellingly answered, but on balance it appears that he came to believe in his divinity. His megalomania cost him more than just his credibility with his men, however—that character flaw must surely affect our evaluation of his "greatness."

When he first became king Alexander had merely called himself a descendant of Zeus, given that he traced his lineage back to Zeus and Heracles, as did the other members of the Argead ruling family. He took care to perform his religious duties carefully, and he was a model of piety, dutifully sacrificing at the tombs of Protesilaus and Achilles on the eve of his Persian expedition, for example, as well as to various gods and heroes as that campaign progressed. The visit to Didyma in 334, which prompted Apollo to begin speaking again after considerable silence and declare that Alexander was a son of Zeus, was a game changer. While Alexander's visit to the Oracle of Zeus Ammon at Siwah in 331 has been seen as the turning point in his divinity, I would argue that his quest for apotheosis began with Apollo at Didyma.

After he won control of Egypt Alexander, only in his mid-twenties, was worshiped by the native Egyptians. The psychological effect on him must have been tremendous. To find out if what Apollo had claimed was true, and if the Egyptians were right, Alexander needed to consult Zeus himself, to learn, as Aristobulus stated, "his own origin more precisely or at least be in a position to say he had learned it."[30] Since Alexander and the priest of Zeus Ammon at Siwah met in private, we do not know exactly what transpired. A delighted Alexander emerged from the meeting to proclaim to his men that Zeus had acknowledged him as his son, but as Aristobulus's comment indicates, he would have said that even if the Oracle had rejected Alexander's question about his divine kinship. After Siwah Alexander the man morphed into Alexander the god.

Yet the question still remains whether Alexander's proclamation at Siwah was all for show or whether he genuinely believed it. He knew that his army's next battle against Darius at Gaugamela would be its toughest because it was a battle Darius had to win no matter the cost. To rally his men before the fighting Alexander delivered a rousing speech and appealed to the gods as Son of Zeus to give them a sign. An eagle duly landed on the Persian line, which he immediately said was sent from his divine father to show that he was on the invaders' side. His reaction might be genuine belief or quickly seizing a providential opportunity afforded by the circling bird. But better indications exist that Alexander actually believed he was a god.

Most prominent is his controversial attempt to introduce *proskynesis* at his court in Bactria in 327. Alexander would have been well aware that his action would provoke hostility among his men, who regarded the custom as sacrilegious and as free men objected to its slave-like posture. The belief that he was striving to create equality among all of his subjects and intended *proskynesis* to be a common form of greeting cannot be correct, because he also knew that his men derided the Persians when they prostrated themselves before him and would never themselves stoop—literally—to the same lows. That leaves us with only one explanation: he intended *proskynesis* to acknowledge his divine status, regardless of the hostile reaction.

From then on it was a downward spiral into megalomania as Alexander openly flaunted his divinity, alienating his men in a way that Philip never had. The Porus medallion, struck after the Battle of the Hydaspes River in 326, was the first representation of Alexander on a coin; significantly it depicted him clasping a thunderbolt as the Son of Zeus.[31] Also in India, Alexander's break with Heracles, born a mortal and deified only on death, and association with Dionysus, who was born a god, speaks volumes, as does the march across Carmania in 324 when he dressed as Dionysus and orchestrated a *proskynesis* of sorts by standing atop a wagon, thereby positioning himself above his men for symbolic effect.[32] More ominous is the contemporary Ephippus's account that in the final years of the reign,

> Alexander came to wear even sacred clothing as it suited him. Sometimes he wore the purple robe, cloven sandals, and horns of Ammon as if he were the god; other times he would pretend to be Artemis, whose cloak he often wore when he was driving his chariot, together with a Persian robe, which showed off the goddess' bow and javelin above his shoulders. Sometimes he would appear as if he were Hermes. And at other times, almost every day in fact, he wore a purple cloak, a tunic with a white stripe, and a cap with the royal diadem on it. In private with his friends he wore the sandals of Hermes, the petasus on his head, and in his hand he held the caduceus. Very often he wore a lion's skin and carried a club, just like Heracles.... Alexander used to have the floor sprinkled with exquisite perfumes and fragrant wine. Myrrh and other kinds of incense were burnt before him. All those in his

presence stayed silent or spoke just a few words of good omen because of their fear, for he was a very violent man, with no regard for human life, and appeared to be a person of melancholic constitution.[33]

The manner of dress and especially the burning of incense and the reverential silence in Alexander's presence indicate a cult to him while alive. Certainly cults for him were found on the Greek mainland, Asia Minor, and farther afield, but these were more likely political than the result of genuine belief on their adherents' parts.[34]

It is noteworthy that among the reasons for the later mutiny at Opis in 324 was the men's dissatisfaction with Alexander's orientalism and divinity. They contemptuously told him that if he wanted to invade Arabia (his next campaign), he could do so with his father Zeus—and one of his reasons for invading Arabia was to be worshiped as a god. Finally, he allegedly asked the Indian philosophers how a man could become a god, to which they had replied: by doing something a man cannot do. Alexander's military exploits to date and the empire he had forged in so short a time were indeed superhuman: it looked as though he had done what no man could do. In the end, a fateful June day in Babylon proved his mortality after all.

THE RETURN OF NEARCHUS

The Macedonian army arrived at Salmus, the capital of Carmania, by winter 324. There a group of dirty, haggard, and malnourished men asked to be admitted into Alexander's presence. No one recognized them until their leader introduced himself: Nearchus. The Macedonian admiral had put in at Carmania's main harbor, Harmozeia (Hormuz), about five days' march from Salmus; he had survived a 1,000-mile, 60-day voyage along the Makran coast with the loss, astonishingly, of only one ship. Alexander broke down and wept tears of joy before calling for sacrifices to Zeus, Apollo, Poseidon, Heracles, and the other gods of the sea as a thank offering for the fleet's safe return. He also held a festival with games and musical events to celebrate not only that but also—astonishingly—his conquest of

India and safe passage through the Gedrosian Desert. Still, his men allowed Alexander his triumph and even egged him on to kiss his lover the eunuch Bagoas when he won the singing and dancing competition. It would be interesting to know whether any jealously existed between Alexander's closest boyhood friend and lover Hephaestion and Bagoas over Alexander's affections.

Nearchus's men had been forced to survive on only fish and dates until they arrived off the Carmanian coast and could pillage the natives' arable crops, fruits, and vines. They had plenty of stories to tell, which enthralled the Macedonians, Alexander especially, for hours.[35] But Nearchus's experiences had a more practical value for Alexander: despite all manner of trials and tribulations, a fleet had navigated an unknown coastline without depending on a land army to furnish it with provisions or protection.

Nearchus wrote an account of his epic travels, which Arrian later used as the basis of his *Indica*. As exciting as Nearchus' adventure had been, its impact on the locals he had encountered along the way stood in sobering contrast.[36] The Makran coastal people known as the "fish-eaters" (west of Karachi), who scraped water out of sand with long, claw-like fingers and ate only stranded fish, were sent packing when Nearchus arrived at their homes and stole all their meager supplies of food and water. As the Macedonians progressed westward they seized sheep and goats on which local inhabitants depended for their food, but worse was their conduct at a tiny impoverished town named Cyiza. Its people offered them fish, dates, and cakes, but Nearchus and his men overpowered them and forced them to hand over all their wheat, barley, and fish meal or suffer extermination. They must certainly have suffered starvation after they left—in fact, all who over the years had borne the brunt of Alexander and his army in their territory must have suffered considerable losses to their livestock, provisions, and reserves.

By now Alexander had laid plans for the invasion of Arabia. His reasons ranged from the economic to the personal. Among other things the land was fertile, and he planned to establish colonies on the lush islands of Tylus (Bahrain) and Icarus (Falaika). He may also have wanted to control the lucrative spice trade with Arabia Felix and even as far as Yemen. Personally, there was his "never-ending thirst for fresh conquests," as Arrian would have it,[37] and the fact that the Arabs were "the only bar-barians of these areas that had not sent an embassy to him or done any-thing in terms of their position and they had showed him no respect."[38] Since Bactria Alexander had fallen back on this last reason for making war on a people, which he interpreted as a sign of rebellion.[39] Further, the Arabs worshiped only Uranus and Dionysus, because Uranus was the greatest god and because Dionysus's expedition to India had brought him great fame. Alexander believed himself more than worthy to be con-sidered by the Arabs as a third god because he had performed deeds on a par with those of Dionysus.[40] His men, however, thought differently, as yet another mutiny soon proved.

14.

ALEXANDER'S FINAL YEARS

A LEXANDER LEFT SALMUS AND marched northward to Pasargadae, which he had first visited in 330. When the satrap of Persis, Phrasaortes, had died in 327 or 326, a certain Orxines succeeded him, but without the king's affirmation. As Alexander approached Pasargadae Orxines met him and gave him expensive gifts to win his favor, but the king was not swayed. He soon had his chance to get rid of him when he visited the tomb of Cyrus the Great in Pasargadae and discovered it looted and that the broken skeleton of the Great King was scattered unceremoniously on its floor. He instructed Bagoas to accuse Orxines of maladministration and desecration. Bagoas needed little encouragement: he was still smarting from Orxines snubbing him by giving presents to the king but not "the king's whores."[1] The unfortunate Orxines was crucified without trial. As a sign of his respect for Cyrus, Alexander tasked Aristobulus with rebuilding the tomb and ensuring that his remains were properly interred.

FROM PASARGADAE TO SUSA

Before he left Pasargadae Alexander appointed Peucestas, who had bravely protected him during the siege of Malli, as satrap of Persis—of all of Alexander's Macedonian appointees he was the only one who learned Persian and embraced Persian manners. Then the king marched south to Persepolis, where he joined Hephaestion, who had traveled there with the baggage train and elephants by an easier route. The stay in Persepolis was marked this time by the ritual suicide by self-immolation of the Brahman sage Calanus, who had joined Alexander's retinue at Taxila. Calanus had fallen ill in Pasargadae and at Persepolis resolved to die. He asked for a large pyre to be built, close to the shell of the former palace, and to the blaring of trumpets, the cheers of the assembled men, and the war cries of the elephants, Calanus ascended the pyre and sat on it without making a sound or movement while the flames engulfed him. In his honor Alexander held games and festivities, including a drinking contest. The alcohol intake of the Macedonians had been steadily increasing during their time in Central Asia, but this competition was excessive even by their standards. After it, 35 men died immediately, and six, not long after; the winner (unfortunately named Champion), who drank 12 quarts of wine, died four days later.[2]

After sobering up, a march of 24 days along the Royal Road took Alexander and his army from Persepolis to Susa, where they arrived in late February or March 324. Peucestas visited him here, as did Nearchus, who after his epic voyage along the Makran coast had taken a fleet to the mouth of the Euphrates. He had not been able to map the coastline in the same sort of detail as in his earlier expedition because strong tides and currents had kept him in open waters; all he had found was nothing more than a few shallow harbors that could not accommodate a war fleet. Nevertheless, Alexander rewarded him with a crown for his tremendous navigational accomplishments and also gave crowns to Peucestas for his heroism at Malli and Leonnatus for his victory over the Oreitae.

At Susa Alexander was forced to take drastic action to remedy the military and economic problems that his Dissolution Decree had caused. Unable to draft the thousands of ex-mercenaries in his army who were still roaming Asia and conscious of the danger posed by the ever-increasing numbers of them at Taenarum in Greece, he decided on a simple solution: send them home. To this end he issued what is commonly called the Exiles Decree, ordering all Greek exiles (not just mercenaries), excluding murderers, antidemocrats, and the Thebans (probably because he still remembered their defiance in 335), to return to their home cities and authorizing Antipater to use force against any city that refused to comply: "King Alexander to the exiles from the Greek cities. We have not been the cause of your exile, but, apart from those of you who are under a curse, we shall be the cause of your return to your own native cities. We have written to Antipater about this so that if any cities are not willing to restore you, he may force them."[3]

The decree was to be officially proclaimed by royal messenger at the Olympic Games of July 31 to August 4 (324). This wide-sweeping measure could hardly be kept a secret, and exiles started to make their way back to the mainland well before the games. The decree is another example of Alexander's pragmatism: it solved the immediate problems presented by the marauding mercenaries in the eastern half of the Macedonian Empire and to some degree stabilized it. At the same time it helped to shore up his support base in Greece while he was away campaigning in Arabia since the returned exiles would owe him their loyalty. On the other hand, it was a unilateral decision that rode roughshod over the provisions of the League of Corinth, which had guaranteed the autonomy of cities in their domestic affairs. The individual cities were naturally angry over this and worried about the social and economic chaos that tens of thousands of returning exiles would bring with them, especially as Greece was still recovering from a recent famine. They therefore sent embassies to the king at Babylon pleading for its repeal, which presumably explains why Antipater took no action against them until Alexander issued his ruling.

THE MASS MARRIAGE AT SUSA
AND THE "UNITY OF MANKIND"

Waiting for Alexander at Susa were the Persian royal princesses who had fallen into his hands after Issus in 333 and whom he had instructed to receive a Greek education and learn Greek. At that time he had deliberately taken over Darius's role as protector and father, in which capacity he had promised to find them husbands. He had not forgotten his promise. The stage was therefore set at Susa for the famous mass marriage in which Alexander and 91 senior personnel were forced to marry Persian royal women. Many of the bridegrooms would have left wives back home in Macedonia, but that mattered little as they were polygamists. The elaborate ceremony followed Persian custom, with the bridegrooms sitting on high-backed chairs to receive a toast, after which their brides entered and kissed their respective fiancés to solemnize the marriage.

Alexander married Stateira, the eldest daughter of Darius III, and Parysatis, the youngest daughter of Artaxerxes III.[4] The other daughter of the late Darius, Drypetis, was married to Hephaestion. The actual marriages took place on one day and were followed by five days of lavish, celebratory performances by conjurors, rhapsodes, harp-players, flute-players, and tragic and comic actors. To celebrate the unions Alexander personally paid off all of his soldiers' debts incurred over the years, which cost him over 20,000 talents. The rank-and-file debtors were delighted with their king's generosity but not so those who had been forced into their interracial marriages. After Alexander's death the following year almost all of them divorced their wives—we know of only one man, Seleucus, who stayed married. Seleucus's wife was Spitamenes of Bactria's daughter Apame (the only Central Asian Iranian woman among the brides at Susa).

One ancient writer claimed that Alexander organized the mass marriage at Susa to unite the races—in much the same way as his integration of foreigners into his army and administration, his bid to introduce *proskynesis* at his court, and his marriage to Roxane.[5] There are still some modern scholars who concur, and in Oliver Stone's *Alexander* movie a brotherhood of mankind is uppermost in the king's mind. Nothing could be further from the truth: Alexander had no such idealistic intention, let alone actual policy, and as in all matters he was always the pragmatist.[6]

He used foreigners in his army to help maintain his numbers and especially for their specialist military skills, for example, mounted archers and javelin men. When he did so they remained in their own ethnic divisions to set them apart from the squadrons of his own men; only toward the end of his reign, when Alexander constituted a new army, as we shall see, did he slowly absorb them into existing companies, such as the Arachotians, Bactrians, and Sogdianians into the Companion Cavalry. Later, he included nine Persians in the royal *agema* and 20,000 Asians under Peucestas, who joined the army at Babylon in 323.[7] In his administration, native noblemen provided a vital liaison role between the mass of the subject peoples and Alexander, given their knowledge of local affairs and linguistic skills. Alexander intended them to help promote and maintain Macedonian rule. In this regard he married Roxane to exploit the influence of her father, Oxyartes of Bactria. Finally, Alexander's attempt to enforce *proskynesis* on his men had less to do with social protocol and more to do with his pretensions to personal divinity.

Pragmatism was likewise at the core of the mass marriage. He intended these multiple marriages to pollute the Persian bloodline, thereby ending that ethnic identity, so that there could never be another challenger to the self-proclaimed King of Asia. Since the easternmost satrapies and India had thrown off Macedonian rule as soon as Alexander had left them, it was imperative for him to maintain control over his new kingdom of Asia, which meshed together Europe and the former Persian Empire. The marriages thus brought about a new class of commanders and administrators, one of mixed Irano-Macedonian blood, who would not be seen as foreign conquerors.[8] That no Greek women were brought out from the mainland to marry Persian noblemen and that a few months later Alexander forbade his discharged veteran soldiers from taking their Asian wives and children back home with them speak volumes (although he promised to return sons to fathers after they received a Greek education).

The Susa marriage was destined to have a long legacy: together with his brutal destruction of the sacred books of the *Avesta*, it is why present-day Zoroastrians of Iran call Alexander "the accursed."[9]

THE OPIS MUTINY

From Susa Alexander followed the Tigris River north into Mesopotamia to Opis, which he reached by midsummer. There he announced that Craterus (Antipater's son-in-law) would lead several thousand of the veterans and wounded soldiers back to their homes in Greece. They were to receive honorable discharges and full pay on their long trek, with an added bonus of one talent each when they arrived home. Alexander's decision appeared sensible enough in the circumstances—the Arabian expedition was likely to be a long and hard-fought one, and he needed all his men to be fighting fit. However, the men's reaction was startling: they mutinied, sarcastically telling him that if he wanted to keep marching, he could do so with his father Ammon. Their comments indicate their bitterness over his pretensions to personal divinity and continued orientalism. The straw that broke the camel's back, though, came in 324, when the 30,000 youths from Lydia, Lycia, Syria, Egypt, and the northeast satrapies joined the army at Susa. Their numbers had been steadily building over the years as Alexander traversed Asia. The king dubbed them the *epigonoi*—successors—even calling them a counterbalance (*antitagma*) to the Macedonian phalanx.[10] Acceptance of a mixed Macedonian–Iranian army was intolerable for the men who had loyally followed his arduous journey from Asia Minor to India. Interpreting his discharge order as a sign that he no longer had confidence in them and preferred foreigners to the traditional army, his troops rebelled.

This time Alexander acted more forcefully than at the Hyphasis River in 326. He called on his hypaspists, who were still loyal to him, to execute 13 of the most vocal protesters on the spot and then delivered a long, critical harangue to the rebellious troops, which Arrian quotes in his narrative of the mutiny. Alexander began by rightly praising Philip for what he had done for his people and country (quoted on p. 106) but followed that with a self-centered account of how he had built the vast empire that his father had only been crafting, the wounds he had suffered along the way, and how he had bestowed greater glory on the Macedonians than Philip:

> These services which my father rendered you, great as they are when considered by themselves alone, are actually small in comparison with our own.... I opened up for you the Hellespontine straits, although at that time the Persians controlled the sea, and after my cavalry victory over the satraps of Darius I added all Ionia to your empire and all Aeolis, both Phrygias and Lydia; I captured Miletus by siege, and gave you the enjoyment of all the other countries that voluntarily surrendered to my power. All the benefits from Egypt and Cyrene, which I won without a blow, go to you; "hollow" Syria, Palestine, Mesopotamia, are your possessions; Babylon, Bactria, Susa are yours, and yours are the wealth of the Lydians, the treasures of the Persians, the bounty of India and the outer sea. It is you

who are satraps, generals and taxiarchs. If you consider me, what is there still in my possession after these exertions but this purple and diadem? I have acquired nothing for myself; no one can point to treasures of mine, but only to your possessions or what is kept in trust for you, for I have nothing to gain by keeping them for my own use; I eat the same food as you do, I sleep as you do, except that my food is not, I think, as luxurious as some of you consume, and that I know that on your behalf I am wakeful, so that you may be able to slumber soundly. But, you may say, the exertions and hardships were yours and all these acquisitions were mine, while I direct you without any personal exertion or hardship!...Come then, let any of you strip and display his own wounds, and I will display mine in turn; in my case there is no part of the body, or none in front, that has been left unwounded, and there is no weapon of close combat, no missile whose scars I do not bear on my person, but I have been wounded by the sword hand to hand, shot by arrows and struck by a catapult, and I am often struck by stones and clubs for your interest, your glory and your riches, while I lead you as conquerors through every land and sea, river, mountain and plain.... And now it was my intention to send away only men unfit for war, to be the envy of those at home but, as you all desire to go, let all of you begone, return to your homes and report that your king, Alexander, defeated Persians, Medes, Bactrians, Sacae, subdued Uxians, Arachotians, Drangians, conquered Parthyaeans, Chorasmians, Hyrcanians as far as the Caspian sea, went over the Caucasus beyond the Caspian gates, crossed the river Oxus and the Tanais, and even the river Indus which no one but Dionysus had crossed before, and the Hydaspes and Acesines and Hydraotes, and would have crossed the Hyphasis as well but for your apprehensions, and that he burst out on the great sea by both mouths of the Indus, and came through the Gedrosian desert, where no one had ever before gone with an army, and acquired Carmania and the land of the Oritans as he passed through, while the fleet had already sailed along the coast from India to Persia, and that when you returned to Susa you deserted him and went off, handing him over to the protection of the barbarians he had conquered. This is a report that will perhaps win you a fine reputation with men and will doubtless be holy in the sight of heaven. Begone![11]

His attempt to shame his men into submission this way fell on deaf ears, so he removed himself to the palace to play another waiting game.

Another two-day standoff followed, but on the third day Alexander decided to force the issue. He did not intend to exploit religion again as at the Hyphasis River; instead, he threatened to replace senior Macedonian personnel with Persians and actually began that process. In addition he transferred Macedonian titles for his Foot Companions and Companion Cavalry onto Persian troops. His action had the desired effect. In great shame the men dropped their arms before the palace and begged him to forgive them. He did so, and in tears he and his men reconciled.

As a further means to reconciliation Alexander held an enormous banquet, attended by at least 9,000 people. He sat at the head table, flanked by senior Macedonian military and civilian officials; next to him were Persians, and next to them were members of other races. At the end of the meal, the king stood and, as Arrian stated, prayed for "various blessings and especially that the Macedonians and Persians should enjoy harmony as partners in government."[12] This so-called banquet of reconciliation and Alexander's prayer for concord (*homonoia*), which implied equality in the administration of the new Macedonian Empire, has also been considered part of a unity of mankind policy. Again, however, Alexander was simply being pragmatic. Among other things, in ending the Opis mutiny he had exploited the enmity between Macedonians and foreigners, and the seating arrangement at the banquet emphasized a clear pecking order. His prayer was likewise practical: he needed a united army for the invasion of Arabia to succeed as well as harmony among his subjects.

Perhaps even prayers were a lost cause. The extent of the animosity between Macedonians and foreigners—even Greeks—had been ably demonstrated by the clash between a Macedonian soldier, Corrhagus, and a Greek wrestler, Dioxippus, while Alexander was recovering from the wound he sustained at Malli.[13] Corrhagus had challenged Dioxippus to a fight after he had criticized the latter for not fighting in battle with them. Dioxippus quickly got the drop on Corrhagus, and Alexander had to order him to stop. Needless to say, Dioxippus's days were numbered: after being falsely accused of stealing a goblet from Alexander, he wrote a letter of protest to the king and committed suicide.

Alexander had successfully ended another mutiny, but this time he took pains to ensure that the army remained loyal to him in the future. He still discharged the veterans and wounded soldiers—10,000 infantrymen and 1,500 cavalrymen in all—who left for Greece under Craterus's command—a convenient means for Alexander to rid himself of the increasingly hostile general. Alexander had been incorporating native troops into his armed forces for some years, which correspondingly decreased the Greco-Macedonian element to his army. He intended these fresh troops to accept the army base as their home, not their own lands, thereby reducing the chance of mutinying to return to where they had been born and raised.[14] Just as the invasion of Bactria was a new phase in the Macedonian invasion of Asia, so the inclusion of increasing numbers of foreign troops to replace his own men was a new phase in the Macedonian army, one that grew directly out of Alexander's *pothos* to continue campaigning where he could.

Craterus set off from Susa for Cilicia, where he would winter before transporting the men across to Greece. Once there, according to Arrian, he was to assume Antipater's duties,[15] while the latter, now aged 73, was to take 10,000 reinforcements to Alexander at Babylon. Antipater had done a sterling job in keeping the Greeks as well as the Illyrians and the Paeonians passive while Alexander was in Asia.[16] He had faced acerbic opposition from Olympias, who had criticized him endlessly in letters to her son, which strained relations between him and Alexander. Olympias had finally withdrawn from meddling in political affairs in 324 when she went to live in Epirus, but that did not stop her complaints to Alexander. He might have summoned Antipater to him because he had finally given in to his mother, whom he trusted implicitly.[17] Antipater's criticism of Alexander's divine pretensions did not help him either.

Antipater, by now in his seventies, probably suspected Alexander's motives and, with no wish to suffer the fate of the other Old Guard generals, refused to leave Macedonia. Instead, he sent his eldest son, Cassander, to tell Alexander that he could not spare the men, given the growing tensions in Greece. There was some truth to this excuse because of potential threats from the mercenaries collecting at Taenarum and Antipater's lack of manpower from the many reinforcements he had needed to send to Alexander over the years.[18]

THE DEATH OF HEPHAESTION

From Susa Alexander marched to Ecbatana, arriving there in the autumn of 324. There, he held a festival, complete with 3,000 athletic, dramatic, and musical performers, in honor of Dionysus, the god with whom he now associated himself. Then after a drinking party Hephaestion fell ill and quickly developed a fever. His doctor, Glaucias, ordered him to bed and to eat a carefully planned diet. Hephaestion was the model patient for an entire week, but then he tired of the imposed diet and ate a whole chicken, washed down by half a gallon of chilled wine. The sickness returned, and he died the same day.

The death of his friend and lover, whom he had first met as a page at Philip's court, caused Alexander intense anguish.[19] He immediately had the unfortunate Glaucias crucified and issued a directive that the entire empire was to be in mourning for three days, during which he sat by Hephaestion's body and refused to eat. In Homeric fashion he cut off his hair—just as Achilles had done when the corpse of Patroclus was brought to him—and ordered lavish funeral games to be held in Hephaestion's memory, in which 3,000 athletes and entertainers competed. He also dispatched an embassy to the Oracle of Zeus Ammon at Siwah requesting that Hephaestion be honored with a hero cult—making him a demigod—for his achievements. Finally, he had Hephaestion's body solemnly transported to Babylon, Alexander's next destination, to be interred in a gigantic brick ziggurat over 200 feet high at an estimated cost of 10,000 talents. Alexander did not live long enough to oversee its construction.

Alexander's grief was excessive but understandable. Hephaestion was more than just Alexander's most senior military commander: he was his closest friend and confidant. The two of them were lovers, for it was said that the only thing that conquered Alexander was Hephaestion's thighs. The native peoples of course cared little for his loss, and they were furious when Alexander ordered all of the Persian sacred fires to be quenched during the mourning period, something that took place only on the death of a Great King. This blatant disregard of religious beliefs explains yet again why the Persians would always view Alexander as a mere conqueror.

Alexander was now feeling increasingly isolated. True, he had other boyhood friends in his retinue, Ptolemy and Nearchus to name but two, but he did not share the same depth of intimacy with them as he had with Hephaestion. Moreover, there was perhaps little love lost between Hephaestion and the other men, who may well have resented his meteoric rise to power from mere boyhood friend to chiliarch, the most powerful individual after Alexander.[20] Even Alexander's act of marrying Hephaestion to a daughter of Darius had set him apart from the other senior staff. Alexander had no desire to replace Hephaestion with someone who had resented his late friend, which is probably why he allowed the office of chiliarch to remain vacant for the remainder of his reign, although he did now come to favor Perdiccas.

During the winter Alexander waged a 40-day campaign against the Cossaeans of the Zagros mountain range that bordered on Media (in modern Lorestan), southwest of Ecbatana, which Plutarch claimed he undertook to take his mind off Hephaestion.[21] This military operation was the very last one he ever undertook. The Cossaeans controlled important communications routes and levied a toll on anyone traveling between Ecbatana and Babylon. Alexander starved the various tribes into surrender, after which he may have decided to abolish their right to charge passage, as with the Uxians in 331. Despite his victory against the Cossaeans, the toll of years of warfare and battle was affecting his men, just as it must have affected the Macedonians back home. This often neglected aspect calls for comment.

THE EXPERIENCE OF WAR AND BATTLE

As the fourth century progressed combat became more frequent, and the nature of warfare changed considerably, mostly due to Alexander's exploits in Asia.[22] Cities increasingly employed professional mercenaries to fight for them rather than relying on their own citizens. This was a problem Demosthenes frequently addressed in his speeches against Philip to rouse his countrymen to war. Their reluctance to serve personally stemmed from apathy and perhaps also a loss of battle skills from relying on mercenaries. In Asia, however, Alexander fought practically every year—often several times in one year—from mere skirmishes to full-scale pitched battles, sieges, and guerilla warfare.

How did all these years of fighting affect Macedonia and its people? After all, Macedonia was at war or involved in military operations in some form or another outside its borders every year that Philip and Alexander were kings with the exception of 337. That was the year Philip established the League of Corinth, and his only activities were diplomatic. While Philip was not involved in any military exploits in 336, the year of his assassination, he nevertheless had sent a vanguard army into Asia to prepare the way for the main invading force that summer under his leadership, and it was still there and on active military duty when Alexander took over the reins of power in the same year.

Despite the many years of warfare that led to Macedonia becoming an imperial power, the Macedonians on the mainland did not live in fear of invasion or attack because Philip had checked incursions from foreign tribes and interference by Greek cities. When Alexander invaded Asia there was no Persian reprisal against Macedonia or Greece as might be expected from an enemy. Alexander's kingdom prospered thanks to Philip's economic reforms and his creation of a professional army that no longer used conscript framers, thereby allowing farmers to work their lands and provide food. Alexander likewise stimulated the economy by sending back money from his vast hauls in Asia to the state treasury.

Presumably the Macedonians—and others who provided troops for the army—grieved over the deaths and injuries of family members, lovers, friends, and fellow countrymen in the war in Asia. As far as Macedonia proper goes—Upper and Lower Macedonia, that is—it is not inconceivable that everyone knew someone serving in the army. Then again, perhaps they did not lament their dead. The Athenians mourned their losses—as Pericles's funeral speech delivered at the end of the first year of the Peloponnesian War shows—but the Spartans saw death in battle as the only honorable way for men to die. There is the classic anecdote of a

Spartan mother waving her son off to battle and telling him to return home carrying his shield or lying dead on it, and in Sparta only mothers who died in childbirth and men who died in battle were allowed epitaphs. Like the Spartans, the Macedonians were a militaristic society, and it does not follow that they wept for their dead as other Greeks did. Likewise families of soldiers serving with Alexander might not have anxiously awaited news of their loved ones and devoured every scrap of news that came from Asia, unlike families of combatants in more recent times.

The troops in the field had a very different experience of course. Alexander's generalship skills and personal sufferings with his men have been noted a number of times. We happen to know more about them because ancient writers were more concerned with him and less concerned with the rank-and-file army. Attempts have been made to compare the battlefield experiences of surviving soldiers and their families of the Vietnam War (specifically the My Lai massacre of 1968) with ancient combat in order to shed light on the nature of violence and its impact on ancient society and culture.[23] Similarities are traced between the modern era and the ancient, such as the effect of war on families, the increasing brutality and level of atrocities of men who were morally upright before going to war, the reaction to fighting and injury, and even the ways of memorializing the fallen soldier (in Classical Athens the funeral oration; more recently, the Vietnam Wall in Washington, D.C., for example).[24]

While this is undoubtedly a fascinating—and profoundly gut-wrenching—study, it has limitations when it comes to soldiers in the field. We cannot interview survivors or their families from the ancient world. Nor do we have any journals or letters from the ancient front that tell us exactly what it was like for those who fought there and how it affected them. That a soldier in the recent era tragically suffers from PTSD does not mean that his ancient counterpart did. Moreover, Macedonians, Illyrians, Thracians, and even Greeks were not the sort of "decent" people who in modern times had never experienced fighting before joining the army and who became more savage as time wore on. Alexander's troops were already experienced soldiers long before they stepped onto the Asian shore. Yet they did become more bloodthirsty over time. However, certain of their reactions allow us, I think, a glimpse into how warfare and combat affected them, supporting some of the analogies made to more recent warfare outlined above.

We can only imagine the brutality of the fighting when two opposing lines of infantry or cavalry detachments clashed and everyone was fighting for their lives. Philip, for example, had been shot in an eye at the siege of Methone in 354; Cleitus had chopped off the arm of the Persian about to decapitate Alexander at the Granicus River in 334; Alexander had almost died when he was shot in the chest by an arrow at the siege of Malli in 325; and Darius had cut off the hands of the Macedonian sick and wounded and cauterized them with pitch before Issus in 333. Dismemberments and terrible wounds from weaponry on both sides must have been common in all battles and sieges, and mercy killings of soldiers whose lives could not be saved occurred after conflicts.

Survivors must have felt a sense of rage, which would explain the mass slaughters that characterized Alexander's later reign when he and his men were faced with any resistance. They must also have felt a sense of despondency over the years as march followed march, fight followed fight, with no end in sight, and opposition from new enemy combatants never ceased. It is no surprise that the wounds they suffered, their weakening bodies, the resulting damage to their arms and armor, and their general psychological malaise were all reasons Coenus gave at the Hyphasis River mutiny for returning home. In this respect Alexander's men suffered more than they had under Philip—apart from their defeat in 353 at the hands of Onomarchus of Phocis, after which they fled back to Macedonia, and in 339 by the Triballi, they had always been victorious and stayed loyal to Philip. In fact, in 353 it may have been the Illyrians and Paeonians in the army who first took off, seeing in the reversal the chance to unite with their own people and attack a vulnerable Philip.[25] Of course Philip's army fought only on the mainland against foes and on terrain they largely knew. Had he lived to invade Asia he would presumably have encountered the same levels of resistance and hardship as Alexander.

Soldiers who did make it back home from Alexander's campaign in Asia were quick to show their thanks to the gods, as a dedicatory inscription set up by some returning Boeotian cavalrymen in perhaps 329 attests (discussed on p. 302). Alexander frequently performed thank offerings to the gods for victory and for the lives of the men who had not died in the conflict, but not just as a means of exhortation. Religion and warfare were closely intertwined, and several gods were consciously courted for their support in battle, including Zeus and Athena. Yet religion did not prevent the men from becoming increasingly bloodthirsty under the steady combat and thinking little of their wholesale massacre of native peoples. The level of violence that can be seen in Central Asia and India in particular was arguably stimulated by Alexander, who "gloried in battle and killing, and had an awesome proficiency in the technique of slaughter."[26] He had allowed his men a free hand to loot and kill indiscriminately in Persepolis, but that was in line with the panhellenic invasion for revenge. From Bactria to India, though, he adopted a no-prisoners policy, which at times included noncombatants such as refugees. His mass killing of the Indian mercenaries at Massaga, to whom he had given his word on their safety, is symptomatic of his lack of concern for human life. Exposed to such butchery for so long, his men adapted to it. Thus it is no surprise that on their own initiative they savagely murdered every man, woman, and child at Malli because of Alexander's wound.

As time passed the troops grew discontented with Alexander's continual march eastward with no end in sight and the way he was changing before their eyes. Perhaps if he had remained true to Macedonian custom, they may have endured the hard fighting in harsh and unfamiliar terrain. However, the psychological stress brought on by the incessant conflicts and drenching monsoons, their weakened constitutions (as Coenus's remark implies), and their desperation to return home led to mutiny at the Hyphasis River. That they deliberately disobeyed their oath of allegiance to Alexander as king emphasizes how they were at the very end of their tether.

When yet more fighting took place in India, the men's weariness and lack of commitment to a war they had not seen as a strategic necessity for a long time were seen in their initial lackluster performance at the siege of Malli. Yet their pride in being part of the conquering Macedonian army did not abate—the major reason for their second mutiny, at Opis in 324, was over Alexander's plans to replace them with foreign troops. They may well have had enough of the bitter experiences of warfare and did not want to follow him in his grandiose plan of invading Arabia, but they still felt a fierce loyalty to their army. After Alexander's death the Macedonian army of Philip and Alexander would change forever, and men previously united in combat under the one king fought under different generals against one another. Macedonia thus continued to be at war—and the soldiers and their families continued to suffer.

OMENS AND EMBASSIES

Still, in 323 Alexander crossed the Tigris River and approached Babylon, where a group of Chaldaean philosophers met him and bluntly told him to go away or suffer death. They are not likely to have been acting in his best interests, since the Babylonians may have suspected and had no enthusiasm for Alexander's plan to move the capital of his empire to their city (which made sense geographically). Alexander heeded the warning, even to the extent of setting up his camp outside the city walls, but the court philosopher Anaxarchus persuaded him to change his mind. One again he entered the city and took up residence in the palace of Nebuchadnezzar.

The omens about his demise continued. One time an unknown man donned Alexander's cloak and diadem and sat on the throne in the palace. The eunuchs next to the throne were forbidden to touch him, so all they could do was beat their chests and rip their clothes in despair. Alexander ordered the man to be tortured to find out whether he was part of a plot against him, but all the man said was that he had acted impetuously. Even so, there was a general feeling that his action was a bad omen. Sometime later, as Alexander sailed through the marshes that contained the tombs of the Assyrian kings, his hat blew off and fell on some reeds by one of the tombs. One of the sailors swam to retrieve it and to save it from getting wet put it on his head. Alexander rewarded him with a talent and then had his head chopped off because of an omen that the head of someone else wearing the hat should not be protected.

It was from Babylon that he intended to launch his Arabian campaign, but before that he needed to settle some diplomatic business. Various embassies from the Greek mainland, Thrace, Illyria, Scythia, Spain, the Etruscans, and supposedly Carthage and Rome had journeyed to Babylon to meet with him. He saw each one in a particular order of business: first, those who had come on religious matters; second, those that brought him tokens of their submission; third, those with territorial disputes and private matters; and finally, those in connection with the Exiles Decree.

The business of the embassies is unknown, with the exception of those about the Exiles Decree. Those from Scythia and Thrace were most likely trying to regain Alexander's goodwill following their revolt in 326, during which the rebels defeated Zopyrion, his general in Thrace, in a battle at the river Borysthenes in Scythia. The Carthaginian embassy may well have brought him an offer of friendship, prompted by his blunt warning to the Carthaginian delegates at Tyre in 331 that he would one day deal with their city. The Carthaginians may well have been concerned that after Arabia he would attack Carthage.

The Roman embassy may have been an invention of later Roman writers.[27] At this time, in 323, Rome was still struggling to achieve dominance in Italy. It had defeated the Etruscans and annexed their lands and was currently at war against the Samnites to its southeast. Possibly the Romans were seeking Alexander's help in the Samnite war, although that is unlikely. Possibly they wanted to assure Alexander that, having conquered the Etruscans, they would take steps to curb the rampant Etruscan piracy in the Adriatic, about which the Athenians had complained to Alexander as hegemon of the League of Corinth. This would explain why the Etruscans sent an embassy to Babylon to ingratiate themselves with this seemingly unstoppable conqueror. On the other hand, the Roman embassy may be fiction, invented at a later date by Alexander's eulogists to depict his foresight, for when he met their embassy he was said to have prophesied the future greatness of Rome as an imperial power.[28]

The ambassadors from the Greek cities took Alexander gold crowns and appeared before him wearing crowns, which bespoke of his divinity. Their action did not mean that they believed he was a god but was most likely a ploy to earn his favor and bolster their appeals over the Exiles Decree. After all, Alexander's surprising leniency toward the Spartans after Agis's war of 330 may have been because they diplomatically acknowledged his divinity. Perhaps also the Greeks were cynically exploiting the extraordinary honors afforded to Hephaestion, which had led some states (Athens included) to institute their own heroic cult to him.[29] Nevertheless he rejected all their pleas. His rejection, together with the subversive activities of the former imperial treasurer, Harpalus, threw the western half of his empire into disarray and put Greece on the verge of open revolt (Map 1).

EVENTS IN MAINLAND GREECE
AND THE MACEDONIAN HEGEMONY

In 324 Harpalus had fled from Babylon to Athens with 6,000 mercenaries, 5,000 talents of money, and 30 warships, believing that only an orchestrated revolt would save him from Alexander. When he had first appeared off Attica the Athenians had denied him entry into their city. He sailed to Taenarum, where he left most of his men and ships, and returned to Athens as a suppliant—he had received citizenship for a gift of grain to the city during a recent famine. The Athenians could not refuse a citizen who was seeking asylum and admitted him; he immediately offered his considerable resources to the Athenians if they would call the Greeks to arms. The ensuing "Harpalus affair" jeopardized Macedonian rule far more so than Agis's abortive war, given the widespread hostile reaction to the Exiles Decree.[30]

As we have seen, Demosthenes had stayed out of the political limelight following his victory over Aeschines in the Crown trial of 330. Now he addressed the Assembly about Harpalus and in doing so demonstrated how much his policy toward Macedonia had changed because of Macedonian rule. His speech is not extant, but aware of what types of reprisals Alexander or Antipater could take against Athens, he convinced the Athenians to imprison Harpalus, confiscate the money he had brought with him (apparently 700 talents), and send an embassy to Alexander to ask what they should do with him. Demosthenes had earlier met with Nicanor, the royal messenger who had proclaimed the Exiles Decree at Olympia, and may have received some pointers from him about placating

Alexander. That is why he had Harpalus imprisoned and further persuaded the Athenians to vote divine honors on Alexander so that the embassy could report all this news to him at Babylon.

After the embassy left Athens Harpalus suddenly escaped from custody and fled to Crete, where he was murdered. His flight led to the discovery of only a portion of the money he claimed he had brought back with him to Athens, and the people suspected several politicians, including Demosthenes, of taking bribes to effect his escape. Demosthenes protested his innocence and called for the Areopagus, one of the oldest councils in the constitution, to inquire into the matter. Demosthenes had favorable political relations with the council, which may explain why it took six months to investigate the allegation and may even have wanted to let the matter drop. However, the return of the unsuccessful embassy over the Exiles Decree, coupled with the people demanding a report, prompted the Areopagus to accuse Demosthenes and some other politicians of corruption. There is no evidence that Demosthenes took anything from Harpalus, nor could the Areopagus cite any in its report, and Harpalus probably lied about the amount. Nevertheless, Demosthenes was put on trial in March 323, found guilty, and fled into a self-imposed exile until after Alexander's death the same year. That he was a political victim is shown by the fact that some of the others accused were acquitted at their trials.

The Harpalus affair and the Greek response to the Exiles Decree are important for the political demise of Demosthenes, the contemptuous attitude Alexander held for the Greeks, the impotency of the League of Corinth, and the Greek attitude to the Macedonian hegemony.[31] The Athenians in the age of Philip would have seen Harpalus's offer of arms and money as a godsend, and if Philip had issued an Exiles Decree, the Greeks would have lost little time uniting and preparing to fight to the end to resist it. Now, in 324, the Greek cities resorted to diplomacy, not military action, and instead of welcoming Harpalus with open arms the Athenians saw him as a liability and sent an embassy to Alexander to resolve the situation. Greece in the 320s was very different from Greece in the 350s and 340s thanks to the Battle of Chaeronea, which really had brought about the end of Greek *autonomia* and *eleutheria*. The League of Corinth had allowed the Greeks some semblance of autonomy in their domestic affairs, but that was just a charade—the unilateral Exiles Decree, which directly interfered in the constitutions and lives of practically every Greek city, proved that.[32]

At the same time Macedonian rule afforded the Greeks a period of prolonged (if enforced) peace that they had never experienced before thanks to the bellicose nature of the poleis system and the unpopularity of the large cities. Even in the days of Philip a number of smaller states had welcomed Macedonian intervention in Greece, tired as they were of the bitter rivalries of the powerful cities that caused so much disruption. It is perhaps worthwhile reflecting on the idea that if there had been no Macedonian domination, the weaknesses in the polis system and the xenophobic attitude of the states would surely have brought *autonomia* and *eleutheria* to an end in some other way.

With this Macedonian peace came prosperity for Greece. Cities from Athens to those of the Peloponnese benefited to the extent that they were able to inaugurate costly building programs.[33] In Athens, Lycurgus, one of the city's public treasurers, ordered the construction of a naval arsenal, 400 triremes, the Panathenaic Stadium, the Theater of Dionysus, and various gold and silver ornaments for the Panathenaea festival. His public works were meant to symbolize a new age in Athenian history after the doom and gloom of recent decades, one of optimism to echo the greatness of Periclean Athens at the height of the Athenians' fifth-century empire.[34] To this end Lycurgus compiled new editions of the fifth-century tragedies of Aeschylus, Sophocles, and Euripides and set up bronze statues of these great tragedians in the city, which were likewise meant to conjure up past glories.[35] However grudgingly, the Greeks had to acknowledge the fruits of the peace afforded by Macedonian rule.

Still, they were also aware of their absolute impotence in political and military affairs. That realization, no matter how much money was accumulating in treasuries or how many buildings were being constructed, must have been the hardest pill to swallow.

15.

DEATH IN BABYLON AND

ALEXANDER'S LEGACY

IN THE MEANTIME PREPARATIONS for the invasion of Arabia continued, which included the construction of more warships and an enormous harbor at Babylon capable of accommodating 1,000 vessels. Alexander held competitions with golden wreaths as prizes for the rowers and helmsmen, many hired from Phoenicia and Syria, as part of their training and preparation. By May he was satisfied with all the arrangements, but then the last round of drinking parties beckoned to him, one of which proved fatal.

ALEXANDER'S DEATH

Later in May Alexander received word that Zeus Ammon at Siwah had granted Hephaestion a heroic cult. In great delight he held a huge celebratory feast, at which the attendees downed copious quantities of unmixed wine. As the king prepared to retire to his bedchamber a man named Medeius of Larisa (in Thessaly) convinced him to continue drinking. Never one to refuse a drink, Alexander agreed, toasting "the health of everyone at the dinner, as many as 20 altogether, and he received the same number of toasts from everyone."[1] He finished off by drinking a pitcher, reputed to hold 12 pints, but dropped it as his body went into violent spasms and then collapsed. He died some days later.[2] Perhaps his generals and attendants did not express the same degree of anguish as later painters of this scene would have us believe (Figure 24).

FIGURE 24

Karl Theodor von Piloty, *Death of Alexander the Great*. BPK, Berlin/Neue Pinakothek, Bayerische Staatsgemaeldesammlungen/Art Resource, New York.

Alexander's last days were recorded in his *Royal Diaries* (*Ephemerides*), a daily journal purportedly written by his secretary, Eumenes of Cardia.[3] Its authenticity is suspect because it may have been composed after his death to rebut a belief that he was poisoned. The *Ephemerides* relate that Medeius did persuade Alexander to continue drinking after the banquet had long since finished and that Alexander collapsed after drinking the large pitcher of wine. From then he deteriorated rapidly over the following week:

On the 18th of Daesius he slept in his bathroom because he had a fever. The next day he had a bath and then went to his bedroom and played dice with Medeius for the rest of the day. When it grew late he had a bath, sacrificed to the gods as was his duty, ate some food, and had a fever all night. On the 20th he took another bath, performed his customary sacrifice, but stayed in the bathroom to listen to Nearchus's tales of his voyage and the great sea. He did the same on the 21st although the fever was worse and he was very sick during the night and throughout the following day. He ordered his bed moved next to his large bath, and here he discussed vacant posts in the army and who was experienced enough to fill them with his senior staff. On the 24th his fever was high and violent and he had to be carried outside to perform the sacrifices, at which point he bade his senior officers to remain in the palace's court and the battalion commanders and companies remain outside for the night. On the 25th they carried him to the palace on the other side of the river, where he got some sleep, but the fever remained high. When his commanders came to his bedside he could not speak, and the same held true on the 26th. Then men outside were convinced he had died so they rushed the palace doors shouting all the time and threatening his Companions until they gave way and opened the doors to admit them. One by one, without cloak or armor, they all filed slowly past the king's bed. In the meantime Python and Seleucus were sent to the temple of Serapis to ask whether they should take Alexander there, but the god told them to leave him where he was. On the 28th, as evening fell, he died.[4]

It was June 11, to give the modern equivalent of the date.[5] Alexander was but a few weeks shy of his thirty-third birthday. Perhaps a little before he lost his voice he gave his signet ring (the Persian seal) to Perdiccas, who had become his second-in-command, so that the business of imperial administration would continue uninterrupted.

What killed Alexander?[6] Common explanations include poison (hence murder), disease, or natural causes. Shortly after her son's death Olympias accused Antipater and his son Cassander of poisoning Alexander, presumably because they were disenchanted with Alexander's orientalism and pretensions to divinity. Antipater's son Iolaus, one of the king's cupbearers at court, was said to have actually dropped the poison, smuggled by Cassander to Babylon, into Alexander's drink. This scenario has support from the fact that the Athenians voted honors for Iolaus and Olympias later desecrated his tomb.[7] Possibly Antipater was part of a plot of several senior commanders to remove Alexander and, even at this time, divide the empire among themselves.[8] However, there is only circumstantial evidence for poisoning, and Olympias's accusation is hardly surprising given her dislike of Antipater.[9] Then again, Alexander's symptoms, especially the abdominal spasms, are consistent with an intake of arsenic or strychnine, both of which are tasteless in the unmixed wine that the

Macedonians drank.[10] These poisons are usually fast acting though, whereas Alexander took several days to die.

There is always a tendency with prominent historical figures—especially someone as charismatic and superhuman as Alexander—to believe that they died from unnatural causes, thereby giving rise to all manner of conspiracy theories. The real cause of Alexander's death may never be known, but disease or natural causes cannot be excluded. Malaria has been posited, but Alexander would have built up a resistance to it because it was prevalent throughout Macedonia while he was growing up and he did not contract it during his 22 years of living in the country.[11] That leaves us with the excessive amount of alcohol he consumed in his lifetime compounded by his many wounds (especially the near-fatal punctured lung at Malli), weakened bodily constitution, and punishing lifestyle. Today, survivors of wounds of the magnitude Alexander had received change their lifestyles dramatically, often eating differently, eliminating alcohol, or avoiding overexertion. Alexander did none of these things but continued as before. His body was unable to take it and simply gave out, accelerated by his heavy drinking, in which case acute alcoholic pancreatitis is a viable candidate for his demise.

Alexander's corpse was carefully removed from the couch on which he had died and embalmed—a clear break from Macedonian tradition. The reason for embalming the body was understandable because it was to be formally buried at Aegae and therefore needed to be preserved for its long journey. Once there it would have been burned on a pyre and interred in a tomb, perhaps even next to that of Philip. The embalming procedure did not take place until six days after Alexander died. Once embalmed Alexander's body was anointed with oils and other scents and laid inside a golden coffin, which in turn was placed inside a stone sarcophagus, over which was draped purple cloth. A magnificent funeral wagon was built—so elaborate it was believed to have taken almost two years to build—to transport Alexander to Macedonia. Throughout this period the deceased king lay in state, during which time the wars for personal dominion had begun among his generals.

The funeral cortège finally departed Babylon but never made it to Aegae. At some point on its journey Ptolemy, who had taken control of

Egypt after Alexander's death and who was then in a bitter power struggle with Perdiccas, seized it. Perdiccas might have Alexander's signet ring, but possession of Alexander's body gave Ptolemy an enormous political advantage over all the other generals, and he was not prepared to relinquish it. This is also seen in the coinage he struck, featuring the head of Alexander with the horns of Ammon, the aegis, and the diadem. Ptolemy buried Alexander in Memphis, but in 306, when he moved to Alexandria, he removed Alexander's body to a tomb in that city.

Alexander's tomb in Alexandria became a focal point for powerful visitors throughout the centuries. One celebrated visitor was Octavian, the future emperor Augustus. After the defeat of Antony and Cleopatra in the Battle of Actium in 31, Octavian went to Egypt to take possession of that country. He was asked if he wanted to see the tombs of the Ptolemies and famously replied, "I wish to see a king, not corpses."[12] After viewing Alexander's body he was alleged to have put a golden wreath on its head—perhaps to make amends, if there is any truth to the story, for accidentally snapping off Alexander's nose as he bent over his face![13] Alexander's tomb is still undiscovered.[14]

AFTERMATH

On Alexander's death his men abandoned the invasion of Arabia; in Greece the Exiles Decree was consigned to oblivion—only Tegea in Arcadia ever took back its exiles (Map 1)[15]—and in Athens the money Harpalus had left behind when he fled was used to hire mercenaries at Taenarum as a precursor to another Greek revolt. The Macedonian Assembly also rejected the late king's extravagant final plans, which he had outlined in his notebooks (*hypomnemata*) and which were read out by Perdiccas:

> Perdiccas found orders for the completion of Hephaestion's pyre, which called for heavy expenditure, and for all his other designs, which, numerous and grandiose, required an inordinate outlay of money. He therefore decided it was expedient to leave them unfulfilled. But not to appear to have diminished Alexander's prestige on his own authority, he brought the

proposal concerning these matters before the common council of the Macedonians. The greatest and most significant projects in the *hypomnemata* were the following. There was the construction of a thousand warships, larger than triremes, in Phoenicia, Syria, Cilicia, and Cyprus. These were for a campaign against the Carthaginians and the other peoples living along the coast of Libya and Iberia and the area next to these along the coast as far as Sicily. There was the laying of a road along the coast of Libya as far as the Pillars of Hercules and the provision, at strategic points, of ports and dockyards sufficient for an expedition of such proportions. Next there was the building of six very expensive temples, each costing 1,500 talents. As well as this there was to be the establishment of cities and a transfer of populations from Asia to Europe, and in reverse from Europe to Asia, with the aim of bringing the largest continents into harmonious and familial unity through intermarriage and family ties. The aforementioned temples were to be built at Delos, Delphi and Dodona. There were also to be temples in Macedonia: to Zeus at Dium, to Artemis Tauropolus at Amphipolis, and to Athena in Cyrnus. At Ilium, too, a temple of the last-mentioned goddess was to be constructed, one that could not take second place to another. Alexander's father Philip was to have a tomb as great as the largest of the pyramids in Egypt, which some people count among the greatest works in the world. When these *hypomnemata* were read out, the Macedonians, although they reacted favorably to the mention of Alexander, realized nevertheless that the projects were excessive and impractical, and decided against bringing the aforementioned ones to fruition.[16]

Perdiccas was also said to have read out Alexander's will, but it is likely that he forged that document and possibly also the *hypomnemata* to help his own political ambitions in the struggles with the other generals.[17] If so, then many or possibly even all of these overblown "final plans" may never have crossed Alexander's mind.

Alexander's death also led many of the inhabitants he had settled in his new cities, especially in Central Asia, to quit their so-called homes and attempt to return to the Greek mainland—or in the case of the natives, to their original Asian homes. Their isolation and probably distaste for local practices had proved too much, and their departures may well have led to the abandonment or downscaling of many of Alexander's foundations.[18]

On the Greek mainland Alexander's death was first disbelieved. The Athenian orator Demades supposedly quipped that if Alexander were really dead, the whole world would smell his corpse.[19] But once the Greeks knew it to be true they revolted from the Macedonian hegemony, confident that the splits among Alexander's generals and the lack of a proper heir would be to their advantage. Certainly Demosthenes did not hesitate, for while in exile for his alleged role in the Harpalus affair he campaigned to persuade the Greeks to unite under Athens. His activities earned his recall to Athens.

This revolt, which is called the Lamian (or Hellenic) War, was ultimately unsuccessful.[20] Antipater was not prepared to lose control of Greece, and the following year, 322, he defeated the Greeks in battle at Crannon in Thessaly. The Athenians, who had led the revolt, were treated harshly. Among other things, Antipater abolished their democracy, imposed a Macedonian garrison in the city, and hunted down anti-Macedonian politicians such as Hyperides and Demosthenes. To escape capture Demosthenes committed suicide on the island of Calauria (modern Poros). It was an ignoble end to Athens's proud history and Greece's greatest orator.[21]

The Macedonian Empire was likewise a victim of Alexander's death. His generals had crowded by his bedside in Babylon to ask him about his successor since Roxane was still pregnant. They wanted to know to whom he intended to leave his kingdom, but, so one tradition goes, all he said was, "to the best."[22] Since he had previously given Perdiccas his signet ring, Perdiccas believed that he was the best, but the other generals did not agree. Only the sheer force of Alexander's personality had kept these men united, and now, without the king, their differing personalities and conflicting ambitions came to the fore. Eager to rule in their own right they divided everything up among themselves while no doubt being well aware that just as Alexander had established the empire by conquest, so they, too, would need to fight to continue ruling their respective areas.

To add to the disunity and chaos there were rival factions among the generals that supported Alexander's half-brother Arrhidaeus (then about

35 years old and still suffering some type of mental incapacity), proclaiming him Philip III, and the baby boy that Roxane gave birth to, Alexander (IV). For the next three decades the empire that Philip had founded and Alexander had so brilliantly enlarged was ripped apart in the wars of the successors (Map 5).[23] In 317 Olympias had Philip III and his wife, Eurydice, murdered, and in 311 Cassander (Antipater's son) had Alexander IV and Roxane put to death to strengthen his hold over Macedonia. Eventually, in 276, Antigonus Gonatas (grandson of Alexander's commander Antigonus Monophthalmus) fought back an invasion of Greece by the Celts (whom the Romans called Gauls), which gave him control of the mainland. In the same year he established the Antigonid dynasty, which ruled Macedonia until the Romans brought it to an end in 168. By this time the three great kingdoms of the Hellenistic period had formed: Ptolemaic Egypt, Seleucid Syria, and Antigonid Greece. Macedonia, however, would always remain a shadow of its former self, eventually becoming a province of the Roman Empire in 148.

WHAT DID THE MACEDONIANS THINK OF THEIR EMPIRE IN 323—AND ALEXANDER?

The Macedonians likely welcomed their new, dominant position on the mainland at the end of Philip's reign in 336, even if it, and the impending invasion of Asia, had impacted aspects of their kingship. While Alexander was away they witnessed manpower losses far greater than in the time of Philip, but they still prospered from his economic stimulation policies and the money that Alexander regularly sent back to the treasury. Even though there was political friction between Antipater and Olympias, which increased the longer Alexander was away, those barons present in Macedonia took no steps to support one over the other, and the people continued with their daily lives and business. Any concerns they had about instability in political affairs necessarily dissipated when Olympias withdrew to Epirus in 324.

As news of Alexander's military successes filtered back to the mainland the Macedonians came to understand that they were living in a new era.

Demosthenes of Athens certainly did—until the Battle of Issus in 333 he had hoped that the Persians would kill the young king and Greece could again reassert its independence. After that battle he realized that his hope was futile. If he grasped the implications of Alexander's victories for the Macedonian hegemony of Greece, so too must the Macedonians.

From Asia Callisthenes was transmitting back to the mainland all manner of stories about Alexander's actions, often exaggerated for effect. The people were not in a position to judge their veracity, so when, for example, Alexander supposedly wrote to Antipater that he and Darius had fought each other at Issus and the Great King had actually wounded him, they had no reason to doubt him. In their eyes he continued to be a traditional warrior king, leading from the front and involving himself in the thick of fighting. The information he sent back from the various surveyors and civilian naturalists he had taken with him was beneficial to intellectuals and scientists—Aristotle for one—thereby adding to his standing.

Yet, when stories began to make their way back of Alexander's changing habits and how he treated his senior staff, the Macedonians must have paused. What could they have made of the news, for example, that Alexander had executed Philotas and Parmenion on specious charges, that he had murdered Cleitus in cold blood, that he had started to wear Persian clothing, that he believed he was a god, and that his army had mutinied on him? Equally worrying must have been the news of his close encounters with death, as at the Granicus River and Malli, with no heir to succeed him. Those present with the king could appreciate his generalship and charisma—as well as fear him—because they witnessed his skills, character, and emotions firsthand. The Macedonians back home could not make any such observations: all they heard about was a king who had forsaken his own people and customs to share in those of the "barbarians."

The people's adverse reaction perhaps explains why the Macedonian mints at Pella, Amphipolis, and Philippi produced no coins of Alexander after the Battle of Issus, in contrast with those of Philip during his reign.[24] All of the remaining Alexander coinage was struck personally by him in the East or was posthumous. Likewise the dearth of artistic evidence on the mainland is also revealing of attitudes to Macedonia's new role in the Greek world and the impact of the army on the empire. Mention has already been made of the Philippeion and its status for Philip (pp. 107–108), but for Alexander's campaigns memorials are to be found only in the East during his lifetime and on the mainland only after his death. There was no "Alexandreion" or even a statue of Alexander to connect him to his Asian campaign on the mainland. The king himself erected monumental altars to the 12 Olympian gods on the banks of the Hyphasis River to mark his eastern boundary and altars to Ocean and Earth on an island in the Southern Ocean to mark the southern. There is a dedicatory inscription to Zeus Soterios set up by 23 cavalrymen from Orchomenus in Boeotia for their safe return home in perhaps 329. It is not meant to memorialize Alexander in any way and is more important for Boeotian military history.[25] We have to wait until after Alexander's death for artistic connections to his exploits in Persia, such as a mural (now lost) from the early third-century B.C. Kinch tomb at Lefkadia that depicted a Macedonian cavalryman galloping after a fleeing Persian who tries to use his shield for protection.[26]

Fighting the Persians obviously lent itself to all manner of exciting representations, as the Alexander mosaic (Figure 16) and Alexander sarcophagus (Figure 22) attest. That we do not have more examples from the mainland suggests only one thing: Alexander was more admired abroad as a conqueror than at home as a king.

LEGACY—AND EVALUATION

With Homeric heroes as idols and ancestors and a fierce determination not just to emulate their love of combat and thirst for adventure but to outdo them, Alexander's life was destined to be one of fighting and valor. His strategic and tactical genius in someone so young coupled with a deep intellect make him one of history's foremost conquerors. Even if parts of his empire were in revolt by the end of his reign and it collapsed entirely on his death, for a time he was ruler of one of the largest empires of antiquity.[27]

In their battles for supremacy Alexander's generals, who became the early Hellenistic rulers, exploited both his image and any association they had with him for political purposes—thus Perdiccas had his signet ring, but Ptolemy had his corpse entombed in Egypt.²⁸ This intense competition explains the explosion of coins with Alexander's image on them—virtually all of the coins with his portrait were posthumous.²⁹ As the Hellenistic period gave way to the Roman era, Alexander's military exploits and the vast numbers of enemy dead came to excite admiration—hardly a surprise in a society that granted a successful general a triumph through the streets of Rome only if he had killed at least 5,000 of the enemy. In fact, the first attested reference to Alexander as "great" occurs in a Roman comedy of the first century B.C.³⁰ Apart from his political and military legacy Alexander also has a legacy as a subject in philosophy, especially Cynic and Roman, where his deeds supported arguments about moral considerations.³¹

The chivalry of the medieval period eagerly embraced the young heroic king. The so-called *Alexander Romance*, supposedly an account of his life and reign possibly composed by Callisthenes, was rewritten many times in the Middle Ages and translated into numerous Western and Eastern languages. The various versions invented adventures and adapted Alexander to fit their own social and historical backgrounds. As a document the *Alexander Romance* (as all the versions are collectively known) is far from a serious historical work, but it stands as a testament to Alexander's legendary status and power (see the appendix). In early modern Europe through to the age of the Enlightenment Alexander fever likewise gripped rulers—thus, for example, LeBrun painted a series of portraits of Louis XIV as Alexander, and Racine compared Louis with Alexander in his tragedy *Alexander the Great*. Alexander, however, fared less well in Dante's estimation—he relegated him to the seventh circle of hell or Violence (*Inferno* 12.98–100). In the modern era Alexander has been the subject of TV documentaries, movies, and songs and even has had hotel suites named after him.³²

Alexander's greatest legacy is not found in literature or popular culture; it is found in the new world of the Hellenistic period, which due to his pioneering campaigns opened up trade, commerce, travel, and social and cultural exchanges between East and West.³³ Yet that period was heralded by the collapse of his Macedonian Empire. Even after the wars of the successors and the establishment of the Antigonid dynasty in Macedonia in 276, the country would never again be as powerful as in the days of Philip and his son. The ultimate reason for the collapse had nothing to do with its size or the problems associated with a multicultural subject population, such as plagued the Romans; rather, Alexander did not have a successor in place. His legacy for his kingdom, then, stands in stark contrast to that of Philip. Might that outweigh his demonstrated genius on the battlefield, for which he was dubbed "great," and if so, how "great" was he?[34]

Alexander's generalship and leadership skills earned for him legendary status. We cannot question his success in battling armies that far outnumbered his own and marching through unknown terrain covering thousands of miles, as well as having to adapt to new challenges, which ranged from guerilla warfare in Afghanistan to war elephants in India. The odds were always against him in the battles he fought and the sieges he waged, yet he never panicked or chose to run away and fight another day. He seemed to know in advance that his strategy, no matter how audacious, no matter the gamble psychologically on the foe, would pay off—and it did.

He pushed his men hard, sometimes too hard, but his great leadership skills were shown time and again by the way he never shirked from suffering as they did and always strove to be a source of inspiration for them. He put his own life in danger as at Malli and refused water in the Gedrosian Desert because everyone was suffering from dehydration. Through it all he kept his men marching and fighting and his senior staff committed, no matter how reluctantly, to his campaigns despite the intensity of their personality clashes. In tandem with his military prowess was his personal quest for honor, which also defined his generalship and relationship with his men.[35] In these respects Alexander's greatness shines through.

Yet it is well to remember that his army grew increasingly resentful of his orientalism and favoring of Asian officials, his pretensions to personal divinity, and his self-directed reasons for marching into new and hostile regions. The men's mood and Alexander's unpopularity led them twice to mutiny and members of his retinue to plot to kill him.[36] Nor can every military exercise be lauded—the disastrous march across the Gedrosian Desert for one. Further, Alexander almost died at the Granicus River and at the siege of Malli, which threw his men into great panic—not just because their king might be dead but because no other general had the unwavering support of everyone to lead them home. The aftermath of his death proved that.

Even more important was the nature of the actual empire. Certainly Alexander defeated his enemies in epic battles and sieges, but ultimately he did not conquer them, nor did he impose long-term, stable rule. The single empire he created was more mirage than reality, as the wars of his successors, who turned his inchoate empire into a number of distinct empires that survived for over 200 years, proved. True, the League of Corinth controlled the western half of his empire, and he did take viable steps to administer the eastern half of it, prudently working through the Iranian, Bactrian, and Indian aristocracy to promote his rule among the locals. However, his native subjects never saw him as anything but an invader, not just because he cut back their power but because he underestimated—or never grasped—such things as how native religion bound satraps to their Great King in a way they were never bound to Alexander, or the symbolic standing of satrapal cities, which he viewed as mere treasuries. He generally disregarded social customs and even abolished some if they personally offended him, and he failed to appreciate the standing of the Brahmans in Indian society, which enraged the people and prompted their revolt. His insistence on all things Greek at his festivals was likewise resented.

Moreover, Alexander was never continuously present as king in any one part of his empire because he was always campaigning in another, and in 323 he had his eyes set on Arabia and after that possibly the western Mediterranean. In wanting to outdo his father's exploits Alexander undertook the campaigns he did and strove to be recognized as a god on earth, no matter the cost.[37] It is no surprise, when we think about it, that he experienced near-constant disloyalty on the part of the satraps he appointed and revolts. Defeated in battle does not mean conquered, nor does it permit a new rule to come into being and a stable society. Where Alexander went wrong, and in particular why, impacts his "greatness"—and serves as a lesson for commanders and makers of strategy in culturally different regions of the world today.[38]

Further, Alexander was not just a general: he was a king. He displayed many of the personal traits of his father, but his orientalism, pretensions to personal divinity, and harsh treatment of critics meant that he never enjoyed the same close bonds as his father with his subjects and army. Despite the dissatisfaction that his adoption of Persian dress and status as Son of Zeus caused among his men, he seemed to care little, as his attempt to introduce *proskynesis*, for example, demonstrated. He was deeply loyal to his friends, but that loyalty was not always reciprocated, as conspiracies proved, causing him considerable distress and a sense of loneliness. In time he grew distrustful of everyone but Hephaestion and dealt swiftly and brutally with critics—Philotas and Parmenion, Callisthenes, and Cleitus were killed for standing up to a ruler whom they saw as less the traditional warrior king and more an oriental potentate. Even the death of Coenus, whose voicing of dissatisfaction at the Hyphasis River had blocked Alexander from marching deeper into India, was suspiciously coincidental. Nor did Alexander provide an heir. His son Heracles from the marriage to Barsine was illegitimate, and his marriage to Roxane was a case of too little too late.

Ancient writers were likewise critical of Alexander's voracious appetite for conquest at all costs. The contemporary Aristobulus remarked that he "was insatiably ambitious of ever acquiring fresh territory"; Plutarch claimed that while Alexander was at Babylon he once reflected that he had no idea what to do for the rest of his life, and in Curtius's opinion Alexander could cope better with warfare than peace and leisure and that "to track down and ferret out peoples removed almost to the limits of human habitation seemed a difficult undertaking, and yet his craving for renown and his insatiable lust for reputation permitted him to think nothing inaccessible or remote."[39]

Then again, perhaps Alexander had little choice but to keep campaigning because he had no legal or constitutional authority in the East and his power there rested solely on military conquest.[40] Yet he did not intend to stop at India: he was on the eve of invading Arabia when he died and after that may well have turned to Carthage and the western Mediterranean.

Away in the West, Antipater had done a sterling job in maintaining Macedonian rule over Greece, but the Exiles Decree was met with resistance that, had the king not died, might have plunged the western half of the empire into chaos. Despite this, and despite being absent from his kingdom for a decade, Alexander had made no plans to return.

Alexander's personal character also changed for the worst. He believed himself invincible, which explained his actions that endangered his own life and jeopardized his campaign and army. He came to have a total disregard for human life and a propensity for mass slaughter and even genocide, especially in Central Asia, which have led to preposterous comparisons with Hitler and Stalin.[41] The passage from Ephippus quoted earlier (pp. 268–269) speaks of him dressing as Ammon or other gods and of incense burned in his presence and the observing of a reverential silence as one would do for a god. The passage ends: "all those in his presence stayed silent or spoke just a few words of good omen because of their fear, for he was a very violent man, with no regard for human life, and appeared to be a person of melancholic constitution."[42] Those at court thus lived in a reign of terror, always afraid that they might say the wrong thing and suffer the king's wrath. The episode of Apollodorus, commander of the garrison at Babylon, whom Alexander called to him in 325 after returning from India, is indicative of this.[43] Apollodorus saw Alexander's punishment of the corrupt governors firsthand, and he wrote to his brother, a seer, to ask him if he could foresee his own fate. The brother reported unfavorable omens about Hephaestion (who died soon after), which Apollodorus immediately took to the king. It was his way of showing his personal loyalty and so avoiding any suspicion Alexander might have of him.

Alexander's drinking habits were criticized in the *Ephemerides* (daily records):

The things about Alexander that are not good: On the 5th of the month Dius they say that he drank in Eumaeus' quarters, and on the 6th he slept from the drinking, but then he got up and for the rest of the day discussed the following day's activities with his senior staff. On the 7th day as a guest of Perdiccas he drank with him, and slept again on the 8th day. Then on the

15th of the same month he also slept, but the next day attended to business as he was wont to do after drinking. On the 24th he dined at Bagoas's house, which was 10 stades from the palace, and on the 28th he rested. Thus one of two conclusions has to be right: either Alexander's drinking on so many days of the month caused him actual harm or those who wrote about these things are lying.[44]

The Macedonians were heavy drinkers, but as the above extract shows, Alexander was not drinking himself into a stupor every day and cannot be called an alcoholic in the modern sense of the term. Nor did alcohol ever impair his strategic and tactical planning or battle prowess. Still, it is worth noting that Alexander's drinking was part of the aspects of his life that were "not good" and that it was during a furious, drunken argument in 327 that he lost control of his senses and killed Cleitus.

To conclude, I return to the remarks of Diodorus and Justin on Philip and Alexander, which were discussed as part of the summary of Philip's kingship on pp. 117–119.[45] I can now add what they said about Alexander. Given his superhuman accomplishments, it is surprising that Justin merely remarks: "so it was that [Alexander] did battle with no adversary without defeating him, besieged no city without taking it, and attacked no tribe without crushing it entirely.... In the end he was brought down not by the valor of an enemy but by a plot hatched by his own men and the treachery of his fellow countrymen."[46] This is considerably briefer than his long necrology comparing Philip with Alexander. Furthermore, Justin makes it plain that Alexander died the victim of a conspiracy, a far cry from the death that the would-be fourth-century Homeric hero doubtless craved. Even briefer is Diodorus, who at the end of his account of the reign simply states that Alexander "accomplished greater deeds than any, not only of the kings who had lived before him but also of those who were to come later down to our time."[47] This too contrasts with his remarks that Philip "made himself the greatest of the kings in Europe in his time" and "won for himself the greatest empire in the Greek world."[48]

Why do these ancient writers hold such different views about Philip and Alexander? Part of the answer lies in the Roman perceptions of Alexander at the time they were writing and their appreciation of what makes a worthy ruler.[49] In the first century B.C. philhellenism had dropped out of fashion in Rome (not to be embraced again until the second century A.D.), and the Romans were hostile to both Greek values and Alexander. This background influenced Diodorus and Trogus (whose account Justin follows) to look beyond mere conquest and think like the Romans in terms of the nature of kingship, what a good king should be, how he should serve his country, and especially his legacy. Here Philip's legacy certainly outshone that of Alexander.[50] Indeed, if Philip had not laid "the basis for a worldwide empire," the son would not have been able to "bring to completion the glorious enterprise," as Justin remarked.[51] Put more bluntly: without Philip, no Alexander the Great.

That was why Philip had won "the greatest empire in the Greek world" because on his death he controlled all of Greece as far as the Hellespont. In conquering Persia and building an empire from Greece to India Alexander had indeed "accomplished greater deeds than any"—but he was unable to reconcile his kingship with his subjects, and instability in his empire was growing toward the end of his life, which did little good for Macedonia. A great conqueror does not necessarily make a great king— as the demise of Macedonia's empire and the end of the Argead dynasty demonstrated on Alexander's death. His legacy was not so much the distinguished intellectual and cultural achievements of the Hellenistic period but, rather, the wars of his successors, whose ambitions changed his empire into a collection of competing dynasties that shaped the political fortunes of the eastern Mediterranean and Near East for more than 200 years.

APPENDIX: THE SOURCES

OF INFORMATION

ANCIENT WORKS

THE EVIDENCE FOR CLASSICAL Macedonian history falls into four categories: literary (written histories and speeches), numismatic (coins), epigraphic (inscriptions), and archaeological (tombs, artifacts, and paintings): see P. J. Rhodes, "The Literary and Epigraphic Evidence to the Roman Conquest," K. Dahmen, "The Numismatic Evidence," and C. L. Hardiman, "Classical Art to 221 BC," in Roisman and Worthington (eds.), *Companion to Macedonia*, pp. 23–40, 41–62, and 505–521, respectively. On the archaeological evidence from cities, see the relevant essays in R. Lane Fox (ed.), *Brill's Companion to Ancient Macedon* (Leiden: 2011).

The Macedonians left next to no written records. The exceptions were Marsyas of Pella (*FGrH* 135/156), possibly a royal page, who wrote an account of Macedonia's kings from earliest times to 331, and Theagenes, who composed a treatise on Macedonian toponyms and urban settlements, especially in Lower Macedonia. Their works survive only in fragments. For our knowledge of Macedonian history, politics, society, and culture from literary evidence, we have to rely on Greek and Roman writers, who often present a biased or incomplete picture.

The veracity of the contemporary speeches by Athenian orators is doubtful because rhetoric was not history. In the case of Philip, for example, Aeschines very often depicted him in a favorable light, whereas

Demosthenes thought little of misrepresenting his actions and the threat he posed to Greek freedom. In addition, both orators were political enemies, and each one strove to denigrate the other's motives and actions, even if this meant manipulating the truth, thereby affecting their value as source material: see J. Buckler, "Demosthenes and Aeschines," in Ian Worthington (ed.), *Demosthenes: Statesman and Orator* (London: 2000), pp. 114–158. Aeschines and Demosthenes have next to nothing to say about Alexander the Great, on which we have a smaller number of speeches, some only fragmentary, principally by the orators Demades, Dinarchus, and Hyperides.

Contemporaneous with Philip and Alexander and in the generation after their deaths were some 40 writers who wrote about Macedonian affairs: see L. Pearson, *The Lost Histories of Alexander the Great* (New York: 1960). Their accounts are not extant, but later writers who used them as source material quoted or paraphrased from them. For Philip, the most important is Theopompus of Chios, who wrote a *Philippica* (*History of Philip*) in the late 330s and early 320s, in which he was critical of that king for his apparent drunkenness; his insatiable appetite for women, men, and boys; his destruction of Greek cities; and even his incontinence: see M. A. Flower, *Theopompus of Chios* (Oxford: 1994). Also important is a fragment from a biography written by the third-century B.C. Peripatetic biographer Satyrus, which provides our only information for the names of Philip's wives, the order in which he married them, and how his seventh and final marriage created a rift between him and Olympias: see A. D. Tronson, "Satyrus the Peripatetic and the Marriages of Philip II," *JHS* 104 (1984), pp. 116–126.

The most important of the contemporary sources for Alexander was the *Ephemerides*, the royal journal, which was a daily record of Alexander's actions, including his final days, perhaps kept by his secretary, Eumenes of Cardia. Other early writers include the philosopher and court historian Callisthenes of Olynthus, who accompanied Alexander on his campaign and thus had firsthand knowledge of events and the king's actions until he was condemned to death in 327, and the general Ptolemy, son of Lagus, who had known Alexander since boyhood and fought alongside him in Asia. Ptolemy published his work when he was ruler of

Egypt and focused more on the military aspects of Alexander's reign, elevating his own personal role in some important military engagements. Finally, Cleitarchus of Colophon (Asia Minor), who wrote after Alexander's death, was critical of the king as well as being more interested in sensational stories, and Aristobulus of Cassandreia, an engineer, also published after the king's death and made observations on his character.

Numismatic evidence from Philip's reign shows his propaganda and the kingdom's increasing economic prosperity, given that he minted both silver and gold denominations, which became the strongest of the Greek currencies. Almost all of the coins featuring Alexander are posthumous, but they show that his successors consciously identified themselves with their former king for political capital. The epigraphic evidence is more meager. Of special note are the inscriptions relating to the League of Corinth and Alexander's dealings with the Greeks of Asia Minor and the nearby islands. The archaeological evidence that has been unearthed over the past three or four decades from urban and rural sites is of stunning importance, especially at the sanctuary to Zeus at Dium and the tombs at Derveni and Vergina (Aegae). In the last complex are the probable tombs of Philip II and Alexander IV (Alexander the Great's son).

The above types of evidence may be called "primary sources" because they were written in the era of Philip and Alexander. The connected narratives of the reigns of these kings date from the first century B.C. to the fourth century A.D. and can be called "secondary sources." They have strengths and weaknesses depending on how they used the primary material and were influenced by the Roman background against which they were written: see A. B. Bosworth, *From Arrian to Alexander* (Oxford: 1988) and *Alexander and the East. The Tragedy of Triumph* (Oxford: 1996), with N. G. L. Hammond, *Three Historians of Alexander the Great* (Cambridge: 1983) and *Sources for Alexander the Great* (Cambridge: 1993); D. Spencer, *The Roman Alexander: Reading a Cultural Myth* (Exeter: 2002); P. Cartledge, *Alexander the Great: The Hunt for a New Past* (London: 2003), pp. 267–294; and S. Asirvatham, "His Son's Father? Philip II in the Second Sophistic," in Carney and Ogden (eds.), *Philip and Alexander*, pp. 193–204.

The earliest of these histories was written by Diodorus Siculus (of Sicily) while living in late Republican Rome. His *Universal History* of

40 books (only 15 survive) covered the period from mythical times to Caesar's campaigns in Gaul of 54 B.C. He wrote of Philip's reign in book 16 and of Alexander's in book 17. Diodorus followed Cleitarchus for the most part; although he is guilty of some chronological errors, telescoping of events, and questionable troop numbers in Alexander's battles, for example, he was careful in his treatment of the earlier source material, and his history is generally reliable: see further, K. Sacks, *Diodorus Siculus and the First Century* (Princeton: 1990).

Lucius Flavius Arrianus Xenophon (Arrian) hailed from Nicomedia in the Roman province of Bithynia (Asia Minor) and was governor of the province of Cappadocia in the reign of Emperor Hadrian in the second century A.D. He was a Greek and wrote an *Anabasis of Alexander* in Greek in seven books (no doubt influenced by Xenophon's *Anabasis*), which have all survived. Although Arrian singled out in particular Ptolemy and Aristobulus, not least because they had actually been with Alexander, he ultimately preferred Ptolemy's less romanticized version. In doing so Arrian excluded some of the more sensational aspects of Alexander's kingship, in which he was less interested, in favor of military discussion. Ptolemy embellished his role in some of Alexander's engagements, which thus calls Arrian into doubt on occasion.

Quintus Curtius Rufus wrote a *Historiae Alexanderi Magni* in Latin in 10 books sometime in the mid– to later first century A.D. The first two books have not survived, but the remaining eight are virtually complete. Curtius, who follows Ptolemy and Cleitarchus, makes numerous factual, geographical, and chronological errors and in many respects uses Alexander's character as a vehicle to criticize despotic emperors such as Caligula, Claudius, and Nero: see further, E. Baynham, *The Unique History of Quintus Curtius Rufus* (Ann Arbor: 1998).

In the first century B.C. Gnaeus Pompeius Trogus, a Roman historian from Gaul, wrote a *Historiae Philippicae* in 44 books, which has not survived. At some point in the second to fourth century A.D. Marcus Junianus Justinus (Justin), a Roman historian about whom nothing is known, prepared an epitome of it, also in Latin. Justin's description of Philip's reign runs from the end of book 7 to the end of 9, while that of Alexander takes up the whole of books 11–12. It is not possible to compare Justin's epitome with Trogus's original, although the attachment to Cleitarchus's work presumably indicates that Trogus had followed it, but recent scholarship has elevated Justin's historical value: see M. Alonso-Núñez, "An Augustan World History: The *Historiae Philippicae* of Pompeius Trogus," *G&R*² 34 (1987), pp. 56–72 and J. Yardley, *Justin and Pompeius Trogus. A Study of the Language of Justin's* Epitome *of Trogus* (Toronto: 2003).

In the second century A.D. the biographer Plutarch of Chaeronea wrote a series of "parallel lives" of influential Greeks and Romans to the end of the Roman Republic in which he paired a particular individual with another man. Those of Demosthenes (paired with Cicero), Alexander (paired with Caesar), and Phocion (paired with Cato the Younger) provide a great deal of information about Philip and Alexander. However, because of the genre of biography, Plutarch was less interested in factual accuracy and unromantic details and more interested in sensationalism, gossip, and the morality of his subjects: see J. M. Mossman, "Tragedy and Epic in Plutarch's *Alexander*," *JHS* 108 (1988), pp. 83–93; T. Duff, *Plutarch's "Lives." Exploring Vice and Virtue* (Oxford: 1999); and C. Pelling, *Plutarch and History* (London: 2002).

Other writers in a variety of genres also provide information, such as the geographer Strabo (first century B.C.–first century A.D.), the Greek historian Polybius (second century B.C.), and even the Roman historian Livy (first century B.C.). Two other records, however, deserve further mention. First is Plutarch's treatise *On the Fortune or the Virtue of Alexander*, which is a rhetorical exercise that discusses Alexander as a warrior king and as an intellectual and idealist. It provides details of some aspects of Alexander's life and events but runs afoul of being taken seriously because the author ascribes to Alexander a desire to unite the races and impose Greek civilization on the peoples he conquered.

Second is the so-called *Alexander Romance*, which possibly originated with Callisthenes but was substantially reworked and added to in the third and subsequent centuries, especially the medieval period. Versions of the *Romance* are found in Latin, Syriac, Arabic, Ethiopic, and Persian, not to mention Icelandic and Irish. Indeed, in the Middle Ages only the Gospels have the edge in most numbers of translations. The *Romance* is really fiction, since it contains many unhistorical and anachronistic events. For example, depending on the version, Alexander is the son of the last Egyptian pharaoh, Nectanebo (to legitimize his claim to rule Egypt); visits Jerusalem in no fewer than five *Romance*s to consult with the High Priest; searches for the water of life; goes underwater in a bathysphere; meets a tribe of headless men; flies in a balloon; or fights as a Christian knight or a Muslim warrior: see C. Mossé, *Alexander: Destiny and Myth*, trans. J. Lloyd (Edinburgh: 2004), pp. 176–188 and R. Stoneman, "The *Alexander Romance*: From History to Fiction," in J. R. Morgan and R. Stoneman (eds.), *Greek Fiction. The Greek Novel in Context* (London: 1994), pp. 117–129.

For Alexander's representation in various legends in the East, see R. Stoneman, *Legends of Alexander the Great* (London: 1994) and *Alexander the Great: A Life in Legend* (New Haven: 2008).

COLLECTIONS AND TRANSLATIONS

The fragments of the early literary writers or primary sources are collected in F. Jacoby, *Die Fragmente der griechischen Historiker* (*The Fragments of the Greek Historians*). The Greek texts of the Alexander historians are in vol. IIB, nos. 117–153 (Berlin: 1927), and vol. IIIB, nos. 742–743 (Berlin: 1930); there is a commentary in German on them in IID (Berlin: 1927), pp. 403–542. They are translated in C. A. Robinson, *The History of Alexander the Great* 1 (Providence: 1953) and about a third of them are reprinted (in translation) in Ian Worthington, *Alexander the Great: A Reader*, 2nd ed. (London: 2011). A new edition of Jacoby's *Fragmente*, with original texts, facing English translations, and new, critical commentaries, is being published by E. J. Brill Academic Publishers as *Brill's New Jacoby*, editor-in-chief Ian Worthington.

The most up-to-date translations of the contemporary Greek orators are in the University of Texas Oratory of Classical Greece series, under the general editorship of Michael Gagarin, which I have used in this book and cited in the notes.

The following are recommended translations of the later narrative writers or secondary sources:

Arrian

The Campaigns of Alexander, trans. A. de Sélincourt, Penguin Classics (Harmondsworth: 1971)

Arrian, "*History of Alexander*," trans. P. A. Brunt, 2 vols., Loeb Classical Library (Cambridge: 1976 and 1983)

Arrian, "*The Anabasis*" and "*The Indica*," trans. M. Hammond and J. E. Atkinson, Oxford World Classics (Oxford: 2013)

Quintus Curtius Rufus

Quintus Curtius, "*History of Alexander*," trans. J. C. Rolfe, 2 vols., Loeb Classical Library (Cambridge: 1946)

The History of Alexander, trans. J. Yardley, Penguin Classics (Harmondsworth: 1984)

Curtius Rufus. "*Histories of Alexander the Great*," Book 10, trans. J. E. Atkinson and J. Yardley (Oxford: 2009)

Diodorus Siculus

Diodorus Siculus 15.20–16.65, trans. C. L. Sherman, Loeb Classical Library, vol. 7 (Cambridge: 1952)

Diodorus Siculus 16.66–17, trans. C. Bradford Welles, Loeb Classical Library, vol. 8 (Cambridge: 1963)

Plutarch

Plutarch, "*The Age of Alexander*," trans. Ian Scott-Kilvert, Penguin Classics (Harmondsworth: 1973)

Plutarch's "*Lives—Demosthenes and Alexander*," trans. B. Perrin, Loeb Classical Library, vol. 7 (Cambridge: 1919)

Plutarch's "*Lives—Phocion*," trans. B. Perrin, Loeb Classical Library, vol. 8 (Cambridge: 1919)

On the Fortune or the Virtue of Alexander, in *Moralia*, trans. F. C. Babbitt, Loeb Classical Library, vol. 4 (Cambridge: 1936)

The Greek Alexander Romance, trans. R. Stoneman, Penguin Classics (Harmondsworth: 1991)

Justin

R. Develin and W. Heckel, *Justin: Epitome of the "Philippic History" of Pompeius Trogus* (Atlanta: 1994)

J. Yardley and W. Heckel, *Justin. Epitome of the "Philippic History" of Pompeius Trogus,"* 1: *Books 11–12: Alexander the Great* (Oxford: 1997)

There are also collections of abridged translations from the above in J. Roisman, *Alexander the Great: Ancient and Modern Perspectives* (Lexington: 1995) and W. Heckel and J. Yardley, *Alexander the Great. Historical Sources in Translation* (Malden: 2003).

For the numismatic evidence, see G. Le Rider, *Le monnayage d'argent et d'or de Philippe II frappé en Macédoine de 359 à 294* (Paris: 1977); A. Stewart, *Faces of Power. Alexander's Image and Hellenistic Politics* (Berkeley and Los Angeles: 1993), pp. 9–21; and K. Dahmen, *The Legend of Alexander the Great on Greek and Roman Coins* (London: 2007). See also V. Poulios, "Macedonian Coinage from the 6th Century to 148 BC," in J. Vokotopoulou (ed.), *Greek Civilization: Macedonia, Kingdom of Alexander the Great* (Athens: 1993), pp. 83–103.

For collections of inscriptions, see M. N. Tod, *Greek Historical Inscriptions* 2 (Oxford: 1948), which has a Greek text and English commentary; L. Moretti, *Inscrizioni Storiche Ellenistiche* (Florence: 1967 and 1976), with Greek text and Italian commentary; and P. J. Rhodes and R. Osborne, *Greek Historical Inscriptions, 404–323* BC (Oxford: 2003), with Greek text, facing English translation, and English commentary. Many of these inscriptions are translated (with notes) in P. E. Harding, *From the End of the Peloponnesian War to the Battle of Ipsus* (Cambridge: 1985). For texts, translations, and detailed discussion of the epigraphical evidence relating to Alexander's dealings with the Greeks, see A. J. Heisserer, *Alexander the Great and the Greeks* (Norman: 1980). The Research Centre for Greek and Roman Antiquity in Athens, part of the National Hellenic Research Foundation, has collected epigraphic and other evidence from all over ancient Macedonia, which it publishes in its *Meletemata* series.

The archaeological evidence is too plentiful to list. See, for example, M. Andronikos, "Archaeological Discoveries in Macedonia," in J. Vokotopoulou (ed.), *Greek Civilization: Macedonia, Kingdom of Alexander the*

Great (Athens: 1993), pp. 5–11 (see too pp. 32–67 and 197–241) and the essays on various cities in Fox, *Brill's Companion to Ancient Macedon*. Of especial note are M. Andronikos, *Vergina: The Royal Tombs* (Athens: 1984; repr., 2004); S. Drougou and C. Saatsoglou-Paliadeli, *Vergina. Wandering through the Archaeological Site* (Athens: 2004); and D. Pandermalis, *Dion. The Archaeological Site and Museum* (Athens: 1997). See also A. Cohen, *The Alexander Mosaic. Stories of Victory and Defeat* (Cambridge: 1997); and on Alexander's portraiture: M. Bieber, "The Portraits of Alexander," *G&R*[2] 12 (1965), pp. 183–188; E. von Schwarzenberg, "The Portraiture of Alexander," in E. Badian (ed.), *Alexandre le Grand, Image et Réalité*, Fondation Hardt, Entretiens 22 (Geneva: 1976), pp. 223–278; A. Stewart, "Alexander in Greek and Roman Art," in Roisman (ed.), *Companion to Alexander*, pp. 31–66, and especially *Faces of Power*.

TIMELINE

431–404: The Peloponnesian War: Athens defeated and Sparta triumphant.

404–371: The Spartan hegemony of Greece: ends with Thebes defeating Sparta at the Battle of Leuctra (371).

383 or 382: Birth of future Philip II, son of King Amyntas III of Macedonia and Eurydice.

378: Athens founds the Second Athenian Confederacy.

371–362: The Theban hegemony of Greece: ends with an Athenian-led coalition defeating Thebes at the Battle of Mantinea (362).

368–365: Philip a hostage in Thebes.

364?: Philip governor of Amphaxitis(?); he marries Phila of Elimeia (first wife).

359: Death of Perdiccas III and 4,000 Macedonians battling the Illyrians. Macedonian Assembly acclaims Philip (II) king; Philip arranges an armistice(?) with the Illyrians and marries Audata (second wife); he nullifies threats from Paeonians, Thracians, and Athenians; he begins military reforms.

358: Philip defeats Illyrians and Paeonians; he unites Upper and Lower Macedonia; he makes alliance with Thessaly to secure his southern border; he marries Philinna of Larissa (third wife).

357: Philinna gives birth to son Arrhidaeus; Philip allies with Epirus; he marries Olympias of Epirus (fourth wife); Athens declares war on Philip; Philip allies with Chalcidean League.

356: Olympias gives birth to Alexander; Philip annexes Crenides and renames it Philippi, Macedonia's first colony; Phocis seizes Delphi, sparking Third Sacred War (355–346).

355: Amphictyonic Council formally declares sacred war against Phocis; Philip besieges Methone (Thermaic Gulf).

354: Philip blinded in right eye at Methone; he makes agreement with Cersebleptes of Thrace.

353: Philip intervenes in Thessaly; he is defeated by Onomarchus of Phocis.

352: Battle of the Crocus Field in Thessaly at which Philip defeats Onomarchus; Philip elected archon of Thessaly; he marries Nicesipolis (fifth wife); he returns to Pella; he campaigns in Thrace against Cersebleptes.

351: Philip returns from Thrace; in Athens, Demosthenes delivers first *Philippic* against Philip.

350: Philip possibly campaigns in Paeonia and Illyria and invades Epirus.

349: Philip invades the Chalcidice; he has to intervene in Thessaly; Athens makes alliance with Olynthus against Philip.

348: Philip returns to the Chalcidice; fall of Olynthus; Philip proposes peace with Athens; Aeschines, Demosthenes's political opponent, debuts in the Assembly.

347: Cersebleptes and Athens challenge Philip's influence in Thrace.

346: Peace of Philocrates ends war between Philip and Athens over Amphipolis; Third Sacred War ends in defeat of Phocis; Philip receives the two Phocian votes on the Amphictyonic Council; Philip elected President of the Pythian Games; Isocrates's *To Philip* implores him to invade Asia.

345: Philip moves population groups in Macedonia; he founds new towns on his northwestern frontier; he campaigns against Pleurias of Illyria(?).

344: Philip sends Python of Byzantium to Athens to amend terms of the Peace of Philocrates; Demosthenes's second *Philippic* rejects Philip's proposal; Philip moves to control Thessaly.

343:     Philip deposes Arybbas of Epirus and installs his brother-in-law Alexander as king; possible plot to burn the Athenian dockyards.

342:     Philip hires Aristotle to tutor Alexander; he intervenes on
Euboea; he conquers Thrace; he defeats the Getae in the
north and marries Meda (sixth wife); escalating tensions
between Athens and Philip in the Thracian Chersonese.

341:     Diopeithes of Athens campaigns in the Thracian Chersonese;
Philip demands his recall; Demosthenes's *On the Chersonese*
and the third and fourth *Philippics* support Diopeithes and
urge war against Philip; Philip threatens Athenian interests
in Chersonese.

340:     Philip besieges Perinthus, Selymbia, and Byzantium; he appoints
Alexander regent of Macedonia; Demosthenes's last surviving
political speech, *To Philip's Letter*, calls for war; Philip captures
the Athenian grain fleet; Athens declares war on Philip.

339:     Philip campaigns in Scythia but returning home is badly
wounded in battle against the Triballi; outbreak of the Fourth
Sacred War against Amphissa in Locris; Philip appointed
general of the Amphictyonic troops; he spends winter con-
valescing.

338:     Philip enters Greece; he seizes Elatea to control Thermopylae; Demosthenes brokers alliance with Thebes against Philip;
end of Fourth Sacred War; Battle of Chaeronea between
Philip and an Athenian/Theban-led coalition of troops gives
Philip mastery of Greece; end of second war between Philip
and Athens; Philip summons delegates from Greek states to
Corinth to announce Common Peace; work on his Philippeion at Olympia begins(?).

337:     Second meeting of Greeks (except Sparta) at Corinth;
Common Peace sworn to and League of Corinth formally
constituted with Philip as hegemon; Macedonian hegemony
of Greece assured; Philip announces invasion of Asia; he
marries Cleopatra (seventh wife); Alexander and Olympias
leave Pella but soon return; Pixodarus affair.

336: Philip sends advance force to Asia Minor; marriage of Cleo-patra (Philip's daughter) to Alexander of Epirus at Aegae; assassination of Philip (July); Alexander (III) succeeds to the throne; Alexander begins purge of rivals; burial of Philip at Aegae (modern Vergina); revolt of the Greeks from the League of Corinth crushed by Alexander; he resurrects League of Corinth and father's plan to invade Asia.

335: Alexander campaigns against the Triballi and Illyrians; revolt of Thebes; he razes it to the ground; purge of rivals ends.

334: Alexander invades Asia (summer); Battle of the Granicus River; sieges of Miletus and Halicarnassus.

333: Alexander conquers coastal Asia Minor; he undoes the Gordian knot; Persian counteroffensive at sea; Alexander almost dies at Tarsus; Battle of Issus.

332: Alexander besieges Tyre and Gaza; conquest of the Levant; he secures Egypt.

331: Alexander founds Alexandria; he visits Oracle of Zeus Ammon at Siwah; Agis III of Sparta calls on Greeks to defy Macedonian rule; Battle of Gaugamela; Alexander takes control of Babylon and Susa; Battle at the Persian Gates.

330: Antipater defeats Agis; Alexander enters Persepolis; he burns palace to the ground; death of Darius III at Hecatompylus; Bessus, satrap of Bactria, proclaims himself Great King (Artaxerxes V); Alexander invades Bactria and Sogdiana; so-called Philotas conspiracy at Phrada leads to executions of Philotas and Parmenion.

329: Alexander captures Bessus; start of massive revolt of Bactria and Sogdiana.

328: Alexander fighting in Bactria and Sogdiana; murder of Cleitus; Alexander besieges the Sogdian rock.

327: Final victory over Bactrian rebels; Alexander marries Roxane at Maracanda (spring); he attempts to introduce *proskynesis* at Bactra; Pages' Conspiracy; execution of Callisthenes; march to India; siege of the Rock of Aornus.

326: Battle of the Hydaspes River; mutiny at the Hyphasis River; Alexander campaigns against the Malli and is near-fatally wounded.

325: Alexander sails down the Indus into the Indian Ocean; he leaves India, which revolts; disastrous march through the Gedrosian Desert; voyage of Nearchus along the Makran coast.

324: Mass marriage at Susa; the Exiles Decree causes furor on the mainland; mutiny at Opis; Hephaestion dies at Ecbatana.

323: Alexander arrives in Babylon; he intends to invade Arabia; Alexander dies (June 11); Greeks revolt from Macedonian hegemony; Alexander's generals divide up his empire; beginning of the wars of the successors.

322: Antipater reimposes Macedonian rule over Greece and demands surrender of anti-Macedonian politicians; Demosthenes commits suicide on Calaura (Poros) to avoid capture.

CAST OF PRINCIPAL CHARACTERS

AESCHINES: Aeschines was an Athenian orator and statesman who was born in the 390s and advocated maintaining peace with Philip II in the second half of the 340s, which brought him into conflict with Demosthenes. Aeschines's unsuccessful prosecution of Demosthenes in 330 led to his departure from Athens. The year of his death is not known.

AGIS III: Agis was a king of Sparta who, in the late 330s, with Persian support, mounted a serious challenge to the Macedonian hegemony of Greece. In 331 he called the Greeks to arms against Antipater, Alexander's deputy in Greece, but Antipater defeated and killed him the following year at Megalopolis (in Arcadia).

ALEXANDER III (THE GREAT): Alexander was the son of Philip II and Olympias of Epirus and was born in 356. He became king of Macedonia in 336 and died in Babylon in 323. He invaded Asia in 334, toppling the Achaemenid ruling dynasty and establishing an empire that stretched from Greece to what the Greeks called India (Pakistan and Kashmir). His next campaign, an invasion of Arabia, was abandoned on his death.

ALEXANDER IV: Alexander IV, son of Alexander III and Roxane, was born after his father's death in 323. Although proclaimed king as Alexander IV, he shared the throne with his half-brother Philip III Arrhidaeus. He was, however, a pawn in the wars of Alexander's generals, and after he was imprisoned in Amphipolis for a time he and his mother were put to death in 311.

ALEXANDER OF EPIRUS: Alexander of Epirus was the brother of Olympias, taken by Philip to live in Pella in 350 until he came of age in 343.

In that year Philip invaded Epirus, expelled the king (Arybbas), and installed Alexander as ruler. Always loyal to Philip, Alexander of Epirus married Cleopatra, daughter of Philip and Olympias (thus Alexander's niece) at Aegae in 336. In 330 Alexander took part in an ill-fated campaign in Italy, where he was killed.

ANTIPATER: Antipater, born to a noble family perhaps in the 390s, served as a general under Philip and was the first to proclaim Alexander king when Philip was assassinated in 336. When Alexander left for Asia in 334 he appointed Antipater his guardian (*epitropos*) of Macedonia and deputy hegemon of the League of Corinth. Antipater served Alexander well, among other things ending Agis of Sparta's attempt to topple the Macedonian hegemony of Greece. He clashed frequently with Olympias, and in 324 Alexander may have decided to replace him with Craterus. Antipater died in 319.

ARIOBARZANES: Ariobarzanes was a Persian nobleman and satrap of Persis, whose adroit use of the terrain kept Alexander at bay at the Persian Gates in 331 for one month. Eventually, Alexander was able to surround his troops and defeat them in battle. Ariobarzanes and survivors escaped to Persepolis, but as Alexander's men approached the city they killed them.

ARISTOTLE: One of the greatest philosophers of ancient Greece, Aristotle was born at Stageira (Chalcidice) in 384. Philip II hired him to tutor his son Alexander from 343 to 340. Alexander and Aristotle remained in contact while the former was in Asia, but Alexander did not share Aristotle's view that Greeks should rule "barbarians," and relations between the two of them cooled because of this. Aristotle moved to Athens, where he founded the Lyceum in the 330s. He died in 322.

ARTABAZUS: Artabazus, satrap of Hellespontine Phrygia, revolted from Artaxerxes II in the 350s and, with his family, fled for refuge to Pella. His young daughter Barsine met a young Alexander there; years later, after Issus in 333, they became lovers. Artabazus returned to Persia in 343. He served Darius III loyally and then Alexander after the Great King's death in 330. Alexander made Artabazus satrap of Bactria in 329, but two years later he resigned and shortly after died.

ARTAXERXES III "OCHUS": Artaxerxes III "Ochus" was Great King of Persia from 359 until 338. He was assassinated in 338 on the orders of a eunuch named Bagoas (not the Bagoas who was Alexander's eunuch and lover). Alexander married one of his daughters at Susa in 324.

ARTAXERXES IV "ARSES": Artaxerxes IV "Arses," son of Artaxerxes III, ruled from 338 to 336. Bagoas, who had arranged the death of his father, installed Arses as Great King, but in 336 Bagoas had him killed.

ATTALUS: Macedonian nobleman who adopted the young Cleopatra who later married Philip II in 337 (his seventh marriage). At the wedding banquet Attalus toasted that Macedonia might finally have a legitimate heir, which infuriated the named heir, Alexander. Attalus married the daughter of Parmenion and was one of the commanders of the advance force that went to Asia Minor in 336. The following year Alexander III had Attalus, still in Asia Minor, put to death.

BAGOAS: A Persian eunuch of great beauty, Bagoas was given to Alexander by the Persian Nabarzanes at Zadracarta in 330. Alexander became infatuated with him, and he and Bagoas enjoyed a sexual relationship.

BARSINE: Barsine first encountered Alexander as a young boy in the 350s when she lived for a time with her father, Artabazus, satrap of Hellespontine Phrygia, at Pella. She later married Mentor of Rhodes and, when he died, his brother Memnon. After Issus in 333, Parmenion captured her at Damascus and sent her to Alexander. The king supposedly lost his virginity to her. They lived in a de facto relationship, and she bore him a son, Heracles.

BESSUS: The powerful satrap of Bactria, Bessus supported Darius III at Gaugamela in 331. In 330 he was one of the conspirators who overthrew Darius III (but not one of his assassins), and because of his blood ties with the Achaemenids he proclaimed himself Artaxerxes V. The threat he posed to Alexander caused the king to pursue him into Bactria. In 329 Bessus was betrayed, and Alexander had him executed.

CALLISTHENES: Probably the nephew of Aristotle, Callisthenes hailed from Olynthus and was a philosopher who accompanied Alexander on his Asian campaign as court historian. He most likely embellished his account of Alexander's exploits for propaganda reasons. He defied Alexander's attempts to introduce *proskynesis* at Bactra in 327, after which the king implicated him in the Pages' Conspiracy; he either was executed or died in prison.

CLEITUS: A Macedonian nobleman, also known as "the Black," Cleitus served under Philip and was one of Alexander's generals in Asia. He saved the king's life at the Granicus River in 334. However, his criticisms of Alexander's orientalism led to a drunken argument between the two of them at Maracanda in 328, which ended with Alexander killing him in cold blood.

CLEOPATRA: As probably a young teenager Cleopatra was adopted by Attalus. She married Philip II in 337. Her name may then have been changed to Eurydice. The ancient sources say that this was the only time Philip married out of love. Cleopatra earned Olympias's enmity, and after Philip's death in 336 Olympias had Cleopatra and her infant child (possibly a boy named Caranus) put to death.

COENUS: Coenus was the son-in-law of Parmenion and one of Alexander's commanders. He defiantly spoke up to Alexander during the mutiny at the Hyphasis River in 326, which forced the king to abandon his attempt to reach the Ganges. Later, Coenus was found dead.

CRATERUS: One of the "Old Guard" generals of Philip II, Craterus was also the son-in-law of Antipater. He served Alexander well, especially in Bactria and India, and in 324 at Opis Alexander tasked him with leading back to Greece the 10,000 veteran and wounded soldiers whom he discharged from his army. Alexander may have selected him for this mission also to replace Antipater.

DARIUS III: Darius III was the Great King of Persia and last of the Achaemenid line, who came to the throne in 336 and died in 330. Ancient sources and even some modern accounts portray him unflatteringly as a weak king and coward in battle since he twice fled his line (Issus in 333 and Gaugamela in 331). However, he was an able administrator and strategist. As support for him waned because of his losses to Alexander, he was murdered by some of his satraps in 330 at Hecatompylus.

DEMOSTHENES: Demosthenes was an Athenian orator, born in about 384, who was Philip's most vocal opponent. In a series of speeches beginning with the first *Philippic* (in 351), Demosthenes urged the Athenians to fight Philip, even after the two sides made peace in 346. During Alexander's reign Demosthenes was far less vocal, and in 323 he fled Athens into a self-imposed exile following his disgrace in the Harpalus affair. He was later recalled but fled Athens again when Greek resistance in the Lamian War after Alexander's death collapsed. To escape capture, he committed suicide in 322. Demosthenes's rhetorical style makes him the greatest of the Greek orators whose works survive.

HARPALUS: A Macedonian nobleman and boyhood friend of Alexander, Harpalus became imperial treasurer, a post created by the king. Harpalus fled back to Greece before Issus in 333, perhaps out of fear that the Macedonians might lose, perhaps because he had embezzled money, possibly even both, but Alexander forgave him. Harpalus established his headquarters at Babylon, but his grandiose actions earned him Alexander's enmity, and in 324 he fled to Athens hoping to incite a revolt. Unsuccessful, he left for Crete, where he was murdered.

HEPHAESTION: Hephaestion was another of Alexander's boyhood friends, whose close relationship with the king likely turned into a physical one. Hephaestion was made co-commander of the Companion Cavalry (with Cleitus) after the demise of Philotas in 330 and was later appointed chiliarch (second-in-command). When he died in 324 in Ecbatana Alexander was grief-stricken; among other things, he ordered the whole empire to be in mourning and arranged for Hephaestion to become a demigod with his own cult.

HERMOLAUS: Hermolaus was one of the young pages or personal attendants of the king. Hermolaus's action in preempting Alexander's spearing of a boar in 327 caused him to be flogged and, seeking revenge, to orchestrate the so-called Pages' Conspiracy at Bactra in the same year.

ISOCRATES: Isocrates was an Athenian orator who was head of Athens's most famous and influential school of rhetoric. In 346 to he wrote the *To Philip*, a letter to the Macedonian king urging him to unite the Greeks and invade Asia. Philip could not do so then, but possibly Isocrates put the notion of such a campaign into Philip's mind. Isocrates died in 338 (aged 98), the same year as Chaeronea, still advocating for an invasion of Asia.

MAZAEUS: Mazaeus was a Persian nobleman who was satrap of Cilicia and Syria and who commanded the Persian right wing at Gaugamela. He surrendered Babylon without incident to Alexander in 330, for which he was appointed satrap of Babylonia, the first Persian aristocrat to receive this office from the king.

MEMNON: Memnon was born in Rhodes and became a mercenary commander in the pay of Artabazus, satrap of Hellespontine Phrygia; he married his daughter Barsine and later served Darius III. Though he was a gifted strategist, Memnon's advice on how to defeat the Macedonian army at the Granicus River was overruled, to the Persians' detriment. Memnon was later in charge of the Persian fleet and also mounted a formidable defense when Alexander besieged Halicarnassus in 333. He died at the siege of Mytilene in the same year.

NEARCHUS: Nearchus hailed from Crete and was another of Alexander's boyhood friends. He was made satrap of Lycia and Pamphylia but then tapped as admiral of the fleet. His most famous voyage was the mapping of the Makran coast to the Persian Gulf, in 324, a 1,000-mile epic voyage that took him 60 days with minimal losses, a stirring account of which is found in Arrian's *Indica*.

OLYMPIAS: Olympias was a princess of Epirus who married Philip II in 357 as part of a diplomatic alliance between Macedonia and Epirus. In 356 Olympias gave birth to Alexander (III). She disliked Philip greatly and may even have played a role in his assassination. She frequently clashed with Antipater when Alexander was in Asia but withdrew to Epirus from 331 to 317. In that year she returned to interfere in Macedonian politics but was herself put to death in 316.

PARMENION: Parmenion, a nobleman, was the most senior of Alexander's generals and arguably the greatest. Parmenion served under Philip and was part of an advance force sent to Asia Minor when the king was killed. He declared his loyalty to Alexander, but over time his criticisms of Alexander's orientalism, and the military and diplomatic clashes the two men had, earned him the king's disfavor. In 330 Alexander implicated him in the so-called Philotas conspiracy, even though he was then in Ecbatana, and had him put to death.

PHILIP II: Philip was the son of Amyntas III and Eurydice and was born in about 383. He became king of Macedonia in 359 and was assassinated in 336. In that time he transformed Macedonia from an economically, politically, and militarily weak kingdom on the periphery of Greece into a superpower, in the process conquering the lands adjoining his borders as well as Thrace and Greece, and even made plans to invade Asia.

PHILIP III ARRHIDAEUS: Arrhidaeus, son of Philip II and his third wife, Philinna of Thessaly, was born in 357. He suffered some type of mental incapacity, and his younger brother Alexander (the future Alexander III) became heir. Arrhidaeus lived at Pella; on Alexander's death in 323 he was proclaimed king as Philip III Arrhidaeus. However, he shared regnal power with Alexander IV, son of Alexander III and Roxane. Arrhidaeus was a pawn in the wars of Alexander's generals, and he and his wife, Eurydice, were executed in 317.

PHILOTAS: The son of Parmenion, Philotas was commander of the Companion Cavalry but, like his father, was critical of Alexander's orientalism. In 330 a plot to kill Alexander was supposedly revealed to Philotas, who dismissed it. When Alexander found out, he did not simply rebuke Philotas for not informing him but, rather, implicated him in it. Because of his arrogance none of the other senior staff liked Philotas, and none spoke up for him—his father, Parmenion, at the time was in Ecbatana. Philotas was put on trial, found guilty, and executed.

PORUS: The Indian prince Porus ruled the territory between the Hydases and Acesines rivers. In 326 he brought Alexander to battle at the Hydaspes River, where he was soundly defeated. He survived, and his bravery motivated Alexander to reconfirm and even extend his lands, although he likely became a vassal to Alexander. Porus never repaid the favor and helped India revolt in 325.

PTOLEMY: A nobleman and boyhood friend of Alexander, Ptolemy was made a general and served Alexander loyally, including taking Bessus into custody in 329. When Alexander's corpse was being transported from Babylon to Aegae, Ptolemy kidnapped it and buried it in Egypt, which he had taken on Alexander's death. He held Egypt throughout the wars of the successors, in the process founding the Ptolemaic dynasty. His firsthand account of Alexander's exploits after the destruction of Thebes in 335 is one of the major primary sources for Arrian's later narrative of the reign (see the appendix).

ROXANE: Roxane (Roshanak, "Beautiful Star") was a Bactrian noblewoman, daughter of Oxyartes, who married Alexander at Maracanda in 327. When Alexander died in 323 Roxane was pregnant with their child; she gave birth to a boy, Alexander IV, who was used as a pawn in the wars of the successors. Both of them were put to death in 311.

SPITAMENES: Spitamenes, a Sogdian nobleman, was arguably Alexander's greatest foe because of his brilliance in guerilla warfare. In 329 Spitamenes seized Bessus and surrendered him to Ptolemy, but his action was a hollow one. Soon after he encouraged the whole of Bactria and Sogdiana to revolt and besieged Macedonian troops in Maracanda. He decisively defeated a relief force sent by Alexander (the greatest Macedonian defeat in Asia) and for the next two years harried the invaders mercilessly. In 327 Coenus defeated him in battle, after which his troops (the Massagetae) beheaded him.

NOTES

INTRODUCTION

1. See I. Morris and W. Scheidel (eds.), *The Dynamics of Ancient Empires* (Oxford: 2009).

2. For details of the lives and activities of all the individuals discussed in this book, see W. Heckel, *Who's Who in the Age of Alexander the Great* (Malden: 2006).

1. GREECE AND MACEDONIA

1. P. Green, *The Greco-Persian Wars* (Berkeley and Los Angeles: 1996).

2. Thucydides 1.123.6 for Sparta's reaction to Athens's power. On the war: D. Kagan, *The Peloponnesian War* (London: 2003); L. Tritle, *The Peloponnesian War* (Westport: 2004).

3. P. Cartledge, *Agesilaos and the Crisis of Sparta* (Baltimore: 1987); C. D. Hamilton, *Agesilaus and the Failure of Spartan Hegemony* (Ithaca: 1991); cf. J. Buckler, *Aegean Greece in the Fourth Century BC* (Leiden: 2003), pp. 12–295.

4. J. Buckler, *The Theban Hegemony* (Cambridge: 1980); cf. Buckler, *Aegean Greece*, pp. 296–350, 359–366 and "Alliance and Hegemony in Fourth-Century Greece: The Case of the Theban Hegemony," in J. Buckler and H. Beck (eds.), *Central Greece and the Politics of Power in the Fourth Century BC* (Cambridge: 2008), pp. 127–139.

5. E. M. Burke, "Athens after the Peloponnesian War: Restoration Efforts and the Role of Maritime Commerce," *Class. Antiquity* 9 (1990), pp. 1–13.

6. G. L. Cawkwell, "The Foundation of the Second Athenian Confederacy," *CQ*² 23 (1973), pp. 56–60; J. Buckler, "Sphodrias' Raid and the Evolution of the Athenian League," in J. Buckler and H. Beck (eds.), *Central Greece and the Politics of Power in the Fourth Century BC* (Cambridge: 2008), pp. 79–84. Charter: P. J. Rhodes and R. Osborne (eds.), *Greek Historical Inscriptions, 404–323 BC* (Oxford: 2003), no. 22 (pp. 92–105). Confederacy: J. Cargill, *The Second Athenian League* (Berkeley: 1981); G. L. Cawkwell, "Notes on the Failure of the Second Athenian Confederacy," *JHS* 101 (1981), pp. 40–54; G. T. Griffith, "Athens in the Fourth Century," in P. D. A. Garnsey and C. R. Whittaker (eds.), *Imperialism in the Ancient World* (Cambridge: 1978), pp. 127–144.

7. G. L. Cawkwell, "Athenian Naval Power in the Fourth Century," *CQ*² 34 (1984), pp. 334–345; J. S. Morrison, "Athenian Sea-Power in 323/2 B.C.: Dream and Reality," *JHS* 107 (1987), pp. 88–97.

8. G. L. Cawkwell, "Eubulus," *JHS* 83 (1963), pp. 47–67.

9. Plutarch, *Moralia* 1011b, with J. J. Buchanan, *Theorika* (New York: 1962); cf. Cawkwell, "Eubulus," pp. 53–58 and M. H. Hansen, "The Theoric Fund and the *Graphe Paranomon* against Apollodorus," *GRBS* 17 (1976), pp. 235–246.

10. Justin 8.1.1–2.

11. Polis problems and critics: N. G. L. Hammond, *Philip of Macedon* (London: 1994), pp. 64–78.

12. R. Billows, "Cities," in A. Erskine (ed.), *A Companion to the Hellenistic World* (Malden: 2003), pp. 196–215; cf. R. Waterfield, *Dividing the Spoils. The War for Alexander the Great's Empire* (Oxford: 2011), pp. 76–80.

13. Up-to-date discussions of Macedonia's history, society, and culture, with analysis of the evidence: Roisman and Worthington (eds.), *Companion to Macedonia*; R. Lane Fox (ed.), *Brill's Companion to Ancient Macedon* (Leiden: 2011)—the latter features mostly archaeological studies of cities and is not as comprehensive as the former.

14. Geographical descriptions: N. G. L. Hammond, *A History of Macedonia* 1 (Oxford: 1972), pp. 3–211; E. N. Borza, *In the Shadow of Olympus: The Emergence of Macedon* (Princeton: 1990), pp. 28–50; C. G. Thomas, *Alexander the Great in His World* (Malden: 2006), pp. 22–32. See too C. Edson, "Early Macedonia," *Anc. Macedonia* 1 (1970), pp. 17–44; M. Sivignon, "The Geographical Setting of Macedonia," in M. B. Sakellariou (ed.), *Macedonia, 4000 Years of Greek History and Civilization* (Athens: 1983), pp. 12–26; C. G. Thomas, "The Physical Kingdom," in Roisman and Worthington (eds.), *Companion to Macedonia*, pp. 65–80.

15. On the dynasty, cf. Thomas, *Alexander*, pp. 55–69.

16. Diodorus 7.16. Identification of Aegae with Vergina: Hammond, *History of Macedonia*, pp. 156–157; N. G. L. Hammond, "The Location of Aegae," *JHS* 117 (1997), pp. 177–179. See too P. B. Faklaris, "Aegae: Determining the Site of the First Capital of the Macedonians," *AJA* 98 (1994), pp. 609–616.

17. Griffith in N. G. L. Hammond and G. T. Griffith, *A History of Macedonia* 2 (Oxford: 1979), pp. 383–404; N. G. L. Hammond, *The Macedonian State: The Origins, Institutions and History* (Oxford: 1992), pp. 21–24, 60–70, 166–170; Thomas, *Alexander*, pp. 55–69; C. J. King, "Kingship and Other Political Institutions," in Roisman and Worthington (eds.), *Companion to Macedonia*, pp. 374–391.

18. W. Heckel, "King and 'Companions': Observations on the Nature of Power in the Reign of Alexander," in Roisman (ed.), *Companion to Alexander*, pp. 197–225, discussing various factions on pp. 200–205; see too G. Weber, "The Court of Alexander the Great as Social System," in Heckel and Tritle (eds.), *New History*, pp. 83–98.

19. P. Briant, "Chasses royales macédoniennes et chasses royales perses: Le thème de la chasse au lion sur *la chasse de Vergina*," *Dialogues d'Histoire Ancienne* 17 (1991), pp. 211–255 and "Les chasses d'Alexandre," *Anc. Macedonia* 5 (1993), pp. 267–277; E. Carney, "Hunting and the Macedonian Elite: Sharing the Rivalry of the Chase (Arrian 4.13.1)," in D. Ogden (ed.), *The Hellenistic World: New Perspectives* (London: 2002), pp. 59–80.

20. E. A. Fredricksmeyer, "The *Kausia*: Macedonian or Indian?" in Worthington (ed.), *Ventures*, pp. 136–158.

21. E. N. Borza, "The Symposium at Alexander's Court," *Anc. Macedonia* 3 (1983), pp. 45–55; E. Carney, "Symposia and the Macedonian Elite: The Unmixed Life," *Syllecta Classica* 18 (2007), pp. 129–180; F. Pownall, "The Symposia of Philip II and Alexander III of Macedon: The View from Greece," in Carney and Ogden (eds.), *Philip and Alexander*, pp. 55–65; N. Sawada, "Macedonian Social Customs," in Roisman and Worthington (eds.), *Companion to Macedonia*, pp. 392–408; R. A. Tomlinson, "Ancient Macedonian Symposia," *Anc. Macedonia* 1 (1970), pp. 308–315.

22. Ephippus, *FGrH* 126 F 1 (= Athenaeus 3.120e).

23. Demosthenes 2, *Olynthiac* 2.18–19.

24. *Ephemerides, FGrH* 117 F 2b (= Athenaeus 10.434b).

25. J. Roisman, "Honor in Alexander's Campaign," in Roisman (ed.), *Companion to Alexander*, pp. 316–321, on the shameful nature of symposia and lack of honor among the attendees, which contrasted to Alexander's value of honor in himself and others.

26. W. S. Greenwalt, "Polygamy and Succession in Argead Macedonia," *Arethusa* 22 (1989), pp. 19–45; cf. D. Ogden, *Alexander the Great. Myth, Genesis and Sexuality* (Exeter: 2011), pp. 111–115.

27. Details of his wives and reasons for marrying are in a fragment from a biography of Satyrus, quoted in Athenaeus 13.557b–e; cf. 13.560c: see A. D. Tronson, "Satyrus the Peripatetic and the Marriages of Philip II," *JHS* 104 (1984), pp. 116–126.

28. Cf. Thucydides 2.80.5; Isocrates 4, *Panegyricus* 3; Demosthenes 15, *On the Freedom of the Rhodians* 15; Dinarchus 1, *Against Demosthenes* 24. Greek perceptions of Macedonians: E. Badian, "Greeks and Macedonians," in B. Barr-Sharrar and E. N. Borza (eds.), *Macedonia and Greece in Late Classical and Early Hellenistic Times* (Washington: 1982), pp. 33–51; E. N. Borza, "Greeks and Macedonians in the Age of Alexander. The Source Traditions," in R. W. Wallace and E. M. Harris (eds.), *Transitions to Empire. Essays in Honor of E. Badian* (Norman: 1996), pp. 122–139; J. M. Hall, "Contested Ethnicities: Perceptions of Macedonia within Evolving Definitions of Greek Identity," in I. Malkin (ed.), *Ancient Perceptions of Greek Ethnicity* (Cambridge: 2001), pp. 159–186. See too S. Asirvatham, "Perspectives on the Macedonians from Greece, Rome, and Beyond," in Roisman and Worthington (eds.), *Companion to Macedonia*, pp. 100–104.

29. Demosthenes 9, *Philippic* 3.30–31; cf. Demosthenes 3, *Olynthiac* 3.16.

30. E. N. Borza, "The Philhellenism of Archelaus," *Anc. Macedonia* 5 (1993), pp. 237–244.

31. M. Andronikos, "Art during the Archaic and Classical Periods," and J. Touratsoglou, "Art in the Hellenistic Period," in M. B. Sakellariou (ed.), *Macedonia, 4000 Years of Greek History and Civilization* (Athens: 1983), pp. 92–110 and 170–191, respectively; C. L. Hardiman, "Classical Art to 221 BC," in Roisman and Worthington (eds.), *Companion to Macedonia*, pp. 505–521.

32. Cf. Plutarch, *Eumenes* 14.10–11, for the Macedonian language.

33. L. M. Danforth, *The Macedonian Conflict* (Princeton: 1995); cf. L. M. Danforth, "Alexander the Great and the Macedonian Conflict," in Roisman (ed.), *Companion to Alexander*, pp. 347–364; H. Poulton, *Who Are the Macedonians?* (Bloomington: 2000).

34. Summarized in Ian Worthington, *Philip II of Macedonia* (New Haven: 2008), pp. 216–219; Thomas, *Alexander*, pp. 32–36; J. Engels, "Macedonians and Greeks," in Roisman and Worthington (eds.), *Companion to Macedonia*, pp. 81–98.

35. Polybius 28.8.9.

36. E. M. Anson, "The Meaning of the Term *Makedones*," *Anc. World* 10 (1984), pp. 67–68.

37. Religious beliefs and the gods: P. Christesen and S. C. Murray, "Macedonian Religion," in Roisman and Worthington (eds.), *Companion to Macedonia*, pp. 428–445.

38. N. G. L. Hammond, "Literary Evidence for Macedonian Speech," *Historia* 43 (1994), pp. 131–142.

39. P. Cartledge, *Alexander the Great: The Hunt for a New Past* (London: 2003), pp. 45, 49–50, 106, 132–136, 152–153, with T. Whitmarsh, "Alexander's Hellenism and Plutarch's Textualism," *CQ²* 52 (2002), pp. 174–192.

40. G. T. Griffith, "The Macedonian Background," *G&R²* 12 (1965), pp. 125–139; Ian Worthington, "Alexander, Philip, and the Macedonian Background," in Roisman (ed.), *Companion to Alexander*, pp. 69–98; M. Zahrnt, "The Macedonian Background," in Heckel and Tritle (eds.), *New History*, pp. 7–25.

41. E. N. Borza, "The Natural Resources of Early Macedonia," in Adams and Borza (eds.), *Macedonian Heritage*, pp. 1–20 and *Shadow of Olympus*, pp. 50–57; see too Hammond, *History of Macedonia*, pt. 1.

42. Economy: P. Millett, "The Political Economy of Macedonia," in Roisman and Worthington (eds.), *Companion to Macedonia*, pp. 472–504.

43. E. N. Borza, "Timber and Politics in the Ancient World. Macedon and the Greeks," *Proceedings of the American Philosophical Society* 131 (1987), pp. 32–52.

44. Thomas, *Alexander*, pp. 132–141; see too H. Dell, "Philip and Macedonia's Northern Neighbours," in M. B. Hatzopoulos and L. D. Loukopoulos (eds.), *Philip of Macedon* (Athens: 1980), pp. 90–99. Macedonia before Philip: Edson, "Early Macedonia," pp. 17–44; Hammond, *History of Macedonia*; Hammond and Griffith, *History of Macedonia*, pp. 3–200; Hammond, *Macedonian State*, pp. 89–99; Borza, *Shadow of Olympus*, pp. 3–197; R. M. Errington, *A History of Macedonia*, trans. C. Errington (Berkeley and Los Angeles: 1990), pp. 1–38. See too S. Sprawski, "From the Bronze Age to Alexander I," and J. Roisman, "Classical Macedonia to Perdiccas III," in Roisman and Worthington (eds.), *Companion to Macedonia*, pp. 127–144 and 145–165, respectively.

45. J. Wilkes, *The Illyrians* (Oxford: 1995).

46. Amyntas: Hammond and Griffith, *History of Macedonia*, pp. 172–180; Borza, *Shadow of Olympus*, pp. 180–189; Errington, *History of Macedonia*, pp. 29–34; W. S. Greenwalt, "Amyntas III and the Political Stability of Argead Macedonia," *Anc. World* 18 (1988), pp. 35–44.

47. M. B. Hatzopoulos, "Succession and Regency in Classical Macedonia," *Anc. Macedonia* 4 (1986), pp. 279–292.

48. Worthington, *Philip II*, pp. 20–22.

2. PHILIP II AND THE RISE OF MACEDONIA

1. Philip's reign in detail: N. G. L. Hammond and G. T. Griffith, *A History of Macedonia* 2 (Oxford: 1979), pp. 203–698; J. R. Ellis, *Philip II and Macedonian Imperialism* (London: 1976); G. L. Cawkwell, *Philip of Macedon* (London: 1978); N. G. L. Hammond, *Philip of Macedon* (London: 1994); Ian Worthington, *Philip II of Macedonia* (New Haven: 2008) (also comparing and contrasting him to Alexander the Great). Focusing on Philip as general and tactician: R. A. Gabriel, *Philip II of Macedon: Greater than Alexander* (Washington: 2010). See too E. N. Borza, *In the Shadow of Olympus: The Emergence of Macedon* (Princeton: 1990), pp. 198–230; R. M. Errington, *A History of Macedonia*, trans. C. Errington (Berkeley and Los Angeles: 1990), pp. 38–91; S. Müller, "Philip II," in Roisman and Worthington (eds.), *Companion to Macedonia*, pp. 166–185. See too C. G. Thomas, *Alexander the Great in His World* (Malden: 2006), pp. 69–88; A. B. Bosworth, *Conquest and Empire. The Reign of Alexander the Great* (Cambridge: 1988), pp. 5–18.

2. Sources: see the appendix; cf. Worthington, *Philip II*, pp. 210–215.

3. Griffith in Hammond and Griffith, *History of Macedonia*, pp. 699–701; J. R. Ellis, "The Stepbrothers of Philip II," *Historia* 22 (1973), pp. 350–354.

4. Education: E. Carney, "Elite Education and High Culture in Macedonia," in Heckel and Tritle (eds.), *Crossroads*, pp. 47–63.

5. Diodorus 15.67; Justin 6.9.7, 7.5.2; cf. Plutarch, *Pelopidas* 26.5.

6. Justin 7.5.2; cf. Plutarch, *Pelopidas* 26.5.

7. E. Carney, *Women and Monarchy in Macedonia* (Norman: 2000), pp. 59–60.

8. Diodorus 16.3.1.

9. Diplomacy versus military action: T. T. B. Ryder, "The Diplomatic Skills of Philip II," in Worthington (ed.), *Ventures*, pp. 228–257; G. L. Cawkwell, "The End of Greek Liberty," in R. W. Wallace and E. M. Harris (eds.), *Transitions to Empire. Essays in Honor of E. Badian* (Norman: 1996), pp. 98–121. Military prowess: G. T. Griffith, "Philip as a General and the Macedonian Army," in M. B. Hatzopoulos and L. D. Loukopoulos (eds.), *Philip of Macedon* (Athens: 1980), pp. 58–77.

10. Philip's actions in detail: Worthington, *Philip II*, pp. 23–25.

11. Carney, *Women and Monarchy*, pp. 57–58.

12. J. Heskel, "Philip II and Argaios: A Pretender's Story," in R. W. Wallace and E. M. Harris (eds.), *Transitions to Empire. Essays in Honor of E. Badian* (Norman: 1996), pp. 37–56.

13. L. Rawlings, *The Ancient Greeks at War* (Manchester: 2007)—with no treatment of Philip or Alexander! See too H. van Wees, *Greek Warfare: Myths and Realities* (London: 2004); A. Chaniotis, *War in the Hellenistic World: A Social and Cultural History* (Oxford: 2005), much of which is relevant to Classical warfare; cf. P. Hunt, *War, Peace, and Alliance in Demosthenes' Athens* (New York: 2010).

14. Rawlings, *Ancient Greeks at War*, pp. 64–67.

15. V. D. Hanson, *The Western Way of War. Infantry Battle in Classical Greece* (New York: 1989).

16. V. D. Hanson, *Warfare and Agriculture in Classical Greece* (Berkeley and Los Angeles: 1998).

17. Rawlings, *Ancient Greeks at War*, pp. 177–202.

18. Philip's military reforms: Hammond and Griffith, *History of Macedonia*, pp. 405–449; J. F. C. Fuller, *The Generalship of Alexander the Great* (repr.; New Brunswick: 1960), pp. 39–54; Thomas, *Alexander*, pp. 141–158; Worthington, *Philip II*, pp. 26–32; Gabriel, *Philip II*, pp. 62–92. On the Macedonian army, see too N. V. Sekunda, "The Macedonian Army," in Roisman and Worthington (eds.), *Companion to Macedonia*, pp. 446–471.

19. Gabriel, *Philip II*, pp. 62–63.

20. Griffith in Hammond and Griffith, *History of Macedonia*, pp. 705–709; A. W. Erskine, "The *Pezêtairoi* of Philip II and Alexander III," *Historia* 38 (1989), pp. 385–394.

21. N. G. L. Hammond, "Training in the Use of the Sarissa and Its Effect in Battle 359–333 BC," *Antichthon* 14 (1980), pp. 53–63.

22. E. W. Marsden, "Macedonian Military Machinery and Its Designers under Philip and Alexander," *Anc. Macedonia* 2 (1977), pp. 211–223; P. T. Keyser, "The Use of Artillery by Philip II and Alexander the Great," *Anc. World* 15 (1994), pp. 27–49; Gabriel, *Philip II*, pp. 88–92.

23. N. G. L. Hammond, "Royal Pages, Personal Pages, and Boys Trained in the Macedonian Manner during the Period of the Temenid Monarchy," *Historia* 39 (1990), pp. 261–290; E. Carney, "The Role of the *Basilikoi Paides* at the Argead Court," in T. Howe and J. Reames (eds.), *Macedonian Legacies: Studies in Ancient Macedonian History and Culture in Honor of Eugene N. Borza* (Claremont: 2008), pp. 145–164.

24. Diodorus 16.1.5.

25. Diodorus 16.4.3, 17.7.5.

26. N. G. L. Hammond, "The Battle between Philip and Bardylis," *Antichthon* 23 (1989), pp. 1–9; Gabriel, *Philip II*, pp. 105–109.

27. J. R. Ellis, "The Dynamics of Fourth-Century Macedonian Imperialism," *Anc. Macedonia* 2 (1977), pp. 103–114 and "The Unification of Macedonia," in M. B. Hatzopoulos and L. D. Loukopoulos (eds.), *Philip of Macedon* (Athens: 1980), pp. 36–47. Philip's economic reforms: Worthington, *Philip II*, pp. 7–8, 30, 33–34, 40, 45–48, 50, 78–79, 110, 117, 124, 135, 168–169, 196–197; Griffith in Hammond and Griffith, *History of Macedonia*, pp. 657–671; N. G. L. Hammond, "Philip's Innovations in Macedonian Economy," *SO* 70 (1995), pp. 22–29, in answer to H. Montgomery, "The Economic Revolution of Philip II—Myth or Reality?" *SO* 60 (1985), pp. 37–47; P. Millett, "The Political Economy of Macedonia," in Roisman and Worthington (eds.), *Companion to Macedonia*, pp. 472–504.

28. A. B. Bosworth, "Philip II and Upper Macedonia," *CQ*² 21 (1971), pp. 93–105. See too H. Dell, "The Western Frontier of the Macedonian Monarchy," *Anc. Macedonia* 1 (1970), pp. 115–126 and "Philip and Macedonia's Northern Neighbours," in M. B. Hatzopoulos and L. D. Loukopoulos (eds.), *Philip of Macedon* (Athens: 1980), pp. 90–99; W. S. Greenwalt, "Macedonia, Illyria and Epirus," in Roisman and Worthington (eds.), *Companion to Macedonia*, pp. 279–305.

29. Thessaly: H. D. Westlake, *Thessaly in the Fourth Century BC* (repr.; Chicago: 1993); M. Sordi, *La Lega Thessala fino ad Alessandro* (Rome: 1958). Jason: S. Sprawski, *Jason of Pherai* (Cracow: 1999). Philip's involvement in Thessaly: G. T. Griffith, "Philip of Macedon's Early Interventions in Thessaly (358–352 B.C.)," *CQ²* 20 (1970), pp. 67–80; C. Ehrhardt, "Two Notes on Philip of Macedon's First Interventions in Thessaly," *CQ²* 17 (1967), pp. 296–301; S. Sprawski, "Were Lycophron and Jason Tyrants of Pherae? Xenophon on the History of Thessaly," in C. Tuplin (ed.), *Xenophon and His World* (Stuttgart: 2004), pp. 437–452.

30. Carney, *Women and Monarchy*, pp. 61–62; cf. D. Ogden, *Alexander the Great. Myth, Genesis and Sexuality* (Exeter: 2011), pp. 115–121. Justin at 9.8.2 and 13.2.11 calls her a common whore.

31. S. Sprawski, "All the King's Men. Thessalians and Philip II's Designs on Greece," in D. Musial (ed.), *Society and Religions. Studies in Greek and Roman History* (Toruń: 2005), pp. 31–49 and "Philip II and the Freedom of the Thessalians," *Electrum* 9 (2003), pp. 61–64; E. Badian, "Philip II and the Last of the Thessalians," *Anc. Macedonia* 6 (1999), pp. 109–121. On relations between Macedonia and Thessaly, including Philip's reign, see D. Graninger, "Macedonia and Thessaly," in Roisman and Worthington (eds.), *Companion to Macedonia*, pp. 306–325.

32. Carney, *Women and Monarchy*, pp. 62–67, 79–81.

33. M. B. Hatzopoulos, "Succession and Regency in Classical Macedonia," *Anc. Macedonia* 4 (1986), pp. 279–292.

34. Greenwalt, "Macedonia, Illyria and Epirus," pp. 279–305, for Macedonia's relations with Epirus.

35. P. J. Rhodes and R. Osborne (eds.), *Greek Historical Inscriptions, 404–323 BC* (Oxford: 2003), no. 47.

36. Macedonia's relations with Thrace: Z. Archibald, "Macedonia and Thrace," in Roisman and Worthington (eds.), *Companion to Macedonia*, pp. 326–341.

37. Siege: Worthington, *Philip II*, pp. 41–42. Siege warfare: Rawlings, *Ancient Greeks at War*, pp. 128–143.

38. Aeschines 2, *On the False Embassy* 70, and 3, *Against Ctesiphon* 54; Isocrates 5, *To Philip* 2; Diodorus 16.8.2–3.

39. Plutarch, *Alexander* 3.8.

40. R. Sealey, "Athens after the Social War," *JHS* 75 (1955), pp. 74–81 and *Demosthenes and His Time: A Study in Defeat* (Oxford: 1993); Hunt, *War, Peace, and Alliance in Demosthenes' Athens*, pp. 259–264.

41. Siege: Worthington, *Philip II*, pp. 48–49; Gabriel, *Philip II*, pp. 121–123.

42. Duris, *BNJ* 76 F 36 (javelin); Theopompus, *BNJ* 115 F 52; Demosthenes 18, *On the Crown* 67; Justin 7.6.14–15.

43. Plutarch, *Alexander* 3.2; Olympias's impregnation: Plutarch, *Alexander* 2.6. On the eye injury and its role in later traditions of Philip, see A. S. Riginos, "The Wounding of Philip II of Macedon: Fact and Fabrication," *JHS* 114 (1994), pp. 106–114.

44. Excellent discussion in Gabriel, *Philip II*, pp. 127–132.

45. Diodorus 16.35.2–3.

3. THE NEW PLAYER IN GREEK POLITICS

1. Third Sacred War: J. Buckler, *Philip II and the Sacred War* (Leiden: 1989) and *Aegean Greece in the Fourth Century BC* (Leiden: 2003), pp. 397–429, 442–452. Previous sacred wars (in 595–586 and in the mid-fifth century): H. W. Parke and J. Boardman, "The Struggle for the Tripod and the First Sacred War," *JHS* 77 (1957), pp. 276–282; J. K. Davies, "The Tradition about the First Sacred War," in S. Hornblower (ed.), *Greek Historiography* (Oxford: 1994), pp. 193–212.

2. The name comes from the word *amphictyony* (those that dwell around or near), but by the Classical period states more geographically distant had joined the league.

3. The Phocians claimed that they were innocent because the land belonged to them and in support cited Homer, *Iliad* 2.517–519.

4. Diodorus 16.38.4.

5. E. Carney, *Women and Monarchy in Macedonia* (Norman: 2000), pp. 60–61.

6. Ian Worthington, *Philip II of Macedonia* (New Haven: 2008), pp. 65–66.

7. Diodorus 16.35.5; cf. Justin 8.2.3–4.

8. Revenge: G. Squillace, "Consensus Strategies under Philip and Alexander: The Revenge Theme," in Carney and Ogden (eds.), *Philip and Alexander*, pp. 69–75.

9. Style of Philip's return and change in his attitude to the Greeks: Ian Worthington, "Alexander, Philip, and the Macedonian Background," in Roisman (ed.), *Companion to Alexander*, pp. 94–96, and *Philip II*, pp. 61–62; cf. J. R. Ellis, "The Dynamics of Fourth-Century Macedonian Imperialism," *Anc. Macedonia* 2 (1977), pp. 103–114; J. Buckler, "Philip II's Designs on Greece," in R. W. Wallace and E. M. Harris (eds.), *Transitions to Empire. Essays in Honor of E. Badian* (Norman: 1996), pp. 77–97.

10. Ian Worthington, *Demosthenes of Athens and the Fall of Classical Greece* (Oxford: 2013).

11. M. H. Hansen, *Athenian Democracy in the Age of Demosthenes*, 2nd ed. (Norman: 1999).

12. M. H. Hansen, *The Athenian Assembly in the Age of Demosthenes* (Oxford: 1987).

13. Ian Worthington, "Rhetoric and Politics in Classical Greece: Rise of the *Rhêtores*," in Ian Worthington (ed.), *A Companion to Greek Rhetoric* (Malden: 2007), pp. 255–271.

14. Worthington, *Demosthenes of Athens*, pp. 70–89, 98–126.

15. Worthington, *Demosthenes of Athens*, pp. 118–122.

16. Demosthenes 4, *Philippic* 1.40–41; translation: J. Trevett, *Demosthenes, Speeches 1–17* (Austin: 2011), ad loc.

17. Cf. L. Rawlings, *The Ancient Greeks at War* (Manchester: 2007), pp. 218–220.

18. A. Moreno, *Feeding the Democracy: The Athenian Grain Supply in the Fifth and Fourth Centuries BC* (Oxford: 2007).

19. P. Hunt, *War, Peace, and Alliance in Demosthenes' Athens* (New York: 2010), pp. 35–39.

20. The story that Philip had a pederastic relationship with him (Justin 8.6.6–8) is based on a hostile tradition: Worthington, *Philip II*, p. 70.

21. Demosthenes 1, *Olynthiac* 1.12–13; translation: Trevett, *Demosthenes, Speeches 1–17*, ad loc.

22. N. G. L. Hammond, *The Macedonian State: The Origins, Institutions and History* (Oxford: 1992), p. 198.

23. Justin 8.3.10, with J. R. Ellis, "The Stepbrothers of Philip II," *Historia* 22 (1973), pp. 350–354.

24. Worthington, *Philip II*, pp. 74–82; R. A. Gabriel, *Philip II of Macedon: Greater than Alexander* (Washington: 2010), pp. 150–157, with G. L. Cawkwell, "The Defence of Olynthus," *CQ*² 12 (1962), pp. 122–140 and J. M. Carter, "Athens, Euboea and Olynthus," *Historia* 20 (1971), pp. 418–429.

25. Worthington, *Demosthenes of Athens*, pp. 132–141.

26. Demosthenes 9, *Philippic* 3.11.

27. Demosthenes 9, *Philippic* 3.26.

28. Cawkwell, "Defence of Olynthus," pp. 130–140; Worthington, *Philip II*, pp. 80–82.

29. J. R. Ellis, *Philip II and Macedonian Imperialism* (London: 1976), pp. 101–103 and "Philip and the Peace of Philokrates," in Adams and Borza (eds.), *Macedonian Heritage*, pp. 43–59; G. L. Cawkwell, "The Peace of Philocrates Again," *CQ*² 28 (1978), pp. 93–104; N. G. L. Hammond and G. T. Griffith, *A History of Macedonia* 2 (Oxford: 1979), pp. 329–347; Worthington, *Philip II*, pp. 82–85.

30. Diodorus 16.58.3.

31. Worthington, *Philip II*, pp. 84–86, 88, 90, 95, 98–101, 142; G. L. Cawkwell, "Philip and Athens," in M. B. Hatzopoulos and L. D. Loukopoulos (eds.), *Philip of Macedon* (Athens: 1980), pp. 100–110; T. T. B. Ryder, "The Diplomatic Skills of Philip II," in Worthington (ed.), *Ventures*, pp. 251–257.

32. E. M. Harris, *Aeschines and Athenian Politics* (Oxford: 1995); R. Lane Fox, "Aeschines and Athenian Politics," in R. Osborne and S. Hornblower (eds.), *Ritual, Finance, Politics. Athenian Democratic Accounts Presented to David Lewis* (Oxford: 1994), pp. 135–155. On the rivalry with Demosthenes: J. Buckler, "Demosthenes and Aeschines," in Ian Worthington (ed.), *Demosthenes: Statesman and Orator* (London: 2000), pp. 114–158.

33. The principal contemporary sources for the peace negotiations and the end of the Third Sacred War are the two speeches *On the False Embassy*, which Demosthenes and Aeschines gave at Aeschines's trial in 343, and their speeches in the Crown trial of Demosthenes in 330. The information in them is often distorted because of their personal enmity and different attitudes to the peace: Buckler, "Demosthenes and Aeschines," pp. 121–132, 148–154. On Demosthenes's ability to switch policy around the Peace of Philocrates, cf. T. T. B. Ryder, "Demosthenes and Philip II," in Ian Worthington (ed.), *Demosthenes: Statesman and Orator* (London: 2000), pp. 58–72.

34. Lead-up to the Assembly and meeting: Harris, *Aeschines and Athenian Politics*, pp. 63–77; and especially A. Efstathiou, "The 'Peace of Philocrates': The Assembles of 18th and 19th Elaphebolion," *Historia* 53 (2004), pp. 385–407.

35. Harris, *Aeschines and Athenian Politics*, pp. 96–97.

36. Justin 8.5.3.

37. Amount: Worthington, *Philip II*, p. 102. It was to be repaid in annual installments of 60 talents, beginning in 343. In 341 it was reduced to 30 talents, and after 337, to only 10: P. J. Rhodes and R. Osborne (eds.), *Greek Historical Inscriptions, 404–323 BC* (Oxford: 2003), no. 67.

4. THE GATHERING WAR CLOUDS

1. Demosthenes 5, *On the Peace* 13–14.

2. Ian Worthington, *Demosthenes of Athens and the Fall of Classical Greece* (Oxford: 2013), pp. 186–187.

3. Support for Philip: Ian Worthington, *Philip II of Macedonia* (New Haven: 2008), pp. 104, 121–122.

4. E. Carney, "Elite Education and High Culture in Macedonia," in Heckel and Tritle (eds.), *Crossroads*, pp. 47–63.

5. G. Xanthakis-Karamanos, *Studies in Fourth-Century Tragedy* (Athens: 1980); R. Green, *Theatre in Ancient Greek Society* (London: 1994), pp. 50–62; see too chapter 14, p. 292.

6. Theopompus, *BNJ* 115 F 294.

7. Translation and commentary: F. Natoli, *The Letter of Speusippus to Philip II* (Stuttgart: 2004). See also M. M. Markle, "Support of Athenian Intellectuals for Philip: A Study of Isocrates' *Philippus* and Speusippus' *Letter to Philip*," *JHS* 96 (1976), pp. 80–99.

8. C. G. Thomas, *Alexander the Great in His World* (Malden: 2006), pp. 123–130.

9. Aeschines 2, *On the False Embassy* 34–35; translation: C. Carey, *Aeschines* (Austin: 2000), ad loc.

10. Worthington, *Demosthenes of Athens*, pp. 38–41.

11. F. Papazoglou, *Les villes de Macédoine à l'époque romaine* (Paris: 1988); M. Siganidou, "Urban Centres in Macedonia," in J. Vokotopoulou (ed.), *Greek Civilization: Macedonia, Kingdom of Alexander the Great* (Athens: 1993), pp. 29–31. Border: H. Dell, "The Western Frontier of the Macedonian Monarchy," *Anc. Macedonia* 1 (1970), pp. 115–126; A. B. Bosworth, "Philip II and Upper Macedonia,"

CQ^2 21 (1971), pp. 93–105; see too W. S. Greenwalt, "Macedonia, Illyria and Epirus," in Roisman and Worthington (eds.), *Companion to Macedonia*, pp. 279–305.

12. Justin 8.5.7–6.2. J. R. Ellis, "Population-Transplants by Philip II," *Makedonika* 9 (1969), pp. 9–17.

13. S. Sprawski, "Philip II and the Freedom of the Thessalians," *Electrum* 9 (2003), pp. 55–66.

14. Demosthenes 18, *On the Crown* 295; cf. Demosthenes 6, *Philippic* 2.22, 9, *Philippic* 3.26, 19, *On the False Embassy* 260.

15. Demosthenes 6, *Philippic* 2.17–19; translation: J. Trevett, *Demosthenes, Speeches 1–17* (Austin: 2011), ad loc.

16. Aeschines 3, *Against Ctesiphon* 83; Plutarch, *Demosthenes* 9.5–6; Athenaeus 223d–224b.

17. Background and charges: E. M. Harris, *Aeschines and Athenian Politics* (Oxford: 1995), pp. 115–120; T. T. B. Ryder, "Demosthenes and Philip II," in Ian Worthington (ed.), *Demosthenes: Statesman and Orator* (London: 2000), pp. 58–72; J. Buckler, "Demosthenes and Aeschines," in ibid., pp. 121–132, 134–140.

18. Demosthenes 18, *On the Crown* 132–133; cf. Dinarchus 1, *Against Demosthenes* 63; Plutarch, *Demosthenes* 14.5.

19. Diodorus 16.71.1–2, with Worthington, *Philip II*, pp. 122–125; R. A. Gabriel, *Philip II of Macedon: Greater than Alexander* (Washington, D.C.: 2010), pp. 182–185.

20. E. Carney, *Women and Monarchy in Macedonia* (Norman: 2000), pp. 67–68.

21. This speech has been considered spurious, but see Ian Worthington, "The Authenticity of Demosthenes' Fourth *Philippic*," *Mnemosyne* 44 (1991), pp. 425–428.

22. Siege: Worthington, *Philip II*, pp. 131–132; Gabriel, *Philip II*, pp. 190–194.

23. Worthington, *Philip II*, pp. 132–133; Gabriel, *Philip II*, pp. 194–198.

24. [Demosthenes] 12, *Philip's Letter* 23, with J. Buckler, "Philip II's Designs on Greece," in R. W. Wallace and E. M. Harris (eds.), *Transitions to Empire. Essays in Honor of E. Badian* (Norman: 1996), pp. 87–89 and G. L. Cawkwell, *Philip of Macedon* (London: 1978), p. 137.

25. Philochorus, *FGrH* 328 F 162.

26. Plutarch, *Moralia* 331b, with A. S. Riginos, "The Wounding of Philip II of Macedon: Fact and Fabrication," *JHS* 114 (1994), pp. 116–118. For an alternative description of the wound, see Gabriel, *Philip II*, pp. 13–14.

5. THE DOWNFALL OF GREECE

1. J. Buckler, "Philip II's Designs on Greece," in R. W. Wallace and E. M. Harris (eds.), *Transitions to Empire. Essays in Honor of E. Badian* (Norman: 1996), pp. 77–97.

2. Background: Ian Worthington, *Philip II of Macedonia* (New Haven: 2008), pp. 136–137.

3. Aeschines 3, *Against Ctesiphon* 116.

4. Demosthenes 18, *On the Crown* 143–155. Aeschines's role at the meeting and possible exploitation by Philip: E. M. Harris, *Aeschines and Athenian Politics* (Oxford: 1995), pp. 126–130; P. D. Londey, "The Outbreak of the Fourth Sacred War," *Chiron* 20 (1990), pp. 239–260.

5. J. Roisman, *The Rhetoric of Conspiracy in Ancient Athens* (Berkeley and Los Angeles: 2006), pp. 133–145.

6. J. Trevett, "Demosthenes and Thebes," *Historia* 48 (1999), pp. 184–202; *contra* G. L. Cawkwell, "Demosthenes' Policy after the Peace of Philocrates II," CQ^2 13 (1963), pp. 206–209.

7. Plutarch, *Demosthenes* 18.2.

8. Both sides' fighting capabilities: N. G. L. Hammond, *Philip of Macedon* (London: 1994), pp. 149–151; cf. Worthington, *Philip II*, pp. 147–149; R. A. Gabriel, *Philip II of Macedon: Greater than Alexander* (Washington: 2010), pp. 214–216.

9. Plutarch, *Alexander* 9.3.

10. Diodorus 16.86.1.

11. Plutarch, *Camillus* 19.5, 8. Battle: N. G. L. Hammond and G. T. Griffith, *A History of Macedonia* 2 (Oxford: 1979), pp. 596–603; Worthington, *Philip II*, pp. 149–151; Gabriel, *Philip II*, pp. 214–222; N. G. L. Hammond, "The Victory of Macedon at Chaeronea," in *Studies in Greek History* (Oxford: 1973), pp. 534–557; cf. J. Ma, "Chaironeia 338: Topographies of Commemoration," *JHS* 128 (2008), pp. 172–191.

12. P. A. Rahe, "The Annihilation of the Sacred Band at Chaeronea," *AJA* 85 (1981), pp. 84–87; J. Buckler, "A Note on the Battle of Chaeronea," in J. Buckler and H. Beck (eds.), *Central Greece and the Politics of Power in the Fourth Century BC* (Cambridge: 2008), pp. 254–258.

13. Story: Theopompus, *BNJ* 115 F 236 (= Athenaeus 435b–c). Theopompus, *BNJ* 115 F 282, says that Philip rushed into battle drunk, but that is a biased view. Mockery of Demosthenes: Diodorus 16.87.1–2; Plutarch, *Demosthenes* 20.3; Plutarch, *Moralia* 715c; *contra* Justin 9.4.1–3. See further Worthington, *Philip II*, pp. 152–154.

14. See p. 312.

15. G. L. Cawkwell, "The End of Greek Liberty," in R. W. Wallace and E. M. Harris (eds.), *Transitions to Empire. Essays in Honor of E. Badian* (Norman: 1996), pp. 98–121.

16. Lycurgus 1, *Against Leocrates* 50.

17. Justin 9.3.11.

18. Plutarch, *Demosthenes* 19.1.

19. Plutarch, *Alexander* 2–3 for the various stories, on which D. Ogden, *Alexander the Great. Myth, Genesis and Sexuality* (Exeter: 2011), pp. 7–56, is essential.

20. Hegesias, *FGrH* 142 F 3 (= Plutarch, *Alexander* 3.5–9).

21. Ogden, *Alexander the Great*, pp. 29–56, for the view that the snake myth, at least, was first put out by Ptolemy I in his struggles with the other successors.

22. M. Bieber, "The Portraits of Alexander," *G&R²* 12 (1965), pp. 183–188; E. von Schwarzenberg, "The Portraiture of Alexander," in E. Badian (ed.), *Alexandre le Grand, Image et Réalité*, Fondation Hardt, Entretiens 22 (Geneva: 1976), pp. 223–278; A. Stewart, "Alexander in Greek and Roman Art," in Roisman (ed.), *Companion to Alexander*, pp. 31–66, and *Faces of Power. Alexander's Image and Hellenistic Politics* (Berkeley and Los Angeles: 1993), especially pp. 21–78, 105–130; C. Mihalopoulos, "The Construction of a New Ideal. The Official Portraiture of Alexander the Great," in Heckel and Tritle (eds.), *New History*, pp. 275–293.

23. A. B. Bosworth, *Conquest and Empire. The Reign of Alexander the Great* (Cambridge: 1988), pp. 19–23; Ian Worthington, *Alexander the Great: Man and God*, rev. ed. (London: 2004), pp. 30–43; J. R. Hamilton, "Alexander's Early Life," *G&R²* 12 (1965), pp. 125–139.

24. T. S. Brown, "Alexander's Book Order (Plut. *Alex.* 8)," *Historia* 16 (1967), pp. 359–368; N. V. Sekunda, "Philistus and Alexander's Empire (Plutarch, *Vita Alexandri* 8.3)," in J. Pigoń (ed.), *The Children of Herodotus: Greek and Roman Historiography and Related Genres* (Newcastle: 2009), pp. 181–189.

25. A. R. Anderson, "Bucephalas and His Legend," *AJPh* 51 (1930), pp. 1–21.

26. E. Badian, "Alexander the Great and the Scientific Exploration of the Oriental Part of His Empire," *Anc. Society* 22 (1991), pp. 127–138; for those accompanying Alexander, see L. Tritle, "Alexander and the Greeks. Artists and Soldiers, Friends and Enemies," in Heckel and Tritle (eds.), *New History*, pp. 121–140.

27. Quote: Plutarch, *Moralia* 329b. Slavery as natural: Aristotle, *Politics* 1252a 32, 1254b 20, 1253b 32, 1278b 33; barbarians as slaves: Aristotle, *Politics* 1252b 8. See also A. H. Chroust, "Aristotle and the Foreign Policy of Macedonia," *Review of Politics* 34 (1972), pp. 367–394.

28. Plutarch, *Alexander* 7.5.

29. Plutarch, *Alexander* 8.3–4, 78.2.

30. Worthington, *Philip II*, pp. 154–163, citing bibliography.

31. Possible fragment of this treaty: Ian Worthington, "*IG* ii² 236 and Philip's Common Peace of 337," in L. G. Mitchell and L. Rubinstein (eds.), *Greek Epigraphy and History: Essays in Honour of P. J. Rhodes* (Swansea: 2008), pp. 213–223.

32. Demosthenes 18, *On the Crown* 285; Plutarch, *Demosthenes* 21.2. The speech (60) is extant: see Ian Worthington, *Demosthenes of Athens and the Fall of Classical Greece* (Oxford: 2013), pp. 259–262, citing bibliography.

33. Background: Worthington, *Philip II*, pp. 158–171.

34. Justin 9.5.3.

35. T. T. B. Ryder, *Koine Eirene* (Oxford: 1965), pp. 102–106; S. Perlman, "Fourth Century Treaties and the League of Corinth of Philip of Macedon," *Anc. Macedonia* 4 (1986), pp. 437–442 and "Greek Diplomatic Tradition and the Corinthian League of Philip of Macedon," *Historia* 34 (1985), pp. 153–174. See too P. J. Rhodes and R. Osborne (eds.), *Greek Historical Inscriptions, 404–323 BC* (Oxford: 2003), no. 76, with commentary (pp. 376–379). The league as an example of early international law: P. Hunt, *War, Peace, and Alliance in Demosthenes' Athens* (New York: 2010), pp. 217–236.

36. N. G. L. Hammond, "The *Koina* of Epirus and Macedonia," *ICS* 16 (1991), pp. 183–192.

6. PHILIP'S ASSASSINATION AND LEGACY

1. J. M. Cook, *The Persian Empire* (London: 1983); M. Dandamaev, *A Political History of the Achaemenid Empire* (Leiden: 1989); P. Briant, *From Cyrus to Alexander: A History of the Persian Empire*, trans. P. T. Daniels (Winona Lake: 2002).

2. Interactions: S. J. Bouzek and I. Ondřejova, "Some Notes on the Relations of the Thracian, Macedonian, Iranian and Scythian Arts in the Fourth Century B.C.," *Eirene* 24 (1987), pp. 67–93; S. A. Paspalas, "On Persian-Type Furniture in Macedonia: The Recognition and Transmission of Forms," *AJA* 104 (2000), pp. 531–560; O. Palagia, "Hephaestion's Pyre and the Royal Hunt of Alexander," in A. B. Bosworth and E. J. Baynham (eds.), *Alexander the Great in Fact and Fiction* (Oxford: 2000), pp. 167–206. Similarities: C. G. Thomas, *Alexander the Great in His World* (Malden: 2006), pp. 173–186; P. Cartledge, *Alexander the Great: The Hunt for a New Past* (London: 2003), pp. 190–191; M. J. Olbrycht, "Macedonia and Persia," in Roisman and Worthington (eds.), *Companion to Macedonia*, pp. 345–351.

3. Arrian 2.14.5. Revenge: G. Squillace, "Consensus Strategies under Philip and Alexander: The Revenge Theme," in Carney and Ogden (eds.), *Philip and Alexander*, pp. 76–80.

4. E. A. Fredricksmeyer, "On the Final Aims of Philip II," in Adams and Borza (eds.), *Macedonian Heritage*, pp. 85–98.

5. Diodorus 16.53.2. See too T. T. B. Ryder, "The Diplomatic Skills of Philip II," in Worthington (ed.), *Ventures*, pp. 228–257; and G. L. Cawkwell, "The End of Greek Liberty," in R. W. Wallace and E. M. Harris (eds.), *Transitions to Empire. Essays in Honor of E. Badian* (Norman: 1996), pp. 98–121.

6. Onesicritus, *BNJ* 134 F 2 (= Plutarch, *Alexander* 15.2); Plutarch, *Moralia* 327d–e. Opis speech: Arrian 7.9.6; Curtius 10.2.24. For the mutiny, see pp. 277–280.

7. Ian Worthington, *Philip II of Macedonia* (New Haven: 2008), pp. 169–170.

8. Polybius 3.6.12–13 states that Philip used the excuse of panhellenism to hide his intent. Philip's aims: Worthington, *Philip II*, pp. 166–169. Panhellenic propaganda: M. Faraguna, "Alexander and the Greeks," in Roisman (ed.), *Companion to Alexander*, pp. 107–115.

9. Arrian 7.9.2–5; translation: P. A. Brunt, *Arrian, "History of Alexander"* 2, Loeb Classical Library (Cambridge: 1983), ad loc. N. G. L. Hammond, *Alexander the Great: King, Commander and*

Statesman, 2nd ed. (Bristol: 1989), p. 248, argues that the speech is mostly authentic; cf. B. Nagle, "The Cultural Context of Alexander's Speech at Opis," *TAPhA* 126 (1996), pp. 151–172.

10. Worthington, *Philip II*, pp. 164–166, citing bibliography.

11. E. Carney, *Women and Monarchy in Macedonia* (Norman: 2000), pp. 70–75.

12. Athenaeus 13.557b–e; cf. 13.560c, quoting Satyrus's biography. Other reasons for marrying now: Worthington, *Philip II*, pp. 172–174, citing bibliography.

13. Plutarch, *Alexander* 9.5–6. See Athenaeus 13.557d and 560c for the view that this marriage more than anything else put a rift in Philip's household, with W. Heckel, "Philip and Olympias (337/6 BC)," in G. S. Shrimpton and D. J. McCargar (eds.), *Classical Contributions: Studies in Honor of M. F. McGregor* (Locust Valley: 1981), pp. 51–57, and Worthington, *Philip II*, pp. 175–176. Olympias during Philip's reign: Carney, *Women and Monarchy*, pp. 62–67, 79–81; Thomas, *Alexander*, pp. 88–97; generally, E. Carney, *Olympias, Mother of Alexander the Great* (London: 2006), and "Alexander and His 'Terrible Mother,'" in Heckel and Tritle (eds.), *New History*, pp. 189–202.

14. On the incident and Attalus's remark: Worthington, *Philip II*, pp. 176–178.

15. Plutarch, *Alexander* 9.10; Justin 9.7.4.

16. Cf. Justin 9.7.7: she tried to persuade her brother to go to war against Philip.

17. Cf. Plutarch, *Alexander* 10.1–3; Worthington, *Philip II*, pp. 177–180, 182–186; E. A. Fredricksmeyer, "Alexander and Philip: Emulation and Resentment," *CJ* 85 (1990), pp. 300–315.

18. See Cartledge, *Alexander*, pp. 98–106.

19. D. Ogden, *Alexander the Great. Myth, Genesis and Sexuality* (Exeter: 2011), pp. 115–121.

20. Plutarch, *Demosthenes* 10.3.

21. C. Mossé, *Alexander: Destiny and Myth*, trans. J. Lloyd (Edinburgh: 2004), pp. 94–107.

22. Diodorus 16.92.5, 95.1. Philip's statue has wrongly been taken to indicate that he believed himself divine: Worthington, *Philip II*, pp. 228–233.

23. Diodorus 16.93.1–2.

24. Aristotle, *Politics* 5.1311b1–3; Diodorus 16.93–94, 17.2.3–6; Plutarch, *Alexander* 10.4–7; Plutarch, *Moralia* 327c; Justin 9.6.4–7.14; cf. Arrian, *FGrH* 156 FF 9 and 22, with Worthington, *Philip II*, pp. 181–186, citing bibliography.

25. Plutarch, *Alexander* 10.6.

26. Justin 9.7.1; see also 9.7.1–11. Justin's account has been rejected, for example, by Hammond, *Alexander*, pp. 40–41.

27. See too P. Green, *Alexander of Macedon* (Harmondsworth: 1974), pp. 108–109; Cartledge, *Alexander*, pp. 94–96.

28. A. B. Bosworth, "Philip II and Upper Macedonia," *CQ*² 21 (1971), pp. 93–105.

29. Plutarch, *Alexander* 77.8.

30. W. S. Greenwalt, "The Search for Arrhidaeus," *Anc. World* 10 (1985), pp. 74–76; E. Carney, "The Trouble with Philip Arrhidaeus," *AHB* 15 (2001), pp. 63–89.

31. Worthington, *Philip II*, pp. 177–178.

32. Legacy: Worthington, *Philip II*, pp. 194–208 and "Worldwide Empire vs Glorious Enterprise: Diodorus and Justin on Philip II and Alexander the Great," in Carney and Ogden (eds.), *Philip and Alexander*, pp. 165–174; A. B. Bosworth, *Conquest and Empire. The Reign of Alexander the Great* (Cambridge: 1988), pp. 5–18; Cartledge, *Alexander*, pp. 219–235; R. A. Gabriel, *Philip II of Macedon: Greater than Alexander* (Washington: 2010), pp. 243–251; see too M. Zahrnt, "The Macedonian Background," in Heckel and Tritle (eds.), *New History*, pp. 7–25.

33. Ryder, "Diplomatic Skills of Philip II," pp. 228–257; J. Buckler, "Philip II's Designs on Greece," in R. W. Wallace and E. M. Harris (eds.), *Transitions to Empire. Essays in Honor of E. Badian* (Norman: 1996), pp. 77–97; Cawkwell, "End of Greek Liberty," pp. 98–121.

34. Theopompus, *FGrH* 115 F 237 (= Athenaeus 77d–e); Demosthenes 18, *On the Crown* 295–296.

35. Cynical diplomacy to achieve a goal is one thing, but it is going too far to call it part of his inexorable imperialistic tendencies that made him a classical Hitler: A. Adams, "Philip *Alias* Hitler," *G&R* 10 (1941), pp. 105–113. G. Maclean Rogers, *Alexander: The Ambiguity of Greatness* (New York: 2004), pp. 280–283, compares Alexander to Hitler and Stalin, though Rogers does say that he was not their precursor.

36. Diodorus 16.95, clearly echoing Theopompus's line in the proem to his *Philippica* that Europe had never produced such a man as Philip: Theopompus, *BNJ* 115 F 27.

37. Justin 9.8, with Worthington, "Worldwide Empire," pp. 165–174.

7. ALEXANDER'S EARLY KINGSHIP—AND PERSIA

1. Arrian, *Preface* 2.

2. Plutarch, *Demosthenes* 22.3.

3. Arrian 1.25.2; Plutarch, *Moralia* 327c.

4. A. B. Bosworth, *Conquest and Empire. The Reign of Alexander the Great* (Cambridge: 1988), pp. 25–27; Ian Worthington, *Alexander the Great: Man and God*, rev. ed. (London: 2004), pp. 44–46; J. R. Ellis, "The First Months of Alexander's Reign," in B. Barr-Sharrar and E. N. Borza (eds.), *Macedonia and Greece in Late Classical and Early Hellenistic Times* (Washington: 1982), pp. 69–73.

5. J. R. Ellis, "Amyntas Perdikka, Philip II and Alexander the Great," *JHS* 91 (1971), pp. 15–24; P. Green, *Alexander of Macedon* (Harmondsworth: 1974), pp. 111–112, 135–136; and Ian Worthington, "Alexander's Destruction of Thebes," in Heckel and Tritle (eds.), *Crossroads*, pp. 65–86.

6. Alexander may have implicated them to draw attention from himself: E. Badian, "The Death of Philip II," *Phoenix* 17 (1963), pp. 244–250. They had little if any claim to the throne: A. B. Bosworth, "Philip II and Upper Macedonia," *CQ²* 21 (1971), pp. 96–97.

7. W. Heckel, "King and 'Companions': Observations on the Nature of Power in the Reign of Alexander," in Roisman (ed.), *Companion to Alexander*, pp. 197–225.

8. M. Andronikos, *Vergina: The Royal Tombs and the Ancient City* (Athens: 1984; repr., 2004) and "The Royal Tombs at Aigai (Vergina)," in M. B. Hatzopoulos and L. D. Loukopoulos (eds.), *Philip of Macedon* (London: 1980), pp. 188–231; cf. S. Drougou and C. Saatsoglou-Paliadeli, *Vergina. Wandering through the Archaeological Site* (Athens: 2004).

9. J. H. Musgrave, R. A. H. Neave, and A. J. N. W. Prag, "The Skull from Tomb II at Vergina: King Philip II of Macedon," *JHS* 104 (1984), pp. 60–78; A. J. N. W. Prag, "Reconstructing the Skull of Philip of Macedon," in E. C. Danien (ed.), *The World of Philip and Alexander* (Philadelphia: 1990), pp. 17–37 and "Reconstructing King Philip II: The 'Nice' Version," *AJA* 94 (1990), pp. 237–247.

10. On the controversy: Ian Worthington, *Philip II of Macedonia* (New Haven: 2008), pp. 234–241, citing bibliography; to which add E. N. Borza and O. Palagia, "The Chronology of the Royal Macedonian Tombs at Vergina," *Jahrbuch des Deutsche Archaeologischen Instituts* 122 (2007), pp. 81–125.

11. Diodorus 17.3.6–4.9; Arrian 1.1.2–3. Background: Bosworth, *Conquest and Empire*, pp. 188–192; Worthington, *Alexander*, pp. 50–53.

12. P. A. Brunt, "The Aims of Alexander," *G&R²* 12 (1965), pp. 205–215, argues that Alexander's invasion was merely his inheritance from Philip; cf. N. G. L. Hammond, "The Kingdom of Asia and the Persian Throne," *Antichthon* 20 (1986), pp. 73–85. E. A. Fredricksmeyer, "On the Final Aims of Philip II," in Adams and Borza (eds.), *Macedonian Heritage*, pp. 85–98 and "Alexander the Great and the Kingship of Asia," in A. B. Bosworth and E. J. Baynham (eds.), *Alexander the Great in Fact and Fiction* (Oxford: 2000), pp. 136–166, suggests that Philip wanted to establish an absolute monarchy and his own deification.

13. Plutarch, *Alexander* 14.4.

14. Plutarch, *Alexander* 14.1–3; cf. Plutarch, *Moralia* 331f, 605d, 782a; Diogenes Laertius 6.32.

15. Diodorus 17.9.5; cf. Arrian 1.7.1–2; Justin 11.2.

16. Worthington, "Alexander's Destruction of Thebes," pp. 65–86.

17. Aeschines 3, *Against Ctesiphon* 239–240; cf. 133, 155–156. Dinarchus 1, *Against Demosthenes* 10, 18–20, 24–26, with Ian Worthington, *A Historical Commentary on Dinarchus. Rhetoric and Conspiracy in Later Fourth-Century Athens* (Ann Arbor: 1992), 1.18–21, on pp. 139–143, 160–170 and "Intentional History: Alexander, Demosthenes and Thebes," in L. Foxhall and H.-J. Gehrke (eds.), *Intentional History: Spinning Time in Ancient Greece* (Stuttgart: 2010), pp. 239–246.

18. Plataea, Thespiaea, and Orchomenus had been destroyed by Thebes in the 370s and 360s but were restored by Philip after Chaeronea; Thebes had been Phocis's bitter enemy in the Third Sacred War.

19. Siege: N. G. L. Hammond, *Alexander the Great: King, Commander and Statesman*, 2nd ed. (Bristol: 1989), pp. 58–65; Bosworth, *Conquest and Empire*, pp. 32–33, 194–196; Worthington, *Alexander*, pp. 58–63.

20. Ptolemy, *FGrH* 138 F 3 (= Arrian 1.8.1).

21. L. Rawlings, *The Ancient Greeks at War* (Manchester: 2007), pp. 218–220.

22. Diodorus 17.14.4; Plutarch, *Alexander* 11.12.

23. Aristobulus, *BNJ* 139 F 2b (= Plutarch, *Moralia* 259d–260d).

24. J. Roisman, "Honor in Alexander's Campaign," in Roisman (ed.), *Companion to Alexander*, pp. 279–321.

25. Aeschines 3, *Against Ctesiphon* 133; Dinarchus 1, *Against Demosthenes* 24; Polybius 4.23.8, 5.10. 6–8, 9.28.8, 34.1.

26. Hegesias, *FGrH* 142 T 3.

27. The sources give differing numbers, but five names are common to all: Demosthenes, Lycurgus, Polyeuctus, Ephialtes, Charidemus: see A. B. Bosworth, *A Historical Commentary on Arrian's History of Alexander, 1: Books 1–3* (Oxford: 1980), pp. 92–96.

28. Aristobulus, *BNJ* 139 F 3 (= Plutarch, *Demosthenes* 23.5–6).

29. Ian Worthington, *Demosthenes of Athens and the Fall of Classical Greece* (Oxford: 2013), pp. 281–293.

30. Quoted by M. J. Olbrycht, "Macedonia and Persia," in Roisman and Worthington (eds.), *Companion to Macedonia*, p. 352. See too B. Due, "Alexander's Inspirations and Ideas," in J. Carlsen et al. (eds.), *Alexander the Great. Reality and Myth* (Rome: 1993), pp. 53–60.

31. Diodorus 17.17.3, 5. On Antipater, see R. M. Errington, *A History of Macedonia*, trans. C. Errington (Berkeley and Los Angeles: 1990), pp. 92–94; E. Baynham, "Antipater: Manager of Kings," in Worthington (ed.), *Ventures*, pp. 331–356; D. L. Gilley and Ian Worthington, "Alexander the Great, Macedonia and Asia," in Roisman and Worthington (eds.), *Companion to Macedonia*, pp. 199–205.

32. E. Baynham, "Why Didn't Alexander Marry a Nice Macedonian Girl before Leaving Home? Observations on Factional Politics at Alexander's Court in 336–334 BC," in T. Hillard (ed.), *Ancient History in a Modern University* 1 (Sydney: 1998), pp. 148–155; cf. E. D. Carney, *Women and Monarchy in Macedonia* (Norman: 2000), pp. 97–100.

33. Athenaeus 435a. On the story: D. Ogden, *Alexander the Great. Myth, Genesis and Sexuality* (Exeter: 2011), pp. 144–146.

34. Plutarch, *Alexander* 21.7.

35. For example, W. W. Tarn, *Alexander the Great* 2 (Cambridge: 1948), pp. 322–326 (Tarn passes over all of Alexander's sexual relations because he found them distasteful!). The myth of the sexless Alexander: Ogden, *Alexander the Great*, pp. 174–184, with pp. 124–154 on his wives and dalliances; cf. D. Ogden, "Alexander's Sex Life," in Heckel and Tritle (eds.), *New History*, pp. 203–217. See too E. D. Carney, "Women in Alexander's Court," in Roisman (ed.), *Companion to Alexander*, pp. 227–252.

8. FROM EUROPE TO ASIA

1. Alexander's campaign and the Persian attitude and resistance: P. A. Brunt, "Persian Accounts of Alexander's Campaigns," *CQ*² 12 (1962), pp. 141–155; M. Brosius, "Alexander and the Persians," in Roisman (ed.), *Companion to Alexander*, pp. 169–193; P. Cartledge, *Alexander the Great: The Hunt for a New Past* (London: 2003), pp. 189–206; M. J. Olbrycht, "Macedonia and Persia," in Roisman and Worthington (eds.), *Companion to Macedonia*, pp. 342–369; P. Briant, *Alexander the Great and His Empire*, trans. A. Kuhrt (Princeton: 2010), "Conquête territoriale et stratégie idéologique: Alexandre le Grand et l'idéologie monarchique achéménide," in J. Wolski (ed.), *Actes du colloque international sur L'idéologie monarchique dans l'antiquité* (Cracow: 1980), pp. 37–83, "The Empire of Darius III in Perspective" and "Alexander and the Persian Empire, between 'Decline' and 'Renovation,'" in Heckel and Tritle (eds.), *New History*, pp. 141–170 and 171–188, respectively; cf. "'Alexandre et l'hellénisation de l'Asie': l'Histoire au passé et au présent," *Studi Ellenistici* 16 (2005), pp. 9–69.

2. Callisthenes: L. Pearson, *The Lost Histories of Alexander the Great* (New York: 1960), pp. 22–49; L. Prandi, *Callistene: Uno storico tra Aristotele e i re macedonici* (Milan: 1985).

3. Composition: A. B. Bosworth, *Conquest and Empire. The Reign of Alexander the Great* (Cambridge: 1988), pp. 259–266; W. Heckel, *The Conquests of Alexander the Great* (Cambridge: 2008), pp. 24–28. Alexander's army: Bosworth, *Conquest and Empire*, pp. 259–277; D. Engels, *Alexander the Great and the Logistics of the Macedonian Army* (Berkeley and Los Angeles: 1978); N. G. L. Hammond, *Alexander the Great: King, Commander and Statesman*, 2nd ed. (Bristol: 1989), pp. 24–34, 153–164; R. D. Milns, "The Army of Alexander the Great," in E. Badian (ed.), *Alexandre le Grand, Image et Réalité*, Fondation Hardt, Entretiens 22 (Geneva: 1976), pp. 87–136; N. V. Sekunda, "The Macedonian Army," in Roisman and Worthington (eds.), *Companion to Macedonia*, pp. 446–471; W. W. Tarn, *Alexander the Great* 2 (Cambridge: 1948), pp. 135–198. Heckel, *Conquests*, app. 1 (pp. 153–157), gives a useful list of Alexander's officers and their commands.

4. Numbers: J. F. C. Fuller, *The Generalship of Alexander the Great* (repr.; New Brunswick: 1960), p. 88; P. Green, *Alexander of Macedon* (Harmondsworth: 1974), pp. 156–158; Hammond, *Alexander*, pp. 67–68; Heckel, *Conquests*, p. 158—see also his app. 2 (pp. 158–163) for troop numbers during the reign. Fuller, *Generalship*, app. 2 (pp. 153–157), lists Alexander's officers and their commands. The following numbers and dispositions are those of Fuller.

5. Diodorus 17.4.5; cf. Plutarch, *Alexander* 15.1.

6. Number: Polyaenus 5.44.4.

7. Diodorus 17.17.2.

8. Keeping to Philip's original intention: P. A. Brunt, "The Aims of Alexander," *G&R*² 12 (1965), pp. 205–215. Marching to the ends of the earth: W. Heckel, "Alexander the Great and the 'Limits of the Civilised World,'" in Heckel and Tritle (eds.), *Crossroads*, pp. 147–174; cf. Briant, *Alexander*, pp. 24–38. Variations on the panhellenic appeal: M. Faraguna, "Alexander and the Greeks," in Roisman (ed.), *Companion to Alexander*, pp. 107–109.

9. Xenophon, *Anabasis* 1.8.22.

10. C. Nylander, "Darius III—The Coward King. Point and Counterpoint," in J. Carlsen et al. (eds.), *Alexander the Great. Reality and Myth* (Rome: 1993), pp. 145–159; E. Badian, "Darius III," *HSCPh* 100 (2000), pp. 241–268; Briant, *Alexander*, pp. 42–44, 48–52.

11. Numbers: Green, *Alexander*, pp. 498–500; Heckel, *Conquests*, pp. 47–48, 159.

12. Battle: Bosworth, *Conquest and Empire*, pp. 39–44; Fuller, *Generalship*, pp. 147–154; Green, *Alexander*, pp. 173–180; Hammond, *Alexander*, pp. 65–69, 73–77; Heckel, *Conquests*, pp. 46–51; E. Badian, "The Battle of the Granicus: A New Look," *Anc. Macedonia* 2 (1977), pp. 271–293; A. M. Devine, "Demythologizing the Battle of the Granicus," *Phoenix* 40 (1986), pp. 265–278 and "A Pawn-

Sacrifice at the Battle of the Granicus: The Origins of a Favorite Stratagem of Alexander the Great," *Anc. World* 18 (1988), pp. 3–20; N. G. L. Hammond, "The Battle of the Granicus River," *JHS* 100 (1980), pp. 73–88.

13. Green, *Alexander*, pp. 488–512, for issues with the battle.

14. C. G. Thomas, *Alexander the Great in His World* (Malden: 2006), p. 53.

15. Devine, "Pawn-Sacrifice," pp. 3–20.

16. Aristobulus, *BNJ* 139 F 5 (= Plutarch, *Alexander* 16.15). Lysippus carved a bronze monument of the fallen cavalrymen at Dium, the Macedonian religious center in the foothills of Olympus, although the group included a portrait of Alexander!

17. Alexander's generalship: A. R. Burn, "The Generalship of Alexander," *G&R*² 12 (1965), pp. 140–154; Fuller, *Generalship*; Cartledge, *Alexander*, pp. 157–188, 219–266; A. M. Devine, "Alexander the Great," in J. Hackett (ed.), *Warfare in the Ancient World* (New York: 1989), pp. 104–129; D. L. Gilley and Ian Worthington, "Alexander the Great, Macedonia and Asia," in Roisman and Worthington (eds.), *Companion to Macedonia*, pp. 186–207; B. Strauss, "Alexander: The Military Campaign," in Roisman (ed.), *Companion to Alexander*, pp. 133–156; cf. J. Roisman, "Honor in Alexander's Campaign," in Roisman, ed., *Companion to Alexander*, pp. 279–321; and W. Heckel, "A King and His Army," in Heckel and Tritle (eds.), *New History*, pp. 69–82.

18. Heckel, *Conquests*, p. 50; A. M. Devine, "Alexander's Propaganda Machine: Callisthenes as the Ultimate Source for Arrian, *Anabasis* 1–3," in Worthington (ed.), *Ventures*, pp. 89–104.

19. Diodorus 17.21.4.

20. Arrian 1.16.7; Plutarch, *Alexander* 16.17–18.

21. M. M. Kholod, "On the Financial Relations of Alexander the Great and the Greek Cities in Asia Minor: The Case of *Syntaxis*," in A. Mehl, A. V. Makhlayuk, and O. Gabelko (eds.), *Ruthenia Classica Aetatis Novae. A Collection of Works by Russian Scholars in Ancient Greek and Roman History* (Stuttgart: 2013), pp. 83–92.

22. Engels, *Alexander the Great and the Logistics of the Macedonian Army*.

23. Not all saw his action as rash: Diodorus 17.23.1 cryptically refers to "those who say that Alexander's strategic conception was sound when he dismissed his fleet."

24. Siege: Bosworth, *Conquest and Empire*, pp. 47–49; Fuller, *Generalship*, pp. 200–206; Hammond, *Alexander*, pp. 81–83.

25. Arrian 1.25; Justin 11.7.12. Diodorus 17.32.1–2 places this episode later at Tarsus; most likely it was at Phaselis: Bosworth, *Conquest and Empire*, p. 50.

26. Callisthenes, *FGrH* 124 F 31; Arrian, 1.26.1–2; Plutarch, *Alexander* 17.3–5.

27. Xenophon, *Anabasis* 1.4.18.

28. Myth's impact on the historical and legendary Alexander: D. Ogden, *Alexander the Great. Myth, Genesis and Sexuality* (Exeter: 2011), pp. 65–67, 76–77. See too E. A. Fredricksmeyer, "Alexander, Midas, and the Oracle at Gordium," *CPh* 56 (1961), pp. 160–168.

29. Aristobulus, *BNJ* 139 F 7b (= Plutarch, *Alexander* 18.2–4).

30. S. Ruzicka, "War in the Aegean, 333–331 BC: A Reconsideration," *Phoenix* 42 (1988), pp. 131–151.

31. V. Ehrenberg, *Alexander and the Greeks* (Oxford: 1938); E. Badian, "Alexander the Great and the Greeks of Asia," in E. Badian (ed.), *Ancient Society and Institutions. Studies Presented to V. Ehrenberg on His 75th Birthday* (Oxford: 1966), pp. 37–69; N. G. L. Hammond and F. W. Walbank, *A History of Macedonia* 3 (Oxford: 1988), pp. 72–76; Bosworth, *Conquest and Empire*, pp. 250–258; Faraguna, "Alexander and the Greeks," pp. 109–115; K. Nawotka, "Freedom of Greek Cities in Asia Minor in the Age of Alexander the Great," *Klio* 85 (2003), pp. 15–41; M. M. Kholod, "The Garrisons of Alexander the Great in the Greek Cities of Asia Minor," *Eos* 97 (2010), pp. 249–258.

32. P. J. Rhodes and R. Osborne (eds.), *Greek Historical Inscriptions, 404–323 BC* (Oxford: 2003), no. 84A; in detail, see A. J. Heisserer, *Alexander the Great and the Greeks* (Norman: 1980), pp. 79–95; cf. Faraguna, "Alexander and the Greeks," pp. 113–115.

33. Kholod, "Garrisons of Alexander the Great," pp. 249–258.

9. ALEXANDER: MASTER STRATEGIST AND EMERGING GOD

1. Diodorus 17.31.2; Arrian 2.8.8; Curtius 3.2.4–9; Justin 11.9.1; Plutarch, *Alexander* 18.6.

2. Lead-up and battle: A. B. Bosworth, *Conquest and Empire. The Reign of Alexander the Great* (Cambridge: 1988), pp. 58–62; J. F. C. Fuller, *The Generalship of Alexander the Great* (repr.; New Brunswick: 1960), pp. 154–162; N. G. L. Hammond, *Alexander the Great: King, Commander and Statesman*, 2nd ed. (Bristol: 1989), pp. 94–111; W. Heckel, *The Conquests of Alexander the Great* (Cambridge: 2008), pp. 57–65; Ian Worthington, *Alexander the Great: Man and God*, rev. ed. (London: 2004), pp. 95–102; A. M. Devine, "The Strategies of Alexander the Great and Darius III in the Issus Campaign (333 BC)," *Anc. World* 12 (1985), pp. 25–38 and "Grand Tactics at the Battle of Issus," *Anc. World* 12 (1985), pp. 39–59; N. G. L. Hammond, "Alexander's Charge at the Battle of Issus in 333 B.C.," *Historia* 41 (1992), pp. 395–406; C. L. Murison, "Darius III and the Battle of Issus," *Historia* 21 (1972), pp. 399–423.

3. Ptolemy, *FGrH* 138 F 6 (= Arrian 2.11.8).

4. P. Briant, *Alexander the Great and His Empire*, trans. A. Kuhrt (Princeton: 2010), p. 52.

5. Plutarch, *Alexander* 34.1.

6. M. Brosius, "Alexander and the Persians," in Roisman (ed.), *Companion to Alexander*, pp. 179–181.

7. E. A. Fredricksmeyer, "Alexander the Great and the Kingship of Asia," in A. B. Bosworth and E. J. Baynham (eds.), *Alexander the Great in Fact and Fiction* (Oxford: 2000), pp. 136–166.

8. Chares, *FGrH* 125 F 6 (= Plutarch, *Moralia* 341c).

9. A. Cohen, *The Alexander Mosaic. Stories of Victory and Defeat* (Cambridge: 1997); A. Stewart, *Faces of Power. Alexander's Image and Hellenistic Politics* (Berkeley and Los Angeles: 1993), pp. 130–157.

10. Curtius 10.5.18–25. Although note that a reason (*the* reason?) for her sadness was the question of whether she would face another period of captivity and loss of status as after Issus.

11. Aristobulus, *BNJ* 139 F 11 (= Plutarch, *Alexander* 21.7).

12. Diodorus 17.40.3 suggests that their refusal was because of their loyalty to Darius.

13. Siege: Bosworth, *Conquest and Empire*, pp. 65–67; Fuller, *Generalship*, pp. 206–216; Hammond, *Alexander*, pp. 113–117; Worthington, *Alexander*, pp. 105–111; E. F. Bloedow, "The Siege of Tyre in 332 BC: Alexander at the Crossroads in His Career," *La Parola del Passato* 301 (1990), pp. 255–293; P. Romane, "Alexander's Siege of Tyre," *Anc. World* 16 (1987), pp. 79–90.

14. Arrian 2.24.4.

15. Siege: Bosworth, *Conquest and Empire*, pp. 67–68; Fuller, *Generalship*, pp. 216–218; Heckel, *Conquests*, pp. 68–71; Worthington, *Alexander*, pp. 111–112; P. Romane, "Alexander's Siege of Gaza," *Anc. World* 18 (1988), pp. 21–30.

16. N. G. L. Hammond, *The Genius of Alexander the Great* (London: 1997), p. 96, rejects the episode: "Alexander always honored the brave." Yet plenty of brave men faced Alexander during his reign and were ruthlessly killed.

17. See in detail I. A. Ladynin, "The Argeadai Building Program in Egypt in the Framework of Dynasties' XXIX–XXX Temple Building," in K. Nawotka and A. Wojciechowska (eds.), *Alexander the Great and Egypt: History, Art, Tradition* (Wiesbaden: forthcoming).

18. I. A. Ladynin, "Nadpisi na statuetke starshego syna tsarya Nectaneba II: Perevod i kommentariy" [The inscriptions on the statuette of the elder son of King Nectanebo II: Translation and

commentary], in M. A. Chegodaev (ed.), *Yazyki drevneegipetskoy kultury: Problemy perevodimosti* [Languages of the ancient Egyptian culture: Problems of translation] (Moscow: forthcoming).

19. S. Burstein, "Pharaoh Alexander: A Scholarly Myth," *Anc. Society* 22 (1991), pp. 139–145.

20. D. Ogden, *Alexander the Great. Myth, Genesis and Sexuality* (Exeter: 2011), pp. 57–78, explains Alexander's visit to the Oracle because of the imagery of rams, goats, sheep, and impregnations by Zeus that are associated with Macedonia and Alexander and with Ammon, which thus piqued Alexander's interest. See too A. B. Bosworth, "Alexander and Ammon," in K. Kinzl (ed.), *Greece and the Ancient Mediterranean in History and Prehistory* (Berlin: 1977), pp. 51–75.

21. Diodorus 17.52.2; Arrian 3.2.1; Curtius 4.8.1; Plutarch, *Alexander* 26.6.

22. Aristobulus, *BNJ* 139 FF 13–15 (= Arrian 3.3).

23. Callisthenes, *FGrH* 124 F 14b (= Plutarch, *Alexander* 27.3–4).

24. Ptolemy, *FGrH* 138 F 8 (= Arrian 3.3.5).

25. Ptolemy, *FGrH* 138 F 9 (= Arrian 3.4.5).

26. Aristobulus, *BNJ* 139 FF 13–15 (= Arrian 3.3–4).

27. Bosworth, "Alexander and Ammon," pp. 51–75; and D. Kienast, "Alexander, Zeus, and Ammon," in W. Will and J. Heinrichs (eds.), *Zu Alexander d. Gr.: Festschrift G. Wirth* (Amsterdam: 1988), pp. 309–334. Alexander's pretensions to divinity: Bosworth, *Conquest and Empire*, pp. 278–290; Worthington, *Alexander*, pp. 273–283.

28. Later Alexandria: R. MacLeod (ed.), *The Library of Alexandria* (London: 2000); R. Waterfield, *Dividing the Spoils. The War for Alexander the Great's Empire* (Oxford: 2011), pp. 136–139.

29. I. A. Ladynin, "Aleksandr Velikiy i Kleomen iz Navkratisa v drevneegipetskom istochnike? (K interpretazii avtobiograficheskoy nadpisi iz grobnizy Unnefera v Saqqara)" [Alexander the Great and Cleomenes of Naucratis in an ancient Egyptian source? (On the interpretation of the autobiographical inscription from the tomb of Wennefer at Saqqara)], *Mnemon: Issledovania i publicazii po istorii antichnogo mira* [Mnemon: Studies and publications on the history of the ancient world] 12 (2013), pp. 200–225.

10. THE FALL OF THE PERSIAN EMPIRE

1. Possibly the embassy should be placed in Tyre in 331, before Gaugamela: A. B. Bosworth, *Conquest and Empire. The Reign of Alexander the Great* (Cambridge: 1988), pp. 75–76, citing sources.

2. Arrian 2.25.2.

3. Arrian 2.5.8, 7.14.1. C. L. Hardiman, "Classical Art to 221 BC," in Roisman and Worthington (eds.), *Companion to Macedonia*, pp. 509–511.

4. L. Tritle, "Alexander and the Greeks. Artists and Soldiers, Friends and Enemies," in Heckel and Tritle (eds.), *New History*, pp. 121–140.

5. Plutarch, *Moralia* 328b.

6. M. Brosius, "Alexander and the Persians," in Roisman (ed.), *Companion to Alexander*, pp. 169–193.

7. A. J. Sachs and H. Hunger, *Astronomical Diaries and Related Texts from Babylonia* 1 (Vienna: 1988); R. J. van der Spek, "Darius III, Alexander the Great and Babylonian Scholarship," *Achaemenid History* 13 (2003), pp. 289–346. Cf. P. A. Brunt, "Persian Accounts of Alexander's Campaigns," *CQ²* 12 (1962), pp. 141–155.

8. Battle: Bosworth, *Conquest and Empire*, pp. 76–85; P. Cartledge, *Alexander the Great: The Hunt for a New Past* (London: 2003), pp. 179–182; J. F. C. Fuller, *The Generalship of Alexander the Great* (repr.; New Brunswick: 1960), pp. 163–180; N. G. L. Hammond, *Alexander the Great: King, Commander and Statesman*, 2nd ed. (Bristol: 1989), pp. 138–150; W. Heckel, *The Conquests of Alexander the*

Great (Cambridge: 2008), pp. 75–80; E. W. Marsden, *The Campaign of Gaugamela* (Liverpool: 1964); Ian Worthington, *Alexander the Great: Man and God*, rev. ed. (London: 2004), pp. 126–135; A. M. Devine, "Grand Tactics at Gaugamela," *Phoenix* 29 (1975), pp. 374–385, "The Battle of Gaugamela: A Tactical and Source-Critical Study," *Anc. World* 13 (1986), pp. 87–115, and "The Macedonian Army at Gaugamela: Its Strength and the Length of Its Battle-Line," *Anc. World* 19 (1989), pp. 77–80; G. T. Griffith, "Alexander's Generalship at Gaugamela," *JHS* 67 (1947), pp. 77–89.

9. Arrian 3.8.6; Diodorus 17.39.4; Curtius 4.12.13; Plutarch, *Alexander* 31.1.

10. Arrian 3.12.5.

11. Curtius 4.16.26, with Hammond, *Alexander*, p. 149.

12. Callisthenes, *FGrH* 124 F 37 (= Plutarch, *Alexander* 33.9–11).

13. On Persepolis, see conveniently (though dated), D. N. Wilber, *Persepolis. The Archaeology of Parsa, Seat of the Persian Kings* (New York: 1969).

14. Brosius, "Alexander and the Persians," pp. 174–175; A. Kuhrt, "Alexander in Babylon," *Achaemenid History* 5 (1990), pp. 121–130.

15. Sachs and Hunger, *Astronomical Diaries*, no. 329.

16. Curtius 6.6.1–10; Plutarch, *Alexander* 45.1–4. On Alexander's orientalism, see pp. 214–216.

17. N. G. L. Hammond, *The Genius of Alexander the Great* (London: 1997), p. 112.

18. E. A. Fredricksmeyer, "Alexander the Great and the Kingship of Asia," in A. B. Bosworth and E. J. Baynham (eds.), *Alexander the Great in Fact and Fiction* (Oxford: 2000), pp. 136–166.

19. Ian Worthington, "Alexander the Great, Nation-Building, and the Creation and Maintenance of Empire," in V. D. Hanson (ed.), *Makers of Ancient Strategy: From the Persian Wars to the Fall of Rome* (Princeton: 2010), pp. 118–137.

20. E. Badian, "The Administration of the Empire," *G&R²* 12 (1965), pp. 166–182; W. E. Higgins, "Aspects of Alexander's Imperial Administration: Some Modern Methods and Views Reviewed," *Athenaeum* 58 (1980), pp. 129–152; Bosworth, *Conquest and Empire*, pp. 229–250; C. Mossé, *Alexander: Destiny and Myth*, trans. J. Lloyd (Edinburgh: 2004), pp. 113–119; P. Briant, *Alexander the Great and His Empire*, trans. A. Kuhrt (Princeton: 2010), pp. 67–100; cf. 101–138; and Cartledge, *Alexander*, pp. 189–206.

21. Heckel, *Conquests*, app. 3 (pp. 164–165), lists Alexander's satraps and their successors.

22. Plutarch, *Moralia* 328e, with P. Fraser, *Cities of Alexander the Great* (Oxford: 1996): Alexander founded only nine cities.

23. F. L. Holt, "Alexander's Settlements in Central Asia," *Anc. Macedonia* 4 (1986), pp. 315–323.

24. Brosius, "Alexander and the Persians," pp. 169–193; Briant, *Alexander*, pp. 42–66.

25. Cf. Bosworth, *Conquest and Empire*, pp. 244–245; but against this, see Briant, *Alexander*, pp. 96–100.

26. Office of the Secretary of Defense for Net Assessment, *Military Advantage in History* (Washington, D.C.: 2002), p. 80.

27. Bosworth, *Conquest and Empire*, pp. 90–92; Fuller, *Generalship*, pp. 228–234; Worthington, *Alexander*, pp. 146–148; H. Speck, "Alexander at the Persian Gates: A Study in Historiography and Topography," *AJAH²* 1 (2002), pp. 15–23.

28. In his account Ptolemy writes that he (not Philotas) was in charge of the second group tasked with attacking the Persians. However, Ptolemy's job was to polish off any fleeing Persians, so he most likely exaggerated his own role.

29. Diodorus 17.70.

30. L. Rawlings, *The Ancient Greeks at War* (Manchester: 2007), pp. 218–220.

31. E. N. Borza, "Fire from Heaven: Alexander at Persepolis," *CPh* 67 (1972), pp. 233–245; N. G. L. Hammond, "The Archaeological and Literary Evidence for the Burning of the Persepolis Palace," *CQ²* 42 (1992), pp. 358–364; Briant, *Alexander*, pp. 107–111.

32. A. S. Shahbazi, "Iranians and Alexander," *AJAH²* 2 (2003), pp. 5–38.

33. Hammond, *Alexander*, p. 169; H. Sancisi-Weerdenburg, "Alexander and Persepolis," in J. Carlsen et al. (eds.), *Alexander the Great. Reality and Myth* (Rome: 1993), pp. 177–188.

34. E. Poddighe, "Alexander and the Greeks. The Corinthian League," in Heckel and Tritle (eds.), *New History*, pp. 99–120.

35. Ian Worthington, *Demosthenes of Athens and the Fall of Classical Greece* (Oxford: 2013), pp. 275–325.

36. Aeschines 3, *Against Ctesiphon* 164.

37. Bosworth, *Conquest and Empire*, pp. 198–204; N. G. L. Hammond and F. W. Walbank, *A History of Macedonia* 3 (Oxford: 1988), pp. 76–78; E. Badian, "Agis III: Revisions and Reflections," in Worthington (ed.), *Ventures*, pp. 258–292.

38. Plutarch, *Moralia* 219e; Aelian, *VH* 2.19.

39. Worthington, *Demosthenes of Athens*, pp. 294–309.

11. THE WAR IN AFGHANISTAN

1. Herodotus 7.64 on Bactrian participation in the Persian Wars. Alexander in Bactria: F. L. Holt, *Alexander the Great and Bactria: The Formation of a Greek Frontier in Central Asia* (Leiden: 1988), *Thundering Zeus. The Making of Hellenistic Bactria* (Berkeley and Los Angeles: 1999), *Into the Land of Bones: Alexander the Great in Afghanistan* (Berkeley and Los Angeles: 2005), and "Alexander's Settlements in Central Asia," *Anc. Macedonia* 4 (1986), pp. 315–323. See too J. F. C. Fuller, *The Generalship of Alexander the Great* (repr.; New Brunswick: 1960), pp. 234–245; W. Heckel, *The Conquests of Alexander the Great* (Cambridge: 2008), pp. 87–111.

2. W. Heckel, "Alexander the Great and the 'Limits of the Civilised World,'" in Heckel and Tritle (eds.), *Crossroads*, pp. 147–174. Alexander's limit was the Hyphasis River in India.

3. E. Badian, "The Eunuch Bagoas: A Study in Method," *CQ²* 28 (1958), pp. 144–157. D. Ogden, *Alexander the Great. Myth, Genesis and Sexuality* (Exeter: 2011), pp. 167–170 and "Alexander's Sex Life," in Heckel and Tritle (eds.), *New History*, pp. 213–217, cautions accepting the homoerotic relationship at face value.

4. Ogden, *Alexander the Great*, pp. 146–150.

5. Curtius 6.5.29.

6. K. M. Dobbins, "Alexander's Eastern Satrapies," *Persica* 11 (1984), pp. 74–108.

7. Arrian 7.6.2–5; translation: W. Heckel and J. Yardley, *Alexander the Great. Historical Sources in Translation* (Malden: 2003), p. 188. Alexander among Macedonians, Greeks, and Iranians: P. Briant, *Alexander the Great and His Empire*, trans. A. Kuhrt (Princeton: 2010), pp. 101–138; M. J. Olbrycht, "Macedonia and Persia," in Roisman and Worthington (eds.), *Companion to Macedonia*, pp. 355–360; cf. J. Roisman, "Honor in Alexander's Campaign," in Roisman (ed.), *Companion to Alexander*, pp. 279–321.

8. Mixing of dress: N. V. Sekunda, "A Macedonian Companion in a Pompeian Fresco," *Archeologia* (Warsaw) 54 (2003), pp. 29–33.

9. P. Green, *Alexander of Macedon* (Harmondsworth: 1974), p. 335.

10. A. B. Bosworth, *Conquest and Empire. The Reign of Alexander the Great* (Cambridge: 1988), pp. 101–104; Heckel, *Conquests*, pp. 88–92; Ian Worthington, *Alexander the Great: Man and God*, rev. ed. (London: 2004), pp. 164–170; W. L. Adams, "The Episode of Philotas: An Insight," in Heckel and Tritle (eds.), *Crossroads*, pp. 113–126; E. Badian, "The Death of Parmenio," *TAPhA* 91 (1960), pp. 324–338; W. Heckel, "The Conspiracy *against* Philotas," *Phoenix* 31 (1977), pp. 9–21; W. Z. Rubinsohn, "The 'Philotas Affair'—A Reconsideration," *Anc. Macedonia* 2 (1977), pp. 409–420. On conspiracies: E. Badian, "Alexander the Great and the Loneliness of Power," in E. Badian (ed.), *Studies in Greek and Roman History* (Oxford: 1964), pp. 192–205 and "Conspiracies," in A. B. Bosworth and E. Baynham (eds.), *Alexander the Great in Fact and Fiction* (Oxford: 1996), pp. 60–92;

W. Heckel, "King and 'Companions': Observations on the Nature of Power in the Reign of Alexander," in Roisman (ed.), *Companion to Alexander*, pp. 197–225 and "A King and His Army," in Heckel and Tritle (eds.), *New History*, pp. 69–82; cf. Briant, *Alexander*, pp. 119–123.

11. Cf. G. Weber, "The Court of Alexander the Great as Social System," in Heckel and Tritle (eds.), *New History*, pp. 83–98.

12. Curtius 6.7.15: Peucolaus, Nicanor, Aphobetus, Iolaus, Dioxenus, Archepolis, Amyntas, Demetrius, and Calis (the last two at 6.2.37).

13. Plutarch, *Alexander* 49.6–7; cf. Diodorus 17.80.2.

14. Factions and their impact on the king and vice versa: Heckel, "King and 'Companions,'" pp. 197–225.

15. Badian, "Alexander the Great and the Loneliness of Power," pp. 192–205.

16. P. Cartledge, *Alexander the Great: The Hunt for a New Past* (London: 2003), p. 168.

17. Cartledge, *Alexander*, pp. 96–106.

18. Personality:C. Mossé, *Alexander: Destiny and Myth*, trans. J. Lloyd (Edinburgh: 2004), pp. 94–107.

19. Briant, *Alexander*, pp. 178–179, citing bibliography.

20. Heckel, *Conquests*, p. 95.

21. H. W. Parke, "The Massacre of the Branchidae," *JHS* 105 (1985), pp. 59–68.

22. A. B. Bosworth, *Alexander and the East. The Tragedy of Triumph* (Oxford: 1996), pp. 100–108; Heckel, *Conquests*, pp. 100–104; Worthington, *Alexander*, pp. 184–187; A. B. Bosworth, "The Tumult and the Shouting: Two Interpretations of the Cleitus Episode," *AHB* 10 (1996), pp. 19–30; E. Carney, "The Death of Clitus," *GRBS* 22 (1981), pp. 149–160; L. Tritle, "Alexander and the Killing of Cleitus the Black," in Heckel and Tritle (eds.), *Crossroads*, pp. 127–146.

23. Heckel, *Conquests*, p. 102, notes that the song might have honored a harpist named Aristarchus, who died in Balkh, where he had been left with a small garrison, some pages, and sick men, and Cleitus objected to a nonmilitary man being honored in song. Yet why would Alexander appoint a harpist to command garrison troops?

24. Curtius 8.1.30–37; Green, *Alexander*, p. 362.

25. Roisman, "Honor in Alexander's Campaign," pp. 279–321; on the Cleitus incident, see pp. 288, 319–320.

26. Chronology of these months: A. B. Bosworth, "A Missing Year in the History of Alexander the Great," *JHS* 101 (1981), pp. 17–39.

12. PASSAGE TO INDIA

1. Curtius 8.4.21–26; translation: W. Heckel and J. Yardley, *Alexander the Great. Historical Sources in Translation* (Malden: 2003), p. 203. For the later (hostile) tradition on Roxane, providing much of the "evidence" for her life with Alexander, see D. Ogden, *Alexander the Great. Myth, Genesis and Sexuality* (Exeter: 2011), pp. 124–133.

2. Custom: Curtius 8.4.27–29; cf. M. Renard and J. Servais, "A propos du mariage d'Alexandre et de Roxane," *L'Ant. Class.* 24 (1955), pp. 29–50.

3. F. L. Holt, *Alexander the Great and Bactria: The Formation of a Greek Frontier in Central Asia* (Leiden: 1988), p. 66; Ian Worthington, *Alexander the Great: Man and God*, rev. ed. (London: 2004), pp. 188–190.

4. Herodotus 1.134 says that they prostrated themselves; the Persepolis Treasury reliefs illustrate bowing and blowing a kiss.

5. A. B. Bosworth, *Alexander and the East. The Tragedy of Triumph* (Oxford: 1996), pp. 109–112.

6. *Contra* W. Heckel, *The Conquests of Alexander the Great* (Cambridge: 2008), pp. 106–107.

7. Curtius 8.5.5–6; Justin 12.7.1.

8. Chares, *FGrH* 125 F 14b (= Arrian 4.12.3–5).

9. Conspiracy and sources: Bosworth, *Alexander and the East*, pp. 112–114. See too E. Badian, "Alexander the Great and the Loneliness of Power," in E. Badian (ed.), *Studies in Greek and Roman History* (Oxford: 1964), pp. 192–205 and "Conspiracies," in A. B. Bosworth and E. Baynham (eds.), *Alexander the Great in Fact and Fiction* (Oxford: 1996), pp. 60–92; E. N. Borza, "Anaxagoras and Callisthenes: Academic Intrigue at Alexander's Court," in H. J. Dell (ed.), *Ancient Macedonian Studies in Honour of C. F. Edson* (Thessaloníki: 1981), pp. 73–86; E. Carney, "The Conspiracy of Hermolaus," *CJ* 76 (1980), pp. 223–231.

10. Aristobulus, *FGrH* 139 F 30 (= Arrian 4.13.5).

11. Curtius 8.6.7.

12. Borza, "Anaxagoras and Callisthenes," pp. 73–86; cf. Badian, "Conspiracies," pp. 71–72. See too D. Golan, "The Fate of a Court Historian: Callisthenes," *Athenaeum* 66 (1988), pp. 99–120.

13. A. B. Bosworth, "The Indian Campaigns, 327–325 BC," in Roisman (ed.), *Companion to Alexander*, pp. 159–168 and *Alexander and the East*; Heckel, *Conquests*, pp. 112–131; A. K. Narain, "Alexander and India," *G&R²* 12 (1965), pp. 155–165; A. B. Bosworth, "The Indian Satrapies under Alexander the Great," *Antichthon* 17 (1983), pp. 37–46; K. M. Dobbins, "Alexander's Eastern Satrapies," *Persica* 11 (1984), pp. 74–108; cf. E. Badian, "The Administration of the Empire," *G&R²* 12 (1965), pp. 166–182.

14. Arrian 3.8.6; motives: Bosworth, *Alexander and the East*, pp. 154–165.

15. Curtius 8.8.15. On Dionysus, see Diodorus 2.38, 3.63, 4.3, and Arrian 8.5; on Heracles, see Arrian 8.8–9. Alexander and Dionysus: Bosworth, *Alexander and the East*, pp. 119–126 and "Alexander, Euripides and Dionysos: The Motivation for Apotheosis," in R. W. Wallace and E. M. Harris (eds.), *Transitions to Empire. Essays in Honor of E. Badian* (Norman: 1996), pp. 140–166.

16. W. Heckel, "Alexander the Great and the 'Limits of the Civilised World,'" in Heckel and Tritle (eds.), *Crossroads*, pp. 147–174.

17. A. Dihle, "The Conception of India in Hellenistic and Roman Literature," *Proc. Camb. Phil. Soc.* 10 (1964), pp. 15–23.

18. For example, in the confrontation between Alexander and Porus after the Battle of the Hydaspes River (Onesicritus, *BNJ* 134 F 17a = Strabo 15.1.64 [716]) and with the Brahman philosophers: pp. 248 and 258.

19. G. Woodcock, *The Greeks in India* (London: 1966); see too W. W. Tarn, *The Greeks in Bactria and India* (Cambridge: 1951).

20. Bosworth, *Alexander and the East*, pp. 121–126.

21. Woodcock, *Greeks in India*, pp. 21–23, on the identity of the Nysans, with an analogy to present-day Kafirs living by Chitral (Pakistan), whose men wear a hat like the *kausia*, practice viticulture, and hold an annual festival in honor of the god of wine.

22. Arrian 4.27.3–4; Diodorus 17.84; Plutarch, *Alexander* 59.3–4.

23. Onesicritus, *BNJ* 134 F 5 (= Strabo 11.11.3).

24. Archelaus, *FGrH* 123 F 1 (= Solinus 52.18–23).

25. Nearchus, *BNJ* 133 F 11 (= Arrian, *Indica* 16–17).

26. Aristobulus, *BNJ* 139 F 42 (= Strabo 15.62).

27. Siege: Bosworth, *Alexander and the East*, pp. 49–53; J. F. C. Fuller, *The Generalship of Alexander the Great* (repr.; New Brunswick: 1960), pp. 247–252; Worthington, *Alexander*, pp. 202–204.

28. Diodorus 17.87.2; Arrian 5.15.4; Curtius 8.13.6; Plutarch, *Alexander* 62.2.

29. Numbers: N. G. L. Hammond, *Alexander the Great: King, Commander and Statesman*, 2nd ed. (Bristol: 1989), p. 208; Bosworth, *Alexander and the East*, p. 16. For the figure of 25,000: Heckel, *Conquests*, p. 161.

30. Lead-up and battle: Bosworth, *Alexander and the East*, pp. 9–20; Fuller, *Generalship*, pp. 180–199; Hammond, *Alexander*, pp. 208–216; Heckel, *Conquests*, pp. 115–120; F. L. Holt, *Alexander*

the Great and the Mystery of the Elephant Medallions (Berkeley and Los Angeles: 2003), pp. 49–53; Worthington, *Alexander*, pp. 207–212; A. M. Devine, "The Battle of Hydaspes: A Tactical and Source-Critical Study," *Anc. World* 16 (1987), pp. 91–113.

31. Diodorus 17.89.1–3; Arrian 5.18.2–3.

32. Bosworth, *Alexander and the East*, pp. 6–8; K. Dahmen, *The Legend of Alexander the Great on Greek and Roman Coins* (London: 2007), pp. 6–9, 109–110. There are 10 medallions. Holt, in *Alexander the Great and the Mystery of the Elephant Medallions*, conducts a fascinating investigation into them, from their discovery and arrival in museums in the late nineteenth century to present-day interpretations of them. Among other things, he argues that they have been misinterpreted and that they were a victory issue that Alexander awarded his men to commemorate the Hydaspes victory. Against this view, see, for example, Dahmen, *Legend of Alexander the Great*, pp. 6–9. Note also the caution of S. Bhandare, "Not Just a Pretty Face: Interpretations of Alexander's Numismatic Legacy in the Hellenistic East," in H. P. Ray and D. T. Potts (eds.), *Memory as History: The Legacy of Alexander in Asia* (New Delhi: 2007), pp. 208–256.

33. Dahmen, *Legend of Alexander the Great*, pp. 6, 109–110; cf. Heckel, *Conquests*, p. 125.

34. Heckel, *Conquests*, p. 115, citing bibliography.

13. RETREAT FROM INDIA

1. Curtius 9.2.11, with W. Heckel, "Alexander the Great and the 'Limits of the Civilised World,'" in Heckel and Tritle (eds.), *Crossroads*, pp. 147–174. Army discontent: P. Briant, *Alexander the Great and His Empire*, trans. A. Kuhrt (Princeton: 2010), pp. 63–66.

2. Diodorus 17.103.5.

3. A. B. Bosworth, *Alexander and the East. The Tragedy of Triumph* (Oxford: 1996), pp. 74–80.

4. Bosworth, *Alexander and the East*, pp. 186–200; *contra* W. Heckel, *The Conquests of Alexander the Great* (Cambridge: 2008), pp. 120–125, that Alexander did not intend to proceed farther and that the altars he set up at the Hyphasis also marked the extent of Porus's domains.

5. E. Carney, "Macedonians and Mutiny: Discipline and Indiscipline in the Army of Philip and Alexander," *CPh* 91 (1996), pp. 19–44; F. L. Holt, "The Hyphasis Mutiny: A Source Study," *Anc. World* 5 (1982), pp. 33–59.

6. For the suggestion that Alexander orchestrated the mutiny because he wanted to turn back at the Hyphasis, see P. O. Spann, "Alexander at the Beas: Fox in a Lion's Skin," in F. B. Titchener and R. F. Moorton Jr. (eds.), *The Eye Expanded. Life and the Arts in Greco-Roman Antiquity* (Berkeley and Los Angeles: 1999), pp. 62–74; Heckel, "Alexander the Great and the 'Limits of the Civilised World,'" pp. 147–174; Briant, *Alexander*, pp. 37–38.

7. Ian Worthington, "Alexander the Great and the 'Interests of Historical Accuracy': A Reply," *AHB* 13 (1999), pp. 136–140; *contra* F. L. Holt, "The Death of Coenus," *AHB* 14 (2000), pp. 49–55.

8. Bosworth, *Alexander and the East*, pp. 133–145.

9. Bosworth, *Alexander and the East*, p. 144.

10. A. B. Bosworth, *Conquest and Empire. The Reign of Alexander the Great* (Cambridge: 1988), pp. 135–137 and *Alexander and the East*, pp. 133–141; J. F. C. Fuller, *The Generalship of Alexander the Great* (repr.; New Brunswick: 1960), pp. 259–263; Ian Worthington, *Alexander the Great: Man and God*, rev. ed. (London: 2004), pp. 219–221.

11. Aristobulus, *BNJ* 139 F 46 (= Plutarch, *Moralia* 341c).

12. Ptolemy, *FGrH* 138 F 25 (= Arrian 6.10.1).

13. R. Stoneman, "Who Are the Brahmans?," *CQ*² 44 (1994), pp. 500–510 and "Naked Philosophers: The Brahmans in the Alexander Historians and the *Alexander Romance*," *JHS* 105 (1995), pp. 99–114; cf. Bosworth, *Alexander and the East*, pp. 92–97.

14. Onesicritus, *BNJ* 134 F 17a (= Strabo 15.1.63–64).

15. Arrian 7.1.5–2.1; translation: P. A. Brunt, *Arrian, "History of Alexander"* 2, Loeb Classical Library (Cambridge: 1983), ad loc.

16. A. B. Bosworth, "Calanus and the Brahman Opposition," in W. Will (ed.), *Alexander der Grosse: Eine Welteroberung und ihr Hintergrund* (Bonn: 1998), pp. 173–203.

17. G. Woodcock, *The Greeks in India* (London: 1966), p. 45. On Alexander's legacy in India, see the essays in H. P. Ray and D. T. Potts (eds.), *Memory as History: The Legacy of Alexander in Asia* (New Delhi: 2007).

18. D. Engels, *Alexander the Great and the Logistics of the Macedonian Army* (Berkeley and Los Angeles: 1978).

19. Numbers: Bosworth, *Conquest and Empire*, p. 142.

20. Cf. Arrian 6.24.2–3, and on Alexander and Cyrus: M. Brosius, "Alexander and the Persians," in Roisman (ed.), *Companion to Alexander*, pp. 174–175.

21. Bosworth, *Conquest and Empire*, pp. 143–146. Although not everyone would agree: Heckel, *Conquests*, pp. 131–134. March and presentation in the sources: Bosworth, *Alexander and the East*, pp. 169–183—hardly, though, a "hiccup in the career of conquest" (p. 169).

22. Arrian 6.24.1.

23. Aristobulus, *BNJ* 139 F 49a (= Arrian 6.24).

24. Bosworth, *Conquest and Empire*, pp. 148–150, 240–241; P. Cartledge, *Alexander the Great: The Hunt for a New Past* (London: 2003), pp. 199–200; but see W. E. Higgins, "Aspects of Alexander's Imperial Administration: Some Modern Methods and Views Reviewed," *Athenaeum* 58 (1980), pp. 140–152.

25. Curtius 9.10.29; translation: W. Heckel and J. Yardley, *Alexander the Great. Historical Sources in Translation* (Malden: 2003), p. 213.

26. E. A. Fredricksmeyer, "Alexander's Religion and Divinity," in Roisman (ed.), *Companion to Alexander*, pp. 253–278; cf. B. Dreyer, "Heroes, Cults, and Divinity," in Heckel and Tritle (eds.), *New History*, pp. 218–234.

27. Philip's statue in the grand procession at Aegae before his death may indicate that he believed himself divine, but that is unlikely: Ian Worthington, *Philip II of Macedonia* (New Haven: 2008), pp. 228–233.

28. Hyperides 5, *Against Demosthenes* 31.

29. E. Badian, "The Deification of Alexander the Great," in H. J. Dell (ed.), *Ancient Macedonian Studies in Honour of C. F. Edson* (Thessaloníki: 1981), pp. 27–71; J. P. V. D. Balsdon, "The 'Divinity' of Alexander," *Historia* 1 (1950), pp. 363–388; Bosworth, *Conquest and Empire*, pp. 278–290 and "Alexander, Euripides and Dionysos: The Motivation for Apotheosis," in R. W. Wallace and E. M. Harris (eds.), *Transitions to Empire. Essays in Honor of E. Badian* (Norman: 1996), pp. 140–166; L. Edmunds, "The Religiosity of Alexander," *GRBS* 12 (1971), pp. 363–391; E. A. Fredricksmeyer, "Three Notes on Alexander's Deification," *AJAH* 4 (1979), pp. 1–9, "Alexander, Zeus Ammon, and the Conquest of Asia," *TAPhA* 121 (1991), pp. 199–214, and "Alexander's Religion and Divinity"; J. R. Hamilton, "Alexander and His 'So-Called' Father," *CQ*² 3 (1953), pp. 151–157; Worthington, *Alexander*, pp. 273–283.

30. Aristobulus, *FGrH* 139 FF 13–15 (= Arrian 3.3–4).

31. K. Dahmen, *The Legend of Alexander the Great on Greek and Roman Coins* (London: 2007), pp. 6, 109–110; cf. Heckel, *Conquests*, p. 125, for example.

32. D. L. Gilley, "Alexander and the Carmanian March of 324 BC," *AHB* 20 (2007), pp. 9–14.

33. Ephippus, *FGrH* 126 F 5 (= Athenaeus 12.537e–538a).

34. Dreyer, "Heroes, Cults, and Divinity," pp. 218–234.

35. Details on the voyage: Bosworth, *Conquest and Empire*, pp. 150–151.

36. On the following: Bosworth, *Alexander and the East*, pp. 184–185.

37. Arrian 7.19.6.

38. Aristobulus, *BNJ* 139 F 55 (= Arrian 7.19.3–6).
39. Bosworth, *Alexander and the East*, pp. 152–154.
40. Aristobulus, *BNJ* 139 F 55 (= Arrian 7.20.1).

14. ALEXANDER'S FINAL YEARS

1. Curtius 10.1.26, with E. Badian, "The Eunuch Bagoas: A Study in Method," CQ^2 28 (1958), pp. 144–157.

2. Chares, *FGrH* 125 F 19a (= Athenaeus 10.437a–b). See too Plutarch, *Alexander* 70.1.

3. Diodorus 18.8.4. Background and discussion: A. B. Bosworth, *Conquest and Empire. The Reign of Alexander the Great* (Cambridge: 1988), pp. 220–228; M. Faraguna, "Alexander and the Greeks," in Roisman (ed.), *Companion to Alexander*, pp. 124–127; and especially S. Dmitriev, "Alexander's Exile's Decree," *Klio* 86 (2004), pp. 348–381; Ian Worthington, "From East to West: Alexander and the Exiles Decree," in E. Baynham (ed.), *East and West in the World of Alexander: Essays in Honour of A. B. Bosworth* (Oxford: forthcoming 2014). Hammond in N. G. L. Hammond and F. W. Walbank, *A History of Macedonia* 3 (Oxford: 1988), pp. 80–81, sees the decree as merely an announcement and a starting point for discussion, perhaps unlikely because Alexander overruled all the Greek embassies that protested the decree: see below.

4. Diodorus 17.107.6, Curtius 10.3.12, Justin 12.10.9, and Plutarch, *Alexander* 70.2, mention only the marriage to Stateira. On the two women, see D. Ogden, *Alexander the Great. Myth, Genesis and Sexuality* (Exeter: 2011), pp. 133–138, noting the lack of information on their lives compared with Roxane.

5. Plutarch, *Moralia* 329c.

6. W. W. Tarn, "Alexander the Great and the Unity of Mankind," *Proceedings of the British Academy* 19 (1933), pp. 123–166 and *Alexander the Great* 2 (Cambridge: 1948), pp. 399–449; *contra* E. Badian, "Alexander the Great and the Unity of Mankind," *Historia* 7 (1958), pp. 425–444; E. N. Borza, "Ethnicity and Cultural Policy at Alexander's Court," *Anc. World* 22 (1991), pp. 21–25; A. B. Bosworth, "Alexander and the Iranians," *JHS* 100 (1980), pp. 1–21. This belief still emerges today, as Oliver Stone's 2004 movie *Alexander* attests.

7. *Agêma*: Arrian 7.6.4–5; Peucestas's troops: Arrian 7.23.1–4.

8. W. Heckel, *The Conquests of Alexander the Great* (Cambridge: 2008), p. 139; P. Cartledge, *Alexander the Great: The Hunt for a New Past* (London: 2003), p. 105.

9. M. Shaki, "The Denkard Account of the History of the Zoroastrian Scriptures," *Archiv Orientalni* 49 (1981), pp. 114–125; A. S. Shahbazi, "Iranians and Alexander," *AJAH²* 2 (2003), pp. 5–38.

10. Diodorus 17.108.3, but note Heckel, *Conquests*, pp. 140–141.

11. Arrian 7.9.6–10.7; translation: P. A. Brunt, *Arrian, "History of Alexander"* 2, Loeb Classical Library (Cambridge: 1983), ad loc. See too B. Nagle, "The Cultural Context of Alexander's Speech at Opis," *TAPhA* 126 (1996), pp. 151–172.

12. Arrian 7.11.9.

13. Heckel, *Conquests*, pp. 129–130, noting also the Macedonians' suspicion of the Greeks Nearchus and Eumenes after Alexander's death.

14. Bosworth, "Alexander and the Iranians," pp. 13–20.

15. Arrian 7.12.4.

16. E. Baynham, "Antipater: Manager of Kings," in Worthington (ed.), *Ventures*, pp. 331–356; D. L. Gilley and Ian Worthington, "Alexander the Great, Macedonia and Asia," in Roisman and Worthington, eds., *Companion to Macedonia*, pp. 199–205.

17. E. Carney, "Alexander and His 'Terrible Mother,'" in Heckel and Tritle (eds.), *New History*, pp. 189–202.

18. A. B. Bosworth, "Alexander the Great and the Decline of Macedon," *JHS* 106 (1986), pp. 1–12 and "Macedonian Manpower under Alexander the Great," *Anc. Macedonia* 4 (1986), pp. 115–122; *contra* N. G. L. Hammond, *Alexander the Great: King, Commander and Statesman*, 2nd ed. (Bristol: 1989), pp. 153–161; R. Billows, *Kings and Colonists* (Leiden: 1995), pp. 183–212.

19. Alexander and Hephaestion: Ogden, *Alexander the Great*, pp. 155–167.

20. A. W. Collins, "The Office of Chiliarch under Alexander and His Successors," *Phoenix* 55 (2001), pp. 259–283. Arrian 7.14.10 states that Hephaestion became chiliarch in Susa in 324.

21. Plutarch, *Alexander* 72.3–4.

22. L. Rawlings, *The Ancient Greeks at War* (Manchester: 2007); cf. A. B. Bosworth, *Alexander and the East. The Tragedy of Triumph* (Oxford: 1996), pp. 25–30. Changing face of warfare and its effects on armies and cultures: V. D. Hanson, *The Western Way of War. Infantry Battle in Classical Greece* (New York: 1989); and A. Chaniotis, *War in the Hellenistic World: A Social and Cultural History* (Oxford: 2005).

23. L. Tritle, *From Melos to My Lai: A Study in Violence, Culture and Social Survival* (London: 2000). See too Rawlings, *Ancient Greeks at War*, pp. 203–222; Hanson, *Western Way of War*; and J. Shay, *Achilles in Vietnam: Combat Trauma and the Undoing of Character* (New York: 1994).

24. Cf. Chaniotis, *War in the Hellenistic World*, pp. 214–244, but some comments are relevant to Classical memorializations.

25. Ian Worthington, *Philip II of Macedonia* (New Haven: 2008), pp. 61–62.

26. Bosworth, *Alexander and the East*, p. 28.

27. A. B. Bosworth, *From Arrian to Alexander* (Oxford: 1988), pp. 83–93; Heckel, *Conquests*, p. 149, noting Arrian's silence on the matter (7.15.6).

28. Aristus, *FGrH* 143 F 2 (= Arrian 7.15.5).

29. G. L. Cawkwell, "The Deification of Alexander the Great: A Note," in Worthington (ed.), *Ventures*, pp. 293–306; E. Badian, "Alexander the Great between Two Thrones and Heaven: Variations on an Old Theme," in A. Small (ed.), *Subject and Ruler: The Cult of the Ruling Power in Classical Antiquity* (Ann Arbor: 1996), pp. 11–26.

30. On the decree, see the works cited in note 3 above. Harpalus affair: Bosworth, *Conquest and Empire*, pp. 215–220; Ian Worthington, *Demosthenes of Athens and the Fall of Classical Greece* (Oxford: 2013), pp. 311–325; Faraguna, "Alexander and the Greeks," pp. 127–130; E. Poddighe, "Alexander and the Greeks. The Corinthian League," in Heckel and Tritle (eds.), *New History*, pp. 117–120; C. W. Blackwell, *In the Absence of Alexander. Harpalus and the Failure of Macedonian Authority* (New York: 1998); Ian Worthington, *A Historical Commentary on Dinarchus. Rhetoric and Conspiracy in Later Fourth-Century Athens* (Ann Arbor: 1992), pp. 41–77.

31. Ian Worthington, "The Harpalus Affair and the Greek Response to the Macedonian Hegemony," in Worthington (ed.), *Ventures*, pp. 307–330; G. L. Cawkwell, "The End of Greek Liberty," in R. W. Wallace and E. M. Harris (eds.), *Transitions to Empire. Essays in Honor of E. Badian* (Norman: 1996), pp. 98–121.

32. Hammond, *Alexander*, pp. 255–259, paints a different picture, but it is hard to agree with views such as: "It is difficult to find fault with the conduct of Alexander as hegemon of the Greek League" (p. 258).

33. Athens: Bosworth, *Conquest and Empire*, pp. 204–215; E. M. Burke, "Lycurgan Finances," *GRBS* 26 (1985), pp. 251–264; J. Engels, "Anmerkungen zum 'Ökonomischen Denken' im 4. Jahrh. v. Chr. und zur wirtschaftlichen Entwicklung des Lykurgischen Athen," *MBAH* 7 (1988), pp. 90–132; M. Faraguna, *Atene nell'età di Alessandro: Problemi politici, economici, finanziari* (Rome: 1992) and "Alexander and the Greeks," pp. 118–124; F. W. Mitchel, "Athens in the Age of Alexander," *G&R*² 12 (1965), pp. 189–204 and *Lykourgan Athens: 338–322*, Semple Lectures 2 (Cincinnati: 1970); C. Habicht, *Athens from Alexander to Antony*, trans. D. L. Schneider (Cambridge: 1997), pp. 6–35; and see also the

essays on Lycurgus in V. Azoulay and P. Ismard (eds.), *Clisthène et Lycurgue d'Athènes: Autour du politique dans la cité classique* (Paris: 2011). Peloponnese: G. Shipley, "Between Macedonia and Rome: Political Landscapes and Social Changes in Southern Greece in the Early Hellenistic Period," *BSA* 100 (2005), pp. 315–330.

34. M. Faraguna, "Lykourgan Athens?" in V. Azoulay and P. Ismard (eds.), *Clisthène et Lycurgue d'Athènes: Autour du politique dans la cité classique* (Paris: 2011), pp. 67–88; S. D. Lambert, "Connecting with the Past in Lykourgan Athens," in L. Foxhall and H.-J. Gehrke (eds.), *Intentional History: Spinning Time in Ancient Greece* (Stuttgart: Steiner, 2010), pp. 225–238.

35. R. Scodel, "Lycurgus and the State of Tragedy," in C. Cooper (ed.), *Politics of Orality* (Leiden: 2007), pp. 129–154.

15. DEATH IN BABYLON AND ALEXANDER'S LEGACY

1. Nicoboule, *FGrH* 127 F 1 (= Athenaeus 12.434c).

2. Death: Diodorus 17.117.1–3; Arrian 7.24.4–25.1; Plutarch, *Alexander* 75.3; Athenaeus 10.434a–c, 12.537d; A. B. Bosworth, *Conquest and Empire. The Reign of Alexander the Great* (Cambridge: 1988), pp. 171–173; Ian Worthington, *Alexander the Great: Man and God*, rev. ed. (London: 2004), pp. 266–268.

3. E. Badian, "A King's Notebooks," *HSCPh* 72 (1967), pp. 183–204; A. B. Bosworth, "The Death of Alexander the Great: Rumour and Propaganda," *CQ²* 21 (1971), pp. 112–136; A. Chugg, "The Journal of Alexander the Great," *AHB* 19 (2005), pp. 155–175; N. G. L. Hammond, "The Royal Journal of Alexander," *Historia* 37 (1988), pp. 129–150 and "Aspects of Alexander's Journal and Ring in His Last Days," *AJPh* 110 (1989), pp. 155–160; A. E. Samuel, "Alexander's Royal Journals," *Historia* 14 (1965), pp. 1–12.

4. *Ephemerides, FGrH* 117 F 3b (= Plutarch, *Alexander* 76–77.1).

5. L. Depuydt, "The Time of Death of Alexander the Great," *Welt des Orients* 28 (1997), pp. 117–135.

6. The sources and various arguments are collected by P. Doherty, *The Death of Alexander the Great* (New York: 2004), although his thesis that Ptolemy was responsible for Alexander's murder and deliberately styled his account of the reign to exonerate himself is doubtful.

7. Iolas: Plutarch, *Moralia* 849f. Tomb: Diodorus 19.11.8.

8. Bosworth, "Death of Alexander the Great," pp. 134–136.

9. E. Carney, *Olympias, Mother of Alexander the Great* (London: 2006), pp. 63–64.

10. P. Green, *Alexander of Macedon* (Harmondsworth: 1974), pp. 476–477.

11. E. N. Borza, "Some Observations on Malaria and the Ecology of Central Macedonia in Antiquity," *AJAH* 4 (1979), pp. 102–124 and "The Natural Resources of Early Macedonia," in Adams and Borza (eds.), *Macedonian Heritage*, pp. 17–18.

12. Dio 51.16.45, 47; Suetonius, *Augustus* 2.18.

13. Crown: Suetonius, *Augustus* 2.18. Nose: Dio 21.16.5.

14. For its fascinating history, see N. J. Saunders, *Alexander's Tomb. The Two Thousand Year Obsession to Find the Lost Conqueror* (New York: 2006), also discussing how Alexander died. See too A. W. Erskine, "Life after Death: Alexandria and the Body of Alexander," *G&R²* 49 (2002), pp. 163–179.

15. P. J. Rhodes and R. Osborne (eds.), *Greek Historical Inscriptions, 404–323 BC* (Oxford: 2003), no. 101, pp. 526 (text)–527 (translation); Ian Worthington, "The Date of the Tegea Decree (Tod ii 202): A Response to the *Diagramma* of Alexander III or of Polyperchon?" *AHB* 7 (1993), pp. 59–64; S. Dmitriev, "Alexander's Exile's Decree," *Klio* 86 (2004), pp. 351–354.

16. Diodorus 18.4.1–6; translation: W. Heckel and J. Yardley, *Alexander the Great. Historical Sources in Translation* (Malden: 2003), pp. 290–291.

17. A. B. Bosworth, "Ptolemy and the Will of Alexander," in A. B. Bosworth and E. J. Baynham (eds.), *Alexander the Great in Fact and Fiction* (Oxford: 2000), pp. 207–241; W. Heckel, *The Last Days and Testament of Alexander the Great* (Stuttgart: 1998).

18. See P. Fraser, *Cities of Alexander the Great* (Oxford: 1996), for example, pp. 177, 193–195.

19. Plutarch, *Phocion* 22.3.

20. N. G. L. Hammond and F. W. Walbank, *A History of Macedonia* 3 (Oxford: 1988), pp. 107–117. Nomenclature: N. G. Ashton, "The Lamian War—*stat magni nominis umbra*," *JHS* 94 (1984), pp. 152–157.

21. Demosthenes's last days: Ian Worthington, *Demosthenes of Athens and the Fall of Classical Greece* (Oxford: 2013), pp. 326–337.

22. Ptolemy, *FGrH* 138 F 30 (= Arrian 7.26.3).

23. A. B. Bosworth, *The Legacy of Alexander. Politics, Warfare and Propaganda under the Successors* (Oxford: 2002) and "Alexander the Great and the Creation of the Hellenistic Age," in G. R. Bugh (ed.), *The Cambridge Companion to the Hellenistic World* (Cambridge: 2007), pp. 9–27; D. Braund, "After Alexander: The Emergence of the Hellenistic World, 323–281," in A. Erskine (ed.), *A Companion to the Hellenistic World* (Malden: 2003), pp. 19–34; W. L. Adams, "Alexander's Successors to 221 BC," in Roisman and Worthington (eds.), *Companion to Macedonia*, pp. 208–224; R. Waterfield, *Dividing the Spoils. The War for Alexander the Great's Empire* (Oxford: 2011).

24. Cf. Bosworth, *Conquest and Empire*, pp. 244–245.

25. *IG* vii.3206 = *SEG* 41.472, with J. M. Fossey, *Epigraphica Boeotica* 1, *Studies in Boiotian Inscriptions* (Amsterdam: 1991), pp. 86–87.

26. Named after the Danish archaeologist K. F. Kinch, who excavated it in 1887–1892: K. F. Kinch, "Le tombeau de Niausta, Tombeau Macedonien," *Danske Vidensk. Selsk. Skrifter* 7, *Raekke Historisk of Filosofisk Afd.* 4 (1920), pp. 283ff. (not seen).

27. The heroic Alexander is at the heart of R. Lane Fox, *Alexander the Great* (London: 1973); N. G. L. Hammond, *The Genius of Alexander the Great* (London: 1997); and P. Freeman, *Alexander the Great* (New York: 2011), for example, against the more critical evaluations of E. Badian and A. B. Bosworth, whose methodology and interpretations in providing a more "historical" Alexander I follow.

28. A. Meeus, "Alexander's Image in the Age of the Successors," in Heckel and Tritle (eds.), *New History*, pp. 235–250.

29. A. Stewart, *Faces of Power. Alexander's Image and Hellenistic Politics* (Berkeley and Los Angeles: 1993) and "Alexander in Greek and Roman Art," in Roisman (ed.), *Companion to Alexander*, pp. 31–66; K. Dahmen, *The Legend of Alexander the Great on Greek and Roman Coins* (London: 2007).

30. Plautus, *Mostellaria* 775.

31. R. Stoneman, "The Legacy of Alexander in Ancient Philosophy," in Roisman (ed.), *Companion to Alexander*, pp. 325–346.

32. Alexander's legacy and perception in later literature: C. Mossé, *Alexander: Destiny and Myth*, trans. J. Lloyd (Edinburgh: 2004), pp. 165–209; F. L. Holt, *Alexander the Great and the Mystery of the Elephant Medallions* (Berkeley and Los Angeles: 2003), pp. 1–22; see too G. Cary, *The Medieval Alexander* (London: 1956); E. Baynham, "Power, Passion, and Patrons. Alexander, Charles LeBrun, and Oliver Stone," in Heckel and Tritle (eds.), *New History*, pp. 294–310.

33. N. G. L. Hammond, "The Macedonian Imprint on the Hellenistic World," in P. Green (ed.), *Hellenistic History and Culture* (Berkeley and Los Angeles: 1993), pp. 12–23; S. Burstein, "The Legacy of Alexander: New Ways of Being Greek in the Hellenistic Period," in Heckel and Tritle (eds.), *Crossroads*, pp. 217–242; cf. E. Badian, "Alexander the Great and the Scientific Exploration of the Oriental Part of His Empire," *Anc. Society* 22 (1991), pp. 127–138.

34. Worthington, *Alexander*.

35. J. Roisman, "Honor in Alexander's Campaign," in Roisman (ed.), *Companion to Alexander*, pp. 279–321.

36. W. Heckel, "King and 'Companions': Observations on the Nature of Power in the Reign of Alexander," in Roisman (ed.), *Companion to Alexander*, pp. 197–225, argues that Alexander was actually a popular military leader, evidenced, among other things, by so few conspiracies against him. For the opposite view, see E. Badian, "Alexander the Great and the Loneliness of Power," in E. Badian (ed.), *Studies in Greek and Roman History* (Oxford: 1964), pp. 192–205 and "Conspiracies," in A. B. Bosworth and E. Baynham (eds.), *Alexander the Great in Fact and Fiction* (Oxford: 1996), pp. 60–92.

37. Worthington, *Alexander*, pp. 299–303, on the influence of Philip's "ghost."

38. Cf. Ian Worthington, "Alexander the Great, Nation-Building, and the Creation and Maintenance of Empire," in V. D. Hanson (ed.), *Makers of Ancient Strategy: From the Persian Wars to the Fall of Rome* (Princeton: 2010), pp. 118–137.

39. Aristobulus, *BNJ* 139 F 55 (= Arrian 7.19.6); Curtius 6.2.1; Plutarch, *Moralia* 207d; the quotation is Curtius 9.2.8; translation: Heckel and Yardley, *Alexander the Great*, p. 260.

40. Mossé, *Alexander*, p. 134.

41. G. Maclean Rogers, *Alexander: The Ambiguity of Greatness* (New York: 2004).

42. Ephippus, *FGrH* 126 F 5 (= Athenaeus 12.537e–538a).

43. A. B. Bosworth, *Alexander and the East. The Tragedy of Triumph* (Oxford: 1996), pp. 23–24.

44. *Ephemerides*, *FGrH* 117 F 2a (= Aelian, *Varra Historia* 3.23).

45. Ian Worthington, "Worldwide Empire vs Glorious Enterprise: Diodorus and Justin on Philip II and Alexander the Great," in Carney and Ogden (eds.), *Philip and Alexander*, pp. 165–174. Philip also as the greater king: M. Zahrnt, "The Macedonian Background," in Heckel and Tritle (eds.), *New History*, pp. 7–25.

46. Justin 12.16.11.

47. Diodorus 17.117.5.

48. Diodorus 16.95.

49. On how the Romans exploited and manipulated Alexander in their political and cultural life and how that shaped those writing about him, see D. Spencer, *The Roman Alexander: Reading a Cultural Myth* (Exeter: 2002).

50. Summary of their legacies: Ian Worthington, *Philip II of Macedonia* (New Haven: 2008), pp. 204–208.

51. Justin 9.8.

BIBLIOGRAPHY

Adams, A. "Philip *Alias* Hitler." *G&R* 10 (1941), pp. 105–113.

Adams, W. L. "The Episode of Philotas: An Insight." In W. Heckel and L. A. Tritle (eds.), *Crossroads of History. The Age of Alexander*, pp. 113–126. Claremont: 2003.

——. "Alexander's Successors to 221 BC." In J. Roisman and Ian Worthington (eds.), *A Companion to Ancient Macedonia*, pp. 208–224. Malden: 2010.

Alonso-Núñez, M. "An Augustan World History: The *Historiae Philippicae* of Pompeius Trogus." *G&R²* 34 (1987), pp. 56–72.

Anderson, A. R. "Bucephalas and His Legend." *AJPh* 51 (1930), pp. 1–21.

Andronikos, M. "The Royal Tombs at Aigai (Vergina)." In M. B. Hatzopoulos and L. D. Loukopoulos (eds.), *Philip of Macedon*, pp. 188–231. London: 1980.

——. "Art during the Archaic and Classical Periods." In M. B. Sakellariou (ed.), *Macedonia, 4000 Years of Greek History and Civilization*, pp. 92–110. Athens: 1983.

——. "Archaeological Discoveries in Macedonia." In J. Vokotopoulou (ed.), *Greek Civilization: Macedonia, Kingdom of Alexander the Great*, pp. 5–11. Athens: 1993.

——. *Vergina: The Royal Tombs and the Ancient City*. Athens: 1984; repr., 2004.

Anson, E. M. "The Meaning of the Term *Makedones*." *Anc. World* 10 (1984), pp. 67–68.

Archibald, Z. "Macedonia and Thrace." In J. Roisman and Ian Worthington (eds.), *A Companion to Ancient Macedonia*, pp. 326–341. Malden: 2010.

Ashton, N. G. "The Lamian War—*stat magni nominis umbra*." *JHS* 94 (1984), pp. 152–157.

Asirvatham, S. "His Son's Father? Philip II in the Second Sophistic." In E. D. Carney and D. Ogden (eds.), *Philip II and Alexander the Great: Father and Son, Lives and Afterlives*, pp. 193–204. Oxford: 2010.

——. "Perspectives on the Macedonians from Greece, Rome, and Beyond." In J. Roisman and Ian Worthington (eds.), *A Companion to Ancient Macedonia*, pp. 99–124. Malden: 2010.

Atkinson, J. E. *A Commentary on Q. Curtius Rufus' "Historiae Alexandri Magni," Books 3–4; Books 5–7.2*. Amsterdam: 1980 and 1994.

——. "Originality and Its Limits in the Alexander Sources of the Early Empire." In A. B. Bosworth and E. Baynham (eds.), *Alexander the Great in Fact and Fiction*, pp. 307–326. Oxford: 2000.

Azoulay, V., and P. Ismard (eds.). *Clisthène et Lycurgue d'Athènes: Autour du politique dans la cité classique*. Paris: 2011.

Badian, E. "Alexander the Great and the Unity of Mankind." *Historia* 7 (1958), pp. 425–444.

——. "The Eunuch Bagoas: A Study in Method." *CQ²* 28 (1958), pp. 144–157.

———. "The Death of Parmenio." *TAPhA* 91 (1960), pp. 324–338.

———. "Harpalus." *JHS* 81 (1961), pp. 16–43.

———. "The Death of Philip II." *Phoenix* 17 (1963), pp. 244–250.

———. "Alexander the Great and the Loneliness of Power." In E. Badian (ed.), *Studies in Greek and Roman History*, pp. 192–205. Oxford: 1964.

———. "The Administration of the Empire." *G&R*² 12 (1965), pp. 166–182.

———. "Alexander the Great and the Greeks of Asia." In E. Badian (ed.), *Ancient Society and Institutions. Studies Presented to V. Ehrenberg on His 75th Birthday*, pp. 37–69. Oxford: 1966.

———. "A King's Notebooks." *HSCPh* 72 (1967), pp. 183–204.

———. "The Battle of the Granicus: A New Look." *Anc. Macedonia* 2 (1977), pp. 271–293.

———. "The Deification of Alexander the Great." In H. J. Dell (ed.), *Ancient Macedonian Studies in Honour of C. F. Edson*, pp. 27–71. Thessaloníki: 1981.

———. "Greeks and Macedonians." In B. Barr-Sharrar and E. N. Borza (eds.), *Macedonia and Greece in Late Classical and Early Hellenistic Times*, pp. 33–51. Washington: 1982.

———. "Philip II and Thrace." *Pulpudeva* 4 (1983), pp. 51–71.

———. "Alexander the Great and the Scientific Exploration of the Oriental Part of His Empire." *Anc. Society* 22 (1991), pp. 127–138.

———. "Agis III: Revisions and Reflections." In Ian Worthington (ed.), *Ventures into Greek History. Essays in Honour of N. G. L. Hammond*, pp. 258–292. Oxford: 1994.

———. "The Ghost of Empire: Reflections on Athenian Foreign Policy in the Fourth Century." In W. Eder (ed.), *Die athenische Demokratie im 4. Jahrhundert v. Chr.*, pp. 79–106. Stuttgart: 1995.

———. "Alexander the Great between Two Thrones and Heaven: Variations on an Old Theme." In A. Small (ed.), *Subject and Ruler: The Cult of the Ruling Power in Classical Antiquity*, pp. 11–26. Ann Arbor: 1996.

———. "Conspiracies." In A. B. Bosworth and E. Baynham (eds.), *Alexander the Great in Fact and Fiction*, pp. 60–92. Oxford: 1996.

———. "Philip II and the Last of the Thessalians." *Anc. Macedonia* 6 (1999), pp. 109–121.

———. "Darius III." *HSCPh* 100 (2000), pp. 241–268.

Balsdon, J. P. V. D. "The 'Divinity' of Alexander." *Historia* 1 (1950), pp. 363–388.

Baynham, E. "Antipater: Manager of Kings." In Ian Worthington (ed.), *Ventures into Greek History. Essays in Honour of N. G. L. Hammond*, pp. 331–356. Oxford: 1994.

———. "Who Put the Alexander in the *Alexander Romance*? The *Alexander Romance* within Alexander Historiography." *AHB* 9 (1995), pp. 1–13.

———. *The Unique History of Quintus Curtius Rufus*. Ann Arbor: 1998.

———. "Why Didn't Alexander Marry a Nice Macedonian Girl before Leaving Home? Observations on Factional Politics at Alexander's Court in 336–334 BC." In T. Hillard (ed.), *Ancient History in a Modern University* 1, pp. 148–155. Sydney: 1998.

———. "The Ancient Evidence for Alexander the Great." In J. Roisman (ed.), *Brill's Companion to Alexander the Great*, pp. 3–29. Leiden: 2003.

———. "Power, Passion, and Patrons. Alexander, Charles LeBrun, and Oliver Stone." In W. Heckel and L. Tritle (eds.), *Alexander the Great: A New History*, pp. 294–310. Malden: 2009.

———(ed.). *East and West in the World of Alexander: Essays in Honour of A. B. Bosworth*. Oxford: 2014.

Bhandare, S. "Not Just a Pretty Face: Interpretations of Alexander's Numismatic Legacy in the Hellenistic East." In H. P. Ray and D. T. Potts (eds.), *Memory as History: The Legacy of Alexander in Asia*, pp. 208–256. New Delhi: 2007.

Bieber, M. "The Portraits of Alexander." *G&R*² 12 (1965), pp. 183–188.

Billows, R. *Kings and Colonists*. Leiden: 1995.

——. "Cities." In A. Erskine (ed.), *A Companion to the Hellenistic World*, pp. 196–215. Malden: 2003.

Blackwell, C. W. *In the Absence of Alexander. Harpalus and the Failure of Macedonian Authority*. New York: 1998.

Bloedow, E. F. "The Siege of Tyre in 332 BC: Alexander at the Crossroads in His Career." *La Parola del Passato* 301 (1990), pp. 255–293.

——. "Why Did Philip and Alexander Launch a War against the Persian Empire?" *L'Ant. Class.* 72 (2003), pp. 261–274.

Borza, E. N. "Fire from Heaven: Alexander at Persepolis." *CPh* 67 (1972), pp. 233–245.

——. "Some Observations on Malaria and the Ecology of Central Macedonia in Antiquity." *AJAH* 4 (1979), pp. 102–124.

——. "Anaxagoras and Callisthenes: Academic Intrigue at Alexander's Court." In H. J. Dell (ed.), *Ancient Macedonian Studies in Honour of C. F. Edson*, pp. 73–86. Thessaloníki: 1981.

——. "The Natural Resources of Early Macedonia." In W. L. Adams and E. N. Borza (eds.), *Philip II, Alexander the Great, and the Macedonian Heritage*, pp. 1–20. Lanham: 1982.

——. "The Symposium at Alexander's Court." *Anc. Macedonia* 3 (1983), pp. 45–55.

——. "Timber and Politics in the Ancient World. Macedon and the Greeks." *Proceedings of the American Philosophical Society* 131 (1987), pp. 32–52.

——. *In the Shadow of Olympus: The Emergence of Macedon*. Princeton: 1990.

——. "Ethnicity and Cultural Policy at Alexander's Court." *Anc. World* 22 (1991), pp. 21–25.

——. "The Philhellenism of Archelaus." *Anc. Macedonia* 5 (1993), pp. 237–244.

——. "Greeks and Macedonians in the Age of Alexander. The Source Traditions." In R. W. Wallace and E. M. Harris (eds.), *Transitions to Empire. Essays in Honor of E. Badian*, pp. 122–139. Norman: 1996.

——, and O. Palagia. "The Chronology of the Royal Macedonian Tombs at Vergina." *Jahrbuch des Deutsche Archaeologischen Instituts* 122 (2007), pp. 81–125.

Bosworth, A. B. "The Death of Alexander the Great: Rumour and Propaganda." *CQ²* 21 (1971), pp. 112–136.

——. "Philip II and Upper Macedonia." *CQ²* 21 (1971), pp. 93–105.

——. "Alexander and Ammon." In K. Kinzl (ed.), *Greece and the Ancient Mediterranean in History and Prehistory*, pp. 51–75. Berlin: 1977.

——. "Alexander and the Iranians." *JHS* 100 (1980), pp. 1–21.

——. *A Historical Commentary on Arrian's "History of Alexander,"* 1: Books 1–3; 2: Books 4–5.29. Oxford: 1980 and 1995.

——. "A Missing Year in the History of Alexander the Great." *JHS* 101 (1981), pp. 17–39.

——. "The Indian Satrapies under Alexander the Great." *Antichthon* 17 (1983), pp. 37–46.

——. "Alexander the Great and the Decline of Macedon." *JHS* 106 (1986), pp. 1–12.

——. "Macedonian Manpower under Alexander the Great." *Anc. Macedonia* 4 (1986), pp. 115–122.

——. *Conquest and Empire. The Reign of Alexander the Great*. Cambridge: 1988.

——. *From Arrian to Alexander*. Oxford: 1988.

——. *Alexander and the East. The Tragedy of Triumph*. Oxford: 1996.

——. "Alexander, Euripides and Dionysos: The Motivation for Apotheosis." In R. W. Wallace and E. M. Harris (eds.), *Transitions to Empire. Essays in Honor of E. Badian*, pp. 140–166. Norman: 1996.

——. "The Tumult and the Shouting: Two Interpretations of the Cleitus Episode." *AHB* 10 (1996), pp. 19–30.

——. "Calanus and the Brahman Opposition." In W. Will (ed.), *Alexander der Grosse: Eine Welteroberung und ihr Hintergrund*, pp. 173–203. Bonn: 1998.

———. "Ptolemy and the Will of Alexander." In A. B. Bosworth and E. J. Baynham (eds.), *Alexander the Great in Fact and Fiction*, pp. 207–241. Oxford: 2000.

———. *The Legacy of Alexander. Politics, Warfare and Propaganda under the Successors.* Oxford: 2002.

———. "The Indian Campaigns, 327–325 BC." In J. Roisman (ed.), *Brill's Companion to Alexander the Great*, pp. 59–168. Leiden: 2003.

———. "Alexander the Great and the Creation of the Hellenistic Age." In G. R. Bugh (ed.), *The Cambridge Companion to the Hellenistic World*, pp. 9–27. Cambridge: 2007.

Bouzek, S. J., and I. Ondřejova. "Some Notes on the Relations of the Thracian, Macedonian, Iranian and Scythian Arts in the Fourth Century B.C." *Eirene* 24 (1987), pp. 67–93.

Bradford Welles, C. *Diodorus Siculus 16.66–17.* Loeb Classical Library, vol. 8. Cambridge: 1963.

Brauer, G. C. "Alexander in England: The Conqueror's Reputation in the Late Seventeenth and Eighteenth Centuries." *CJ* 76 (1980).

Braund, D. "After Alexander: The Emergence of the Hellenistic World, 323–281." In A. Erskine (ed.), *A Companion to the Hellenistic World*, pp. 19–34. Malden: 2003.

Briant, P. "Conquête territoriale et stratégie idéologique: Alexandre le Grand et l'idéologie monarchique achéménide." In J. Wolski (ed.), *Actes du colloque international sur L'idéologie monarchique dans l'antiquité*, pp. 37–83. Cracow: 1980.

———. "Chasses royales macédoniennes et chasses royales perses: Le thème de la chasse au lion sur *la chasse de Vergina*." *Dialogues d'Histoire Ancienne* 17 (1991), pp. 211–255.

———. "Les chasses d'Alexandre." *Anc. Macedonia* 5 (1993), pp. 267–277.

———. *From Cyrus to Alexander: A History of the Persian Empire.* Trans. P. T. Daniels. Winona Lake: 2002.

———. "'Alexandre et l'hellénisation de l'Asie': l'Histoire au passé et au présent." *Studi Ellenistici* 16 (2005), pp. 9–69.

———. "Alexander and the Persian Empire, between 'Decline and 'Renovation.'" In W. Heckel and L. A. Tritle (eds.), *Alexander the Great: A New History*, pp. 171–188. Malden: 2009.

———. "The Empire of Darius III in Perspective." In W. Heckel and L. A. Tritle (eds.), *Alexander the Great: A New History*, pp. 141–170. Malden: 2009.

———. *Alexander the Great and His Empire.* Trans. A. Kuhrt. Princeton: 2010.

Brosius, M. "Alexander and the Persians." In J. Roisman (ed.), *Brill's Companion to Alexander the Great*, pp. 169–193. Leiden: 2003.

Brown, T. S. "Alexander's Book Order (Plut. *Alex.* 8)." *Historia* 16 (1967), pp. 359–368.

Brunt, P. A. "Persian Accounts of Alexander's Campaigns." *CQ*² 12 (1962), pp. 141–155.

———. "The Aims of Alexander." *G&R*² 12 (1965), pp. 205–215.

———. "Euboea in the Time of Philip II." *CQ*² 19 (1969), pp. 245–265.

———. *Arrian, "History of Alexander."* 2 vols. Loeb Classical Library. Cambridge: 1976 and 1983.

Buchanan, J. J. *Theorika.* New York: 1962.

Buckler, J. *The Theban Hegemony.* Cambridge: 1980.

———. *Philip II and the Sacred War.* Leiden: 1989.

———. "Philip II's Designs on Greece." In R. W. Wallace and E. M. Harris (eds.), *Transitions to Empire. Essays in Honor of E. Badian*, pp. 77–97. Norman: 1996.

———. "Demosthenes and Aeschines." In Ian Worthington (ed.), *Demosthenes: Statesman and Orator*, pp. 114–158. London: 2000.

———. *Aegean Greece in the Fourth Century BC.* Leiden: 2003.

———. "Alliance and Hegemony in Fourth-Century Greece: The Case of the Theban Hegemony." In J. Buckler and H. Beck (eds.), *Central Greece and the Politics of Power in the Fourth Century BC*, pp. 127–139. Cambridge: 2008.

———. "A Note on the Battle of Chaeronea." In J. Buckler and H. Beck (eds.), *Central Greece and the Politics of Power in the Fourth Century* BC, pp. 254–258. Cambridge: 2008.

———. "Philip II, the Greeks, and the King 346–336 B.C." In J. Buckler and H. Beck (eds.), *Central Greece and the Politics of Power in the Fourth Century* BC, pp. 233–253. Cambridge: 2008.

———. "Plutarch on Leuctra." In J. Buckler and H. Beck (eds.), *Central Greece and the Politics of Power in the Fourth Century* BC, pp. 111–126. Cambridge: 2008.

———. "Sphodrias' Raid and the Evolution of the Athenian League." In J. Buckler and H. Beck (eds.), *Central Greece and the Politics of Power in the Fourth Century* BC, pp. 79–84. Cambridge: 2008.

———. "A Survey of Theban and Athenian Relations between 403–371 BC." In J. Buckler and H. Beck (eds.), *Central Greece and the Politics of Power in the Fourth Century* BC, pp. 79–84. Cambridge: 2008.

———. "Thebes, Delphi, and the Outbreak of the Sacred War." In J. Buckler and H. Beck (eds.), *Central Greece and the Politics of Power in the Fourth Century* BC, pp. 213–223. Cambridge: 2008.

Burke, E. M. "Lycurgan Finances." *GRBS* 26 (1985), pp. 251–264.

———. "Athens after the Peloponnesian War: Restoration Efforts and the Role of Maritime Commerce." *Class. Antiquity* 9 (1990), pp. 1–13.

Burn, A. R. "The Generalship of Alexander." *G&R²* 12 (1965), pp. 140–154.

Burstein, S. "Pharaoh Alexander: A Scholarly Myth." *Anc. Society* 22 (1991), pp. 139–145.

———. "The Legacy of Alexander: New Ways of Being Greek in the Hellenistic Period." In W. Heckel and L. A. Tritle (eds.), *Crossroads of History. The Age of Alexander*, pp. 217–242. Claremont: 2003.

Carey, C. *Aeschines*. Austin: 2000.

Cargill, J. *The Second Athenian League*. Berkeley: 1981.

Carney, E. D. "The Conspiracy of Hermolaus." *CJ* 76 (1980), pp. 223–231.

———. "The Death of Clitus." *GRBS* 22 (1981), pp. 149–160.

———. "Macedonians and Mutiny: Discipline and Indiscipline in the Army of Philip and Alexander." *CPh* 91 (1996), pp. 19–44.

———. *Women and Monarchy in Macedonia*. Norman: 2000.

———. "The Trouble with Philip Arrhidaeus." *AHB* 15 (2001), pp. 63–89.

———. "Hunting and the Macedonian Elite: Sharing the Rivalry of the Chase (Arrian 4.13.1)." In D. Ogden (ed.), *The Hellenistic World: New Perspectives*, pp. 59–80. London: 2002.

———. "Elite Education and High Culture in Macedonia." In W. Heckel and L. A. Tritle (eds.), *Crossroads of History. The Age of Alexander*, pp. 47–63. Claremont: 2003.

———. "Women in Alexander's Court." In J. Roisman (ed.), *Brill's Companion to Alexander the Great*, pp. 227–252. Leiden: 2003.

———. *Olympias, Mother of Alexander the Great*. London: 2006.

———. "Symposia and the Macedonian Elite: The Unmixed Life." *Syllecta Classica* 18 (2007), pp. 129–180.

———. "The Role of the *Basilikoi Paides* at the Argead Court." In T. Howe and J. Reames (eds.), *Macedonian Legacies: Studies in Ancient Macedonian History and Culture in Honor of Eugene N. Borza*, pp. 145–164. Claremont: 2008.

———. "Alexander and His 'Terrible Mother.'" In W. Heckel and L. A. Tritle (eds.), *Alexander the Great: A New History*, pp. 189–202. Malden: 2009.

Carter, J. M. "Athens, Euboea and Olynthus." *Historia* 20 (1971), pp. 418–429.

Cartledge, P. *Agesilaos and the Crisis of Sparta*. Baltimore: 1987.

———. *Alexander the Great: The Hunt for a New Past*. London: 2003.

Cary, G. *The Medieval Alexander*. London: 1956.

Cawkwell, G. L. "Aeschines and the Peace of Philocrates." *REG* 73 (1960), pp. 416–438.

———. "A Note on Ps. -Demosthenes 17.20." *Phoenix* 15 (1961), pp. 74–78.

———. "Aeschines and the Ruin of Phocis in 346." *REG* 75 (1962), pp. 453–459.

———. "The Defence of Olynthus." *CQ*² 12 (1962), pp. 122–140.

———. "Demosthenes and the Stratiotic Fund." *Mnemosyne* 15 (1962), pp. 377–383.

———. "Demosthenes' Policy after the Peace of Philocrates I and II." *CQ*² 13 (1963), pp. 120–138, 200–213.

———. "Eubulus." *JHS* 83 (1963), pp. 47–67.

———. "The Crowning of Demosthenes." *CQ*² 19 (1969), pp. 163–180.

———. "The Foundation of the Second Athenian Confederacy." *CQ*² 23 (1973), pp. 56–60.

———. "Epaminondas and Thebes." *CQ*² 22 (1978), pp. 254–278.

———. "The Peace of Philocrates Again." *CQ*² 28 (1978), pp. 93–104.

———. *Philip of Macedon.* London: 1978.

———. "Philip and Athens." In M. B. Hatzopoulos and L. D. Loukopoulos (eds.), *Philip of Macedon*, pp. 100–110. Athens: 1980.

———. "Notes on the Failure of the Second Athenian Confederacy." *JHS* 101 (1981), pp. 40–54.

———. "Athenian Naval Power in the Fourth Century." *CQ*² 34 (1984), pp. 334–345.

———. "The Deification of Alexander the Great: A Note." In Ian Worthington (ed.), *Ventures into Greek History. Essays in Honour of N. G. L. Hammond*, pp. 293–306. Oxford: 1994.

———. "The End of Greek Liberty." In R. W. Wallace and E. M. Harris (eds.), *Transitions to Empire. Essays in Honor of E. Badian*, pp. 98–121. Norman: 1996.

Chaniotis, A. *War in the Hellenistic World: A Social and Cultural History.* Oxford: 2005.

Christesen, P., and S. C. Murray. "Macedonian Religion." In J. Roisman and Ian Worthington (eds.), *A Companion to Ancient Macedonia*, pp. 428–445. Malden: 2010.

Chroust, A. H. "Aristotle and the Foreign Policy of Macedonia." *Review of Politics* 34 (1972), pp. 367–394.

Chugg, A. "The Journal of Alexander the Great." *AHB* 19 (2005), pp. 155–175.

Cohen, A. *The Alexander Mosaic. Stories of Victory and Defeat.* Cambridge: 1997.

Collins, A. W. "The Office of Chiliarch under Alexander and His Successors." *Phoenix* 55 (2001), pp. 259–283.

Connor, W. R. "History without Heroes: Theopompus' Treatment of Philip of Macedon." *GRBS* 8 (1967), pp. 133–154.

Cook, J. M. *The Persian Empire.* London: 1983.

Dahmen, K. *The Legend of Alexander the Great on Greek and Roman Coins.* London: 2007.

———. "The Numismatic Evidence." In J. Roisman and Ian Worthington (eds.), *A Companion to Ancient Macedonia*, pp. 41–62. Malden: 2010.

Dandamaev, M. *A Political History of the Achaemenid Empire.* Leiden: 1989.

Danforth, L. M. *The Macedonian Conflict.* Princeton: 1995.

———. "Alexander the Great and the Macedonian Conflict." In J. Roisman (ed.), *Brill's Companion to Alexander the Great*, pp. 347–364. Leiden: 2003.

Davies, J. K. "The Tradition about the First Sacred War." In S. Hornblower (ed.), *Greek Historiography*, pp. 193–212. Oxford: 1994.

Dell, H. "The Western Frontier of the Macedonian Monarchy." *Anc. Macedonia* 1 (1970), pp. 115–126.

———. "Philip and Macedonia's Northern Neighbours." In M. B. Hatzopoulos and L. D. Loukopoulos (eds.), *Philip of Macedon*, pp. 90–99. Athens: 1980.

Demandt, A. "Politische Aspekete im Alexanderbild der Neuzeit." *Archiv für Kulturgeschichte* 54 (1972), pp. 325–363.

Depuydt, L. "The Time of Death of Alexander the Great." *Welt des Orients* 28 (1997), pp. 117–135.

Develin, R., and W. Heckel. *Justin.* Epitome *of the "Philippic History" of Pompeius Trogus.* Atlanta: 1994.

Devine, A. M. "Grand Tactics at Gaugamela." *Phoenix* 29 (1975), pp. 374–385.

——. "Grand Tactics at the Battle of Issus." *Anc. World* 12 (1985), pp. 39–59.

——. "The Strategies of Alexander the Great and Darius III in the Issus Campaign (333 BC)." *Anc. World* 12 (1985), pp. 25–38.

——. "The Battle of Gaugamela: A Tactical and Source-Critical Study." *Anc. World* 13 (1986), pp. 87–115.

——. "Demythologizing the Battle of the Granicus." *Phoenix* 40 (1986), pp. 265–278.

——. "The Battle of Hydaspes: A Tactical and Source-Critical Study." *Anc. World* 16 (1987), pp. 91–113.

——. "A Pawn-Sacrifice at the Battle of the Granicus: The Origins of a Favorite Stratagem of Alexander the Great." *Anc. World* 18 (1988), pp. 3–20.

——. "Alexander the Great." In J. Hackett (ed.), *Warfare in the Ancient World,* pp. 104–129. New York: 1989.

——. "The Macedonian Army at Gaugamela: Its Strength and the Length of Its Battle-Line." *Anc. World* 19 (1989), pp. 77–80.

——. "Alexander's Propaganda Machine: Callisthenes as the Ultimate Source for Arrian, *Anabasis* 1–3." In Ian Worthington (ed.), *Ventures into Greek History. Essays in Honour of N. G. L. Hammond,* pp. 89–104. Oxford: 1994.

Dihle, A. "The Conception of India in Hellenistic and Roman Literature." *Proc. Camb. Phil. Soc.* 10 (1964), pp. 15–23.

Dmitriev, S. "Alexander's Exile's Decree." *Klio* 86 (2004), pp. 348–381.

Dobbins, K. M. "Alexander's Eastern Satrapies." *Persica* 11 (1984), pp. 74–108.

Doherty, P. *The Death of Alexander the Great.* New York: 2004.

Dreyer, B. "Heroes, Cults, and Divinity." In W. Heckel and L. A. Tritle (eds.), *Alexander the Great: A New History,* pp. 218–234. Malden: 2009.

Drougou, S., and C. Saatsoglou-Paliadeli. *Vergina. Wandering through the Archaeological Site.* Athens: 2004.

Due, B. "Alexander's Inspirations and Ideas." In J. Carlsen et al. (eds.), *Alexander the Great. Reality and Myth,* pp. 53–60. Rome: 1993.

Duff, T. *Plutarch's "Lives." Exploring Vice and Virtue.* Oxford: 1999.

Edmunds, L. "The Religiosity of Alexander." *GRBS* 12 (1971), pp. 363–391.

Edson, C. "Early Macedonia." *Anc. Macedonia* 1 (1970), pp. 17–44.

Efstathiou, A. "The 'Peace of Philocrates': The Assembles of 18th and 19th Elaphebolion." *Historia* 53 (2004), pp. 385–407.

Ehrenberg, V. *Alexander and the Greeks.* Oxford: 1938.

Ehrhardt, C. "Two Notes on Philip of Macedon's First Interventions in Thessaly." CQ^2 17 (1967), pp. 296–301.

Ellis, J. R. "Population-Transplants by Philip II." *Makedonika* 9 (1969), pp. 9–17.

——. "Amyntas Perdikka, Philip II and Alexander the Great." *JHS* 91 (1971), pp. 15–24.

——. "The Stepbrothers of Philip II." *Historia* 22 (1973), pp. 350–354.

——. *Philip II and Macedonian Imperialism.* London: 1976.

——. "The Dynamics of Fourth-Century Macedonian Imperialism." *Anc. Macedonia* 2 (1977), pp. 103–114.

——. "The Unification of Macedonia." In M. B. Hatzopoulos and L. D. Loukopoulos (eds.), *Philip of Macedon,* pp. 36–47. Athens: 1980.

———. "The First Months of Alexander's Reign." In B. Barr-Sharrar and E. N. Borza (eds.), *Macedonia and Greece in Late Classical and Early Hellenistic Times*, pp. 69–73. Washington: 1982.

———. "Philip and the Peace of Philokrates." In W. L. Adams and E. N. Borza (eds.), *Philip II, Alexander the Great, and the Macedonian Heritage*, pp. 43–59. Lanham: 1982.

Engels, D. *Alexander the Great and the Logistics of the Macedonian Army*. Berkeley and Los Angeles: 1978.

Engels, J. "Anmerkungen zum 'Ökonomischen Denken' im 4. Jahrh. v. Chr. und zur wirtschaftlichen Entwicklung des Lykurgischen Athen." *MBAH 7* (1988), pp. 90–132.

———. "Macedonians and Greeks." In J. Roisman and Ian Worthington (eds.), *A Companion to Ancient Macedonia*, pp. 81–98. Malden: 2010.

———. *Philipp II. und Alexander der Grosse*. 2nd ed. Stuttgart: 2012.

———. "Theagenes: Text, Translation, Commentary." In *Brill's New Jacoby*. Online. Leiden: 2007–.

Errington, R. M. "Bias in Ptolemy's History of Alexander." *CQ²* 19 (1969), pp. 233–242.

———. "Arybbas the Molossian." *GRBS* 16 (1975), pp. 41–50.

———. *A History of Macedonia*. Trans. C. Errington. Berkeley and Los Angeles: 1990.

Erskine, A. W. "The *Pezêtairoi* of Philip II and Alexander III." *Historia* 38 (1989), pp. 385–394.

———. "Life after Death: Alexandria and the Body of Alexander." *G&R²* 49 (2002), pp. 163–179.

Faklaris, P. B. "Aegae: Determining the Site of the First Capital of the Macedonians." *AJA* 98 (1994), pp. 609–616.

Faraguna, M. *Atene nell'età di Alessandro: Problemi politici, economici, finanziari*. Rome: 1992.

———. "Alexander and the Greeks." In J. Roisman (ed.), *Brill's Companion to Alexander the Great*, pp. 99–130. Leiden: 2003.

———. "Lykourgan Athens?" In V. Azoulay and P. Ismard (eds.), *Clisthène et Lycurgue d'Athènes: Autour du politique dans la cité classique*, pp. 67–88. Paris: 2011.

Flower, M. A. *Theopompus of Chios*. Oxford: 1994.

Fossey, J. M. *Epigraphica Boeotica, 1: Studies in Boiotian Inscriptions*. Amsterdam: 1991.

Fraser, P. *Cities of Alexander the Great*. Oxford: 1996.

Fredricksmeyer, E. A. "Alexander, Midas, and the Oracle at Gordium." *CPh* 56 (1961), pp. 160–168.

———. "Three Notes on Alexander's Deification." *AJAH* 4 (1979), pp. 1–9.

———. "On the Final Aims of Philip II." In W. L. Adams and E. N. Borza (eds.), *Philip II, Alexander the Great, and the Macedonian Heritage*, pp. 85–98. Lanham: 1982.

———. "Alexander and Philip: Emulation and Resentment." *CJ* 85 (1990), pp. 300–315.

———. "Alexander, Zeus Ammon, and the Conquest of Asia." *TAPhA* 121 (1991), pp. 199–214.

———. "The *Kausia*: Macedonian or Indian?" In Ian Worthington (ed.), *Ventures into Greek History. Essays in Honour of N. G. L. Hammond*, pp. 136–158. Oxford: 1994.

———. "Alexander the Great and the Kingship of Asia." In A. B. Bosworth and E. J. Baynham (eds.), *Alexander the Great in Fact and Fiction*, pp. 136–166. Oxford: 2000.

———. "Alexander's Religion and Divinity." In J. Roisman (ed.), *Brill's Companion to Alexander the Great*, pp. 253–278. Leiden: 2003.

Freeman, P. *Alexander the Great*. New York: 2011.

Fuller, J. F. C. *The Generalship of Alexander the Great*. Repr. New Brunswick: 1960.

Gabriel, R. A. *Philip II of Macedon: Greater than Alexander*. Washington, D.C.: 2010.

Gilley, D. L. "Alexander and the Carmanian March of 324 BC." *AHB* 20 (2007), pp. 9–14.

———, and Ian Worthington. "Alexander the Great, Macedonia and Asia." In J. Roisman and Ian Worthington (eds.), *A Companion to Ancient Macedonia*, pp. 186–207. Malden: 2010.

Golan, D. "The Fate of a Court Historian: Callisthenes." *Athenaeum* 66 (1988), pp. 99–120.

Goukowsky, P. "Recherches récentes sur Alexandre le Grand (1978–1982)." *REG* 96 (1983), pp. 225–241.

Grainger, J. *Alexander the Great Failure: The Collapse of the Macedonian Empire*. London: 2007.

Graninger, D. "Macedonia and Thessaly." In J. Roisman and Ian Worthington (eds.), *A Companion to Ancient Macedonia*, pp. 306–325. Malden: 2010.

Green, P. *Alexander of Macedon*. Harmondsworth: 1974.

———. *The Greco-Persian Wars*. Berkeley and Los Angeles: 1996.

Green, R. *Theatre in Ancient Greek Society*. London: 1994.

Greenwalt, W. S. "The Search for Arrhidaeus." *Anc. World* 10 (1985), pp. 69–77.

———. "Amyntas III and the Political Stability of Argead Macedonia." *Anc. World* 18 (1988), pp. 35–44.

———. "Polygamy and Succession in Argead Macedonia." *Arethusa* 22 (1989), pp. 19–45.

———. "Macedonia, Illyria and Epirus." In J. Roisman and Ian Worthington (eds.), *A Companion to Ancient Macedonia*, pp. 279–305. Malden: 2010.

Griffith, G. T. "Alexander's Generalship at Gaugamela." *JHS* 67 (1947), pp. 77–89.

———. "The Macedonian Background." *G&R*² 12 (1965), pp. 125–139.

———. "Philip of Macedon's Early Interventions in Thessaly (358–352 B.C.)." *CQ*² 20 (1970), pp. 67–80.

———. "Athens in the Fourth Century." In P. D. A. Garnsey and C. R. Whittaker (eds.), *Imperialism in the Ancient World*, pp. 127–144. Cambridge: 1978.

———. "Philip as a General and the Macedonian Army." In M. B. Hatzopoulos and L. D. Loukopoulos (eds.), *Philip of Macedon*, pp. 58–77. Athens: 1980.

Gunderson, L. L. "Alexander and the Attic Orators." In H. J. Dell (ed.), *Ancient Macedonian Studies in Honor of C. F. Edson*, pp. 183–192. Thessaloníki: 1981.

Habicht, C. *Athens from Alexander to Antony*. Trans. D. L. Schneider. Cambridge: 1997.

Hall, J. M. "Contested Ethnicities: Perceptions of Macedonia within Evolving Definitions of Greek Identity." In I. Malkin (ed.), *Ancient Perceptions of Greek Ethnicity*, pp. 159–186. Cambridge: 2001.

Hamilton, C. D. *Agesilaus and the Failure of Spartan Hegemony*. Ithaca: 1991.

Hamilton, J. R. "Alexander and His 'So-Called' Father." *CQ*² 3 (1953), pp. 151–157.

———. "Alexander's Early Life." *G&R*² 12 (1965), pp. 125–139.

———. *A Commentary on Plutarch's Life of Alexander*. Oxford: 1969.

———. "Cleitarchus and Diodorus 17." In K. Kinzl (ed.), *Greece and the Ancient Mediterranean in History and Prehistory. Studies Presented to F. Schachermeyr on His Eightieth Birthday*, pp. 126–146. Berlin: 1977.

Hammond, N. G. L. *Epirus*. Oxford: 1967.

———. *A History of Macedonia* 1. Oxford: 1972.

———. "The Victory of Macedon at Chaeronea." In *Studies in Greek History*, pp. 534–557. Oxford: 1973.

———. "Philip's Tomb in Historical Context." *GRBS* 19 (1978), pp. 331–350.

———. "The Battle of the Granicus River." *JHS* 100 (1980), pp. 73–88.

———. "Training in the Use of the Sarissa and Its Effect in Battle 359–333 BC." *Antichthon* 14 (1980), pp. 53–63.

———. *Three Historians of Alexander the Great*. Cambridge: 1983.

———. "The Kingdom of Asia and the Persian Throne." *Antichthon* 20 (1986), pp. 73–85.

———. "The Royal Journal of Alexander." *Historia* 37 (1988), pp. 129–150.

———. *Alexander the Great: King, Commander and Statesman*. 2nd ed. Bristol: 1989.

———. "Aspects of Alexander's Journal and Ring in His Last Days." *AJPh* 110 (1989), pp. 155–160.

———. "The Battle between Philip and Bardylis." *Antichthon* 23 (1989), pp. 1–9.

———. "Royal Pages, Personal Pages, and Boys Trained in the Macedonian Manner during the Period of the Temenid Monarchy." *Historia* 39 (1990), pp. 261–290.

———. "The *Koina* of Epirus and Macedonia." *ICS* 16 (1991), pp. 183–192.

———. "The Sources of Justin on Macedonia to the Death of Philip." *CQ*² 41 (1991), pp. 496–508.

———. "The Various Guards of Philip II and Alexander III." *Historia* 40 (1991), pp. 396–417.

———. "Alexander's Charge at the Battle of Issus in 333 B.C." *Historia* 41 (1992), pp. 395–406.

———. "The Archaeological and Literary Evidence for the Burning of the Persepolis Palace." *CQ*² 42 (1992), pp. 358–364.

———. *The Macedonian State: The Origins, Institutions and History.* Oxford: 1992.

———. "The Macedonian Imprint on the Hellenistic World." In P. Green (ed.), *Hellenistic History and Culture*, pp. 12–23. Berkeley and Los Angeles: 1993.

———. *Sources for Alexander the Great.* Cambridge: 1993.

———. "Literary Evidence for Macedonian Speech." *Historia* 43 (1994), pp. 131–142.

———. *Philip of Macedon.* London: 1994.

———. "Philip's Innovations in Macedonian Economy." *SO* 70 (1995), pp. 22–29.

———. *The Genius of Alexander the Great.* London: 1997.

———. "The Location of Aegae." *JHS* 117 (1997), pp. 177–179.

———, and G. T. Griffith. *A History of Macedonia* 2. Oxford: 1979.

———, and F. W. Walbank. *A History of Macedonia* 3. Oxford: 1988.

Hansen, M. H. "The Theoric Fund and the *Graphe Paranomon* against Apollodorus." *GRBS* 17 (1976), pp. 235–246.

———. *The Athenian Assembly in the Age of Demosthenes.* Oxford: 1987.

———. *The Athenian Democracy in the Age of Demosthenes.* 2nd ed. Norman: 1999.

Hanson, V. D. "Epameinondas, the Battle of Leuktra and the 'Revolution' in Greek Battle Tactics." *Class. Antiquity* 7 (1988), pp. 190–207.

———. *The Western Way of War. Infantry Battle in Classical Greece.* New York: 1989.

———. *Warfare and Agriculture in Classical Greece.* Berkeley and Los Angeles: 1998.

Hardiman, C. L. "Classical Art to 221 BC." In J. Roisman and Ian Worthington (eds.), *A Companion to Ancient Macedonia*, pp. 505–521. Malden: 2010.

Harding, P. E. *From the End of the Peloponnesian War to the Battle of Ipsus.* Cambridge: 1985.

———. "Rhetoric and Politics in Fourth-Century Athens." *Phoenix* 41 (1987), pp. 25–39.

Harris, E. M. *Aeschines and Athenian Politics.* Oxford: 1995.

Hatzopoulos, M. B. "Succession and Regency in Classical Macedonia." *Anc. Macedonia* 4 (1986), pp. 279–292.

Heckel, W. "The Conspiracy *against* Philotas." *Phoenix* 31 (1977), pp. 9–21.

———. "Marsyas of Pella: Historian of Macedon." *Hermes* 108 (1980), pp. 444–462.

———. "Philip and Olympias (337/6 BC)." In G. S. Shrimpton and D. J. McCargar (eds.), *Classical Contributions: Studies in Honor of M. F. McGregor*, pp. 51–57. Locust Valley: 1981.

———. *The Last Days and Testament of Alexander the Great.* Stuttgart: 1998.

———. "Alexander the Great and the 'Limits of the Civilised World.'" In W. Heckel and L. A. Tritle (eds.), *Crossroads of History. The Age of Alexander*, pp. 147–174. Claremont: 2003.

———. "King and 'Companions': Observations on the Nature of Power in the Reign of Alexander." In J. Roisman (ed.), *Brill's Companion to Alexander the Great*, pp. 197–225. Leiden: 2003.

———. *Who's Who in the Age of Alexander the Great.* Malden: 2006.

———. *The Conquests of Alexander the Great.* Cambridge: 2008.

———. "A King and His Army." In W. Heckel and L. A. Tritle (eds.), *Alexander the Great: A New History*, pp. 69–82. Malden: 2009.

———, and L. A. Tritle (eds.). *Crossroads of History. The Age of Alexander.* Claremont: 2003.

———, and J. Yardley. *Alexander the Great. Historical Sources in Translation.* Malden: 2003.

Heisserer, A. J. *Alexander the Great and the Greeks.* Norman: 1980.

Heskel, J. "Philip II and Argaios: A Pretender's Story." In R. W. Wallace and E. M. Harris (eds.), *Transitions to Empire. Essays in Honor of E. Badian*, pp. 37–56. Norman: 1996.

Higgins, W. E. "Aspects of Alexander's Imperial Administration: Some Modern Methods and Views Reviewed." *Athenaeum* 58 (1980), pp. 129–152.

Holt, F. L. "The Hyphasis Mutiny: A Source Study." *Anc. World* 5 (1982), pp. 33–59.

———. "Alexander's Settlements in Central Asia." *Anc. Macedonia* 4 (1986), pp. 315–323.

———. *Alexander the Great and Bactria: The Formation of a Greek Frontier in Central Asia*. Leiden: 1988.

———. *Thundering Zeus. The Making of Hellenistic Bactria*. Berkeley and Los Angeles: 1999.

———. "The Death of Coenus." *AHB* 14 (2000), pp. 49–55.

———. *Alexander the Great and the Mystery of the Elephant Medallions*. Berkeley and Los Angeles: 2003.

———. *Into the Land of Bones: Alexander the Great in Afghanistan*. Berkeley and Los Angeles: 2005.

Hunt, P. *War, Peace, and Alliance in Demosthenes' Athens*. New York: 2010.

Jacoby, F. *Die Fragmente der griechischen Historiker*. Berlin/Leiden: 1926–.

Jähne, A. "Alexander der Grosse. Persönlichkeit, Politik, Ökonomie." *Jahrbuch für Wirtschaftgeschichte*, 1978: pp. 245–264.

Jouguet, P. *Alexander the Great and the Hellenistic World*. Trans. M. R. Dobie. Repr. Chicago: 1985.

Kagan, D. *The Peloponnesian War*. London: 2003.

Keyser, P. T. "The Use of Artillery by Philip II and Alexander the Great." *Anc. World* 15 (1994), pp. 27–49.

Kholod, M. M. "The Garrisons of Alexander the Great in the Greek Cities of Asia Minor." *Eos* 97 (2010), pp. 249–258.

———. "On the Financial Relations of Alexander the Great and the Greek Cities in Asia Minor: The Case of *Syntaxis*." In A. Mehl, A. V. Makhlayuk, and O. Gabelko (eds.), *Ruthenia Classica Aetatis Novae. A Collection of Works by Russian Scholars in Ancient Greek and Roman History*, pp. 83–92. Stuttgart: 2013.

Kienast, D. "Alexander, Zeus, and Ammon." In W. Will and J. Heinrichs (eds.), *Zu Alexander d. Gr.: Festschrift G. Wirth*, pp. 309–334. Amsterdam: 1988.

Kinch, K. F. "Le tombeau de Niausta, Tombeau Macedonien." *Danske Vidensk. Selsk. Skrifter 7, Raekke Historisk of Filosofisk Afd.* 4 (1920), pp. 283ff.

King, C. J. "Kingship and Other Political Institutions." In J. Roisman and Ian Worthington (eds.), *A Companion to Ancient Macedonia*, pp. 374–391. Malden: 2010.

Kuhrt, A. "Alexander in Babylon." *Achaemenid History* 5 (1990), pp. 121–130.

Ladynin, I. A. "Aleksandr Velikiy i Kleomen iz Navkratisa v drevneegipetskom istochnike? (K interpretazii avtobiograficheskoy nadpisi iz grobnizy Unnefera v Saqqara)" [Alexander the Great and Cleomenes of Naucratis in an ancient Egyptian source? (On the interpretation of the autobiographical inscription from the tomb of Wennefer at Saqqara)]. *Mnemon: Issledovania i publicazii po istorii antichnogo mira* [Mnemon: Studies and publications on the history of the ancient world] 12 (2013), pp. 200–225.

———. "The Argeadai Building Program in Egypt in the Framework of Dynasties' XXIX–XXX Temple Building." In K. Nawotka and A. Wojciechowska (eds.), *Alexander the Great and Egypt: History, Art, Tradition*. Wiesbaden: forthcoming.

———. "Nadpisi na statuetke starshego syna tsarya Nectaneba II: Perevod i kommentariy" [The inscriptions on the statuette of the elder son of King Nectanebo II: Translation and commentary]. In M. A. Chegodaev (ed.), *Yazyki drevneegipetskoy kultury: Problemy perevodimosti* [Languages of the ancient Egyptian culture: Problems of translation]. Moscow: forthcoming.

Lambert, S. D. "Connecting with the Past in Lykourgan Athens." In L. Foxhall and H.-J. Gehrke (eds.), *Intentional History: Spinning Time in Ancient Greece*, pp. 225–238. Stuttgart: 2010.

Lane Fox, R. *Alexander the Great*. London: 1973.

———. "Aeschines and Athenian Politics." In R. Osborne and S. Hornblower (eds.), *Ritual, Finance, Politics. Athenian Democratic Accounts Presented to David Lewis*, pp. 135–155. Oxford: 1994.

——— (ed.). *Brill's Companion to Ancient Macedon*. Leiden: 2011.

Le Rider, G. *Le monnayage d'argent et d'or de Philippe II frappé en Macédoine de 359 à 294*. Paris: 1977.

Londey, P. D. "The Outbreak of the Fourth Sacred War." *Chiron* 20 (1990), pp. 239–260.

Ma, J. "Chaironeia 338: Topographies of Commemoration." *JHS* 128 (2008), pp. 172–191.

MacLeod, R. (ed.). *The Library of Alexandria*. London: 2000.

Markle, M. M. "Support of Athenian Intellectuals for Philip: A Study of Isocrates' *Philippus* and Speusippus' *Letter to Philip*." *JHS* 96 (1976), pp. 80–99.

Marsden, E. W. *The Campaign of Gaugamela*. Liverpool: 1964.

———. "Macedonian Military Machinery and Its Designers under Philip and Alexander." *Anc. Macedonia* 2 (1977), pp. 211–223.

McQueen, E. I. "Some Notes on the Anti-Macedonian Movement in the Peloponnese in 331 B.C." *Historia* 37 (1978), pp. 52–59.

Meeus, A. "Alexander's Image in the Age of the Successors." In W. Heckel and L. A. Tritle (eds.), *Alexander the Great: A New History*, pp. 235–250. Malden: 2009.

Mihalopoulos, C. "The Construction of a New Ideal. The Official Portraiture of Alexander the Great." In W. Heckel and L. A. Tritle (eds.), *Alexander the Great: A New History*, pp. 275–293. Malden: 2009.

Miller, S. G. "The Philippeion and Macedonian Hellenistic Architecture." *Athenische Mitteilungen* 88 (1973), pp. 189–218.

Millett, P. "The Political Economy of Macedonia." In J. Roisman and Ian Worthington (eds.), *A Companion to Ancient Macedonia*, pp. 472–504. Malden: 2010.

Milns, R. D. "The Army of Alexander the Great." In E. Badian (ed.), *Alexandre le Grand, Image et Réalité*, pp. 87–136. Fondation Hardt, Entretiens 22. Geneva: 1976.

Mitchel, F. W. "Athens in the Age of Alexander." *G&R*² 12 (1965), pp. 189–204.

———. *Lykourgan Athens: 338–322*. Semple Lectures 2. Cincinnati: 1970.

Mitchell, L. G., and L. Rubinstein (eds.). *Greek Epigraphy and History: Essays in Honour of P. J. Rhodes*. Swansea: 2008.

Montgomery, H. "The Economic Revolution of Philip II—Myth or Reality?" *SO* 60 (1985), pp. 37–47.

Moreno, A. *Feeding the Democracy: The Athenian Grain Supply in the Fifth and Fourth Centuries* BC. Oxford: 2007.

Moretti, L. *Inscrizioni Storiche Ellenistiche*. Florence: 1967 and 1976.

Morris, I., and W. Scheidel (eds.). *The Dynamics of Ancient Empires*. Oxford: 2009.

Morrison, J. S. "Athenian Sea-Power in 323/2 B.C.: Dream and Reality." *JHS* 107 (1987), pp. 88–97.

Mossé, C. *Alexander: Destiny and Myth*. Trans. J. Lloyd. Edinburgh: 2004.

Mossman, J. M. "Tragedy and Epic in Plutarch's *Alexander*." *JHS* 108 (1988), pp. 83–93.

Müller, S. "Philip II." In J. Roisman and Ian Worthington (eds.), *A Companion to Ancient Macedonia*, pp. 166–185. Malden: 2010.

Murison, C. L. "Darius III and the Battle of Issus." *Historia* 21 (1972), pp. 399–423.

Musgrave, J. H., R. A. H Neave, and A. J. N. W. Prag. "The Skull from Tomb II at Vergina: King Philip II of Macedon." *JHS* 104 (1984), pp. 60–78.

Nagle, B. "The Cultural Context of Alexander's Speech at Opis." *TAPhA* 126 (1996), pp. 151–172.

Narain, A. K. "Alexander and India." *G&R*² 12 (1965), pp. 155–165.

Natoli, F. *The Letter of Speusippus to Philip II*. Stuttgart: 2004.

Nawotka, K. "Freedom of Greek Cities in Asia Minor in the Age of Alexander the Great." *Klio* 85 (2003), pp. 15–41.

Nouhaud, M. *L'Utilisation de L'Histoire par les Orateurs Attiques*. Paris: 1982.

Nylander, C. "Darius III—The Coward King. Point and Counterpoint." In J. Carlsen et al. (eds.), *Alexander the Great. Reality and Myth*, pp. 145–159. Rome: 1993.

Office of the Secretary of Defense for Net Assessment. *Military Advantage in History*. Washington, D.C.: 2002.

Ogden, D. "Alexander's Sex Life." In W. Heckel and L. A. Tritle (eds.), *Alexander the Great: A New History*, pp. 203–217. Malden: 2009.

———. *Alexander the Great. Myth, Genesis and Sexuality*. Exeter: 2011.

Olbrycht, M. J. "Macedonia and Persia." In J. Roisman and Ian Worthington (eds.), *A Companion to Ancient Macedonia*, pp. 342–369. Malden: 2010.

Palagia, O. "Hephaestion's Pyre and the Royal Hunt of Alexander." In A. B. Bosworth and E. J. Baynham (eds.), *Alexander the Great in Fact and Fiction*, pp. 167–206. Oxford: 2000.

Pandermalis, D. *Dion. The Archaeological Site and Museum*. Athens: 1997.

Papazoglou, F. *Les villes de Macédoine à l'époque romaine*. Paris: 1988.

Parke, H. W. "The Massacre of the Branchidae." *JHS* 105 (1985), pp. 59–68.

———, and J. Boardman. "The Struggle for the Tripod and the First Sacred War." *JHS* 77 (1957), pp. 276–282.

Paspalas, S. A. "On Persian-Type Furniture in Macedonia: The Recognition and Transmission of Forms." *AJA* 104 (2000), pp. 531–560.

Pearson, L. *The Lost Histories of Alexander the Great*. New York: 1960.

Pelling, C. *Plutarch and History*. London: 2002.

Perlman, S. "Greek Diplomatic Tradition and the Corinthian League of Philip of Macedon." *Historia* 34 (1985), pp. 153–174.

———. "Fourth Century Treaties and the League of Corinth of Philip of Macedon." *Anc. Macedonia* 4 (1986), pp. 437–442.

Poddighe, E. "Alexander and the Greeks. The Corinthian League." In W. Heckel and L. A. Tritle (eds.), *Alexander the Great: A New History*, pp. 99–120. Malden: 2009.

Poulios, V. "Macedonian Coinage from the 6th Century to 148 BC." In J. Vokotopoulou (ed.), *Greek Civilization: Macedonia, Kingdom of Alexander the Great*, pp. 83–103. Athens: 1993.

Poulton, H. *Who Are the Macedonians?* Bloomington: 2000.

Pownall, F. "The Symposia of Philip II and Alexander III of Macedon: The View from Greece." In E. D. Carney and D. Ogden (eds.), *Philip II and Alexander the Great: Father and Son, Lives and Afterlives*, pp. 55–65. Oxford: 2010.

Prag, A. J. N. W. "Reconstructing King Philip II: The 'Nice' Version." *AJA* 94 (1990), pp. 237–247.

———. "Reconstructing the Skull of Philip of Macedon." In E. C. Danien (ed.), *The World of Philip and Alexander*, pp. 17–37. Philadelphia: 1990.

Prandi, L. *Callistene: Uno storico tra Aristotele e i re macedonici*. Milan: 1985.

Rahe, P. A. "The Annihilation of the Sacred Band at Chaeronea." *AJA* 85 (1981), pp. 84–87.

Rawlings, L. *The Ancient Greeks at War*. Manchester: 2007.

Ray, H. P., and D. T. Potts (eds.). *Memory as History: The Legacy of Alexander in Asia*. New Delhi: 2007.

Renard, M., and J. Servais. "A propos du mariage d'Alexandre et de Roxane." *L'Ant. Class.* 24 (1955), pp. 29–50.

Rhodes, P. J. "The Literary and Epigraphic Evidence to the Roman Conquest." In J. Roisman and Ian Worthington (eds.), *A Companion to Ancient Macedonia*, pp. 23–40. Malden: 2010.

——, and R. Osborne (eds.). *Greek Historical Inscriptions, 404–323 BC*. Oxford: 2003.

Riginos, A. S. "The Wounding of Philip II of Macedon: Fact and Fabrication." *JHS* 114 (1994), pp. 103–119.

Robinson, C. A. *The History of Alexander the Great*. 2 vols. Providence: 1953.

Roebuck, C. "The Settlement of Philip II with the Greek States in 338 B.C." *CP* 43 (1948), pp. 73–92.

Rogers, G. Maclean. *Alexander: The Ambiguity of Greatness*. New York: 2004.

Roisman, J. "Ptolemy and His Rivals in His History of Alexander." *CQ²* 34 (1984), pp. 373–385.

——. *Alexander the Great: Ancient and Modern Perspectives*. Lexington: 1995.

——(ed.). *Brill's Companion to Alexander the Great*. Leiden: 2003.

——. "Honor in Alexander's Campaign." In J. Roisman (ed.), *Brill's Companion to Alexander the Great*, pp. 279–321. Leiden: 2003.

——. *The Rhetoric of Conspiracy in Ancient Athens*. Berkeley and Los Angeles: 2006.

——. "Classical Macedonia to Perdiccas III." In J. Roisman and Ian Worthington (eds.), *A Companion to Ancient Macedonia*, pp. 145–165. Malden: 2010.

——, and Ian Worthington (eds.). *A Companion to Ancient Macedonia*. Malden: 2010.

Romane, P. "Alexander's Siege of Tyre." *Anc. World* 16 (1987), pp. 79–90.

——. "Alexander's Siege of Gaza." *Anc. World* 18 (1988), pp. 21–30.

Rubinsohn, W. Z. "The 'Philotas Affair'—A Reconsideration." *Anc. Macedonia* 2 (1977), pp. 409–420.

Russell, D. A. *Plutarch*. London: 1973.

Ruzicka, S. "War in the Aegean, 333–331 BC: A Reconsideration." *Phoenix* 42 (1988), pp. 131–151.

Ryder, T. T. B. *Koine Eirene*. Oxford: 1965.

——. "The Diplomatic Skills of Philip II." In Ian Worthington (ed.), *Ventures into Greek History. Essays in Honour of N. G. L. Hammond*, pp. 228–257. Oxford: 1994.

——. "Demosthenes and Philip II." In Ian Worthington (ed.), *Demosthenes: Statesman and Orator*, pp. 45–89. London: 2000.

Sachs, A. J., and H. Hunger. *Astronomical Diaries and Related Texts from Babylonia* 1. Vienna: 1988.

Sacks, K. *Diodorus Siculus and the First Century*. Princeton: 1990.

——. "Diodorus and His Sources: Conformity and Creativity." In S. Hornblower (ed.), *Greek Historiography*, pp. 213–232. Oxford: 1994.

Samuel, A. E. "Alexander's Royal Journals." *Historia* 14 (1965), pp. 1–12.

Sancisi-Weerdenburg, H. "Alexander and Persepolis." In J. Carlsen et al. (eds.), *Alexander the Great. Reality and Myth*, pp. 177–188. Rome: 1993.

Saunders, N. J. *Alexander's Tomb. The Two Thousand Year Obsession to Find the Lost Conqueror*. New York: 2006.

Sawada, N. "Macedonian Social Customs." In J. Roisman and Ian Worthington (eds.), *A Companion to Ancient Macedonia*, pp. 392–408. Malden: 2010.

Schultz, P. "Leochares' Argead Portraits in the Philippeion." In P. Schultz and R. von den Hoff (eds.), *Early Hellenistic Portraiture: Image, Style, Context*, pp. 205–233. Cambridge: 2007.

Scodel, R. "Lycurgus and the State of Tragedy." In C. Cooper (ed.), *Politics of Orality*, pp. 129–154. Leiden: 2007.

Scott-Kilvert, I. *Plutarch, "The Age of Alexander."* Penguin Classics. Harmondsworth: 1973.

Sealey, R. "Athens after the Social War." *JHS* 75 (1955), pp. 74–81.

——. *Demosthenes and His Time: A Study in Defeat*. Oxford: 1993.

Seibert, J. *Alexander der Grosse*. Darmstadt: 1972.

Sekunda, N. V. "A Macedonian Companion in a Pompeian Fresco." *Archeologia* (Warsaw) 54 (2003), pp. 29–33.

——. "Philistus and Alexander's Empire (Plutarch, *Vita Alexandri* 8.3)." In J. Pigoń (ed.), *The Children of Herodotus: Greek and Roman Historiography and Related Genres*, pp. 181–189. Newcastle: 2009.

———. "The Macedonian Army." In J. Roisman and Ian Worthington (eds.), *A Companion to Ancient Macedonia*, pp. 446–471. Malden: 2010.

Shahbazi, A. S. "Iranians and Alexander." *AJAH²* 2 (2003), pp. 5–38.

Shaki, M. "The Denkard Account of the History of the Zoroastrian Scriptures." *Archiv Orientalni* 49 (1981), pp. 114–125.

Shay, J. *Achilles in Vietnam: Combat Trauma and the Undoing of Character*. New York: 1994.

Sherman, C. L. *Diodorus Siculus 15.20–16.65*. Loeb Classical Library, vol. 7. Cambridge: 1952.

Shipley, G. "Between Macedonia and Rome: Political Landscapes and Social Changes in Southern Greece in the Early Hellenistic Period." *BSA* 100 (2005), pp. 315–330.

Shrimpton, G. S. "Theopompus' Treatment of Philip in the *Philippica*." *Phoenix* 31 (1977), pp. 123–144.

Siganidou, M. "Urban Centres in Macedonia." In J. Vokotopoulou (ed.), *Greek Civilization: Macedonia, Kingdom of Alexander the Great*, pp. 29–31. Athens: 1993.

Sivignon, M. "The Geographical Setting of Macedonia." In M. B. Sakellariou (ed.), *Macedonia, 4000 Years of Greek History and Civilization*, pp. 12–26. Athens: 1983.

Sordi, M. *La Lega Thessala fino ad Alessandro*. Rome: 1958.

Spann, P. O. "Alexander at the Beas: Fox in a Lion's Skin." In F. B. Titchener and R. F. Moorton Jr. (eds.), *The Eye Expanded. Life and the Arts in Greco-Roman Antiquity*, pp. 62–74. Berkeley and Los Angeles: 1999.

Speck, H. "Alexander at the Persian Gates: A Study in Historiography and Topography." *AJAH²* 1 (2002), pp. 15–23.

Spencer, D. *The Roman Alexander: Reading a Cultural Myth*. Exeter: 2002.

———. "Roman Alexanders. Epistemology and Identity." In W. Heckel and L. A. Tritle (eds.), *Alexander the Great: A New History*, pp. 251–274. Malden: 2009.

———. "You Should Never Meet Your Heroes: Growing Up with Alexander, the Valerius Maxiumus Way." In E. D. Carney and D. Ogden (eds.), *Philip II and Alexander the Great: Father and Son, Lives and Afterlives*, pp. 175–191. Oxford: 2010.

Sprawski, S. *Jason of Pherai*. Cracow: 1999.

———. "Philip II and the Freedom of the Thessalians." *Electrum* 9 (2003), pp. 55–66.

———. "Were Lycophron and Jason Tyrants of Pherae? Xenophon on the History of Thessaly." In C. Tuplin (ed.), *Xenophon and His World*, pp. 437–452. Stuttgart: 2004.

———. "All the King's Men. Thessalians and Philip II's Designs on Greece." In D. Musial (ed.), *Society and Religions. Studies in Greek and Roman History*, pp. 31–49. Toruń: 2005.

———. "From the Bronze Age to Alexander I." In J. Roisman and Ian Worthington (eds.), *A Companion to Ancient Macedonia*, pp. 127–144. Malden: 2010.

Squillace, G. "Consensus Strategies under Philip and Alexander: The Revenge Theme." In E. D. Carney and D. Ogden (eds.), *Philip II and Alexander the Great: Father and Son, Lives and Afterlives*, pp. 69–80. Oxford: 2010.

Stewart, A. *Faces of Power. Alexander's Image and Hellenistic Politics*. Berkeley and Los Angeles: 1993.

———. "Alexander in Greek and Roman Art." In J. Roisman (ed.), *Brill's Companion to Alexander the Great*, pp. 31–66. Leiden: 2003.

Stoneman, R. "The *Alexander Romance*: From History to Fiction." In J. R. Morgan and R. Stoneman (eds.), *Greek Fiction. The Greek Novel in Context*, pp. 117–129. London: 1994.

———. *Legends of Alexander the Great*. London: 1994.

———. "Who Are the Brahmans?" *CQ²* 44 (1994), pp. 500–510.

———. "Naked Philosophers: The Brahmans in the Alexander Historians and the *Alexander Romance*." *JHS* 105 (1995), pp. 99–114.

———. "The Legacy of Alexander in Ancient Philosophy." In J. Roisman (ed.), *Brill's Companion to Alexander the Great*, pp. 325–346. Leiden: 2003.

――. *Alexander the Great: A Life in Legend*. New Haven: 2008.

Strauss, B. "Alexander: The Military Campaign." In J. Roisman (ed.), *Brill's Companion to Alexander the Great*, pp. 133–156. Leiden: 2003.

Syme, R. "The Date of Justin and the Discovery of Trogus' *Historia*." *Historia* 37 (1988), pp. 358–371.

Tarn, W. W. "Alexander the Great and the Unity of Mankind." *Proceedings of the British Academy* 19 (1933), pp. 123–166.

――. *Alexander the Great*. 2 vols. Cambridge: 1948.

――. *The Greeks in Bactria and India*. Cambridge: 1951.

Thomas, C. G. *Alexander the Great in His World*. Malden: 2006.

――. "The Physical Kingdom." In J. Roisman and Ian Worthington (eds.), *A Companion to Ancient Macedonia*, pp. 65–80. Malden: 2010.

Tod, M. N. *Greek Historical Inscriptions* 2. Oxford: 1948.

Tomlinson, R. A. "Ancient Macedonian Symposia." *Anc. Macedonia* 1 (1970), pp. 308–315.

Touratsoglou, J. "Art in the Hellenistic Period." In M. B. Sakellariou (ed.), *Macedonia, 4000 Years of Greek History and Civilization*, pp. 170–191. Athens: 1983.

Townsend, R. F. "The Philippeion and Fourth-Century Athenian Architecture." In O. Palagia and S. V. Tracy (eds.), *The Macedonians in Athens, 322–229 BC*, pp. 93–101. Oxford: 2003.

Trevett, J. "Demosthenes and Thebes." *Historia* 48 (1999), pp. 184–202.

――. *Demosthenes, Speeches 1–17*. Austin: 2011.

Tritle, L. *From Melos to My Lai: A Study in Violence, Culture and Social Survival*. London: 2000.

――. "Alexander and the Killing of Cleitus the Black." In W. Heckel and L. A. Tritle (eds.), *Crossroads of History. The Age of Alexander*, pp. 127–146. Claremont: 2003.

――. *The Peloponnesian War*. Westport: 2004.

――. "Alexander and the Greeks. Artists and Soldiers, Friends and Enemies." In W. Heckel and L. A. Tritle (eds.), *Alexander the Great: A New History*, pp. 121–140. Malden: 2009.

Tronson, A. D. "Satyrus the Peripatetic and the Marriages of Philip II." *JHS* 104 (1984), pp. 116–126.

van der Spek, R. J. "Darius III, Alexander the Great and Babylonian Scholarship." *Achaemenid History* 13 (2003), pp. 289–346.

van Wees, H. *Greek Warfare: Myths and Realities*. London: 2004.

von Schwarzenberg, E. "The Portraiture of Alexander." In E. Badian (ed.), *Alexandre le Grand, Image et Réalité*, pp. 223–278. Fondation Hardt, Entretiens 22. Geneva: 1976.

Waterfield, R. *Dividing the Spoils. The War for Alexander the Great's Empire*. Oxford: 2011.

Weber, G. "The Court of Alexander the Great as Social System." In W. Heckel and L. A. Tritle (eds.), *Alexander the Great: A New History*, pp. 83–98. Malden: 2009.

Welles, C. B. "Alexander's Historical Achievement." *G&R²* 12 (1965), pp. 216–228.

Westlake, H. D. *Thessaly in the Fourth Century BC*. Repr. Chicago: 1993.

Whitmarsh, T. "Alexander's Hellenism and Plutarch's Textualism." *CQ²* 52 (2002), pp. 174–192.

Wilber, D. N. *Persepolis. The Archaeology of Parsa, Seat of the Persian Kings*. New York: 1969.

Wilkes, J. *The Illyrians*. Oxford: 1995.

Woodcock, G. *The Greeks in India*. London: 1966.

Worthington, Ian. "The Authenticity of Demosthenes' Fourth *Philippic*." *Mnemosyne* 44 (1991), pp. 425–428.

――. "Greek Oratory, Revision of Speeches and the Problem of Historical Reliability." *Class. et Med.* 42 (1991), pp. 55–74.

――. *A Historical Commentary on Dinarchus. Rhetoric and Conspiracy in Later Fourth-Century Athens*. Ann Arbor: 1992.

――. "The Date of the Tegea Decree (Tod ii 202): A Response to the *Diagramma* of Alexander III or of Polyperchon?" *AHB* 7 (1993), pp. 59–64.

———. "The Harpalus Affair and the Greek Response to the Macedonian Hegemony." In Ian Worthington (ed.), *Ventures into Greek History. Essays in Honour of N. G. L. Hammond*, pp. 307–330. Oxford: 1994.

——— (ed.). *Ventures into Greek History. Essays in Honour of N. G. L. Hammond*. Oxford: 1994.

———. "Alexander the Great and the 'Interests of Historical Accuracy': A Reply." *AHB* 13 (1999), pp. 136–140.

———. "Alexander, Philip, and the Macedonian Background." In J. Roisman (ed.), *Brill's Companion to Alexander the Great*, pp. 69–98. Leiden: 2003.

———. "Alexander's Destruction of Thebes." In W. Heckel and L. A. Tritle (eds.), *Crossroads of History. The Age of Alexander*, pp. 65–86. Claremont: 2003.

———. *Alexander the Great: Man and God*. Rev. ed. London: 2004.

——— (ed.). *A Companion to Greek Rhetoric*. Malden: 2007.

———. "Rhetoric and Politics in Classical Greece: Rise of the *Rhêtores*." In Ian Worthington (ed.), *A Companion to Greek Rhetoric*, pp. 255–271. Malden: 2007.

———. "*IG* ii² 236 and Philip's Common Peace of 337." In L. G. Mitchell and L. Rubinstein (eds.), *Greek Epigraphy and History: Essays in Honour of P J. Rhodes*, pp. 213–223. Swansea: 2008.

———. *Philip II of Macedonia*. New Haven: 2008.

———. "Alexander the Great, Nation-Building, and the Creation and Maintenance of Empire." In V. D. Hanson (ed.), *Makers of Ancient Strategy: From the Persian Wars to the Fall of Rome*, pp. 118–137. Princeton: 2010.

———. "Intentional History: Alexander, Demosthenes and Thebes." In L. Foxhall and H.-J. Gehrke (eds.), *Intentional History: Spinning Time in Ancient Greece*, pp. 239–246. Stuttgart: 2010.

———. "Worldwide Empire vs Glorious Enterprise: Diodorus and Justin on Philip II and Alexander the Great." In E. D. Carney and D. Ogden (eds.), *Philip II and Alexander the Great: Father and Son, Lives and Afterlives*, pp. 165–174. Oxford: 2010.

———. *Alexander the Great: A Reader*. 2nd ed. London: 2011.

———. *Demosthenes of Athens and the Fall of Classical Greece*. Oxford: 2013.

———. "From East to West: Alexander and the Exiles Decree." In E. Baynham (ed.), *East and West in the World of Alexander: Essays in Honour of A. B. Bosworth*. Oxford: 2014.

Xanthakis-Karamanos, G. *Studies in Fourth-Century Tragedy*. Athens: 1980.

Yardley, J. C. *Justin and Pompeius Trogus. A Study of the Language of Justin's* Epitome *of Trogus*. Toronto: 2003.

———, and W. Heckel. *Justin. Epitome of the "Philippic History" of Pompeius Trogus, 1: Books 11–12: Alexander the Great*. Oxford: 1997.

Yunis, H. *Demosthenes Speeches 18 and 19*. Austin: 2005.

Zahrnt, M. "The Macedonian Background." In W. Heckel and L. A. Tritle (eds.), *Alexander the Great: A New History*, pp. 7–25. Malden: 2009.

SELECT INDEX

CPSIA information can be obtained
at www.ICGtesting.com
Printed in the USA
LVHW09*1942180818
587392LV00007B/159/P